The Economic Emergence of Modern Japan explains how Japan succeeded in transforming an agricultural economy into an advanced industrial economy. This volume brings together chapters from *The Cambridge History of Japan*, Volumes 5 and 6, and *The Cambridge Economic History of Europe*, Volume 7, part 2. Each of the seven chapters, written by leading specialists in Japanese economic history, explains in an authoritative, detailed analysis how institutions, the behavior of individuals and firms, and official policies changed in order to enable Japan to accumulate capital, adopt new technology, ensure a skilled labor force, and increase exports of manufactured goods. The authors pay special attention to distinctive Japanese institutions and policies, the effect of the Tokugawa legacy, the impact of various wars, and the global economy.

The economic emergence of modern Japan

THE ECONOMIC EMERGENCE OF MODERN JAPAN

Edited by
KOZO YAMAMURA
University of Washington

CAMBRIDGE
UNIVERSITY PRESS

University Printing House, Cambridge CB2 8BS, United Kingdom

One Liberty Plaza, 20th Floor, New York, NY 10006, USA

477 Williamstown Road, Port Melbourne, VIC 3207, Australia

4843/24, 2nd Floor, Ansari Road, Daryaganj, Delhi - 110002, India

79 Anson Road, #06-04/06, Singapore 079906

Cambridge University Press is part of the University of Cambridge.

It furthers the University's mission by disseminating knowledge in the pursuit of education, learning and research at the highest international levels of excellence.

www.cambridge.org
Information on this title: www.cambridge.org/9780521589468

First published 1997

A catalogue record for this publication is available from the British Library

Library of Congress Cataloging in Publication data
The economic emergence of modern Japan / edited by Kozo Yamamura.
p. cm.
Includes bibliographical references and index.
ISBN 0-521-57117-0 (hardback). – ISBN 0-521-58946-0 (paperback)
1. Japan – Economic conditions – 1868– I. Yamamura, Kōzō.
HC462.7.E34 1997
330.952 – dc20 96-31272

ISBN 978-0-521-58946-8 Paperback

CONTENTS

PREFACE

This volume presents seven essays that I believe collectively serve as a reliable and readable Japanese economic history from the last several decades of the Tokugawa period (1800–68) to the early 1970s. The first four chapters are selected from Volumes 5 and 6 of the *The Cambridge History of Japan*, published respectively in 1989 and 1988,[1] and the remaining three chapters were published in *The Cambridge Economic History of Europe, Part II* in 1978.[2] As I describe below, these three chapters are included in this volume, despite the date of their publication, because I believe they remain valuable in describing and analyzing those aspects of the Japanese economy that they cover.

In Chapter 1, "Economic Change in the Nineteenth Century," E. Sydney Crawcour presents an authoritative study of the eventful last decades of the Tokugawa period and the tumultuous two decades following the Meiji Restoration of 1868. His analysis, reflecting a thorough command of English and Japanese sources, contains illuminating descriptions and discussions of numerous significant developments that were transforming the economy in many fundamental ways.

The most important topics examined by Crawcour include the reasons for, and characteristics of, several serious economic problems faced by the Tokugawa *bakufu*, the reforms attempted by the *bakufu* to solve them, various effects of opening the economy to foreign trade, and the "continuity and change" seen and development achieved during the 1868–85 period. In dealing with the last topic, Crawcour offers a reflective assessment of the roles played by the Meiji government in helping to bring about the rapid pace of economic development. This chapter skillfully examines all of the most important economic develop-

1 Marius B. Jansen, ed., *The Cambridge History of Japan, Vol. 5, The Nineteenth Century* (Cambridge: Cambridge University Press, 1989) and Peter Duus, ed., *The Cambridge History of Japan, Vol. 6, The Twentieth Century* (Cambridge: Cambridge University Press, 1988).

2 Peter Mathias and M. M. Postan, eds., *The Cambridge Economic History of Europe, Vol. VII, The Industrial Economies; Capital, Labor, and Enterprise, Part 2* (Cambridge: Cambridge University Press, 1978).

ments in the nineteenth century and provides sufficiently detailed descriptions of events and institutions that help readers understand why these developments occurred.

Chapter 2, "Industrialization and Technological Change," also written by Crawcour, examines the thirty-five-year period between 1885 and 1920. This was the period during which modern economic growth based on industrial technology took hold; the Sino-Japanese War of 1894–5 and the Russo-Japanese War of 1904–5, each with very significant fiscal, technological, and other consequences, occurred; and World War I began and ended, transforming the Japanese economy from one that was reliant on light industries to one that boasted heavy and chemical industries. This long but fast-moving chapter offers analyses and detailed descriptions of how the infrastructure for economic growth (banking, transportation, communications, electric power, and education) was built; how traditional sectors (agriculture, traditional industry, commerce, and service) were transformed and how modern sectors (light and heavy engineering industries) grew during the 1885–1913 period; and how significantly World War I changed Japan's industries and international trade. This chapter concludes with Crawcour's assessment of the role of the state in industrialization during the 1885–1920 period.

Chapter 3, "Depression, Recovery, and War, 1920–45" by Takafusa Nakamura, the undisputed doyen among Japanese economic historians, draws upon the author's extensive knowledge of the period. This chapter is not only rich in analyses based on pertinent data and well-chosen illustrative examples, but also is a highly readable narrative of "an unusually stormy and conclusive" twenty-five-year period in Japanese economic history.

The topics analyzed by Nakamura include the causes and manifestations of the post-World War I recession, agricultural stagnation in the 1920s, fiscal and monetary policies of the 1920s and their effects on growth and trade, the manifold effects of the Great Depression, the increasing economic power of *zaibatsu* and its significance, the complex interactions of the 1930s between rapidly changing political realities and economic needs to recover from the Depression and to wage a war, and the economic impact of the full-scale war that began in China in 1937. His analyses and data also show why Japan's gross national expenditures in the 1913–38 period managed to grow at an average rate of 3.9 percent – the highest among all industrial economies – despite many serious problems experienced by the Japanese economy during those twenty-five years.

Chapter 4, "The Postwar Japanese Economy, 1945–1973," is authored by Yutaka Kosai, many of whose works are widely admired for their cogent analysis of Japan's postwar economic performance and the roles that policies played in that performance. This is a chapter for those who wish to read a tightly written, reliable summary of why and how a war-torn economy in 1945 became an economic superpower today.

The chapter is divided into two parts. In the first half, Kosai succinctly summarizes and examines the economic reforms instituted by the Allied Powers (land reform, legalization of collective bargaining, and dissolution of the *zaibatsu*) and Japan's economic policy before the beginning of the Korean War. Kosai is led to conclude that, while the reforms did have various lasting, indirect effects on the Japanese economy, their overall impact was limited as exemplified in the quick emergence of *keiretsu* to take the place of the dissolved *zaibatsu*. And, in reviewing principal economic policies, Kosai carefully examines their effects on labor supply, capital accumulation, price trends, international trade, income distribution, and the growth of demand. He concludes that the policies have been successful.

In the second half of the chapter, Kosai deals with the changes that have occurred in the industrial structure because of policies and technological necessity; the many domestic and international problems that arose as Japan's exports increased rapidly; and the characteristics of Japanese enterprises, that is, *keiretsu,* heavy dependence on bank loans, and distinctive labor-management relations. Kosai ends his chapter with the admonition that "a monolithic picture" of Japanese "industrial policy" is incorrect because Japan's postwar economic policy changed significantly over time and was the outcome of conflicting political and economic interests and significantly changing macroeconomic, technological, and other conditions.

The three essays from *The Cambridge Economic History of Europe* also deal with the Tokugawa legacies up to the end of the "catch-up" industrialization (i.e., the late 1960s and the early 1970s) but are more focused on three broad topics important in analyzing the history of any industrial economy: capital accumulation, factory labor and entrepreneurship, and the ownership and management of firms.

Coauthored by Kazushi Ohkawa and Henry Rosovsky, Chapter 5, "Capital Formation in Japan," is an excellent summary of their seminal *Japanese Economic Growth: Trend Acceleration in the Twentieth Century,*[3] which must be read by all serious students of Japanese economic

3 This book was published by Stanford University Press in 1973, two years after the initial draft of this chapter was written.

history. Although its analytic focus is on capital formation, this chapter, consisting of four parts, offers a good thumbnail sketch of Tokugawa economy and society; a succinct discussion of "the mechanism of Meiji economic growth," that is, an analytic overview of the effects of many Meiji policies and of the capabilities of the Meiji economy to begin and sustain modern economic growth beginning in the 1880s; analyses of "the economics of trend acceleration," or how the rate of Japanese economic growth accelerated as a trend due to the sustained capital formation and adoption of new technology from the beginning of the twentieth century to the end of the rapid growth period in the 1960s; and "an interpretation" that summarizes the central findings of their study on capital accumulation.

Among their findings, the two most important are that (1) private investment, the level of which was determined by profit expectations, was "the main agent of economic modernization as the carrier of new and largely imported technology"; and (2) labor productivity and gross domestic product grew as a trend from the end of the nineteenth century to the mid-1960s due to an unambiguous trend of increase in the capital/labor ratio reflecting the continuing adoption of more efficient new technology.

This chapter requires no more advanced background in economics than do the preceding chapters by Nakamura and Kosai. To read this chapter, the noneconomist reader needs to know that the chapter's analytic underpinning consists of what economists call a growth equation (or an aggregate production function) and a personal saving function. The former, describing the main trend of output growth in the private modern sector, refers to $G(Y) = G(R) + \alpha G(K) + \beta G(L)$. That is, the growth rate of total output (Y) is a sum of the contributions to economic growth made by increases in technological efficiency (R), capital (K), and labor (L). The coefficients α and β, respectively for capital and labor, indicate relative magnitudes of contributions to (or income share in) the growth of total output made by capital and labor. Because technological efficiency (R) cannot be calculated directly from macro or industry data (available in terms of K, L, and Y), it is measured by subtracting $\alpha G(K) + \beta G(L)$ from $G(Y)$. This is to say that technological efficiency is defined as the "residual," that is, what remains unexplained by the contributions made respectively by capital and labor to the growth of total output. The latter, a saving function used in this chapter, refers to $St = A + bYt + cYt - 1$, that is, the saving ratio depends on a constant term, the level of income, and the rate of growth of income.

Chapter 6, "Factory Labor and the Industrial Revolution in Japan" by Koji Taira, is a valuable summary of the findings made and insights gained over many years of research by the author on industrial labor in Japan. This highly readable chapter offers descriptions, illustrated by well-chosen examples, and analyses, both economic and sociological, of three subjects in the periods 1850–90, 1890–1910, and 1910–40.

The first subject is the rarely studied difficulties faced by fledgling Meiji industrial firms in finding stable employees with sufficient skills and in learning how to manage factories. The second subject is the suppressed, thus slowly developing, labor movement and the limited progress made in providing legal protection for industrial workers. And the last subject is the post-World War I development of the Japanese-style management characterized by the significant investment made by large firms to improve the skill level of their employees, seniority-based wages, performance-related bonus payments, and implicit assurance of permanent employment.

Taira's discussions of these subjects by industry (cotton textile, metal working, and engineering) inform readers about the specific problems each industry encountered and how each industry attempted to solve them as Japan raced to achieve its "catch-up" industrialization in the prewar period. Taira also provides a very useful description of how the education system and the level of education attained by Japanese workers changed over time. Throughout the chapter Taira succeeds in enlivening his exposition by strategically inserted, illuminating descriptions of the young women in Meiji textile factories who toiled many hours in harsh conditions, on the important roles played by *oyakata* (master craftsmen) in factories up until the beginning of World War I, and on the slow and tortuous course followed by the Factory Law in pre–World War II Japan.

The final chapter, "Entrepreneurship, Ownership, and Management in Japan" which I contributed, examines who provided the entrepreneurship essential for industrialization and who owned and managed modern enterprises – factories, firms, financial institutions, and enterprise groups (the prewar *zaibatsu* and the postwar *keiretsu*) – in many ways that differed from the patterns and methods seen in the Western industrial economies.

The explicitly stated goal of the examination is to question and suggest a revision of the "orthodox" or dominant view, especially among Japanese economic historians, that Japan's modern economic growth succeeded in a very significant sense because the government and the "community-spirited" bankers and businessmen (motivated to increase collective, national economic interest). This is why the chapter presents many examples of profit-motivated pioneering entrepreneurs of several industries who established and managed profitable firms, and extended description of how *zaibatsu* firms and financial institutions, led by able leaders, succeeded in making oligopolistic profit and in building extensive networks of ownership and management.

However, throughout the chapter, I caution against the danger of unduly underestimating both the roles the government played in Japan's modern economic growth and various distinctive characteristics of ownership and management patterns and practices. This is why I stress the dual character of Japanese industrialization. That is, given the history, culture, and traditions in Japan, its task for industrialization was to produce goods using Western technology while at the same time transforming the society to make it capable of meeting the needs of industrialization.

The central issues raised in this chapter – the significance of the roles of the state in Japan's modern economic growth and the extent of the distinctiveness of Japanese ownership and managerial patterns and methods – remain unresolved.[4] This is evident not only in the differing views of the authors of the chapters in this volume on these issues as readers cannot but note, but also in the ongoing debates among the so-called "revisionists," neoclassical economists, and many others on these issues.[5] This of course is an important reason many scholars and students find the study of Japanese economic history and Japanese economy interesting.

Because of the scholarship of the past few decades that is reflected in the chapters included in this volume, we have today a substantial number of studies of Japan's economic experience in the late Tokugawa (1800–68) and the 1868–1973 periods. This means we have a good foundation for asking new questions in order to increase our

4 An important reason for the differences of the views on the roles of the state and institutions arises in part because the roles changed over time and differed depending on the specific aspects or questions of the Japanese economic experience that are examined. That is one reason why, for example, my view on the roles of the state differ in emphasis between that expressed in this chapter and in "Japan's Deus ex Machina: Western Technology in the 1920s," *Journal of Japanese Studies*, Vol. 12, No. 1 (Winter 1986) and that presented in "Success Ill-gotten? The Role of Meiji Militarism in Japan's Technological Progress," *Journal of Economic History*, Vol. 37, No. 1 (March 1977).

5 The revisionists argue that the state and Japan's distinctive institutions played major and indispensable roles in Japan's economic growth. The best-known work representing this view is Chalmers Johnson, *MITI and the Japanese Miracle: The Growth of Industrial Policy, 1925–75* (Stanford: Stanford University Press, 1982).

understanding of Japan's economic experience of the past as well as the present, which was shaped by its past.

Fortunately, in addition to neoclassical analysis which continues to evolve in many directions, several recent analytic developments can also help us to ask new questions in our efforts to increase our understanding of Japanese economic history. Here let me briefly discuss two analytic approaches – neoinstitutional analysis and Yasusuke Murakami's "anticlassical political-economic analysis" – that I believe most promising. My goals in presenting the following brief discussion are to entice those readers who are yet unfamiliar with these analytic developments to read the works presenting neoinstitutional analysis[6] and Murakami's *An Anticlassical Political–Economic Analysis*[7] and to illustrate why I believe these analytic contributions can provide valuable underpinnings for continued study of Japanese economic history.

Neoinstitutional analysis is built on neoclassical microeconomic theory but has evolved as a useful tool for analyzing institutional changes over time. In this approach, "institution" is defined broadly. For example, in the words of Douglass North, a leading proponent of this approach, it is defined as "humanly devised constraints on human actions that determine the structure of incentives."[8] Thus, institutions include laws, policies, social norms, and even ideologies that collectively shape the incentive structure of individuals and groups to save, to innovate, and to take risks, that is, to determine the performance of an economy.

This approach, evolving over the last three decades, is based on an analytic insight often referred to as the "transaction cost" approach or the "property rights" approach. Simply put, the central insight of this

6 Neoinstitutional analysis evolved as an increasingly coherent analytic approach drawing on the accumulated insights of many economists and political scientists who examined the effects institutions have on the structure of incentives. "Accumulated insights" refers to those contributed during the past 30 years by the large number of scholars who have examined the political and economic behavior of individuals and groups by adopting many overlapping paradigms and theories (e.g., property rights, information, transaction cost, public "choice," "collective actions," "game," "new" industrial organization, etc.).

For those interested in learning about (1) what I referred to as accumulated insights, (2) how they helped give rise to neoinstitutional analysis, and (3) the essential analytic approaches and perspectives of neoinstitutional analysis, by far the best book to consult is Thrainn Eggertsson, *Economic Behavior and Institutions* (Cambridge: Cambridge University Press, 1992). Douglass C. North, *Institutions, Institutional Change, and Economic Performance* (Cambridge: Cambridge University Press, 1990), is an excellent work that also provides rich discussions of (1) and (3) by a leading scholar of neoinstitutional analysis.

7 Yasusuke Murakami, *An Anticlassical Political-Economic Analysis: A Vision for the Next Century* (Stanford: Stanford University Press, 1996) which is a translation of *Han-koten no seiji keizaigaku* (Tokyo: Chūōkōron-sha, 1993).

8 North, *Institutions, Institutional Change, and Economic Performance*, p. 3.

approach is that institutions determine transaction costs: the costs of obtaining information necessary to measure the valuable attributes of what is being traded and the costs of specifying and enforcing property rights (in the broad sense of the phrase, including those in human capital).[9] Transaction costs determine how efficiently or inefficiently an economy performs over time, and thus institutions become principal determinants of economic performance over time.

The above means that, when this approach is adopted, such questions as the following can be asked. Why does an economy have various distinctive institutions affecting its performance? How do institutions change? Why do some inefficient institutions (i.e., those that reduce the performance of an economy) persist in some economies but not in others? As these questions suggest and as an examination of the by now substantial number of works adopting this approach show, this is an approach most useful in analyzing the roles of the government, the most important institution in any economy, and in broadening studies of economic history to include the roles that political and social institutions play in determining the economic performance of a nation.

As the seven chapters in this volume make evident, this neo-institutional approach can assist, I believe, in helping to answer many questions that have been debated by students of Japanese economic history. To what extent did the roles of the Japanese government in the economy from the Meiji period to the present contribute to reducing or increasing transaction costs (thus reducing or increasing the performance of the economy)? Why did those institutions that reduce the performance of the economy persist? How did *zaibatsu* and *keiretsu* reduce or increase transaction costs to promote or reduce Japan's economic performance? Which of the institutions defining Japanese labor-management relations today are efficiency-promoting and which are "path dependent," established in the past and continuing to survive despite their efficiency-reducing effects? I am certain that those who read the seven chapters in this volume and study the neo-institutional approach can ask many other important and interesting questions of Japanese economic history.

Another new analytic approach is the "anticlassical political-economic analysis" of Yasusuke Murakami, a mathematical economist turned social scientist. His analysis, offering well-informed and incisive frontal criticisms of the shortcomings of both classical and neoclassical

9 For an analytically comprehensive definition of transaction costs, see Eggertsson, *Economic Behavior and Institutions*, pp. 14–16.

economic analysis, cannot be summarized in a few pages because it has many economic, political-economic, and even philosophical dimensions. However, for students of economic history, and especially for those interested in Japanese economic history, the core of his anticlassical analysis is the following.

He argues that neoclassical economic analysis is seriously flawed because it is essentially a short-run equilibrium analysis (i.e., markets are assumed to achieve equilibrium because of supply-demand market forces) and fails to include technological change within its analytic framework. Because of these weaknesses, the neoclassical theory, he argues, can only be a tool for analyzing developed economies, not for studying how an economy grows over time. That is, neoclassical analysis is not useful in analyzing the process of industrialization in which technological change plays a dominant role and in which markets are constantly in disequilibrium.

The constant technological change seen in the process of industrialization means, Murakami argues, the cost of production continues to decline as a trend over time as firms adopt one new technology after another as industrialization progresses. And when firms face declining cost, the markets of these firms cannot but be inherently unstable. That is, firms will compete to increase market share to further reduce the cost of production. Those firms that reduce their cost first in a market can and will engage in "domestic dumping" (i.e., engage in "forward pricing" to increase market share).[10] This process leads to markets dominated by monopolists or colluding oligopolists. Thus, if the government of a developing economy wishes to promote the process of industrialization in which a larger number of competitive, increasingly more efficient (cost-reducing) firms participate, it must adopt "developmentalism." Very simply put, developmentalism is the political–economic strategy of promoting industrialization by means of activist government intervention in the economy.

The intervention, according to Murakami's analysis, can include temporary, government-guided cartels among large firms that are rapidly adopting new technology in order to prevent "domestic dumping." Various other policies suggested by Murakami include industry-specific subsidies of various types, trade protection for "infant" industries, and policies to mitigate the unequal distribution of income that often results in the process of industrialization.

10 "Forward pricing" is to price the products of a firm based not on the current production cost but by the lower production cost that the firm anticipates to reach after market share (output) is increased.

Murakami, however, is insistent that developmentalism is to be adopted only by developing economies attempting to catch up with industrialized economies. That is, developmentalist policy intervention must cease when an economy has succeeded in industrializing and has become a developed economy. The two main reasons for this are that as the catch-up process ends, firms are less able to enjoy declining cost (by borrowing new technology from developed economies), and the developmental strategy of trade protection cannot be justified for developed economies if a stable and harmonious world trade regime is to be maintained.

As even the preceding extremely abbreviated summary of a few of the most significant aspects of Murakami's "anticlassical analysis" shows, his analysis enables us to ask many new questions about the Japanese economic experience of the past century. To what extent was Japan a developmentalist economy in the Meiji, interwar, and postwar periods? Did a developmentalist cartel policy to minimize "domestic dumping" contribute to Japanese industrialization? How do the policies of Japan in the prewar and postwar periods differ from the theoretical developmentalism of Murakami and why? In what respects does the Japanese economic history of the past century support Murakami's analysis and in what respect does it not? What were the social costs of developmentalism?

Other, no less important questions can be raised from a study of Japanese economic history, drawing upon the insights of Murakami's anticlassical analysis. Why did or did not Japan succeed in abandoning its developmentalism in recent decades? If Japan is still developmentalist in some respects, is it because developmentalism, once adopted, is difficult to "reverse," contrary to what Murakami believes must occur? Are many of the economic and political challenges Japan faces today, both at home and internationally, the inevitable outcomes of Japan's past economic success based on its developmentalism?

In our efforts to better understand Japanese economic history, we have traveled many miles since the end of World War II. But we still have a long journey to make. That journey, I suggest, may be made more rewarding if we avail ourselves of these two recent analytic contributions and other analytic developments, as well as of the knowledge accumulated to date, including that presented in the seven chapters of this volume. We must always be reminded that knowledge of Japan's economic history is essential in our effort to better understand Japan's modern history and the reasons for the numerous political, economic, and social challenges that confront Japan today at the turn of the century.

CHAPTER 1

ECONOMIC CHANGE IN THE NINETEENTH CENTURY

At the beginning of the nineteenth century, Japan was a preindustrial agricultural economy with technology and living standards not greatly different from those of other preindustrial areas of Asia. If a Frenchman of 1600 had been able to see the Japan of 1800, he would have been impressed by obvious differences in dress, manners, and architecture, but most features of economic life would have been readily understandable to him. Had the same Frenchman visited Japan a century later, he would have been bewildered. By the end of the century, the nation's output of goods and services had increased fourfold, and the proportion contributed by industry had at least doubled, whereas the contribution of agriculture had declined to less than half the total output. Much of the infrastructure necessary for the development of an industrial economy, such as transport, communications, ports, and financial institutions, had been created, and a modest but crucial nucleus of modern factory industry was becoming a viable growth sector. This was a century of economic change, and the change was at an increasing rate.

Explanations for this change represent both a variety of ideologies and a variety of views of the facts. Most Japanese historians have viewed it as a transition from a feudal to a capitalist society within the framework of the Marxian theory of stages of economic development. Even granted that a relative latecomer such as Japan might be able to take advantage of some shortcuts, it was not easy to see how such a change, which took centuries in Europe, could occur within a few decades in Japan. Japanese historians have been divided on how to explain this problem. The Rōnō (laborer and farmer) school, so called from its journal of the same name, made an adjustment at the beginning of the process and, while maintaining the idea that premodern Japan was basically feudal, stressed the emergence of capitalist elements in the century before the Meiji Restoration of 1868, which is usually taken to mark the beginning of Japan's modern period. According to this school, therefore, the gap between the Japan of 1868 and the Japan of the early twentieth century was not as great as that between feudal and capitalist Europe. The Kōza (lectures) school, which took its name from its major publication, *Nihon shihonshugi hattatsu shi kōza* (Lectures on the development of Japanese capitalism),[1] made the adjustment at the latter end and stressed the premodern aspects of the Japanese economy throughout the Meiji period and beyond, as exemplified by the survival of noneconomic factors in the relations between landlords and tenants and between employers and employees, the immaturity of Japanese capitalism, and the absolutist nature of the Meiji state. Neither school seriously questioned the assumption that the process of economic change in Japan was essentially similar to the earlier European experience.

Before the Pacific War, Western observers emphasized the importance of state power in alliance with powerful business groups in exploiting Japanese workers and poor farmers in the interests of building a strong nation as rapidly as possible. Their view may well have been colored by fears of what they saw as "unfair" competition in international trade supported by low wages in Japan. After the war, Western scholars devoted much attention to explaining Japan's economic development in terms of what were identified as preconditions for economic change. In essence, this was an attempt to see whether explanations of economic change in Europe based on such factors as the Protestant ethic and the agricultural revolution could be applied to the Japanese case by identifying analogues to these factors in the Japanese experience. The results were unsatisfactory for two reasons. First, the implied assumption that economic development could not take place in the absence of factors that were thought to be important to European development proved to be invalid. Moreover, when equivalents were found in Japan, such as a merchant ethic analogous to the Protestant ethic, similar conditions were found to exist in other countries, such as China, where modern economic growth did not occur. Second, these studies on the whole took insufficient account of the fact that economic changes in Japan occurred a century or more after the industrialization of western Europe and North America. Not only had the world changed in the meantime, but Japan was able to draw on the experience of the advanced industrial countries.

Since then, explanations of Japan's economic development have mostly been in terms of the quantitative relationships among economic variables such as capital formation, the labor force, technology, the

1 7 vols. (Tokyo: Iwanami shoten, 1932–3).

structure of production and consumption, prices and other aggregates, and the ways in which they affect the rate of growth of national income. In comparison with prewar studies, these quantitative analyses are less explicitly concerned with the role of government and the exercise of power as a means of influencing economic activity. Attention so far has centered more on the behavior of the economic aggregates themselves than on the less quantifiable forces that modified the operation of free-market mechanisms.

There are particular difficulties in applying these quantitative methods to the study of the Japanese economy in the nineteenth century, for most of which quantitative data on a national scale are lacking. What follows in this chapter must therefore be largely descriptive. Because conditions varied widely from one part of Japan to another, descriptions of economic life in one village or region, of which there are many, cannot be taken as representative of the whole country. This chapter will nevertheless attempt to describe the economic system as a whole and the changes in the way that system operated.

THE ECONOMY AT THE BEGINNING OF THE NINETEENTH CENTURY

Japan in 1800 was in most respects typical of a preindustrial Asian country. The population was about 30 million to 33 million, less than a quarter of the present population, and was growing slowly. Some 80 to 85 percent of this population lived in rural villages. Of the remainder, nearly 2 million lived in the three very large cities – Edo (modern Tokyo), Osaka, and Kyoto – and upwards of a million and a half lived in the castle towns, the administrative centers of the domains, that varied in size from a few thousand to nearly 100,000 inhabitants. At least half a million lived in ports and communication centers. For administrative purposes, the bulk of the population was divided into four main classes – samurai, farmers, artisans, and merchants.

With very few exceptions, such as Buddhist or Shinto priests, doctors, and professional teachers, who were outside the four main classes, those who lived in rural villages were officially classed as farmers. They produced all of the country's food including marine products, and industrial crops such as cotton, oilseeds, flax, tobacco, indigo, vegetable wax, and the raw materials for papermaking and sericulture, and they provided nearly all of the tax revenue. But they also produced a large and increasing part of the industrial output and conducted the local trade, commerce, transport, and construction. In some regions, such as around Osaka Bay and along the Inland Sea, villagers officially classed as farmers spent on average as much as half their time in nonagricultural pursuits. In more remote regions where opportunities for industrial employment were fewer, as many as one-third to one-half of the villagers spent the slack agricultural season or periods of a year or more working away from their villages, and at least half of this work was nonagricultural. The importance of industrial and commercial activity was therefore much greater than the classification as farmers of 80 to 85 percent of the population would suggest.

In Edo and the castle towns, about half of the population consisted of samurai and their dependents. As well as forming a standing military force whose function was mainly internal security, the samurai staffed the administrative and clerical levels of the government services. Samurai and their dependents made up some 6 to 7 percent of the country's population, but at any given time at least half of them had only nominal duties. The civilian population of these administrative centers consisted of artisans, wholesale and retail traders, and construction workers whose function was originally to supply the needs of the samurai establishment, but by the early nineteenth century much of the demand for their services came from the civilian population itself and from the growing role that these centers played as entrepôts for the commerce of the surrounding districts. Osaka, with a much smaller samurai establishment, was Japan's commercial center par excellence. Tax rice and essential agricultural and manufactured products were channeled into it and, sometimes after further processing, were redistributed to Edo and other parts of the country. Osaka's highly developed commercial institutions were a key point in the government's system of economic controls. Kyoto, the seat of the imperial court, was the traditional center of the industrial arts and also an important financial market. With the diffusion of such crafts as silk weaving and ceramics to other parts of Japan during the eighteenth century, Kyoto craftsmen specialized in products of high quality and artistic excellence for the court and senior samurai. Unlike the townsmen of Edo, few of whom had been in the city for more than a generation, many of the civilian inhabitants of Kyoto had been established there for two or three centuries before 1800 and were proud of their traditions.

Because of Japan's mountainous geography and long coastline, most interregional traffic went by sea along a chain of ports that ran right around the main islands. Ports like Hakata, Niigata, Sakata, Tsuruga, Obama, Shimonoseki, Shimizu, and Chōshi had populations of ten to twenty thousand and provided services that were adequate for the needs of the Japanese shipping of the time. Nagasaki, the only official international port, was a city of fifty or sixty thousand, not including the Dutch and Chinese settlements. Sakai, the major port for interregional trade, especially with Hokkaido, was about the same size.

The urban population tended to be a shifting one, and information on urban population is much less reliable than that on the rural population. In all, at least 10 percent of the population lived and worked in cities of ten thousand or more, and perhaps another 5 percent lived in towns of five thousand to ten thousand inhabitants.[2]

Urbanization on this scale, while low by modern standards, implies a good deal of commercial activity. Although the theories of the political economy of Tokugawa Japan were predicated on subsistence farming with all the surplus being drawn off in taxes, urban consumption centers had to be supplied with food, clothing, fuel, and other necessities, and thus the system itself required commercial development and production for the market as well as the delivery of taxes in kind. Tokugawa economic policy was aimed at securing these supplies without putting cash into the hands of rural producers who might use it to express their own competing demands for the products of the market. For administrations whose incomes were in taxes in kind but whose expenditures were in the cash market, any growth of civilian demand represented unwelcome competition, and this situation became both a basic problem of economic policy and the source of economic change.

Economic policy and its administration

Under the *bakuhan* system, responsibility for economic policy and its administration was shared by the Tokugawa government (bakufu) and some 270 domain (*han*) administrations. The bakufu held nearly a quarter of the country's land, by ratable value, as its own domain. In addition, it held all the cities of major economic importance containing nearly half the urban population. It also controlled all gold and silver production and had a monopoly of issuing coinage. The bakufu could also give guidance or even issue orders to the daimyo, the titular heads of the domains, who would comply more or less enthusiastically according to their own interests and their relationship with the bakufu; but because they were ultimately responsible to the bakufu for the good government of their domains, they tended to follow its lead. In

2 Sekiyama Naotarō, *Nihon no jinkō* (Tokyo: Shibundō, 1966), pp. 114–15. I have added a figure for samurai and others not included in this source.

general, the economic aim of both the bakufu and the domains was to take in tax as much of the production of their people as they could while maintaining and, if possible, increasing the productive capacity of their territories. In the early years of the *bakuhan* system, these aims of the bakufu and the domains did not seriously conflict with one another, but by 1800 production for the market had developed to a point where competition for the profit on the marketing of these products led to chronic conflict between the policies of the domains and the bakufu and between merchant groups allied with one or the other or seeking independence from both.

The principal aim of the bakufu's economic policy, as of its policy in general, was the maintenance of stability and the preservation of the agricultural economy which was its main source of income. Both the bakufu and the domains believed that the function of the agricultural population was to produce tax revenue, and this belief rather than any interest in the welfare of the villagers underlay their efforts to maintain the viability of the rural village and to increase the production of rice and other crops. Thus in the bakufu territories a village could be punished for failing to get the maximum amount of production from its land, planting commercial crops on land assessed as taxable rice land, or neglecting farming in favor of other occupations. Despite these efforts, the yield from taxes on agriculture had already reached its peak before 1800, and attempts to raise it increasingly encountered strong resistance.

Fiscal policies of both the bakufu and the domains aimed to spend no more than was received as revenue, but this aim was seldom achieved. With their regular income fixed within narrow limits, governments tried to find other sources of income and to limit expenditures as far as possible. In these respects, the situation of the bakufu differed from that of the domains, and the possibilities available to the domains themselves also differed from one another.

The bakufu had separate budgets for rice and cash. Records of these budgets are fragmentary and inconsistent, but all point to a deterioration in the financial position of the bakufu. The regular rice tax income of the bakufu was actually falling at the opening of the nineteenth century. Even in the famine decade of 1782–91 its rice tax receipts averaged 613,000 *koku,* net of collection costs and local administrative expenses, leaving an average annual surplus of just 38,000 *koku*. In the following two decades, receipts rose slightly, but so did expenditures. In the decade of 1812–21, however, rice tax receipts fell sharply to 566,000 *koku* per year, and the bakufu was forced to draw on its stocks. These figures do not appear to include the revenues of the *hatamoto*, or bannermen. Regular cash revenue, including various license fees, also fell over the same period, whereas cash expenditures increased.[3] From time to time the bakufu requested loan subscriptions from the virtually untaxed merchant communities of Edo, Osaka, and some other cities in its domains. Five requests between 1800 and 1813 yielded a total of over half a million *ryō*, about half the amount requested. The cash deficit was financed largely by resort, not to the printing press, as the bakufu did not issue paper currency, but to debasement of the coinage which was subject to rather more practical restraints. Nevertheless, the results were similar, and because about a quarter of the total cash expenditures were financed in this way, inflationary results could be expected.[4] That prices did not rise much until the 1830s and 1840s was due partly to the increasing demand for cash to finance a rising level of cash transactions, as people came to buy more and more things rather than produce them themselves or barter their produce for them, but it also depended largely on price control.

Efforts to reduce expenditures took two forms. First, the bakufu, like the domains, tried to reduce the amount of goods and services bought by itself and its retainers. Official exhortations to frugality were included in its "Regulations for Samurai" and repeated with particular zeal in times of financial crisis, but they seem to have been singularly ineffective.[5] The economic circumstances of the samurai depended on relative movements in the price of rice in which their incomes were denominated and in the prices of the goods and services on which they spent their incomes. As Yamamura has suggested, the real incomes of the bakufu's retainers seem to show no long-term falling trend in the last century of Tokugawa rule, but in the nineteenth century they fell sharply as rice prices fell, whereas the general price level remained relatively stable.[6] Using five-year averages to even out year-to-year fluctuations, the real value of the incomes of bannermen fell by 15 percent between 1791–5 and 1796–1800 and by a further 13 percent between 1796–1800 and 1801–5, and it was a long time before the levels of the last decade of the eighteenth century were

3 *Nihon zaisei keizai shiryō* (Tokyo: Zaisei keisai gakkai, 1922–5), vol. 10, pp. 436–57.

4 Satō Jizaemon, *Kahei hiroku* in *Nihon keizai sōsho* (Tokyo: Nihon keizai sōsho kankōkai, 1914), vol. 32, pp. 327–8.

5 Ishii Ryōsuke, ed., *Tokugawa kinrei kō* (Tokyo: Sōbunsha, 1959), 1st ser., vol. 1, pp. 61–75; and Takayanagi Shinzō and Ishii Ryōsuke, eds., *Ofuregaki Temmei shūsei* (Tokyo: Iwanami shoten, 1958), pp. 481–92.

6 Kozo Yamamura, *A Study of Samurai Income and Entrepreneurship* (Cambridge, Mass.: Harvard University Press, 1974), p. 41.

regained. It was thus in the bakufu's interests to maintain and stabilize the price of rice, while making every effort to prevent rises in the cost of other commodities. These efforts consisted of regulating competing demands for goods from the rural population and attempting to control prices in the cities.

Regulation and control were indeed the cornerstones of economic as of other administration at all levels in Tokugawa Japan and particularly of the economic administration of the bakufu. Economic policies were directed at people rather than at economic variables such as the money supply, incomes, and employment. It was well known, for example, that

> rising prices are due to an overabundance of money. After all, the annual production of goods is fixed while there is no natural limit to the annual amount of increase in the money supply. The greater the increase the worse the effects. It is just like trying to relieve a famine by cutting the meat into smaller portions.[7]

Faced with a deficit, however, the bakufu preferred to regard deficit financing as inevitable and to put the blame for rising prices on the people for spending the money that it thus put into their hands.

The people, particularly the peasant farmers, were regarded as existing and working for the support of the government. All that they produced was, in principle, at its disposal, but because the government accepted responsibility for the peasants' livelihood, it allowed them to keep just so much as they needed to keep body and soul together. In principle, too, every aspect of the village's economic life was controlled, and farmers were required to devote all their efforts to producing food and other useful crops. Any other activity that interfered with this was forbidden. Even if work of any kind was available outside the village, it could not be accepted without permission, and the authorities had to be satisfied that the move would not reduce production from the land. Even an overnight absence from the village required an official exeat. Failure to work from dawn to dusk was described as "laziness" and was a punishable offense. A farmer who failed to cultivate his land so as to produce the maximum crops possible with the existing technology and weather conditions – even though his income might be higher if he devoted his time to other pursuits – not only incurred social penalties but was guilty of dereliction of duty and could be punished for the crime of neglecting his proper duties.

Granted that these regulations were not always strictly enforced, it

7 Satō, *Kahei hiroku*, p. 320.

is clear that the bakufu did not rely on the operation of market forces and indeed regarded them as working against its interests. Restriction of consumption by fiat, wage fixing, compulsory procurement of all essential products at regulated prices, and processing and marketing through organizations that acted in many ways like government agents were the time-honored ways of restricting rural demand, ensuring a steady supply of essential goods to the administrative centers, and keeping prices down. If despite all this, prices in Edo rose, the bakufu simply ordered wholesalers and retailers to reduce them. If the market price of rice fell following a bumper harvest, the bakufu ordered the rice dealers to increase their stocks, sometimes lending them funds to do so. Under such a closely regulated system, the free market operated, as it were, on the fringes and was countenanced only when it was of a petty nature or when it could be made to work to the benefit of the authorities. The situation was in this respect not unlike that in a country such as the People's Republic of China. In terms of producing economic growth, the controlled economy was a failure, but then economic growth was not a principal aim of the policy. As we shall see, even in terms of the economic policy of the time, it failed to achieve the stability that the bakufu desired.

As well as its monopoly of the coinage, control of national commerce and agriculture, and consumption in its own domains, the bakufu controlled foreign trade and most mining and forestry. Foreign trade was officially limited to a small traffic with the Dutch and Chinese through Nagasaki, Japan's only authorized international port, but a considerable trade with the Ryūkyūs operated by Satsuma was tolerated and seems to have included as well as Okinawa sugar, some goods of Chinese, Southeast Asian, or even European origin.

Despite such an array of powers, the financial position of the bakufu and its ability to control the economy declined as the century progressed. The causes of this decline included, as we shall see, the growing fiscal demands of foreign relations and defense, the diminishing power to enforce collection of revenue, a slow but steady fall in the proportion of national product produced by agriculture, a number of poor harvests, and, not the least, the frustration of its system of commercial and financial controls by actions of the domains attempting to shore up their own finances.

Because the domains were denied the right to issue coinage, their deficits represented an increase in their indebtedness, and with rising costs, especially of traveling to and from Edo and maintaining an establishment there, almost all the domains were accumulating a mounting burden of debt despite a range of measures to increase revenue. These included raising the rate of agricultural tax, imposing new taxes, promoting land reclamation, "borrowing" or withholding part of the retainers' stipends, levying contributions from leading merchants of the domain, issuing paper money, encouraging production and processing of industrial crops, and sharing in the profit from their production and sale through monopoly marketing boards operated by the domain itself or through its agents. The scope for increasing revenue by most of these measures was limited. Despite the encouragement of reclamation projects, the output of rice and other staple crops that provided the traditional tax base grew only slowly; and the higher the tax rate was, the more profitable it was for farmers to direct their energies to other kinds of production. Hence the steady flow of edicts forbidding neglect of staple agriculture for other occupations and hence, too, their general lack of effect. Growing and processing industrial crops was far more profitable than was growing rice to be taken in tax. If the taxes were too heavy, the farmers absconded and left the land to go to waste, thus reducing the domain's income and offsetting schemes to increase acreage by expensive land reclamation projects. Even the Satsuma domain, which maintained tighter control than most over its farming population and where alternative occupational opportunities were relatively limited, had by 1820 accumulated debts to the tune of five million *ryō*, equal to about ten years' regular revenue.

In a society that had come to expect that traditional practices would be maintained, imposition of new kinds of tax provoked discontent and sometimes actual rebellion. Levies on merchants and borrowing from retainers tended to alienate the very groups on which the domain authorities relied for support. Denied the right to issue coinage, the domains turned to issuing paper notes. The bakufu had placed strict controls on such issues in 1759, but with the growth of local industry and commerce in the early years of the nineteenth century, there was a demand for means of local payments, and so many domains issued notes backed by cash, rice, or goods. Those notes (*hansatsu*) were legal tender for certain purposes within the domain, and some enjoyed limited acceptance beyond its borders. By the 1860s such issues reached very large proportions, circulated at a heavy discount against cash, and contributed heavily to the inflationary pressures of the last decades of the Tokugawa period. Their direct inflationary effects were, however, largely confined to the domain that issued them, and their effect on national price levels was less than that of the massive increase in bank advances associated with domain borrowing during these decades. At the start of the century, however, the harmful effects of *hansatsu* were not intolerable, even though such issues already involved some conflict with the monetary policies of the bakufu.

Whereas all these measures were to a greater or lesser extent negative, in that they did not promote economic development but rather the opposite, attempts by domains to obtain a share of the profits from production other than staple agriculture had far-reaching consequences. The Tokugawa theory of political economy was rationalized in terms of Confucian maxims that the state could not prosper unless the people were prosperous, understood in the context of subsistence agriculture in which the state's primary function was to maintain law and order rather than to promote economic growth. Promotion of production for the general market, as opposed to encouragement of production for the lord's use, clearly ran counter to the theory. For a domain government to promote such production and trade for its own financial gain was not only ideologically unorthodox but in fact brought the domain into conflict with the bakufu. The reason was that in setting up marketing boards that acquired, either directly or through commercial agents, the more profitable products of the domain at fixed prices and sold them not only locally but on the national market, they competed with the marketing system sponsored and controlled by the bakufu. Nevertheless, some domains had adopted these measures quite early – the Sendai domain's rice and salt monopolies and the Yamaguchi domain's paper monopoly, for example, had been in operation since the seventeenth century.

By the early nineteenth century, many domains had abandoned the orthodoxy of the early Edo period and were actively encouraging new crops and industries, usually in collaboration with merchants from their castle town or from the more advanced Kinki region. From the late eighteenth century, the Tōhoku domains of Aizu, Shinjō, and Yonezawa actively encouraged industrial arts such as weaving and lacquer making, as did the Mito domain in northern Kantō. In the Chūbu region from Kanazawa to Nagoya – with almost a quarter of Japan's arable land, population, and rice production – sericulture, silk and cotton weaving, paper, lacquer ware, and wood and bamboo products were important local industries by 1800. Silk-crepe weaving technology was introduced to Gifu as early as 1730 by a few refugees from a fire in Nishijin. By 1819 Gifu crepe broke the monopoly of the Kyoto industry by marketing its products through the official channels of the powerful Owari domain, to the advantage of the producers, local merchants, and the domain itself. The introduction of striped-cotton weaving in Mino was thanks to another Kyoto fire in the 1780s. Here finance and marketing were through merchants from Ōmi. Tokushima's indigo monopoly, Matsue's ginseng, Uwajima's and Yamaguchi's paper monopolies, and several domains' salt monopolies all brought considerable profits to the domains' treasuries. The operations of these monopoly marketing boards were linked with the issue of local paper currency, as local purchases were paid for in *hansatsu* and sales in the national market were for cash or credits convertible to cash.

Promotion and sale of industrial crops and industrial products by the domains was central to the economic changes taking place in the first decades of the nineteenth century. Those changes were at least as much the results of and reactions to government controls as of spontaneous activity by the population at large. The spread of industrial production in their domains, as commercial agents in the bakufu's cities sought cheaper sources of supply in the countryside, prompted the domain administrations to try to appropriate the profits from it in competition with the city merchants and to promote and control further growth to increase their own resources. Heavy taxes on mainstream agriculture and relatively light taxes on other occupations induced a move from rice culture to industrial crops and processing industries like textiles. This shift was supported from the demand side by a relatively elastic demand for industrial products and a relatively inelastic demand for rice.

Apart from small-scale local peddling, which was countenanced as a form of unemployment relief, commercial activity was controlled at all levels, but control also provoked resistance at all levels. City merchants struggled to maintain the privileges granted to them by the bakufu and to prevent the domains' selling directly to urban consumption centers. Merchants in the castle towns, usually with the backing of their domain authorities, struggled to maintain their privileges against rural merchants. The producers struggled for freedom to sell their products wherever they could obtain the best price, but seldom with much success, as escape from control at one level was generally replaced by control at another. In the process, however, production grew and incomes rose correspondingly, but the increase in income was distributed unevenly. Much went to the city population and helped produce the flowering of city culture that characterized the first years of the century, but a good part went also to the rural traders and manufacturers who came to be characterized as "rich peasants" (*gōnō*).

The village economy

The rural village, the basic unit of administration and taxation, which had once been almost completely self-sufficient, was changing rapidly around 1800, though the pace of change varied from region to region. Variation among regions and even among neighboring villages was so great that it is not possible to speak of a typical or representative village. A village might consist of six or seven households or two hundred or more. In some villages, landholdings were distributed fairly equally; in others the majority held no land at all, and the tax burdens varied from one domain to another and even among neighboring villages. By 1800, regional specialization had produced different patterns of village economic activity from region to region.[8]

Parts of northern Kantō, Tōhoku, and Kyushu and isolated villages throughout the country had changed little in the century before 1800. An average "backward" village consisted of about forty to fifty households, most of which held some land, though the distribution of landholdings could be uneven. In general, however, the scale of farming was limited to what could be cultivated by household labor, generally around half a hectare. Few of the larger landholders were still able to call on the customary labor services of dependent households, and most leased what they could not cultivate to those who held little or no land of their own. Rice was grown to pay taxes in kind, and in an average season, little was left after the tax rice was delivered. For the rest, wheat, barley, soybeans, and coarse grains were grown for household consumption, with the surpluses traded in small local markets or between households. In such areas the opportunities for commercial farming were limited, and industrial employment was also scarce. There was little incentive to use commercial fertilizers or to introduce new technology, and so agricultural productivity rose very slowly – if anything, backward areas were becoming relatively more backward.

Taxation tended to be heavy relative to output, as the domains tried to maintain establishments and styles of living comparable to those of their peers from more prosperous areas. In a poor season some farmers, unable either to pay their taxes or to support themselves, simply walked off their farms and sought employment elsewhere. Because those who remained in the village were held responsible for cultivating and paying the taxes on land so abandoned, this could result in progressive agricul-

8 Horie Eiichi, ed., *Bakumatsu ishin no nōgyō kōzō* (Tokyo: Iwanami shoten, 1963).

tural decline and create serious problems for the domains as well as the farmers. Laws prohibiting farmers from leaving the land were reinforced by prohibitions against neglecting agriculture for more profitable occupations that might have enabled them to hold on. But rather than punish those who had left their land, the bakufu gave subsidies in the form of tools and rations to induce them to return to agriculture; some domains even paid child endowment to try to build up the farm population. Encouragement of agriculture, which was the source of government revenue, and suppression of industry and rural commerce was rationalized by the theory that agriculture was the backbone of the economy, whereas other occupations were unproductive.

In the rice-growing areas of Mutsu and Dewa, improved techniques and some use of commercial fertilizers produced a surplus of rice for sale after taxes were paid. Those who held more land than they could cultivate with the labor of their own households employed labor either by the year or by the day. To operate a commercial farm successfully, however, required some capital, and those with very small holdings either became farm laborers or migrated in search of employment. By 1800 the gap between rich and poor was already widening and was taking a different form, as control over people progressively gave way to control over other resources and the richer were combining commercial farming with trade. To the disgust of one official observer, rich farmers in the Sendai domain never soiled their hands with farm work but lived in luxury, amusing themselves with music, theater, poetry, and archery.[9] Such a life-style must have been for a small if conspicuous minority. In the Kumamoto domain (southern Kyushu) in 1810, a farmer and his wife with just over half a hectare of paddy field and one-third of a hectare of dry field paid half of their crop of rice, barley, and millet in taxes and spent over half of the remainder on wages and food for hired labor. They owned a horse and bought processed foods, tools, equipment, seed, and fertilizer. As a solid owner-cultivator, the farmer's only luxuries were a trip to the temple during the slack season and a new straw hat. At that he would have broken even, had it not been for the horse's falling ill and needing a visit from the veterinarian.[10] Success or failure for a commercial rice grower depended on the quality of his land, his labor costs, and his tax assessment. A substantial farmer with one hectare of good rice land and some dry field in

9 Tamamushi Jūzō, *Jinsei hen,* in Honjō Eijirō, ed., *Kinsei shakai keizai sōsho* (Tokyo: Kaizōsha, 1926), vol. 7.
10 Kodama Kōta, *Kinsei nōmin seikatsu shi* (Tokyo: Yoshikawa kōbunkan, 1958), pp. 276–84.

Mito was able to save six or seven *ryō* a year. Another with the same amount of less productive land could save less than two *ryō*.[11] For those who could accumulate some capital, the region's export of rice, other grains, and dried fish, and its imports of manufactured goods, provided profitable trading opportunities.

In northern Honshū and Kyushu, the inadequacy of subsistence agriculture and rice monoculture as a revenue base was apparent by the middle of the eighteenth century and was highlighted by the crop failures of the 1780s. Many domains encouraged and often financed cultivation and processing of industrial crops such as paper, mulberry, wax, lacquer, and silkworms. The domain monopolized the products and took the lion's share of the proceeds. Although farmers were in effect working for a government enterprise, such innovations also enhanced the viability of the village economy.

In central Honshū, village life was more commercialized; industrial crops were widespread; and village industry was an important source of rural income. A sharp line cannot be drawn between this region and the rice-growing regions of the north. Although the Shōnai domain exported little but rice, other parts of Dewa grew, processed, and exported *benihana* (a red dye), and the Yonezawa domain began to encourage industrial crops, especially sericulture, in the 1790s in an attempt to make up for falling revenues from agriculture. Echigo, just south of Dewa, exported substantial quantities of silk crepe as well as rice. Further south again, the huge Kaga domain produced and exported silk, linen, and cotton cloth, marine products, umbrellas, livestock, lacquer ware, salt, and paper, but rice still accounted for 40 percent of all exports from the domain. The industrial exports themselves were the result of domain development policies dating back to the mid-eighteenth century, and their production and marketing were largely a domain enterprise.

It was in the southern provinces of central Japan from Owari to Harima, and particularly in the provinces of Izumi, Kawachi, and Settsu around Osaka Bay, that village life was most involved with the market. Here farmers worked for profit rather than for the domain administration; indeed with few powerful domains in the area, controls on production were few and ineffective. Many villages specialized in growing cotton and oilseeds to the extent that they imported rice from other areas. These crops required heavy applications of commercial fertilizers, such as oil cake, fish meal, and night soil, and farmers

11 Ibid., p. 284.

carefully balanced their expenditures on fertilizers against the extra income that it could expect to return. An average village in this area consisted of about fifty landholding households and perhaps as many who held little or no land of their own. There was a strong demand for labor, and those with no land of their own found employment in cotton spinning and weaving or as agricultural laborers. Labor was scarce, not, as in the north, because depressed farmers were leaving the area, but because industries were growing rapidly. As a result, wages were relatively high, and those with more land than they could cultivate themselves found it more profitable to rent their surplus land to tenant farmers than to hire labor. Conditions were similar in western Owari where cotton spinning was a major activity.

In all these areas, the villagers spent more time in spinning, weaving, and trading than in farm work. A villager with land sufficient only for a house and garden would have been impoverished in the less commercialized areas of the north, but here he might make a living as a weaver or even be a prosperous trader. Taxes were relatively light, but controls on marketing depressed the prices paid to producers.

The Kantō region, the hinterland of Edo, was developing rapidly in the 1800s as a direct supplier to the Edo market; silk weaving was established in Kiryū, Ashikaga, Hachiōji, and Chichibu; cotton weaving was also widespread; Noda soy sauce was replacing shipments from Osaka; and Edo was supplied with fresh vegetables from its surrounding villages. About a quarter of the rural population was employed in handicrafts and commerce. According to one contemporary source,[12] about half the population indulged in manufacturing, commerce, or sheer idleness, leaving the remaining half to do all the hard agricultural work. Many of these nonagricultural workers had migrated to Kantō from areas farther north where they had been unable to support themselves on their small farms.

All over Japan, village trade was prohibited or discouraged on the grounds that it diverted farmers from their proper work of producing income for the domain and led to luxury and laziness. Some domains permitted peddling so long as it was done on the villagers' own time or when the villager had no other means of support. Where commercial crops were grown with the domain's encouragement or permission, one or more villagers – often village officials – were authorized to collect the produce at the village level and forward it to licensed merchants or domain agents. Retail shops, however, were in principle

12 Buyō Inshi, *Seji kemmonroku* (1816), in *Kinsei shakai keizai sōsho*, vol. 1, pp. 55–6.

restricted to officially nominated towns (*machikata*). This was not easy to enforce, and in many parts of Japan there were villages with shops selling farm equipment, consumer goods of all kinds, and even, according to official reports, luxury goods inappropriate to farmers. The development of rural commerce was affecting the trade of established merchants in the cities and towns, who frequently appealed to the authorities to protect them by forbidding village trade.

The urban economy

Japanese cities were centers of adminstration, consumption, and commerce. Although each domain's castle town or capital combined all three functions, the bakufu's administrative headquarters was in Edo, and its main commercial center, and that of the whole country, was in Osaka. Osaka was the entrepôt to which the products of central and western Japan were sent and from which they were reexported to the great consumption center of Edo and to other parts of the country. This trade was handled by a sophisticated structure of wholesalers (*ton'ya, toiya*) organized in licensed associations (*kabunakama*) which were granted monopoly privileges in return for acting as the bakufu's agents for the control of the national commerce. Shipments from Osaka to Edo were the monopoly of twenty-four groups of authorized wholesalers who were required to consign their goods to ten similarly authorized groups in Edo. This system was under official supervision at every point and operated to keep city consumer prices stable and at the same time to restrict rises in rural incomes. In the century before 1825, this system was effective, and the value of goods channeled through the system rose fourfold or fivefold (much more for some commodities), and prices remained relatively stable. The quantity of cash in circulation at least doubled over this period, with a corresponding profit on the coinage going to the bakufu. That such an increase in the money supply did not produce inflation was due largely to the increased need for money as the volume of transactions increased, but it also reflected the effectiveness of the controls.

Osaka was also the main financial center. At the apex of the financial system of Osaka and of most of the country was a small group of bankers known collectively as the Ten Exchange Houses (Jūnin ryōgae) who performed some of the functions of a central bank, acting as a lender of last resort to correspondent banks, lending to domain governments, controlling the level of bank credits, and controlling the market between gold-denominated cash and silver-denominated bank money. This last was of particular concern to the bakufu. Because wholesale transactions were in silver credit and retail sales in cash, a change in the ratio affected retail price levels. The gold–silver market also reflected the ratio of bank credit to the cash supply. Bank loans financed trade and industry through advances to wholesalers who in turn advanced funds to producers repayable on delivery of the goods. The banks also provided facilities for remittances between Osaka and Edo (and some other centers) by bills of exchange which set off payments by Edo merchants for purchases from Osaka against transfers of official funds from Osaka to Edo. The Osaka banking system also made substantial loans to domains both to cover current deficits and to finance industrial and agricultural development projects.

Industry had once been concentrated in cities, but as the demand for industrial products increased during the eighteenth century, industries such as textiles, pottery, and lacquer ware spread to many parts of Japan. By the 1800s, urban manufacturing was declining, although Kyoto was still the center of high-quality silk weaving and the decorative arts, and Osaka was a major processing center. The construction trades flourished in all the major cities, and the demand for their services was maintained by frequent fires. Artisans in the construction industry were officially under the control of master craftsmen appointed by the bakufu or the domain, a system dating from the time when their function was to build castles and other public buildings; *sake* brewers, wax refiners, oil pressers, and some master weavers were subject to the rules and regulations of their trade associations. The larger cities, especially Edo, contained large numbers of unauthorized immigrants from rural areas who led a hand-to-mouth existence as casual workers, day laborers, and peddlers. Precarious though their livelihood was, they resisted attempts to send them back to their villages, much as the inhabitants of shantytowns on the outskirts of some Third World cities do today.

In each domain, the castle town acted as the commercial as well as the administrative center and performed at the domain level the functions analogous to those that Osaka and Edo performed at the national level. Licensed or "privileged" merchants acted as agents for the collection, distribution, import, and export of goods from the domain, financed and often managed domain enterprises, and backed and managed domain note issues (*hansatsu*).

This description of the Japanese economy at the beginning of the nineteenth century indicates tight economic as well as political control. Staple agriculture was supervised by the local authority in the interests of maintaining revenue. The growing, processing, and marketing of industrial crops were controlled by domain administrations, usually in association with commercial agents inside or outside the domain with whom they shared the profits, leaving small returns to the producers. The national commerce was controlled by the bakufu through licensed associations of merchants in the key cities to maintain adequate supplies of essential goods to Edo and other large cities at stable prices while restricting the growth of incomes and purchasing power in the countryside.

It was clearly in the interests of producers, local merchants, and the domains themselves to evade these controls, as they could usually sell at a higher price in the free market. How effective were the controls? Enforcement became more and more difficult through the first half of the nineteenth century wherever free-market demand was increasing. Faced with a relative decline in their agricultural tax base, moreover, more and more domains adapted to the growth of industry and commerce relative to agriculture by encouraging and exploiting industry and trade as sources of revenue, and those that did not do so soon found increasing difficulty in enforcing controls designed to maintain an economic system that was becoming an anachronism over a growing area of the country. The reforms of the Tempō era represented the last in a series of attempts by the Tokugawa bakufu to salvage its system of economic controls and adapt it to changing economic conditions. Efforts to control economic activity in the interests of the state did not, however, end with the Meiji Restoration, and their changing forms have been a central factor in Japan's economic development ever since.

THE TEMPŌ REFORMS

The transformation of the Japanese village from a community cultivating its land for the benefit of its overlord to a collection of households, each working for its own economic betterment, was well advanced in some regions by the early nineteenth century, and the process accelerated through the century, drawing in more and more areas as it went.

By the 1820s many of the new industrial crops and processing industries introduced by the domains or the city merchants were well established, and output rose quickly, with most of the product marketed through official channels in Osaka or Edo under the control of the bakufu. At about this time, however, the domains, local merchants, and producers themselves could see opportunities to get better prices for their products by selling outside these channels through their own agents in Osaka or Edo or directly to other parts of the country. Almost all the domains were heavily in debt – Satsuma owed thirty-three times its annual revenue in the 1830s, and Chōshū owed twenty-three times its annual income by 1840. A condition of many of these loans was that the domain consigned its produce to its creditors in Osaka, but to do so meant that after the interest and repayments were deducted, little remained. The domains therefore tried to avoid Osaka and to market through other ports or directly to Edo. As a result, shipments to Osaka fell by as much as 30 percent between the 1820s and 1840. In the process, the domains' credit ratings in Osaka fell, and they were forced to seek the cooperation of merchants nearer home and increasingly to rely for revenue on a share of the profits from rapidly growing local industry and trade. Domain restrictions on rural industry and commerce were therefore progressively eased in return for license fees, inspection charges, and other levies or a share in the profits.

Rural traders increased their business at the expense of merchants in the castle towns who had been granted privileges in return for the commercial and financial services they had provided in the eighteenth century or earlier when the rural trade network had not yet developed. These castle town merchants had been the commercial agents and financial backers of the domain monopolies in the late-eighteenth and early-nineteenth centuries, but by the 1830s, even though the total volume of commerce was increasing rapidly, their business was declining as village trade expanded. In Echigo, Shinano, Kii, Tottori, and elsewhere, castle-town merchants complained that they were being ruined by competition from traders in villages where trade was supposed to be forbidden. The response of many domains was to reorganize their marketing boards to include village traders as their grass-roots agents.[13]

By the 1830s a national market had developed for cotton, silk, indigo, wax, paper, sugar, tea, *sake*, pottery, matting, hardware, and lacquer ware apart from and in competition with the bakufu's procurement system, and with new market opportunities opening up, industry and trade became increasingly profitable as compared with agriculture. A survey of the Chōshū domains at the southwestern end of Honshū in 1842 showed that the average gross nonagricultural income

13 See Andō Seiichi, *Kinsei zaikata shōgyō no kenkyū* (Tokyo: Yoshikawa kōbunkan, 1958).

was about as much as the net agricultural income.[14] The main reason for this was that agricultural income was taxed at the rate of 39 percent of net output, whereas nonagricultural income was taxed at less than 10 percent. Agricultural income after tax and production costs were deducted did not even cover reasonable living costs, but nonagricultural pursuits yielded a good profit. On the Inland Sea side of the domain, the proportion of nonagricultural net income was even higher. In northern Honshū about half of farm income came from sericulture, and in Kawachi almost three-quarters came from the cotton industry which by the 1830s produced two million lengths of cloth a year. In the cotton-processing areas of western Owari and Izumi, only 20 percent of output was from agriculture by 1840. Wherever industry developed, it provided cash income which in turn provided the basis for local commerce. In regions such as parts of Tōhoku which enjoyed no comparative advantage in industry, cash income could be obtained only by seeking employment elsewhere, and despite official restrictions, many laborers migrated to the cities or to areas where industry was expanding. In one village in Fukushima, half of the registered landholding families had disappeared by 1841, and 20 percent of the village land was left uncultivated. This was no isolated example – many villages in Tōhoku and outer Kantō were in a similar situation. Often such migration was through personal connections, but in some areas there seem to have been regular labor recruitment agencies.

It should not be imagined that these migrant workers went out in the expectation of making their fortunes. Although it was the existence of employment opportunities elsewhere that made migration possible, it was poverty and hardship that drove people to leave their economically depressed villages, and their willingness to work for little more than subsistence wages tended to keep the general wage level low. Complaints of shortages of wage labor and rising labor costs came mainly from farmers on the outskirts of the major cities who were trying to maintain their relative economic position in areas where nonagricultural activity was expanding rapidly. Overall, however, migration of labor from areas where nonagricultural activity was less

14 *Bōchō fūdo chūshin an.* See Akimoto Hiroya, "Bakumatsu-ki Bōchō ryōkoku no seisan to shōhi," in Umemura Mataji, et al., eds., *Sūryō keizaishi ronshū,* vol. 1: *Nihon keizai no hatten* (Tokyo: Nihon keizai shimbunsha, 1976), pp. 137–58. For a discussion of this document, see Shunsaku Nishikawa, "Grain Consumption: The Case of Chōshū," in Marius B. Jansen and Gilbert Rozman, eds., *Japan in Transition: From Tokugawa to Meiji* (Princeton, N.J.: Princeton University Press, 1986), pp. 421–46.

productive to areas where it was more productive tended to raise average productivity and incomes over the country as a whole.

Cooperation among producers, local traders, and domain authorities could be very productive. In the early nineteenth century, the linen-thread producers of the Kaga domain operated on advances from Ōmi merchants to whom they were forced to sell their thread at low prices. Approaches to the domain to establish a system of finance and marketing that would bring better returns failed, and rather than sell the yarn for such a poor return, the producers, with the assistance of the domain, experimented with weaving their thread into linen crepe. By the 1820s the industry was well established, with finance and marketing facilities arranged by the domain authorities, who opened a marketing office in Edo in 1828. So successful was the venture that in the 1830s the villagers went into cotton weaving as a supplement to linen, for which demand was seasonal. The domain was asked to handle the new product but refused on the ground that the quality was still too uneven. A local merchant involved in the linen trade then offered to finance and market it himself if the domain would lend him the capital. The domain agreed, and by 1861 one district alone was producing a million lengths of cotton a year, and the domain had assumed direct responsibility for quality control and marketing.[15] Even though in such cases, the domain's main object was to secure a source of revenue, the prices to producers and middlemen rose. Producers were no longer prepared to work for the domain for little or no return, and attempts to force them to do so usually provoked vigorous protests. In Kinki and Shikoku where commercial production developed early, such protests were common in the 1790s, and by the 1830s they occurred whenever the producers could get significantly better returns outside the domain monopoly system.

In principle, producers and local merchants were not free to trade unless specifically permitted to do so, and when permission was granted there were usually conditions attached. Local merchants in Okayama gained freedom to export directly from the domain in the 1830s but were required to surrender the hard currency they obtained thereby in return for *hansatsu* which could be used for purchases within the domain but could be converted to cash only at a discount. Although the apparent profits of the local merchants rose, the system operated to help meet the domain's expenses in Edo and Osaka rather

15 Andō, *Kinsei zaikata shōgyō no kenkyū*, pp. 165–70.

than to strengthen the value of its paper currency within the domain, and thus in effect it taxed local trade.

Trading without permission was, however, widespread and difficult to suppress. The authorities were tolerant of peddling by villagers with no other means of support, but larger-scale trading, especially outside the domain or to the detriment of agriculture, was another matter. Nevertheless, there was unauthorized trade (*nukeni*) wherever commercial opportunities presented themselves and restrictions were easier to evade than to police. Having been forced by financial straits to license some village trading in return for license fees in 1825, the Tottori domain found that by 1846 there was so much of it that there was a shortage of cultivators. An attempt to correct the situation by putting the delinquent peasants to forced labor in land reclamation turned out to be a ludicrous anachronism. As the prices to producers rose, it became more and more profitable to leave agriculture for industry and trade, and as rural incomes thereby increased, so did the rural demand for manufactures of all kinds, thus adding fuel to the whole process. By the 1840s most villages in the more advanced regions of Kinki, Chūgoku, and Shikoku were served by shops selling a full range of consumption goods, and villagers bought in cash most of their requirements other than staple grains.

The gains of the domains and the rural producers meant a relative decline in the position of the shogunate. The traditional agricultural tax base was declining as a proportion of total output for domains and shogunate alike, but as possibilities for the domains to profit from the growth of industry and trade increased, the mechanisms by which the shogunate had been able to control national commerce to its advantage became less and less effective. This is indicated by a sharp decline in shipments to Osaka accompanied by rising prices, whose causes were diagnosed in a report prepared in 1841–2 under the direction of Osaka City Magistrate Abe Tōtōmi-no-kami.[16] Based on a survey of twenty-one commodities, the report found that although improper commercial practices were tending to raise prices, more importantly, the development of markets in the countryside was often diverting goods from Osaka and its control system. Attempts to strengthen and extend control to the hinterland of Osaka had failed when they encountered the massive resistance of the 1820s. In eight cases the report found that the operations of the domain monopolies were the major factor. Domains marketed their products elsewhere and forbade private ship-

16 This comprehensive report on problems of price control is printed in full in Osaka-shi sanjikai, ed., *Osaka-shishi* (Osaka: Osaka shiyakusho, 1926), vol. 5, pp. 639–86.

ments to Osaka. If they found it convenient to market in Osaka, they used their monopoly power and the threat of going elsewhere to obtain higher prices. The report recommended abolition of domain monopolies and renewed efforts to enforce regulations requiring producers to ship their products to Osaka, an across-the-board price cut of 20 percent (except for rice), and reorganization of the Osaka licensed trade associations. It appears that the report was never submitted to Edo but was overtaken by the progress of the Tempō reforms.

The reforms

Mizuno Echizen-no-kami Tadakuni, the prime mover of the Tempō reforms, had become governor of Osaka Castle (Osaka jōdai) in 1825, soon after the more-or-less successful protests by thousands of Kinki villagers outraged at being forced to supply the Osaka market at procurement prices to compensate, as they thought, for the increasing evasion of the system elsewhere. Though Mizuno's two-year term in Osaka was relatively quiet, his first years as senior councilor were marked by harvest failures, rising prices, financial crisis, and widespread revolts against the system of government as a whole and especially its economic administration.

Following disastrous harvests, the price of rice in 1836 rose to about double the average of the previous decade and rose by a further 50 percent the next year. But although the rice price subsided over the following three or four years, the prices of other commodities remained high, and in 1840–1 the ratio between the prices paid by the bakufu and its retainers for their purchases as against the price of rice, in which they received a good part of their income, was the highest since the 1770s. At the root of this inflation was the breakdown of trade and price controls in the face of the development of "free" markets, but the situation was aggravated by continuing budget deficits and large issues of currency. If we neglect silver bars (*chōgin*, *mameitagin*) which had gone out of general use by this time, the amount of currency in circulation had increased by about 75 percent in the twenty years before 1838 and was still rising. From 1839 to 1841 new issues of currency, mainly silver quarter-*ryō* pieces (*ichibugin*), totaled close to two million *ryō*, and the gold coinage had been debased to the extent that it was worth only half as much as the better-quality coins of the Keichō, Kyōhō, and Bunsei eras. At the same time, with more and more people earning cash incomes by handicrafts and buying more of their requirements for cash, there was a shortage of the copper currency used for these transactions, and so between 1835 and 1841 the bakufu issued new copper coins to the value of about 580,000 *ryō*. The bakufu seems to have rather overestimated the demand for these coins, because by 1842 their value had fallen further than was thought desirable.

With an increase of about 80 percent in the money supply between 1816 and 1841, substantial inflation could be expected. Although prices rose steeply in famine years, the underlying rise in prices in Edo over the same period was of the order of 50 to 60 percent, or a rather modest 2 percent a year. It seems clear that as well as a growing transaction demand for cash, there was also a considerable rise in the output of goods over the period. That inflation in Edo was relatively modest suggests that most of the increase in currency flowed to the developing rural areas where it was most needed and also that the fall in the flow of goods to Edo through Osaka was largely compensated for by shipments direct from the producing districts in the Kantō hinterland and elsewhere. Nevertheless, deficit financing turned what had until about 1820 been a falling price trend into a rising one.

Although the national output was growing, the bakufu's regular tax income was falling. It had, in fact, been on a declining trend since the mid-eighteenth century. Tax receipts in the famine year of 1836 were the lowest for 125 years, but even when harvests improved, attempts to increase tax revenue met with determined resistance.

The bakufu's first reaction, like that of the domain governments faced with similar problems, was to reduce its own expenditures, suppress competing demands for goods, and try to get more resources back into basic agriculture which was its main source of tax income. The large Kaga domain had embarked on this traditional course as early as 1837 and had anticipated most of the measures taken by the bakufu in the early stages of the Tempō reforms. Faced with financial crisis, the Kaga domain "borrowed" from its samurai by withholding part of their salaries, declared a moratorium on its loans to samurai, introduced price control, imposed export taxes, sent farmers back to their villages, and exhorted villagers to frugality while trying to prevent them from leaving agriculture for other occupations. In an order of 1844 the domain noted that higher wages in weaving were producing a shortage of farm laborers. Village officials should not lightly give permission to engage in industrial employment, and farmers must not pay more than officially determined wage rates – which were graduated from 7,500 *mon* of copper cash (about 1.15 *ryō*) per year for a first-class male farmhand down to 2,000 *mon* for a third-class female servant – and additional seasonal payments must not exceed the customary level.[17] Even though board and lodging were provided, they were at extremely low standards. Farm laboring was a hard life for little reward, and it is hardly surprising that few workers were disposed to accept it if other work were available at even slightly higher wages.

Mizuno himself was trying to implement similar measures in his own domain of Hamamatsu, with very limited success. Nevertheless, such attempts at turning the clock back seem to have been de rigueur for any major reform.

The bakufu announced its reforms in 1841 on the shogun's birthday. A survey of the extent of nonagricultural activity in its villages confirmed that there had been a substantial drift from agriculture, and an order was promptly issued forbidding villagers to engage in nonagricultural work or to seek such work outside the village. The ban was repeated the next year – and the year after and again in 1845 – but all attempts to keep the people down on the farm seem to have been ineffective.

Both the bakufu and the domains attributed the problems of agriculture to a decline in peasant morality leading to neglect of their proper, but unprofitable, work in the fields for more rewarding occupations. Peasants are not what they were, complained a bakufu order. Instead of wearing coarse clothing and tying their hair with straws, they were wearing cotton garments and using hair oil and fancy hair ties. And in wet weather, instead of straw capes they were using raincoats and umbrellas! Peasants would do almost anything to get out of farming, even to the extent of having themeselves disinherited and struck off the village register so that they would be free to leave for more profitable employment elsewhere.[18] Such action could hardly have been taken lightly and indicates the desperation of some of the village population.

Government expenditure, the lifeblood of the Edo merchant community, was slashed; bans were placed on luxuries and amusements; and officials were appointed to police the bans throughout the city. Within a month Echigoya (modern Mitsukoshi Department Store) reported a drop in sales of 5,830 *ryō* from the previous month, Daimaru was down by 2,800 *ryō*, and Shirokiya (modern Tōkyū Department Store) by 3,670 *ryō*. Although all three survived, and indeed survive to this day, this indicated a major business recession.

17 Oda Kichinojō, ed., *Kaga han nōseishi kō* (Tokyo: Tōkō shoin, 1929), pp. 578–9.
18 *Tokugawa kinrei kō*, 1st ser., vol. 5, p. 192.

Even so, prices did not fall far enough for the bakufu, and after a survey of the marketing system based on reports from the wholesale trade associations (*ton'ya nakama*), it became clear that these organizations were no longer effective channels for bringing goods into Edo. Other channels had been developing for some time, bringing in goods from the rapidly growing production of Edo's own hinterland in the Kantō region. The bakufu itself favored this growth in the region in which it could best exercise direct control. By 1821, shipments of soy sauce from Osaka had been replaced by the products of Noda and other parts of the Kantō which were cheaper and whose stronger flavor appealed to Edo tastes. The wholesalers' associations whose business was bound up with the Osaka trade invoked their monopoly privileges in an effort to obstruct the marketing of Kantō products in Edo. But by the 1840s Kantō producers had captured 40 percent of the Edo market for cottonseed oil, and silk textiles from Ashikaga, Kiryū, and elsewhere in Kantō were selling in substantial quantities through Edo merchants who set up business in opposition to the chartered associations. Cotton cloth, tea, and other products of the Kantō region were entering the Edo market in increasing quantities.[19]

With supplies via the Osaka route dwindling, to give preference to Osaka goods in the Edo market meant restricting these growing supplies from Kantō and elsewhere. Moreover, the Kantō region was close to Edo, safe from blockade by sea, and because it was largely in the control of the bakufu either directly or through its retainers and branches, it was a potential base for a bakufu system of monopoly procurement along the lines of those so successfully operated by a number of domains. With such considerations in mind, the bakufu moved early in 1842 to withdraw its support from the Osaka route and to abolish the monopoly privileges of the chartered trade associations (*kabunakama*), beginning with those most closely involved in that trade. Anticipating, though not fully, the confusion likely to follow such a radical departure, the bakufu set up an office under one of the Edo city magistrates, but staffed by civilians, to observe and report on the operation of the new system and to control abuses.

In the spring of 1842 the order to dissolve such trade associations was extended to the domains. By no means all domains complied, and those that did appear to have done so for their own reasons. The Owari (Nagoya) domain, for example, held by one of the senior branches of the Tokugawa family, complied on paper but maintained existing

19 See Hayashi Reiko, "Bakumatsu ishin-ki ni okeru Kantō no shōhin ryūtsū," *Chihōshi kenkyū* 20 (April 1971): 28–41.

controls on a number of trades. The monopoly privileges of its licensed cotton cloth dealers who handled one of the domain's major exports were abolished but were replaced by a marketing board nominally run by the domain itself but with former licensed dealers (*ton'ya*) involved in its operation. Some domains, like Aizu and Satsuma, ignored the order, and the Suwa domain actually licensed a new association of traders to control the marketing of its textiles.[20]

The monopoly marketing boards by which the domains profited from the growth of industry and trade had irked the bakufu for some time, as they were the main mechanism by which the domains were increasing their financial strength relative to that of the bakufu, which was unable to benefit in the same way. At the end of 1842, therefore, it denied domain claims that their monopoly marketing boards were official business and insisted that their products be marketed freely. The response was scarcely encouraging. With agricultural tax income falling and expenses mounting, profits from the marketing boards were essential to keep the domains reasonably solvent. The Matsushiro domain in Shinano, forced for internal reasons to abandon its control of the silk cloth market at this time, found itself heavily in debt within eight years.[21] Suspecting, with some reason, that the bakufu was considering establishing its own monopoly trading system or even moving toward some form of nationwide control of commerce, domains like Chōshū and Satsuma strengthened their own systems rather than relinquishing them.

By early 1843 the thrust of the reform was clearly toward shifting the balance of economic power in favor of the bakufu. At the beginning of the year the bakufu carried out a survey of issues of *hansatsu* (domain notes) but stopped short of banning them. Four months later it tried to restrict the domains' activities by forbidding auctions of goods in ports outside its own territory.

Meanwhile, the bakufu was attempting to reduce both its own expenses and the domains' profits by ordering a general 20 percent price cut in Edo and Osaka, accompanied by cuts in wages and rents. In doing so, it anticipated that the reductions would be passed back to the suppliers, especially the domain marketing boards, which would in turn be forced to lower the prices paid to local suppliers and eventu-

20 See Tsuda Hideo, *Hōken shakai kaitai katei kenkyū josetsu* (Tokyo: Hanawa shobō, 1970), pp. 222–3.

21 Yoshinaga Akira, "Han sembai seido no kiban to kōzō: Matsushirohan sembutsu kaisho shihō o megutte," in Furushima Toshio, ed., *Nihon keizaishi taikei* (Tokyo: Tōkyō daigaku shuppankai, 1965), vol. 4, pp. 225–62.

ally to cut the rates paid to the producers themselves. This would have the added advantage of reducing the relative attractiveness, however small, of industry and trade over agriculture. Had there been no outlets for goods other than the major bakufu cities, this would not have been an unreasonable expectation. In fact, however, a substantial demand had developed in many other parts of the country, and as long as sales could be made there, the domains and rural businessmen were not prepared to cut their margins. Payments to spinners, weavers, and other producers, however, had never been high, and their real incomes had been reduced by inflation. To have reduced them further would certainly have provoked resistance and forced more destitute villagers to move to the cities in search of a livelihood. Thus the supply price of goods did not fall as expected, and Osaka's wholesale prices fluctuated around a level 36 percent above the average of the 1830s.

The price controls were strictly policed under the direction of the Edo city magistrate and financial comptroller Torii Yōzō, Mizuno's right-hand man and a remarkably capable and hardworking official who for those very reasons was generally detested. The result was a substantial diversion of goods from Edo to other markets almost certainly accompanied by some fall in production. Bakufu officials attributed shortages in Edo to the machinations of unscrupulous merchants, but given the extent to which Japan had by then become a commercialized society, they were a natural consequence of its price control policy.

Like other governments, the bakufu seems to have been better at producing recessions than encouraging development. Within six months of the price control order, deteriorating conditions in the countryside were forcing more people out of the villages and exacerbating the problem of destitute itinerants in Edo. At the end of 1842, numbers of these were rounded up and either sent back to their villages or put to work in labor camps. This was followed by a general order to all those in Edo without authorization to return to their villages and their proper agricultural occupations. At this time Ninomiya Sontoku and Ōhara Yūgaku were active in reconstructing Kantō villages on a model in some respects analogous to the modern agricultural cooperative, based on the concept that if farmers were no longer willing to work for their lord, they might still be persuaded that they should work for the good of the village community. This idea, considered novel at the time, achieved only modest success, but it became the prototype for an important element in the organization of modern Japanese society.

By holding down interest rates in its territory, the bakufu had hoped to lighten the burden of debt carried by its retainers. Its effect was, however, to dry up the sources of finance on which they had become dependent, making their financial situation more difficult than ever. In the spring of 1843, therefore, the bakufu took steps to improve their situation and to keep both its retainers and their creditors afloat.

The bakufu itself had made substantial loans to its fief-holding retainers through its Bakuro-chō finance office. Seeing little chance of repayment, the bakufu wrote off half the amount outstanding, or some 200,000 to 250,000 *ryō*, and declared the remainder repayable in easy installments free of interest. Retainers who received their salaries in rice were in the habit of borrowing from their financial agents (*fudasashi*). Some were in debt for large amounts accumulated over generations. To help them, the bakufu worked out an arrangement by which it would lend to its retainers on very favorable terms through the Saruya-chō finance office on condition that the funds be used to repay their debts to the *fudasashi*. The *fudasashi* for their part would follow the example of the bakufu and relieve the financial burdens of their smaller debtors by remitting or lowering interest and arranging for the repayment of capital in small installments. The bakufu pointed out that compared with previous repudiations, this was generous treatment. Before this arrangement was implemented, however, Mizuno was dismissed, and his successor seems to have insisted that all amounts owing to the *fudasashi* be repaid over twenty years free of interest, although the details are unclear. Coming only five years after the *fudasashi* had been ordered to contribute 100,000 *ryō* toward rebuilding part of Edo Castle, it was a serious blow, and a number temporarily closed their doors.[22]

The Mizuno administration seems to have believed that it could finance these rescue operations and put its own finances on a sounder basis by a number of means. As a short-term measure, a forced loan (*goyōkin*) was imposed on the merchant communities of Osaka, Sakai, Hyōgo, and Nishinomiya. Such loans had been raised from time to time, usually to finance rice price support operations. The leading merchants, mainly bankers, were required to lend to the government roughly in proportion to their standing in the business community, for periods of up to twenty years at low rates of interest, very much as Japan's banking system is required to take up government bonds today. The operation of 1843, however, was on a much larger scale than were any of its predecessors. The original target was to raise

22 Koda Shigetomo, *Nihon keizaishi kenkyū* (Tokyo: Ōokayama shoten, 1928) pp. 76–83.

about 2.25 million *ryō* at 2.5 percent repayable over twenty years. Given the lower risk factor, this rate of interest compared favorably with the return on loans to domains. The amount actually taken up was about 1.15 million *ryō*, but even at that it was about twice as much as had ever been raised before. Beyond the financing of the Bakurochō scheme, which was said to require not more than 250,000 *ryō*, no clear reason was given for raising so large a sum, but Mizuno seems to have had in mind some other operation that would require a large amount of capital.[23]

Mizuno was aware of the work of the scholar Satō Shin'en and is said to have commissioned one of his best-known works, *Fukkohō gaigen*.[24] In this and other writings Satō recommended a state monopoly trading system on a national scale, decisively transferring the control of production and the profits of marketing from the domains to the bakufu.

Implementation of some such scheme within the bakufu's own territory was certainly a possibility, and the Kantō region had developed to the point that it could provide a good base. Even before the Osaka loan was finalized, the bakufu announced that it proposed to consolidate its territories by resuming under its direct control all land within a radius of about twenty-five miles of Edo and within about twelve and a half miles of Osaka. Those whose territory was resumed would be compensated with comparable lands elsewhere. One reason for this proposal was the needs of national defense, but another was the need of the bakufu for a strong economic base from which it could compete with the domains and perhaps eventually extend its economic control throughout the country.

Opposition to the plan was widespread among the domains and, combined with opposition from the *hatamoto* who would have been most affected, was sufficient to bring about Mizuno's dismissal. Plans for direct economic control at the national level were abandoned, and reclamation work in Kantō, which if successful would have added considerably to the bakufu's revenue, was stopped. Mizuno's successor, Doi Ōi-no-kami Toshitsura, professed himself unsure of the purpose of the large Osaka loan and suggested that in the circumstances, the money might be returned! Even when Mizuno returned to the government for a few months the following year, plans for, as it were, nationalizing the domains' trading monopolies were not revived.

Nevertheless, the Tempō reforms brought about changes that were

23 Ibid., pp. 437–8.

24 Satō Nobuhiro (Shin'en), *Fukkohō gaigen*, in Takimoto Seiichi, ed., *Nihon keizai taiten* (Tokyo: Shishi shuppansha and Keimeisha, 1928), vol. 19.

irreversible. They made it clear that the process by which economic power was shifting away from the bakufu could not continue without sweeping changes. A realistic program of national defense required the mobilization of resources on a national scale, but the domains were clearly not prepared to surrender their economic powers to the bakufu. At the same time, in dismantling the outworn system of control through the Osaka trade route, the bakufu cleared the way for further changes. These changes were beyond the bakufu's power, but its plans were taken over and largely implemented by the Restoration government some twenty-five years later.

THE OPENING OF FOREIGN TRADE

In the course of the Tempō reforms, the bakufu abandoned attempts to control the economy through the Osaka–Edo marketing system. In its place it had hoped to institute a new system that would give it control of production and commerce throughout the country, but it lacked the political and financial means to carry out its plans in the face of opposition from the domains. The plans were not, however, completely abandoned. Reestablishment of the wholesale traders' associations in 1851 did not represent a return to the pre-Tempō situation, but a move toward more widely based controls. The new associations were not intended to keep out outsiders but to bring them in. Thus they were granted no monopoly privileges, and membership was open to all bona fide traders. Instead of restricting rural traders, the bakufu encouraged them to join the new associations, and in 1852 membership was made compulsory. The jurisdiction of these associations did not extend to the domains' territories, but the new system was comprehensive enough to include all traders through whom the domains sold their goods in the major cities, thus bringing them, nominally at least, under the bakufu's surveillance.

It was into this somewhat uneasy situation that Commodore Matthew Perry arrived in 1853 with instructions to open Japan to foreign trade. The prospect of foreign trade and its actual opening in 1859 dominated the economic as well as the political life of Japan until the Meiji Restoration and beyond. If Japan had been moving toward economic change in the 1840s, the opening of foreign trade ensured that change would be rapid and far-reaching. It produced severe inflation, changed production and relative prices, and focused the struggle between the bakufu and the domains on the issue of control of foreign trade.

The effect of the deflationary measures of the Tempō era was relatively short-lived. By 1850, prices were again rising under the influence of the bakufu's and the domains' deficits and a continuing rise in rural demand. It was the opening of foreign trade, however, that turned comparatively mild price rises into serious and accelerating inflation, and the question of the exchange rate was a major factor.

In the negotiations leading up to the opening of trade, Townsend Harris, representing the United States, insisted that foreign currency – in practice Mexican silver dollars – should exchange for Japanese currency on a weight-for-weight basis. This was the system used in trade with China and other parts of the East where currency, mainly silver, was valued by weight. Silver by weight (*chōgin, mameitagin*) did exist in Japan, and at the official rate of 60 *momme* to the gold *ryō* exchanged for gold at very close to the international ratio of 15.5 to 1, but by the 1850s it formed less than 3 percent of the Japanese currency and was no longer in general use.

The Japanese currency of the 1850s consisted of gold one-*ryō* pieces and smaller-denomination gold coins and silver pieces representing fractions of a gold *ryō*. Most of these latter were silver quarter-*ryō* pieces (*ichibugin*), of which about 200 million had been minted since 1837. As the Japanese negotiators pointed out to Harris, the weight and fineness of these subsidiary coins was immaterial, as they circulated as tokens for one-quarter of a gold *ryō*, irrespective of their intrinsic value, which was much less. If a foreigner were to be allowed to exchange Mexican silver dollars for Japanese token silver coinage by weight, a dollar would exchange for three *ichibu* coins, which in Japan respresented three-quarters of a gold *ryō*. Thus for 1.33 dollars the foreigner would be able to obtain a Japanese gold coin worth over three times that amount, or about 4.59 dollars. Harris's insistence on what he should have realized was a grossly unfair exchange not only complicated the negotiations but also forced the Japanese government to reform its currency in such a way as to make massive inflation inevitable.

The first reaction of the Japanese was to remove the anomaly by reminting the subsidiary silver coinage. Just before the trade was due to start, the bakufu began minting large one-eighth *ryō* silver pieces, two of which weighed rather more than a Mexican silver dollar. At this rate a gold *ryō* would be equivalent to 4.48 Mexican dollars, very close to its value on the international market. Had the bakufu proceeded with its announced intention to remint all its subsidiary silver coinage in this way, it would have reduced the face value of currency in circulation by some 14 million *ryō*, or about 26 percent, with deflationary results. As soon as the new coins appeared at the treaty ports, however, the foreign representatives protested that they were not genuine Japanese coinage in general circulation but a device to prevent foreign traders from making profits in the spirit of the treaties. Forced to withdraw the new coins, the bakufu did all it could to avoid exchange at the anomalous rate specified in the treaties but, under continuing pressure, was unable to prevent the export of up to 500,000 *ryō* of gold over the following six months. In January 1860, however, the bakufu announced that the situation would be corrected by reminting the gold coinage and that in the meantime, silver *ichibu* would exchange in Japan for gold *ryō* at the rate of 13.5 to 1. In April the new gold coins, slightly more than one-third the size of the old ones, were issued at the rate of three new coins for one old one. As a result, the total amount of currency in circulation increased almost 2.5-fold. The British government later apologized for the whole sorry episode, but the damage had been done.

Whether the exchange anomaly introduced by the treaties was removed by reforming (regrading) the silver subsidiary coinage or by reforming (degrading) the gold coinage, the effect on the relationship between the two was the same. The effect on other price relationships, however, was vastly different. The former would have cut the dollar's purchasing power in Japan to one-third and reduced price levels in Japan, or at least would have prevented them from rising. The latter left the exchange value of the dollar intact but led to massive inflation and consequent changes in the distribution of wealth and income in Japan. Within a year the general price level had risen by over 30 percent and by 1866 it was over four times the pretrade level.[25]

Once the exchange situation was resolved, trade grew rapidly. In 1860, the first full year of trade, exports (in terms of Mexican dollars) were 4.7 million and imports 1.7 million. Exports rose to 10.6 million in 1864 and 12.1 million in 1867; and imports, including ships, rose to 8.1 million and 21.7 million, respectively. From the opening of trade until the Restoration, foreign trade resulted in an overall export surplus of just over 4 million. Raw silk was by far the biggest export, accounting for 50 to 80 percent of annual export value. The major imports were woolen and cotton textiles, with arms and vessels becoming important

25 Shimbo Hiroshi, *Kinsei no bukka to keizai hatten: zenkōgyōka shakai e no sūryōteki sekkin* (Tokyo: Tōyō keizai shimpōsha, 1978), p. 282.

(20 percent) as the Restoration approached. The prices of export products rose much faster than those of items not affected by trade. The price of raw silk rose threefold in the first year of trade and doubled again over the following five years. Export demand eventually stimulated a large increase in output, but its initial effect on the Japanese silk-weaving industry was disastrous. In the silk-weaving center of Kiryū, the opening of trade produced an immediate rise in the price of first-grade raw silk, from 94 *ryō* per picul to 267 *ryō* per picul, and in Suwa the price per picul rose from 80 *ryō* to 200 *ryō*. With 30 to 50 percent of production being exported, the shortage of raw material for the Kyoto silk-weaving industry was so severe that the city magistrate anticipated riots and ordered a number of the richer merchants to set up soup kitchens for unemployed weavers.[26]

Currency reform and inflation had the effect of redistributing wealth and income. Reform of the gold currency brought a windfall gain of 200 percent to those who held gold currency, mainly substantial merchants, bankers, and landowners. Inflation benefited traders, especially those engaged in the export trade, but brought hardship to those, such as laborers and lower-ranking samurai, whose incomes were relatively fixed. By 1865 the real wages of carpenters in Osaka were half of what they had been in the 1840s,[27] and high prices and falling real incomes produced a wave of protests and riots in both rural and urban areas. Fuel was added to inflation by a large increase in bank credit. Loans by the banking system to the domain administrations between 1850 and 1867 amounted to about 21 million *ryō*, so large an amount that the value of bank credit instruments in terms of gold cash fell by half over the same period despite the threefold increase in the volume of gold currency.

The effects of the opening of trade on production were far-reaching. Production of raw silk doubled between 1858 and 1863, and new silk-reeling technology spread rapidly. New devices such as the Wakao and *zakuri* reelers, some of them water powered, doubled output per worker and produced raw silk of better and more even quality. Comparable advances were made in the production and processing of tea. These and other industrial crops increasingly replaced rice and other staple food crops, despite official restrictions on converting rice land to other uses. The opening of foreign trade and the

26 Ishii Takashi, *Bakumatsu bōekishi no kenkyū* (Tokyo: Nihon hyōronsha, 1944), pp. 312, 52–4, 176–85, 318.

27 Shimbo, *Kinsei no bukka to keizai hatten*, p. 276. Although these particular wage data may not be representative, the general lag in wages was considerable.

expectations it generated provided an impetus for change throughout the country, notably in areas outside the economically advanced Kinki and Kantō regions, and greatly accelerated the changes in patterns of production and trade that had been proceeding since the beginning of the century.

The opening of foreign trade precipitated a crisis in relations between the bakufu and the domains. The bakufu's plans to impose national economic controls following the Tempō reforms were frustrated by political and financial weakness and domain opposition. If, however, the bakufu could control foreign trade, it could greatly increase its revenue and acquire the resources to organize a nationwide system of trading under its control and thus shift the balance of power decisively in its favor. Because all the ports opened to foreign trade were in bakufu territory, this was by no means a far-fetched scenario.

The bakufu made its first move early in 1860 as foreign trade was beginning to get under way, by declaring that as an interim measure to avoid domestic shortages – such as were affecting the silk-weaving industry – grains, vegetable oil, vegetable wax, textiles, and raw silk were to be sold to bakufu-controlled bodies in Edo which would determine quotas for export. There is clear evidence that the bakufu was planning a much more comprehensive control system that would have supplanted the domain trading corporations and in effect given it a monopoly of domestic as well as overseas trade.[28] An indication of the potential gains involved can be found in an offer by the Kyoto raw silk dealers' association to pay 500,000 *ryō* a year for the right to control that trade. Had the bakufu succeeded in its plan, its revenue would have increased by up to 50 percent. Even the interim measure, however, ran into immediate and stiff opposition from all sections of the raw silk export trade as well as from the domains, and when Harris warned that any form of control or restriction of exports would constitute a violation of the treaty, the bakufu was forced to withdraw once again and allow direct export sales subject to notification and an export permit. Permits seem to have been given freely until 1863, when the bakufu made another attempt to exercise control through export quotas. The result was a drastic fall in deliveries of raw silk and something approaching chaos in Yokohama, where Japanese silk traders whose quotas were restricted paid domain representatives as much as 18 *ryō* per packhorse load to include their consignments with domain silk against which it seems to have been more difficult to enforce the

28 Ishii, *Bakumatsu bōekishi*, pp. 448–67.

quota system. Some resorted to hiring masterless samurai to terrorize the export authorities into issuing licenses. No export permits were processed for about four months, and by February 1864 trade was almost at a halt. Again the bakufu was deluged with complaints from traders, the foreign community, and particularly from domains against whose direct trade the move was ultimately directed. Faced with a warning from the foreign consuls that there was nothing in the treaties to prevent the domains opening their own ports if they wished, the bakufu resumed processing export permits but continued to explore means of enforcing a monopoly of the export trade until October, when the combined foreign flotilla, fresh from the bombardment of Shimonoseki, entered Edo Bay with a show of strength that forced the bakufu to retreat once more.

The bakufu nevertheless continued to explore the idea of a national marketing monopoly right up to its fall, and the question of control of trade was a key factor in forming the attitudes of both the bakufu and individual domains toward foreign relations and the movements leading up to the Restoration.

THE MEIJI RESTORATION: CONTINUITY AND CHANGE

In the context of centuries of Japanese history, the changes following the Restoration appear to have been almost instantaneous and the restrictive apparatus of the old order to have been removed, as it were, at a stroke. But in fact these changes took at least ten turbulent years. The Restoration signaled far-reaching changes but had little immediate impact on the economy other than to exacerbate the existing uncertainty and disruption. Nor did it solve any of the economic problems that had beset the bakufu in its last years. Although the new government appreciated the need for change, the situation was not promising, and for a decade it moved, tentatively at first, from approaching the problems of the economy within the framework inherited from the old system toward entirely new solutions.

One of its first problems was to resolve the struggle for economic control between the central government and the domains. The problem was made more acute by the need to finance the considerable cost of the Restoration itself. Taking up the bakufu's abortive plans to establish a national system of economic control, the Meiji government within six months established an office (Shōhōshi) for the purpose, operating branches (Shōhō kaisho) in Tokyo, Osaka, and Hyōgo. These were organized very much along the lines of the old domain monopolies, with both commercial and financial operations entrusted to merchants of the major trading associations under government supervision. Just as the domains had financed their trading corporations by issuing paper currency, the Meiji government issued its own nonconvertible notes (Dajōkansatsu) through these offices. The system failed and for reasons similar to those that had frustrated earlier attempts by the bakufu. Opposition from the foreign powers prevented control of foreign trade; the new paper currency was not well accepted; and the domains' trading organizations continued to compete with that of the central government.

After only ten months of operation, the Shōhōshi were abolished and replaced by the Tsūhōshi which operated through the trading companies (*tsūshō gaisha*) and finance companies (*kawase gaisha*) established in eight major cities. Formed by substantial merchants and bankers such as the Mitsui and Ono groups under government control, their objectives and functions were similar to those of their predecessors. Although they helped to restore some degree of order to Japanese commercial life, by 1872 changing circumstances had rendered them inappropriate. In preparing for reform of the currency from *ryō* to yen in 1871, the finance companies were ordered to maintain a cash backing of 100 percent for their notes, a requirement that broke some of the participants, and when a new system of national banks was introduced in 1872, they either dissolved or were reorganized as national banks. Abolition of the domains as semiautonomous units in 1871 altered the position of the trading companies by opening the way to entirely new financial and economic policies that would supersede the idea of trade monopolies.[29] After this rather unpromising start, the first decade saw major institutional changes. In retrospect these changes were essential for modern economic growth, but at the time they represented responses to financial necessities rather than a commitment to economic or social progress.

The major preoccupation of the Meiji government was to create a sound fiscal base sufficient for its needs. Neither the bakufu nor a majority of the domains had achieved this, and the new government inherited not only their current fiscal deficits but also a mountain of accumulated debts and further debts that it had itself incurred during the Restoration campaigns. As we have seen, the Meiji government failed in its attempts to augment its income through monopoly corporations, as some domains had done. The most pressing problem was to

29 See Shimbo Hiroshi, *Kōbe keizaigaku sōsho*, vol. 7: *Nihon kindai shin'yō seido seiritsushi ron* (Tokyo: Yūhikaku, 1968).

acquire a stable source of tax revenue, and both the predominance of agriculture in the economy and reluctance to arouse further opposition by imposing revolutionary new taxes ensured that this would take the form of a tax on agriculture. Experience both before and after the Restoration clearly indicated that however redistributed or stabilized, agricultural taxes could not be raised much above their existing level without provoking dangerous levels of resistance.

At that rate the new government could expect at least as big a deficit as those of its predecessor unless it could drastically reduce some item of expenditure. Because some 30 percent of revenue went to pay the samurai's stipends, this was an obvious area for consideration. Other savings had been made. Roughly 20 percent of domain revenue had traditionally been taken by the costs of maintaining establishments in Edo under the system of "alternate attendance" (*sankin kōtai*), and this was no longer necessary. Thus if the yield of agricultural tax could be assured, irrespective of fluctuations in harvests and rice prices, and hereditary samurai stipends reduced or abolished, there seemed some hope of meeting the costs of government, even allowing for new commitments.

Attempts to reduce the fiscal burden of samurai stipends began at the end of 1869 when their total was reduced from 13 million *koku* (1 *koku* equals approximately 180 liters) to 9 million *koku*, and in 1871 the total was further reduced to 4.9 million *koku*. With the reform of the land tax, any hope that samurai may have had of retaining rights to income from land was extinguished, and the Conscription Law of 1873 removed their military *raison d'être*. Those who had refused earlier inducements to surrender their entitlements were required to do so in return for a lump-sum payment, mainly in the form of government bonds redeemable by lot over thirty years beginning in the sixth year after issue. This was well below the samurai's expectations, and the Satsuma Rebellion of 1877 was a forceful expression of their dissatisfaction. Over the next few years, inflation further reduced the real value of their compensation, and by the end of 1880 the market value of 7 percent commutation bonds was only 60.7 percent of their face value. In this way the Meiji government greatly reduced its recurrent expenditure for an outlay of ¥173 million in bonds and ¥730,000 in cash. Redemption of such a large bond issue was itself no easy matter, but without commutation of the samurai's stipends, the government's financial situation would have been hopeless. Those samurai who received comparatively large sums were encouraged to invest in the new national banks by a change in the regulations allowing the use of commutation bonds as capital. Some invested in railway or other joint stock companies, but most were reduced to earning their own living or sinking into poverty.

Reform of the agricultural tax system began in 1873 and took nearly six years to complete. The new tax was payable in cash on the assessed value of land, and the taxpayer was given title to his land. To assess the value of the land, the average crop was valued at the prices used to convert tax payments in kind into payment in cash, with some regard to local market conditions. From the gross value of the crop thus calculated were deducted allowances for seed, fertilizer, and national and local taxes to arrive at the value of the net product, which was capitalized at rates varying from 4 to 6 percent to give the assessed land value. The national land tax was set at 3 percent of this figure, and the local tax at one-third of the national tax.

There has been some discussion as to whether the farmers' tax burden became heavier or lighter as a result of the change. The government's intention was that the total tax yield be as nearly as possible unchanged. Before the reform, however, many domains imposed a number of more-or-less minor taxes in addition to the *seiso,* or tax proper. Villages were also responsible for local works, such as the building and maintenance of roads and bridges, as well as for their own administrative expenses. Because the extent of these is unknown and in any case varied from village to village, a direct comparison is impossible, but it seems likely that the new tax as a proportion of output was no higher, and in most cases lighter, than the old. Because the incidence of the new tax was on the whole more equitable, however, there may well have been cases of previously lightly taxed individuals' having to pay more. Nevertheless there was a good deal of opposition to the new tax, and in 1877 the rate of national tax was reduced to 2.5 percent and the local tax to one-fifth of that rate. This lowered the tax burden considerably, but over the following four years on-farm prices of agricultural products almost doubled while the land tax remained the same. Although there is no indication that the volume of agricultural production fell – it probably rose – the burden of the land tax as a proportion of farm output was by then well under half what it had been before the Restoration.

Although the object of the land tax reform was to secure a stable source of revenue, its effects went far beyond that. Land became a capital asset that could be freely and legally sold, and with taxes fixed in money terms, landowners – and not overlords – received the benefits from agricultural improvements, specialization, falling transport costs, and price rises. These incentives could be expected to have resulted in some increase in the first half of the Meiji period, but it is difficult to measure. Because these benefits went to the landowners, rather than to the cultivating tenants, the more land that a farmer owned in these circumstances, the more he would benefit, and the result was a noticeable concentration of landholdings and an increase in tenancy over this period.

Despite these drastic measures, the government was still heavily in deficit, and between the end of 1877 and the end of 1880 the government note issue rose from ¥105.8 million to ¥124.9 million, largely to cover the cost of suppressing the Satsuma Rebellion. Relaxation of the national bank regulations intended to facilitate the issue of commutation bonds allowed an increase in bank notes over the same period from ¥13.4 million to ¥34.4 million. The paper currency in circulation thus rose by a third in three years, and by the beginning of 1881 it was circulating at a discount of 70 percent against coin.

In the midst of its fiscal problems, the government somehow found the means to start building the infrastructure of communications essential to further development. The government regarded this as a matter of urgency, partly for internal security reasons and partly to forestall foreign investors who had shown a keen interest in direct investment in this area. Beginning with the Tokyo–Yokohama railway financed by a foreign loan, 64 miles of government railways had been built by 1877, and 2,827 miles of telegraph line had been installed by the same year. A semigovernment shipping company was formed in 1870 but failed after about a year of operation. This was followed by a mail steamer service using ships inherited from the bakufu and the domains, but this also failed. In 1875 the government handed over thirty ships free of charge to Iwasaki Yatarō's Mitsubishi Company, along with an operating subsidy of over ¥200,000 a year. This measure too was prompted by internal security considerations and anxiety to eliminate foreign shipping companies, the American Pacific Mail Line and the British P & O Steamship Company which had captured the coastal trade between the treaty ports. Within a year the foreign shipping companies were convinced that their role was over, and further subsidies to Mitsubishi for services during the Satsuma Rebellion put it on the road to becoming one of Japan's largest enterprises and a key participant in the construction of modern industry and commerce.

In land transport, the government-controlled system of packhorses based on post stations was abolished in 1871, and the business was opened to private enterprise. The old system of official couriers was retained with little more than a change of name for the first few years, but a modern-style postal service between Tokyo and Osaka was inaugurated in 1871. In 1872 there were still only 21 post offices, but the number rose to 3,224 by 1874, and in 1877 Japan joined the Universal Postal Union.

In addition to providing these essential physical services, the government created the institutional framework for reorganizing the banking system which culminated in the establishment of a central bank, the Bank of Japan, in 1882. The old financial system, which had served Japan's needs well for many years, had been left in disarray by the events of the Restoration. The government also provided the legal basis for insurance and joint stock companies and encouraged their formation and took the initiative in founding chambers of commerce and trade associations. Until 1885, government activity in the field of infrastructure was at least as great a contribution to economic development as was direct government investment in and promotion of modern industry.

ECONOMIC DEVELOPMENT, 1868–1885

National economic statistics before the 1890s are not available, and although estimates of national income aggregates and levels of production have been prepared back to 1878, the margins for error are great,[30] and the estimating procedures involve assumptions about economic relationships for which little evidence exists. An attempt at quantitative economic analysis of this period would therefore give a spurious impression of accuracy.

The best-documented and most conspicuous area of industrial development is the establishment of new industries based on imported technology. In terms of their proportion of Japan's industrial output at the time, their contribution was negligible, but as vehicles for introducing new technology and modes of production, their long-run significance was immense.

The Meiji government inherited a number of Western-style ironworks, munitions plants, and shipyards from the bakufu and some domains that had developed them for defense purposes.[31] The Saga domain had built Japan's first successful reverberatory iron furnace in

30 See Nakamura Takafusa, *Nihon keizai: Sono seichō to kōzō*, 2nd ed. (Tokyo: Tokyo daigaku shuppankai, 1980), pp. 12–13.

31 See Thomas C. Smith, *Political Change and Industrial Development in Japan: Government Enterprise, 1868–1880* (Stanford, Calif.: Stanford University Press, 1955).

1850 and cast iron guns in considerable numbers from 1853. Satsuma, Mito, and the bakufu itself followed suit. The bakufu's shipyard at Nagasaki built a steamer as early as 1857, and a comprehensive foundry, workshops, and shipyard were under construction at Yokosuka at the time of the Restoration. Satsuma, Saga, and Mito had built steamships, and several other domains had built Western-style sailing vessels. Just before the Restoration, Satsuma had installed a modern integrated cotton-spinning and weaving plant, and Saga had modernized its Takashima coal mine with British technical assistance.

Thus the new government found itself in possession of all Japan's munitions plants and shipyards. In addition it acquired about half of the country's forests and all the major mines, including the Sado gold mines, the Ikuno silver mines, the Miike and Takashima coal mines, the Ani and Innai copper mines, and the Kamaishi, Nakakosaka, and Kosaka iron mines.

Between 1868 and 1881 the government continued to develop these facilities and to establish new ones. Its motives were primarily twofold. First, it gave priority to developing defense industries to meet what it saw as a pressing foreign threat. It keenly appreciated the important role of military power in the negotiations connected with the opening and the conduct of foreign trade and was determined that future negotiations should be on the basis of equality. It was for such reasons that priority was given to munitions plants, although in retrospect their contribution to the development of general engineering proved to be significant. Second, the foreign trade surpluses of the pre-Restoration period soon gave way to mounting deficits. From 1868 to 1880 these deficits totaled ¥77 million, and the prospects for balanced trade were not bright. Foreign yarns and textiles, which in the 1870s made up half of the value of all imports, were much cheaper and of better quality than the Japanese products, and with the demand for them rising, there was an urgent need for import-replacement industries in Japan. Without adequate supporting infrastructure and services, technological background, and the means of mobilizing investment funds on the comparatively large scale required, private Japanese investors could not be relied on to undertake such a task. Direct foreign involvement could not be expected in import-replacement industries, and although it might well have been forthcoming in the production of bulky construction materials such as glass, bricks, and cement, Japanese were convinced that the superiority of foreign enterprise would overwhelm local business and be difficult to control.

It was for these reasons that the government, starting from the Sakai cotton textile mill inherited from the Satsuma domain, bought two more two-thousand-spindle cotton spinning plants in 1878 and installed them in Aichi and Hiroshima. The following year it bought ten more such plants for sale on very easy terms to private investors, mainly people already prominent in the traditional cotton textile industry, and financed the purchase of three more. The indifferent profit performance of these plants was attributed to their small scale, and so later spinning mills were larger. The Senju woolen mill was founded in 1879 for the same import-replacement purposes.

Third, the government hoped that its new nonmilitary industries would have a demonstration effect in familiarizing Japanese with factory production, training administrative and technical staff, and accumulating experience that could be made generally available. Whether or not these industries were expected to make profits is not clear, but in fact most ran at a heavy loss. The government was also active in the promotion and technical improvement of export industries and agriculture. The Tomioka silk filature was established in 1872 to improve technology in Japan's leading export industry, and a number of experimental stations and farms investigated the most modern overseas technology.

It has been estimated that over ¥36.4 million was invested in government enterprises between 1868 and 1881,[32] and in the difficult fiscal circumstances of the time this was a substantial commitment. As we shall see, the nonmilitary enterprises were sold off in the 1880s, and their transfer to private hands was an important factor in the formation of "Meiji capitalism."

The contribution of the new industries to production in the early Meiji period was, however, minimal, and agriculture and traditional industry continued along pre-Restoration lines. Estimation of agricultural production for this period is a serious problem, with important implications for our understanding of the growth process of the following decades. Ohkawa estimated the average annual value of agricultural production between 1878 and 1882 at ¥432 million in current prices.[33] Nakamura, basing his arguments on a reexamination of crop yields and reported acreage, raised this estimate by as much as 80 percent.[34] Ohkawa later revised his estimate to give a value about

32 Ibid., p. 69.

33 Kazushi Ohkawa, *The Growth Rate of the Japanese Economy Since 1878* (Tokyo: Kinokuniya, 1957).

34 James I. Nakamura, *Agricultural Production and the Economic Development of Japan 1873–1922* (Princeton, N.J.: Princeton University Press, 1966).

50 percent higher in real terms than his earlier estimate.[35] The upward revisions were certainly in the right direction, but the question can hardly be said to have been settled.

In 1874 the government ordered a survey of physical production on lines similar to those carried out by the bakufu and the domains before the Restoration.[36] It revealed that agricultural products formed 60 percent of physical output, industrial products 30 percent, and the products of extractive industries (forestry, fishing, and mining) 9 percent. There is a good deal of double counting involved, as the value of silk textiles, for example, includes the value of the raw silk used in their production, which in turn includes the value of the cocoons from which it was reeled.

Of the total value of crops produced, rice accounted for 63 percent, other food crops 23 percent, and industrial crops 12 percent. Most crops were cultivated to some extent in most parts of the country, but production was regionally specialized to the extent that for most crops, about one-ninth of the sixty-three prefectures produced between them one-third to a half of national output. Industrial output consisted mainly of *sake* and processed foods (42 percent) and yarn and textiles (28 percent). The value of *sake* produced was astonishingly large, more than the value of all silk and cotton textiles and three times the value of raw silk output. Commercial production in the economically advanced regions of Kinki, Shikoku, and Kantō was about three times as much per prefecture as in the relatively backward regions of Tōhoku, Kyushu, and the Japan Sea coast.

A survey of the occupational distribution of households in the same year listed 77 percent as "agricultural," with only 3.7 percent (mostly carpenters) as "industrial," 6.7 percent as "commercial," and 9 percent as "miscellaneous, servants, and employees." Clearly a large proportion of handicraft production and trade was the work of households listed as "agricultural."

A survey of nongovernment "factories" in 1884 showed that of 1,981 establishments, 1,237 were in rural villages. Over a third of all "factories" had no more than five workers, and only 176 of them employed more than fifty. Only 72 were steam powered; 47 percent were water powered; and the rest were operated entirely by hand. By industry, textiles accounted for 61 percent, ceramics for 12 percent,

35 Ōkawa Kazushi, ed., *Chōki keizai tōkei*, vol. 1: *Kokumin shotoku* (Tokyo: Tōyō keizai shimpōsha, 1974).

36 This and the following paragraph are based on Yamaguchi Kazuo, *Meiji zenki keizai no bunseki* (Tokyo: Tokyo daigaku shuppankai, 1956), pp. 1–73.

food processing for 9 percent, and metalworking industries for 8 percent.[37]

The outlines that emerge from these surveys are similar to our impressions of Japanese economic life in the 1850s and 1860s. Advances in production of raw silk and tea in response to export demand, some diffusion of indigenous technology, greater specialization, and recovery from the disruption surrounding the Restoration probably raised the real value of farm output above the levels of the early 1860s. Consumption of cotton textiles rose faster than imports, indicating both growth in the domestic industry and some rise in standards of living. Insufficient though the evidence is, however, there are no signs of drastic change or of a sudden spurt in Japanese economic activity.

THE TRANSITION AND ITS NATURE

By 1880 it was clear that inflation was not only a serious fiscal problem but was also hampering economic development. The adverse balance of payments had led to a loss of ¥60 million to ¥70 million of specie, and because silver was depreciating abroad faster than in Japan, most of this was in the form of gold. Japan's reserves of specie had fallen so low that they provided only 4.5 percent backing for the note issue.

When Matsukata Masayoshi became minister of finance in 1881, he took on the task, begun by Ōkuma, of reducing the volume of paper currency in circulation and restoring its parity with specie. Matsukata later recalled the situation as follows:

> At that time [1880] we fell into a condition which filled all classes of the country with anxiety. The real income of the government was reduced by nearly one-half. Among the people, those who lived on interest from government bonds, pensions, and other fixed incomes were suddenly reduced to dire straits. Bonds dropped sharply while commodity prices, especially the price of rice, rose to new heights. The land tax was in reality sharply reduced, while the value of land appreciated greatly. The farmers, who were the only class to profit from these circumstances, took on luxurious habits, causing a great increase in the consumption of luxury goods. . . . Consequently imports from foreign countries were increased and the nation's specie supply further depleted. Merchants, dazzled by the extreme fluctuations in prices, all aimed at making huge speculative profits and gave no heed to productive undertakings. As a result, interest rates were so high that no one could plan an industrial undertaking that required any considerable capital.[38]

37 Ibid., Table 17 facing p. 104. 38 Quoted from Smith, *Political Change*, pp. 96–7.

By drastic retrenchment, new taxes, and skillful financial management helped by what seems to have been a fortuitous cyclical downturn in business conditions,[39] Matsukata's measures reduced the note issue from ¥159.4 million in 1881 to ¥118.5 million by 1885, slightly below the 1877 level. Specie backing rose to 35.7 percent, and the value of paper currency returned very nearly to par. The process produced a severe recession that reversed many of the effects of the inflationary boom, transferring resources back to the government, the banking system, and stronger and more competitive businesses, especially those with government connections who ultimately benefited from the sale of government enterprises forced by financial stringency. The growth of the traditional economy was checked as deflation helped turn resources toward the sectors where they would ultimately be most productively employed. Whether intentionally or not, the Matsukata deflation established the strategy of giving priority to the modern sector which eventually proved successful in its own terms, although inevitably at some cost to the average Japanese both at the time and for many decades later.

But financial management, however skillful, cannot by itself increase the availability of real resources for development. Growth in production no doubt provided some, but what evidence we have suggests that this growth was not nearly as fast as was once thought. The economic transition of the Meiji period thus required some reallocation of existing resources, and the changes that occurred between the Restoration and the end of the Matsukata deflation in fact resulted in the redistribution of both income and wealth.

The commutation of samurai stipends effected a substantial redistribution of income. Before the Restoration, samurai incomes in terms of rice had totaled about nine million *koku*. After allowing for the cost of providing the services that they had performed and of providing for their basic consumption needs, commutation converted income to capital to the value of some three million *koku* a year, enough to cover over half of the total investment in the early Meiji period. Reform of the land tax and the subsequent sequence of inflation and deflation tended to concentrate income in the hands of those rural landowners and businessmen who were likely to invest it.

The monetary changes of the Restoration, particularly the abolition of the silver credit unit, resulted in a large transfer of assets away from

39 Teranishi Shigeo, "Matsukata defure no makuro keizaigakuteki bunseki," *Gendai keizai* 47 (Spring 1982): 78–92.

those who held their assets in that form, mainly conservative bankers and wholesalers closely associated with the old economic order. In the post-Restoration settlement of the bakufu's and the domains' debts, their creditors were forced to write off an estimated ¥47 million, thus transferring assets from the traditional banking system to the government. In the process of redeeming domain paper currency (*hansatsu*), compensation was only about a third of their face value, inflicting heavy losses on the rural population who held them. Most of these changes tended to transfer income and wealth from consumers to potential investors.[40]

One of the most interesting questions that arises from a study of the Japanese economy in the nineteenth century is that of the relationship between the pre-Restoration economy and the transition to modern economic growth. A number of studies have tried to find features and trends in the pre-Restoration economy that might be considered "preconditions" of modern development. In fact these are not very evident. Levels of income per head were on the high side for a preindustrial economy, but they were far below the initial levels in any other country that achieved modern economic growth in the nineteenth century. Moreover, Nakamura's thesis that the Japanese growth rate at this time was not particularly high implies that Japan's success depended significantly and perhaps critically on the ability of the Meiji government and its supporters to restrict consumption in the interests of industrial and military investment. Indeed, consumption over the whole period up to 1945 appears so low and so weakly correlated with national income as to be difficult to reconcile with the usual experience in a free economy.

There has been almost a surfeit of discussion and controversy among Japanese scholars about the nature of Japanese capitalism and the workings of the Japanese economic system, but it has not been widely reflected in Western scholarship, and possibly for good reason. To what extent, however, are we justified in analyzing Japan's early economic growth as though it had taken place in the context of a free-market economy? As we have seen, until the 1870s at least, it was very far from that. Byron Marshall argued that the ethical foundations of classical free-enterprise utilitarianism – faith in the "invisible hand" and the philosophy of laissez faire – were unacceptable in prewar Ja-

40 E. S. Crawcour, "Nihon keizai ikō no arikata: Kinsei kara kindai e," in Shimbo Hiroshi and Yasuba Yasukichi, eds., *Kindai ikōki no Nihon keizai* (*Sūryō keizaishi ronshū*, Vol. 2; Tokyo: Nihon keizai shimbunsha, 1979), pp. 15–28.

pan and that business activity was rationalized in terms of service to the community and the state.[41]

Although traditional economic activity, and the small-business sector that succeeded it, became increasingly free and competitive, Japanese governments have, in the areas that they considered most important, generally put more faith in manipulation than in free competition and the market mechanism. This chapter has suggested that the heritage of manipulation may have contributed as much to Japan's economic development as did the heritage of individual enterprise. As a comparative late developer, Japan was able to take advantage not only of advanced industrial technology but also of advanced techniques of manipulation. Whether the latter should be counted among the "advantages of backwardness" is an interesting question and one that should exercise the minds of all who study the modern development of Japan.

41 Byron K. Marshall, *Capitalism and Nationalism in Pre-war Japan: The Ideology of the Business Elite, 1868–1941* (Stanford, Calif.: Stanford University Press, 1967).

CHAPTER 2

INDUSTRIALIZATION AND TECHNOLOGICAL CHANGE, 1885–1920

ECONOMIC GROWTH, 1885–1920

The stabilization of the economy following the Matsukata deflation of the early 1880s marks the end of a transitional period in Japan's economic development and the beginning of the initial phase of modern economic growth that continued to the end of World War I. By the mid-1880s the costs of the Restoration and its aftermath had largely been met, and a start had been made on building an economic infrastructure. Although economic activity and life-styles were still scarcely touched by modern technology and organization, the seeds of a modern economic sector in industry, trade, and finance, on which Japan's future was to depend, were being sown.

It is from the 1880s that a reasonably reliable and comprehensive set of quantitative estimates (the LTES series) is available.[1] Prepared in the 1960s and subsequently adjusted in some details, these estimates have provided the material for some sophisticated analyses of Japan's experience.[2] The importance of quantitative data for the description and understanding of economic growth scarcely needs emphasizing. There are, however, caveats regarding these estimates. Although based on the consideration and evaluation of all available data, these estimates have been made into a consistent system by reference to an overall model that makes assumptions about the relationships of the various individual series to one another. Gaps in the data for the period before the late 1880s, moreover, can be filled only on the basis of some preconceptions about the speed and direction of growth. If

1 Ohkawa Kazushi, Shinohara Miyohei, and Umemura Mataji, eds., *Chōki keizai tōkei-suikei to bunseki* (hereafter LTES), 14 vols. (Tokyo: Tōyō keizai shinpōsha, 1965–); Kazushi Ohkawa and Miyohei Shinohara with Larry Meissner, eds., *Patterns of Japanese Economic Development: A Quantitative Appraisal* (New Haven, Conn.: Yale University Press, 1979).

2 Good examples are by Ohkawa and Shinohara, eds., *Patterns of Japanese Economic Development;* Kazushi Ohkawa and Henry Rosovsky, *Japanese Economic Growth: Trend Acceleration in the Twentieth Century* (Stanford, Calif.: Stanford University Press, 1973); and Allen C. Kelley and Jeffrey G. Williamson, *Lessons from Japanese Economic Development: An Analytical Economic History* (Chicago: University of Chicago Press, 1974).

these have resulted in inaccurate estimates for the 1880s, the impression they give of growth rates through the first phase of economic growth will be distorted. In fact, it is likely that as James Nakamura suggested,[3] production in traditional sectors for which information is hard to collect, such as agriculture and handicraft industry, has been seriously underestimated for these years. Despite these reservations, the figures become more reliable for later years and, for most of our period, may be accepted as reliable enough to indicate at least the main outlines of production, expenditure, and employment.[4]

International comparisons of output per capita in the early stages of Japan's economic development are impressionistic at best. Simon Kuznets estimated Japan's output per capita for the late 1870s at $74 in 1965 prices, which is between one-quarter and one-third of the levels in advanced countries at a similar initial stage.[5] Ohkawa thought this figure implausibly low and doubled it. The LTES estimates indicate a figure of $172 for 1887, still very low in comparison with initial levels elsewhere. Those who view the process of economic development in Japan as similar to that in other countries may feel that it should have been higher. Ohkawa and Shinohara believe that it could have been as high as $251 but concede that even in 1887, the Japanese economy was at a relatively low level.

By 1920, the end of the period covered in this chapter, gross domestic product in real terms (1934–6 average prices) had risen 2.8 times since 1885. Output of agriculture, forestry, and fisheries grew by 67 percent; commerce, services, and other by 180 percent; mining and manufacturing by 580 percent; transport, communications, and public utilities by over 1,700 percent; and construction by 170 percent. As a result of these differential rates of growth, the share of agriculture, forestry, and fisheries in total output fell from 42 percent to 25 percent; mining and manufacturing rose from 8 percent to 19 percent; and transport, communications, and public utilities rose from 1.5 percent to almost 10 percent, whereas the shares of other sectors changed little. Within these sectors the composition of output and the

3 James I. Nakamura, *Agricultural Production and the Economic Development of Japan* (Princeton, N.J.: Princeton University Press, 1966).

4 For critiques of the early years of the *LTES* series, see Nakamura Takafusa, "Chōki tōkei no seido ni tsuite – 19-seiki Nihon no jakkan no sūji o megutte," *Keizai kenkyū* 30 (January 1979): 1–9; Yasuba Yasukichi, "Senzen no Nihon ni okeru kōgyō tōkei no shinpyōsei ni tsuite," *Ōsaka daigaku keizaigaku* 17 (1977–8), and Nishikawa Shunsaku, " 'Chōki keizai tōkei' no keiryō keizaigaku – Ōkawa hoka *Kokumin shotoku* no tenbō rombun," *Kikan riron keizaigaku* 27 (August 1976): 126–34.

5 Simon Kuznets, *Economic Growth of Nations: Total Output and Production Structure* (Cambridge, Mass.: Harvard University Press, 1971), p. 24.

technical and organizational features of production changed considerably. We shall examine these changes in later sections of this chapter, but we note here that although the greatest absolute increases in output came from the large food and textile sections, which were largely traditional in organization and technique, growth was fastest in modern transport and communications and in the metals and machinery industries in which technical change was most rapid.

Over the same period, the uses to which this growing production was put also changed. Personal consumption, which absorbed 85 percent of the rather low output in 1887, increased 2.4 times by 1920, but because total national expenditure had meanwhile increased 2.6 times, the share of personal consumption fell to 76 percent. Gross domestic fixed-capital formation, a major growth-promoting factor, increased over 6 times, and its share of total national expenditure rose from 9 percent to 21 percent. Japan's involvement with the world economy deepened dramatically, with its exports of goods and services and other foreign earnings rising 9.4 times and its payments for imports of goods and services and other current payments abroad rising nearly 12 times.

From 1885 to 1920, the population increased by 45 percent, and so the per-capita rates of increase were not as high as the total growth rates. Thus, although the total output of the Japanese economy (gross domestic product) rose 2.6 times, output per capita of population rose only 1.8 times. The rise in real personal consumption per capita, a rough measure of the rise in average standards of living, was a relatively modest 67 percent. The gainfully employed population rose by some 22 percent. Whereas the number of workers engaged in agriculture and forestry actually fell by about 1 million, the nonagricultural work force doubled from about 6.5 million to about 13 million, with the biggest increase in manufacturing, followed by commerce, transport and communications, and the service industries.

The Japanese government is widely credited with having played a large part in Japan's economic growth. Except during the Sino-Japanese and Russo-Japanese wars, the government's current and capital expenditures, including military expenditures, was between 7 and 11 percent of gross national expenditures, a rather modest proportion by today's standards. The government's role in capital formation, however, was much larger. From 1897 until the private investment boom during World War I, the government was responsible for 30 to 40 percent of all capital investment. Government investment was, moreover, heavily concentrated in the strategic heavy and engineering industries and in facilities such as railways which contributed in a number of crucial ways to the development of modern industry in Japan.

The economy did not grow at a constant speed between 1885 and 1920. Over the whole span of Japan's modern history the rate of growth has tended to accelerate. Along the way, however, there have been marked variations, often described as cycles, which suggests that they are associated with patterns inherent in the growth process itself. These variations were, however, associated also with specific events. For example, the depressing, though salutary, effects of the Matsukata deflation lasted through the mid-1880s. Recovery was then fairly rapid, based mainly on the development of the textile and traditional handicraft industries, railway building, and the stimulus of the Sino-Japanese War. Establishment of the gold standard in 1897 put a brake on expansion, and growth was much slower until about 1903. The Russo-Japanese War then boosted the heavy and engineering industries, and after a short postwar recession, growth picked up again. World War I effectively removed most of the advanced industrialized nations from competition in world markets as well as in the Japanese market, thus providing Japan with the opportunity to substitute domestically produced goods for imports and to increase exports of manufactures despite the relative backwardness of its manufacturing sector. The result was an unprecedented boom in which all sectors of the economy participated, but those industries in the forefront of modern developments, like engineering, shipbuilding, machine tools, and electrical engineering, grew the fastest. Despite a postwar slump and a succession of economic difficulties throughout the 1920s, the World War I boom firmly established the viability of modern industry in Japan. Although the traditional sectors of agriculture and small business were still responsible for the bulk of output and employment, by 1920 the economy's future growth clearly lay with the modern sector.

In the Meiji era, the traditional and modern sectors had grown concurrently. Although the still-small modern industrial system interacted with the existing economy, the relationship had been complementary rather than competitive. By World War I, however, the demands of the rapidly expanding modern sector increasingly conflicted with the needs of the traditional sector which supplied most of the consumers' needs. Thus there came into being a dual or differential economic structure that included a wide range of technology, productivity, wages, scales of production, profit rates, management practices, and forms of industrial organization. There were also characteristic differences in the nature of the markets in which products were sold and from which capital, labor, technology, intermediate goods, and managerial talent were acquired. Governments after the early Meiji era systematically used all the powers at their disposal to promote the growth of modern industry in what they saw as the national interest, even, if necessary, at the expense of the traditional sector. In the long run this policy made Japan into the advanced industrial country that it is today, but by favoring armaments, investment goods, and exports over consumption goods, for a long time government policy kept the living standards of most Japanese lower than they might have been and contributed to the social and political strains of the turbulent 1930s and 1940s and even later.

The availability of quantitative estimates of many aspects of Japan's economic activity tempts observers to explain its growth solely in terms of those quantitative aggregates and the relationships among them. Economic growth is not, however, a natural phenomenon subject to the operation of mindless natural laws but is the result of purposeful human behavior. What were the motives for economic growth and development in Japan? In one sense there were as many motives as there were individual economic decisions. Japan's leaders did not, however, believe that the sum of decisions about what was best for each individual would achieve the national objectives of promoting industrial development, catching up with the West, and becoming a world power. On the contrary, the importance of national policy and its implementation in shaping the course of Japan's economic development were stressed by the government, accepted by the average Japanese, and increasingly acknowledged in the public utterances of businessmen. As Takahashi Korekiyo said in his 1889 farewell to the students of Tokyo Agricultural College, "Gentlemen, it is your duty to advance the status of Japan, bring her to a position of equality with the civilized powers and then carry on to build a foundation from which we shall surpass them all."[6]

Depending on the relative importance ascribed to public and private motives, Japan's experience has been described as either "growth from above" or "growth from below." These two views should not be regarded as mutually exclusive. The production of goods for domestic consumption, for example, was in general the result of individual decisions and market behavior, but it was also influenced by public decisions about the rate of investment relative to consumption and official encouragement to retain traditional Japanese ways of life. Government decisions on defense and defense-related industries, foreign trade and payments, and education affected both the pace and the

6 Reproduced in Takekazu Ogura, *Can Japanese Agriculture Survive?* 2nd ed. (Tokyo: Agricultural Policy Research Institute, 1980), p. 14. Ironically, Takahashi was assassinated by ultranationalists in 1936 for trying to put a brake on government expenditures.

direction of industrial development. Leading entrepreneurs like Iwasaki Yatarō may have been as devoted to personal profit as were their counterparts elsewhere, but that profit depended heavily on the goodwill of the government. Entrepreneurs were constrained by public opinion, sometimes forcibly expressed, to conform to the image of the nationally minded businessman. In general, the state seems to have played an important role in countries like Japan that began their economic development relatively late. Irrespective of judgments about the motives, methods, and outcomes of public policy in Japan, to explain its economic development without referring to these factors would be to tell only part, and probably a misleading part, of the story.

Before World War I, growth from above and growth from below proceeded together. In any case, the modern sector was so small that its growth did not conflict with the expansion and development of the existing traditional economy. On the contrary, each complemented the other. Agriculture and the handicraft industry produced food and consumption goods for a growing population, as well as most of the exports that helped pay for imports of equipment and raw materials needed by modern industry. After the 1890s, modern industry provided inputs such as fertilizers for agriculture and cotton yarn and dyes for cottage weaving. Productivity rose in both traditional and modern occupations. The expansion and improvement of traditional activities still contributed most of Japan's economic growth, if only because of their overwhelming weight in the economy. The modern sectors of industry and commerce were still small, but it was in these that productivity was the highest and was rising the fastest and expansion was the most rapid. By 1920 the further growth of these modern sectors required some sacrifice of the interests of traditional producers. As the modern sectors expanded, their further growth increasingly required resources to be transferred from less productive traditional employments to new and more productive activities. The further this transfer proceeded, the faster was the growth of total output. This "trend acceleration"[7] became particularly noticeable after the Pacific War, but before World War I the modern sector was still an infant nurtured by the traditional economy rather than the engine of growth that it later became.

This chapter divides at 1913 the period between 1885 and 1920. Before World War I, the building of infrastructure was a large and productive field of investment. Economic growth came mainly from the expansion of existing activities, without any radical innovations in

7 See Ohkawa and Rosovsky, *Japanese Economic Growth*, pp. 39–42.

technology or organization. Most of the developments in the heavy and engineering industries were directly or indirectly related to defense and included government involvement. World War I is treated as a separate phase because it was then that the modern sector, although still small in terms of share of total output, became self-sustaining and began to provide the momentum for further growth. It was also in this period that problems associated with the dual, or differential, structure of the economy began to surface as the interests of new developments began to conflict at some points with those of existing activities.

BUILDING INFRASTRUCTURE, 1885–1913

From 1885 to 1913, Japan's gross national product grew at an average annual rate of somewhere between 2.6 and 3.6 percent.[8] This growth was mainly achieved not by radical technological change but by the diffusion of existing techniques, a series of small technical improvements, increasing specialization, and an economic climate that rewarded producers better than the pre-Meiji system had done. A substantial contribution to economic growth both at this time and later, however, was made by the heavy investment in infrastructure such as ancillary services like banking, transport and communications, public utilities, education, and economic institutions. With the experience of the advanced industrial countries in front of them, Japan's leaders anticipated and provided for future needs for such infrastructure.

Banking

The early decision, embodied in the National Banking Act of 1872 and its amendment in 1876, to base the Japanese banking system on the American model resulted in the establishment of nearly 150 national banks. Organized as joint stock companies, they were the first modern business enterprises in Japan. Along with a large number of small local quasi banks, the new national banks replaced the traditional system of financing productive industry, commerce, land development, and mining.[9]

8 This rather wide range reflects a corresponding degree of doubt about the estimates' accuracy. Ohkawa and Shinohara's *Patterns of Japanese Economic Development*, based on *LTES*, indicates about 2.7 percent whereas Nakamura Takafusa, *Senzenki Nihon keizai seichō no bunseki* (Tokyo: Iwanami shoten, 1971), pp. 5ff, prefers 3.6 percent.

9 For the development of banking in this period see Hugh T. Patrick, "Japan 1868–1914," in *Banking in the Early Stages of Industrialization*, ed. Rondo Cameron et al. (London: Oxford University Press, 1967), pp. 239–89.

The banks' large issues of inconvertible bank notes, however, contributed to the inflation of 1878–81. Consequently, this privilege was withdrawn as part of the Matsukata deflationary policies of the early 1880s, and a new central bank, the Bank of Japan founded in 1882, was granted the sole right to issue paper currency. Ordinary banking functions were gradually taken over by private commercial banks.

A few private banks were large city banks, such as the Mitsui and Konoike banks, which were part of the premodern financial system, or the Sumitomo and Mitsubishi banks, which originated in the financial operations of the large industrial combines (zaibatsu) and became central to their subsequent expansion. Most private banks, however, were relatively small local banks, of which there were about eighteen hundred by the turn of the century. Much of their capital came from local landowners and businessmen, and they did much to foster local production and development as well as to integrate local activity into the national economy and channel local finance into national projects. Recessions in the early 1900s forced consolidations and takeovers of some small banks, but unit correspondent banking on the United States pattern, rather than branch banking of the British type, was still the rule in Japan up to World War I.[10]

The Japanese banking system was nearly complete around 1900, with the establishment of several special-purpose banks that, although their capital was raised by public subscription, operated under government direction and mobilized longer-term finance for enterprises considered to be in the national interest. These special banks, based on German and French models, included the Hypothec Bank of Japan, the Industrial Bank of Japan, the Hokkaido Colonial Bank, and the Bank of Taiwan. The Industrial Bank in particular raised funds at home and abroad for long-term investment, including direct investment in the promotion of Japanese interests on the Asian mainland. In the absence of a developed bond market, the activity of these special banks was an important source of investment funds, even though political influence over the direction of their investment sometimes led to heavy losses.

A postal savings system, introduced as early as 1875, grew rap-

10 Unit banking is a system in which a large number of banks operate only from their head offices or from a small number of local offices. It is sometimes known as *correspondent banking* because the small unit banks are linked to wider financial markets through correspondent banks that act as their agents and hold their deposits. Branch banking is a system in which a few large banks provide banking services over a wide area through a large number of branches. The Japanese banking system of today, like that of France, is best described as a hybrid of these two types in which branch banking by the major city banks predominates.

idly, especially during and after the Russo-Japanese War, because although interest rates were low, it provided a convenient service to small savers. The government used these substantial funds to finance war expenditures and projects of national importance. Following the Savings Bank Act of 1893, many private savings banks were established, and as they paid a somewhat higher rate of interest than did the postal savings system, they attracted a large amount of deposits.

By World War I the banking system had developed, with the government's encouragement, to a point that it could act as an intermediary between savers and investors. Even before the Meiji era, Japan had a well-developed financial system serving trade and commerce and providing circulating capital for handicraft production as well as loans to domains on the security of their tax revenues. These loans were often for quite long terms and were sometimes employed in land reclamation, public works, or industrial development within the domain.[11] This stock of experience doubtlessly facilitated the establishment of a modern banking system at such a relatively early stage of Japan's economic development, but the new system went far beyond the old one. Banks were the first institutions in Japan to be organized on modern joint stock company lines and to use Western business methods. The early banks acted as promoters of commercial and industrial enterprises and were often the agents through which Western business technology was transferred. By the early twentieth century, moreover, the development of a unified national financial system had greatly reduced regional variation in interest rates. Most loans still went to finance trade, commerce, land improvements, agriculture, and local handicraft production, but the larger city banks, the zaibatsu banks, and the special banks played an increasingly important part in developing new factory industries, raising funds abroad, and financing government deficits. As Hugh Patrick pointed out, Japan's modern banking system did not simply develop in response to the needs of economic growth but was created in advance of demand and played a positive part in facilitating economic development.

Railways

Almost from the start, the Meiji government gave high priority to transport and communications, partly for their commercial value, but

11 See E. S. Crawcour and Kozo Yamamura, "The Tokugawa Monetary System: 1787–1868," *Economic Development and Cultural Change* 18 (July 1970): pt 1, pp. 489–518.

also for their value for administration and internal security. Before World War I this sector absorbed more public and private investment than did any other single industry. The development of railways and shipping services provides good examples of how government and private groups combined in various ways to perform tasks of national importance.

Japan's first railway line, linking Tokyo with the port of Yokohama, was built by the government with funds, materials, and technical services provided by Great Britain through the good offices of the British minister, Harry Parkes. The construction of this line was followed by one linking Ōtsu on Lake Biwa with the port of Kobe via Kyoto and Osaka, and another across Honshū from Tsuruga on the Japan Sea to Handa on Ise Bay via the northern shore of Lake Biwa, Gifu, and Nagoya. When Matsukata Masayoshi became minister of finance in October 1881, however, Japan still had less than two hundred miles of railway in operation. As the result of his sharply deflationary fiscal policy, funds to finance further government railway building were scarce despite a clear national need. In 1880 Iwakura Tomomi persuaded a group of peers to invest their commutation bonds in a company to build a trunk railway from Ueno (Tokyo) north to Aomori. Railways, he told them, were a project of national importance, and as the inner bastion of the Imperial House, they should feel bound to invest in them. Summoning the governors of the prefectures along the proposed route, Iwakura directed them to raise subscriptions from suitable people under their administration, but Matsukata's tight money policy was beginning to bite, and so the response was disappointing.[12] The peers themselves asked for a government guarantee of a 10 percent return on their capital but eventually settled for 8 percent. In 1881 they obtained a railway license providing for nationalization after fifty years. When interest rates fell soon afterwards, the guarantee looked generous. With the announcement of profits of 10 percent on the first section of the line, shares were at a premium and further capital was raised without difficulty. The Ueno–Aomori line was completed in 1892, some three years behind schedule but virtually without foreign technical assistance.

12 See speeches by Itō Hirobumi, Ōkuma Shigenobu, and many others involved in railway projects in the late nineteenth century that appeared in *Tetsudō jihō* between 1899 and 1909 and were reprinted in Tetsudō Jihō Kyoku, ed., *10-nen kinen Nihon no tetsudō ron*. This work is included in Noda Masaho, Harada Katsumasa, and Aoki Eiichi, eds., *Meiji-ki tetsudōshi shiryō*, suppl. vol. 1 (Tokyo: Nihon keizai hyōronsha, 1981).

The government guidelines for private railways issued in 1887 provided for nationalization after twenty-five years. By this time railways were such an attractive investment that over the following decade some twenty railway companies were formed, with capital ranging from ¥40,000 to over ¥13 million, much of it raised from local businessmen. Private lines were built where traffic was the densest, and in the absence of competition, charges could be set high. Interest rates and construction costs fell, and operating costs were well below those of the national railways, as indeed they have been ever since. By licensing private railway companies, the government hoped to get lines built quickly. In this it was not disappointed, but most lines were built to serve local needs or in anticipation of immediate profits, and without a coherent overall plan. The Railway Construction Act of 1892 provided for a coordinated national network of trunk lines financed by issues of railway bonds totaling ¥36 million. From 1883 to 1903, operating track rose from a mere 245 miles, most of it built and operated by the state, to 4,500 miles, of which 70 percent was built and operated by private railway companies.[13]

In the late 1890s the government prepared to acquire the major private railways. When Prime Minister Saionji Kinmochi introduced the Railways Nationalization Bill in 1906, he claimed that the government had always favored state operation of the railways because of their national economic and strategic importance and had licensed private companies only because of fiscal exigencies. Although in the early 1870s there had been some support for private enterprise in principle, by the end of the century the importance of the state's role in national development had become widely accepted. By then, moreover, railways were no longer as profitable as they had once been, and most private companies were happy to accept the rather generous takeover terms. After 1906 the government acquired the assets of seventeen companies, including 2,800 miles of trunk line, for a total of ¥476 million.[14] By 1914 the capital investment of the Imperial Japanese Railways amounted to ¥1.007 million, more than the paid-up capital of all industrial companies combined. Through the World War I boom, track in operation increased by about 25 percent, but traffic

13 See Tōyō keizai shinpōsha, ed., *Meiji Taishō kokusei sōran* (Tokyo: Tōyō keizai shinpōsha, 1927), pp. 615–19.

14 For details, see Teishin shō, ed., *Tetsudō kokuyū shimatsu ippan* (1909), reprinted in Takimoto Seiichi and Mukai Shikamatsu, eds., *Nihon sangyō shiryō taikei* (Tokyo: Chūgai shōgyō shinpōsha, 1927), pp. 11, 543–617.

increased much more,[15] and some 90 percent of this traffic was carried by the Imperial Japanese Railways.

The contribution of the railways to Japan's economic development, both then and later, was enormous.[16] They greatly reduced transport costs, thus promoting geographical specialization and mobility of labor and benefiting all sections of the population in the areas they served. They also increased the reach and efficiency of government administration and trained large numbers of engineers and skilled workers.

Shipping

The development of Japan's shipping services is another example of collaboration between the state and private enterprise. During and after the Formosa expedition of 1874, Iwasaki Yatarō's Mitsubishi Company, with the official support of Ōkuma Shigenobu, obtained large subsidies from the government and, with every conceivable form of state aid and protection, used ruthless price cutting to overcome competition from the Imperial Japanese Steamship Mail Company (Nippon teikoku yūbin jōkisen kaisha), itself a recipient of government subsidies. After absorbing this rival, continued subsidies enabled Mitsubishi to eliminate the American Pacific Mail Steamship Company and the British Peninsular and Oriental Steamship Company from coastal steamer traffic, thus obtaining a virtual monopoly. In the climate of the 1881 budget cuts, Ōkuma's opponents in the

15 Table showing traffic increase, 1913–18:

	1913	1918
Freight (million tons/miles)		
National	3,054	5,609
Local	115	334
Total	3,169	5,943
Passengers (million pass./miles)		
National	3,691	6,569
Local	309	687
Total	4,000	7,256

Source: Tōyō keizai shinpōsha, ed., *Meiji Taishō kokusei sōran* (Tokyo: Tōyō keizai shinpōsha, 1927), pp. 617, 618. Local traffic was calculated from revenue figures on the assumption that local railway charges were the same as those of the national railways.

16 For details, see Tetsudōin, ed., *Honpō tetsudō no shakai oyobi keizai ni oyoboseru eikyō* (Tokyo: Tetsudōin, 1930).

government thought that Iwasaki was overcharging for his well-publicized services to the state and that a good part of the government subsidies granted for specific shipping services were being channeled into other projects of his own choosing and for his own enrichment. In the course of a government-orchestrated public outcry, Iwasaki was pilloried for being a self-centered capitalist entrepreneur when he should have realized that he had been granted the subsidies as an agent of the state. In 1882 the government promoted a new state-subsidized shipping concern, the Kyōdō unyu kaisha. With a capital of ¥6 million subscribed largely by shipowners in the Kansai and Echigo regions, the new company was intended to break the monopoly of the Iwasaki "sea monster," but after two years of wasteful competition that almost broke both companies, a government offer of a guaranteed 8 percent return induced them to merge into the Nippon yūsen kaisha (NYK), with Mitsubishi holding just over half the shares.[17] In 1884, Osaka shipowners led by Sumitomo founded the Ōsaka shōsen kaisha (OSK), which also received an annual subsidy of ¥50,000 to operate routes in and around the Inland Sea.

When NYK began operations in 1885 with 58 steamships totaling some 68,700 tons and 13 sailing ships totaling some 4,700 tons, it was clearly understood that the company was to operate as a semigovernment agency and that its ships were to be at the state's disposal in time of war or emergency. The government also stipulated the routes it was to service among Japan's main ports, as well as to the outer islands, Shanghai, Vladivostok, Inchon, and Tientsin. By 1893 Japan's merchant steamer fleet had grown to 642 vessels, with a total tonnage of 102,352 tons. Meanwhile, NYK had considerably raised its fleet's efficiency and began services to Manila, Hong Kong, Southeast Asian ports, and Australia, with a liner service to Bombay to carry Japanese imports of Indian cotton. Before 1900 many NYK masters and chief engineers were foreigners, but by 1920 all officers were Japanese.

Despite these developments, only 14 percent of the steam tonnage entering Japanese ports in 1893 was Japanese. National flag ships carried only 7 percent of exports and less than 9 percent of imports. After the Sino-Japanese War the Diet passed government-initiated bills for further subsidies. Between the Sino-Japanese War and the

17 For details and an assessment of Iwasaki Yatarō, see Yamamura Kozo, "The Founding of Mitsubishi: A Case Study in Japanese Business History," *Business History Review* 41 (1967): 141–60. For monographic treatment of the NYK line, see William D. Wray, *Mitsubishi and the N.Y.K., 1870–1914: Business Strategy in the Japanese Shipping Industry* (Cambridge, Mass.: Harvard University Press, 1985).

Russo-Japanese War, Japan's merchant steamship tonnage doubled with the help of massive subsidies. Although NYK incurred an operating loss of ¥1.8 million in 1903, it was able to pay a 12 percent dividend, owing to government subsidies amounting to 24.3 percent of its paid-up capital. During the Russo-Japanese War, subsidies fell briefly when partly replaced by generous government charters. In 1909, general subsidies were replaced by subsidies for particular overseas routes specified by the government, which controlled services and freight rates.

Between 1883 and 1913, massive government shipping subsidies expanded the merchant steam fleet from 45,000 tons to 1.577 million tons and raised its share of the tonnage entering Japanese ports to just over 50 percent. The cost to the taxpayer was high, partly because the fleets of established mercantile nations with which Japan was competing were also heavily subsidized. Yet the expenditure was considered justified on grounds of national prestige and security. At the same time the benefits were considerable. Construction and maintenance of the merchant fleet provided a stimulus to the heavy engineering industries at a stage when there was otherwise little demand for their products. The early introduction of shipbuilding technology and skills promoted the development of other branches of engineering and, indeed, modern industry in general, enabling Japanese industry to take full advantage of the opportunities presented by World War I.

Posts and telegraphs

Even before the Meiji Restoration, the effectiveness with which government communicated with the population right down to the individual household and the volume of information so communicated seem to have been exceptional for a society at such a comparatively low level of per capita income. These means of communication, designed primarily to serve the government's needs, were energetically developed over the next three decades.

The number of post offices in Japan roughly doubled from about 3,500 in 1883 to over 7,000 in 1913; the number of postal articles handled increased from just over 100 million in 1882 to 551 million in 1897 and 1,664 million (plus 24 million parcels) in 1912.[18] Over this thirty-year period the number of postal articles (excluding parcels) per

18 The statistical information on posts and telecommunications in this section comes from Tōyō keizai shinpōsha, ed., *Meiji Taishō kokusei sōran*, pp. 672–3.

capita rose from about three a year to thirty-two a year, reflecting both the spread of literacy and the growing need for communication beyond the range of word of mouth. By the eve of World War I, mail usage was comparable to that of European nations.

Japan's first telegraph line was built from Tokyo to Yokohama in 1869, and telegraph services were expanded rapidly after 1890, largely for strategic and administrative purposes. The use of this service also grew quickly. From 2.7 million telegrams sent in 1882, the number rose through the Sino-Japanese War to reach 14 million in 1897 and again through the Russo-Japanese War to 27 million by 1907. By 1913 it had risen again to 40 million.

Telephones were introduced in 1890, with just under 400 subscribers connected to 2 exchanges. Here, too, expansion was rapid, and by 1913 there were over 200,000 subscribers connected to 1,046 exchanges. Over this period the average number of calls per subscriber per day rose from seven to twelve, a rather high figure suggesting that many of the telephones were installed in government or business offices.

By 1912, post offices and telecommunications as a whole employed some 84,000 people. The development of these services and the high circulation of newspapers and magazines indicate that Japan was even then becoming an information-based society. Thus the state acquired in this period the means of effective intervention and control in ways that only forty years earlier would have been beyond the capacity of the most advanced nations of Europe. At the same time these developments speeded the movement of goods and services and facilitated the spread and exchange of ideas.

Electric power

Until the 1880s the main alternative to human effort in Japan was water power, which indeed remained well into the twentieth century an important source of power for food processing, silk reeling, and various handicraft industries. Large modern industrial plants for textiles, metals, machinery, ceramics, and food processing, however, were steam-powered from the outset, and by 1887, steam had outstripped water as a source of industrial power. Yet it was not widespread and was so soon replaced by electricity that Japan never experienced a "steam age" like that of Western Europe from the mid-nineteenth century to World War I. The generation and distribution of electric power provided large economies external to individual enterprises and made possible changes in technology, scale, and organization in many industries and even in domestic life, substantially affecting the course of industrialization as a whole.

The first supplies of electric power were for lighting and were provided by private companies that proved extremely profitable from the start. The electric power industry required no state aid or encouragement and was subject to little regulation. The first electric company, the Tokyo Electric Light Company, was formed by Hachisuka Mochiaki and other peers, Shibusawa Eiichi, some of Shibusawa's business associates, and a number of rural businessmen – a group not unlike the backers of early railway development. The company began supplying electricity in 1887 and had installed 21,000 lamps by 1890. With falling charges and more efficient bulbs, electric lighting became increasingly popular. The number of lamps rose from 464,000 in 1905 to over 3 million in 1911 and about 5 million in 1913. Even so, over half of Japanese households were still without electric light. In 1903, electric power companies had a total generating capacity of 25,000 kilowatts. Generators attached to government or private industrial plants and electric railways provided another 25,000 kilowatts, most of which was for power rather than light. By 1913, electric companies produced 80 percent of all electricity. Although two-thirds of their sales were still for lighting, the demand for electricity as a source of power was rising sharply. Between 1911 and 1915, the number of electric motors quadrupled to nearly 43,000, and their total capacity rose from 44,000 horsepower to 182,700 horsepower.

Between the Russo-Japanese War and World War I, electrification was promoted by two technological developments, hydroelectric generation and high-tension transmission. The first hydroelectric generator for public supply had been built in 1892 in connection with a project to provide Kyoto with water by aqueduct from Lake Biwa. By 1910, electric power companies were producing more from hydroelectric than from thermal power, and by World War I, the ratio was two to one. Long-distance transmission technology, introduced into Japan soon after its first use overseas, made possible the development of large hydroelectric sites at a distance from consumption centers. When the Inawashiro Hydroelectric Plant in Fukushima Prefecture was linked to Tokyo in 1914, power was transmitted at 37,500 volts over a distance of 228 kilometers, one of the longest transmission lines in the world at the time.[19]

19 See Minami Ryōshin, *Dōryoku kakumei to gijutsu shinpo: Senzen-ki seizōgyō no bunseki* (Tokyo: Tōyō keizai shinpōsha, 1976), p. 213. Quantitative information on the electric power industry is taken from this work and Minami Ryōshin, *Tetsudō to denryoku*, LTES, vol. 12, 1965.

These technological advances, combined with competition among the power companies, kept charges low, especially for lighting, and thus promoted the use of electricity. By buying power from electric companies and replacing cumbersome shaft-and-belt transmission by motors attached to individual machines, manufacturers raised mechanical efficiency and cut direct power costs. Labor and capital costs were sharply reduced as well. The low capital cost of electric motors compared with that of steam engines or generating plants put the use of electric power within the reach of small plants and even many cottage industries. This change led to new relationships between small plants originating in the traditional sector and larger firms based on imported technology and organization. In some cases smaller firms became suppliers or subcontractors to larger modern establishments. In others the market was divided so that the larger plants concentrated on standardized products and long runs that maximized the economies of scale, leaving other products to small plants using much less capital-intensive methods. The cotton textile industry, for example, was divided between large-scale producers of standard yard goods like sheeting and drill, and small-scale producers of kimono fabrics that differed from the traditional cottage industries only in their use of power looms.

By 1913 the capital stock employed in electricity generation was almost one-third of that employed in the railways. It was the high-technology industry of its time, but before World War I, almost all generating plants were imported and installed under the supervision of foreign engineers and technicians sent out by the manufacturers. The technological transfer effect was therefore slight until the spurt in electrical engineering that took place during the war.

Education

The advantages of an educated, or at least a literate, population for the nation's economic and political development now seem obvious, but they were not widely appreciated in Europe before the mid-nineteenth century. Although traditional Japanese society was relatively literate for its economic level, the early Meiji government devoted few of its own limited resources to education, placing responsibility for elemen-

Summaries of this work are available in Ryōshin Minami, "The Introduction of Electric Power and Its Impact on the Manufacturing Industries: With Special Reference to Smaller Scale Plants," in *Japanese Industrialization and Its Social Consequences*, ed. Hugh Patrick (Berkeley and Los Angeles: University of California Press, 1976), pp. 299–325; and Ryōshin Minami, "Mechanical Power in the Industrialization of Japan," *Journal of Economic History* 37 (December 1977): 935–58.

tary education on local authorities with little more than exhortation from the center. But in the new cabinet system of 1885, the Ministry of Education was given responsibility for the central direction and control of formal education at all levels. As the Imperial Rescript on Education of 1891 proclaimed, the aim of elementary education was to prepare young Japanese to perform their duties as imperial subjects, as laid down in the constitution of the previous year. The purpose of education was not only to impart literacy, numeracy, and basic skills but also to inculcate those virtues of discipline, obedience, harmony, and loyalty that have since been widely represented as traditionally, or even uniquely, Japanese.

From the start, the official emphasis was heavily on elementary education, four years of which became compulsory in 1890. Although financed by local authorities, public education was not yet free, but even so compliance was virtually universal by 1900.[20] Secondary education developed more slowly and on a limited scale. In 1903 only 4 percent (8 percent if miscellaneous semiofficial institutions are included) of the fifteen-to-nineteen age group were receiving education beyond the elementary level. This figure rose to 19.8 percent (27.7 percent) by 1908, but even in 1920 between one-half to three-quarters of young Japanese got no formal education beyond the compulsory elementary level, by then extended to six years. From 1890, secondary education was offered in a multitrack system designed to channel young people into broad occupational categories.

Vocational training was systematized under an ordinance in 1899 but remained patchy. Most training in industrial skills was provided outside the formal education system, at first in schools attached to government industrial establishments or by apprenticeship to craftsmen or associated with "patrons" (*oyabun* or *oyakata*). Despite the proliferation of technical schools, vocational colleges, and institutes after the Russo-Japanese War, as the demand for modern industrial skills expanded during World War I, vocational training tended to become internalized within the larger firms, as it has remained to this day. This development fragmented and internalized the market for skilled labor, placing an unusually high value on those "traditional"

20 Of the ¥41.4 million of public funds spent on education in 1900, 55 percent was allocated to elementary education from village or town ward finances. If we add to this the fees paid by the villagers, it is clear that most of the cost of education was borne by the users. By 1920, total public expenditure on education had risen to ¥313 million, but half was still raised and allocated at the village level. For information on the role of education in Japan's economic development, see Solomon B. Levine and Hisashi Kawada, *Human Resources in Japanese Industrial Development* (Princeton, N.J.: Princeton University Press, 1980).

virtues of loyalty and a sense of obligation to the employer. Concentrating training within the larger firms also reinforced their advantage vis-à-vis the small businesses.

Tertiary education was provided by a small number of national "imperial" universities (Tokyo, 1877; Kyoto, 1897; Kyushu, 1909) that trained personnel primarily for the higher administrative levels of the civil service and secondarily for big business. Then, as since, graduation from Tokyo University's law faculty was the entrée to a distinguished civil service career. After the 1890s, the larger companies followed the government's lead in recruiting university graduates as managerial staff. By 1900 the first generation of self-educated men or managers who had come up through the ranks was being replaced by graduates of Tokyo Imperial and Keio universities or the Tokyo Higher Commercial School (now Hitotsubashi University). Graduates of tertiary institutions were a very small elite who tended to be generalists and administrators rather than scientists or engineers. This shared university background created a sense of solidarity among the top echelons of both government and business.

Japan's education system took shape in the climate of reaction to early uncritical enthusiasm for Western culture, and it was characterized increasingly by nationalist ideology. Its aim, like that of conscription, was to create loyal subjects and docile workers, and it was effective in producing Japanese who not only did what they were told but even believed and felt what they were told to believe and feel. Perhaps a different kind of education might have avoided later political and military disasters, but there can be no doubt that the Japanese education system had positive effects on the nature of the industrial labor force, industrial relations, and the government's ability to manipulate economic life and economic growth. At the relatively liberal tertiary level, this type of education was not calculated to produce innovative scientists or thinkers. But at a time when Japan could draw on and adapt a large international pool of scientific knowledge and when technical competence was more valuable than innovative brilliance, the advantages of its system of education outweighed its disadvantages if judged solely from the standpoint of economic growth.

THE TRADITIONAL SECTOR, 1885–1913

The introduction and growth of industries using technologies and methods of organization developed in the advanced industrial countries were central to Japan's economic development. To understand this development, therefore, we need to distinguish these "modern" activities from the indigenous or "traditional" economy. Conceptually this is not difficult. The modern sector includes manufacturing in factories using inanimate power and equipped with machinery imported from abroad or based on overseas models, whether the output be a new product like soap or a traditional one like cotton yarn or steel produced by new methods. Mining by engineering methods introduced from abroad is "modern," as are railways, merchant shipping, banking and insurance, and utilities like gas and electricity. Government services provided by central and local bureaucracies, education, the police, and the armed services are also part of the modern sector.

The traditional sector consists of agriculture, traditional industry, and traditional commerce and services. Agriculture is classed as traditional, as the techniques and organization of farming and the farmer's way of life have changed very little, despite the greater use of new items like chemical fertilizers. Cottage industries or very small workshops, even though they may use modern materials like chemical dyes and machine-spun yarn or produce new products like pencils or matches, are classed as traditional because here, too, their technology and organization of production did not require a sharp break with traditional practice. Retail trade, the construction industry, and transport by packhorses and riverboats all are traditional. (Transport by rickshaw, a mid-nineteenth-century innovation, may be a borderline case.)

When we try to quantify modern and traditional economic activity, however, two serious problems arise. The first is separating modern from traditional industry. Before 1914, quantitative information was collected and classified by industry – by what was produced rather than how it was produced – and so the statistical information for this period does not generally distinguish between production in a large modern factory and handicraft production by farmers as a side occupation. From time to time, information was collected and classified by size of workplace as measured by the number of workers. This information has been used to distinguish between traditional and modern industry on the assumption that production in plants with five or more (sometimes ten or more) workers could be regarded as modern industry.[21] The results of this procedure must be regarded as impression-

21 Estimates of the occupational distribution of the work force between 1872 and 1920 were made by Hijikata Seibi, "Shokugyō betsu jinkō no hensen o tsūjite mitaru shitsugyō mondai," *Shakai seisaku jihō*, no. 108 (September 1929). His estimates are reproduced in Yamada Yūzō, *Nihon kokumin shotoku suikei shiryō*, rev. ed. (Tokyo: Tōyō keizai shinpōsha, 1957), pp. 152–3. Umemura Mataji prepared revised estimates for occupational distribution

istic. Nevertheless, because modern economic development is the growth of modern, as opposed to traditional, industry, any attempt to analyze that process without differentiating between them will miss the point; econometric analysis that treats Japanese industry as homogeneous can scarcely be taken seriously.

The second problem is separating traditional industry from agriculture, particularly for the early years of our period when a large part of industrial output was produced in rural villages by people classified as farmers. Even in the late 1880s well over half of Japan's cotton yarn and raw silk, for example, is estimated to have been produced in this way. Farming, however, carried greater social prestige than did other rural occupations, and so shopkeepers, pedlars, industrial workers, or entrepreneurs with traditional family links with the land tended to give their occupation as "farmer," even though their own or their families' involvement in agriculture might have been minimal. As manufacturing gradually became more clearly separated from agriculture, fewer nonfarmers were classified as farmers. This statistical anomaly accounts for part of the apparent reduction in the agricultural labor force. Although the transfer of labor and other resources from agriculture to traditional industry was important to the growth of the Japanese economy during this period, the extent of that transfer was less than the official statistics imply.

Although we must acknowledge and emphasize the data's shortcomings, changes in the relative size of the agricultural, traditional nonagricultural, and modern sectors are so central to Japan's economic growth that we must make some attempt to quantify them.

In the early 1880s most – 98 percent – of Japan's 22 million gainfully employed persons were engaged in economic activities that had

between agriculture and nonagriculture for 1872 to 1905 and in the industrial sector between 1880 and 1883 and between 1906 and 1920. See Umemura Mataji, "Sangyō betsu koyō no hendō: 1880–1940-nen," *Keizai kenkyū* 24 (April 1973): 107–16. Umemura's revisions of Hijikata's figures indicate a larger nonagricultural work force in the 1880s, a smaller agricultural work force between 1885 and 1905, and a more pronounced movement of labor out of agriculture during World War I. A revised version of Umemura's estimates appears in Okhawa and Shinohara, eds., *Patterns of Japanese Economic Development*, pp. 392–4; while retaining his estimate of the total labor force, Umemura increased the numbers in agriculture and reduced those in nonagriculture and also raised the numbers in service industries at the expense of manufacturing.

If estimates of occupational distribution by industrial sector, especially for the early years, are still tentative, classification of the labor force into traditional and modern occupations should be regarded as impressionistic. The best are by Nakamura Takafusa, *Senzen-ki Nihon keizai seichō no bunseki*, pp. 338–9, and, for 1920 only, Nakamura Takafusa, "Zairai sangyō no kibo to kōsei–Taishō 9-nen kokusei chōsa o chūshin ni," in *Sūryō keizaishi ronshū*, vol. 1: *Nihon keizai no hatten*, ed. Umemura Mataji et al. (Tokyo: Nihon keizai shinbunsha, 1976), pp. 195–219.

changed little since the Meiji Restoration. Although just over 70 percent were officially classified as farmers, agriculture probably absorbed closer to 60 percent of Japan's labor supply in actual work hours. On the same labor input basis, fishing and the construction industry each employed about 2 percent of the work force, traditional mining and manufacturing roughly one-sixth, and commerce and services a slightly smaller proportion. Only about 400,000 people worked in the modern sector. Of these, more than half were employed by central or local government as bureaucrats, police, servicemen, teachers, or workers in government arsenals and factories. Modern private enterprise employed fewer than 200,000 people. In the early 1880s, over 90 percent of Japan's net domestic product was produced by traditional activities. Agriculture, forestry, and fisheries with just over 70 percent of the labor supply produced just under half of the net domestic product. Traditional production of goods and services other than agricultural accounted for another 45 percent or so, and the modern sector contributed only about 5 percent of output. As Nakamura Takafusa observed, modern industry was like sparsely scattered islands in a sea of traditional industry.[22]

Between 1883 and 1913, Japan's labor force increased from 22 million to 26 million, and its sectoral distribution changed. The official statistics show the number of people engaged in agriculture falling slightly, whereas the nonagricultural labor force almost doubled, but in actual labor input the change was considerably smaller than these figures indicate. Within the nonagricultural sector, modern employment increased four times, whereas employment in traditional occupations rose by only 60 percent. Nevertheless, because of the overwhelming weight of traditional commerce and industry, those sectors absorbed most – over three-quarters – of the increase in the work force. Over these three decades the output of the Japanese economy increased by almost three times. Of this increase, the growth of agricultural output contributed about 20 percent, and other traditional-style production added 40 percent or more. Although the modern sector expanded two or three times as fast as did the traditional sector, it was so relatively small initially that it contributed less than a third of the growth of the national output. These figures are admittedly impressionistic, but the picture they give of the Japanese economy before World War I is not unrealistic. In particular, they highlight the importance of traditional activities and their contribution to economic growth.

22 Nakamura Takafusa, "Shijō kōzō to sangyō soshiki," in *Nihon keizai ron – Keizai seichō 100-nen no bunseki*, ed. Emi Kōichi and Shionoya Yūichi (Tokyo: Yūhikaku, 1973), p. 301.

Agriculture

Because agriculture was such a large part of the Japanese economy at the start of its modern growth, its performance had an important bearing on the growth process. There have been various estimates of what that performance was. Using government statistics, Ohkawa and others estimated the rate of growth of real income produced in agriculture from around 1880 to World War I (1913–17 average) at just over 2.4 percent a year, with a rate of 3.3 percent to the turn of the century and just over 1 percent thereafter.[23] However, government statistics were very inaccurate for the early years. James Nakamura claimed that concealment of output and underreporting of yields had resulted in government figures for the period from 1875 to 1882 that showed only about half the actual output. Correcting for this, he derived an annual rate of growth of agricultural output from 1880 to World War I of between 0.8 and 1.2 percent, with the rate rising rather than falling after the turn of the century.[24] Ohkawa's estimate must be regarded as high because it implies for the early years a per capita caloric intake too low to be credible, but Nakamura's estimate must be regarded as low because it does not allow for any rise in per capita caloric intake as incomes rose. A more recent reworking of the statistics has produced results halfway between the two, indicating the gross farm value of production as growing at an average annual rate of 1.7 percent in constant 1934–36 prices, with the rate rising from 1.5 percent before 1900 to 1.8 percent after the turn of the century.[25] Although this estimate cannot be regarded as final, it is probably accurate enough for our purposes. Although the estimate scarcely indicates the kind of agricultural spurt once thought to be a major element in the initial phase of Japan's economic growth, it suggests a significant acceleration, as compared with the pace of agricultural progress in the century before the Restoration.

The expansion of agricultural output, both before and after 1900, was associated with the increasing use of conventional inputs like land, labor, machinery, and fertilizer, as well as with changes in organization and technology. Changes in composition also affected the value of the total output. From 1880 to 1900, agricultural inputs grew rela-

23 Kazushi Ohkawa et al., *The Growth Rate of the Japanese Economy Since 1878* (Tokyo: Kinokuniya, 1957), p. 17. 24 Nakamura, *Agricultural Production*, p. 115.

25 Umemura Mataji et al., LTES, vol. 9. Their estimates have not been significantly altered by subsequent minor adjustments. See Saburō Yamada and Yujirō Hayami, "Agriculture," in *Patterns of Japanese Economic Development*, pp. 85–103; and Yamada Saburō, "Nōgyō," in *Nihon keizai ron*, pp. 109–10.

tively slowly. The agricultural population appears to have been almost constant, even though actual labor input may well have risen when those who had devoted relatively little of their time to agriculture moved into other sectors. Reported rice paddy area was almost unchanged. Although the area of upland or dry fields increased, because of underreporting in the early years, this increase may have been more apparent than real. In any case, the average annual increase in arable land area was less than 0.5 percent. Fixed capital rose by less than 1 percent a year, and although current inputs rose somewhat faster, even in 1900 the use of commercial fertilizers and pesticides was quite limited.

After 1900 the farming population fell slightly, but the arable land area expanded faster than before; the use of implements, simple machinery, fertilizer, and other current inputs increased rapidly. This more widespread use of implements and fertilizers is consistent with the faster growth of output after the turn of the century, but over the whole period, agricultural output increased much more than did the resources devoted to agriculture. This disparity has sometimes been attributed to the more effective use of resources made possible by improvements in technology or organization. But the pace of such change in agriculture is typically slow, and before World War I, Japan seems to have been no exception.

In fact, the organization of Japanese farming changed little, and the scale of farming remained small. Average arable land per farm household was under one hectare in 1880, rose slowly to about one hectare in 1900, and then remained stable, but the median, or typical, farm was much smaller and changed only marginally in size. The only major organizational change during this period was in the structure of land ownership. With the removal of legal obstacles to land transfer, ownership tended to become more concentrated, and the relative supply of land and labor was such that those with more land than they could cultivate themselves found it advantageous to lease the surplus to tenants rather than to hire workers. Thus the proportion of land farmed by tenants increased gradually throughout the period, from about 35 percent in the early 1880s to about 45 percent by World War I, with the rate of increase highest in periods of economic depression. Between 1884 and 1886, in the aftermath of the Matsukata deflation, foreclosures – many for the nonpayment of taxes – transferred almost one-eighth of the country's cultivated land into the hands of creditors. By the end of the century, landlords, who had not been a particularly influential group at the beginning of the Meiji era, annually collected rents equivalent to almost a quarter of Japan's rice crop. With land taxes falling in real terms, the revenue lost by the government accrued mainly to landlords, who by 1900 had become a major source of local investment and enterprise as well as a powerful force in both local affairs and national politics.

Another significant organizational change was the establishment of village cooperatives under the industrial cooperatives (*sangyō kumiai*) legislation of 1900. Although these were voluntary organizations, they had become almost universal in rural villages by 1914. Together with the landlords, they acted as intermediaries between the farmers and the markets for materials and products, as vehicles for the introduction of new technology and equipment, and as channels of communication with the government in a wide range of matters. These cooperatives were intended to strengthen the competitiveness of the small farmers, to help them survive in an increasingly capitalist environment, and to forestall the widening inequality and social unrest that might result from the unfettered operation of free competition. Although the lot of most farmers, especially tenants, was seldom happy and sometimes desperate, the cooperatives did improve productivity and reduce social tension.

Technological innovation in agriculture before the 1900s was limited. Early attempts to introduce European farming methods were not successful and were abandoned in the 1880s in favor of measures to promote and improve traditional small-scale farming through the combined efforts of the Ministry of Agriculture and Commerce, landowners, and expert farmers. Rather than introducing new technology, these measures encouraged the dissemination of existing expertise by pooling local knowledge and transferring it from the more advanced regions of Kinki and north Kyushu to the relatively backward regions in the east and north. Rising rice yields and narrowing variations within and among districts may indicate some diffusion of improved plant varieties, better seed selection, and more productive cultivation practices.[26] Nevertheless, change seems to have been marginal except in sericulture, in which an important technological development made possible a silkworm hatch in the late summer–autumn season as well as in the spring, thus increasing the output of cocoons by utilizing labor from farming families during what had been a slack season. By 1900 this "second crop" contributed over one-third of all Japan's co-

26 See Yujirō Hayami with Masakatsu Akino, Masahiko Shintani, and Saburō Yamada, *A Century of Agricultural Growth in Japan, Its Relevance to Asian Development* (Minneapolis: University of Minnesota Press, and Tokyo: Tokyo University Press, 1965), pp. 113–31.

coons. From 1880 to 1900 the growth of sericulture accounted for 20 percent of the growth of the gross value of agricultural production. If sericulture is excluded, the growth rate of agricultural output over this period is reduced to about 1.3 percent, but even this seems high compared with a 0.4 percent rate of growth of total inputs. What we know of technical progress seems scarcely sufficient to account for such a difference. It may well be that the growth of conventional inputs, especially labor, has been underestimated.

Between 1900 and 1920 the average growth rate of agricultural production (gross value) rose to 1.8 percent a year. Although the farm population fell, all other inputs increased considerably: arable land by 0.7 percent a year, farm implements and machinery by 2.0 percent, and current inputs by 4.7 percent, including a massive increase in the use of commercial fertilizers. Technological change, too, speeded up after the turn of the century. With government supervision and support, landowners realigned plots and improved drainage to raise fertility. A fourfold increase in the application of fertilizers would have been largely wasted without new plant strains and deep plowing. New varieties such as Shinriki, which were highly responsive to fertilizers, were propagated rapidly in the 1900s, and the development of the reversible short-bottomed plow in 1900 made deep plowing practicable. Soon after, the introduction of a rotary weeder, which was used between straight equidistant rows of plants, greatly increased efficiency.

Apparently these changes were not greeted with universal enthusiasm, however, for some fourteen improvements were made compulsory under instructions issued in 1903 to the agricultural associations by the Ministry of Agriculture and Commerce. These included use of the brine flotation method of seed selection, oblong seed beds, and their conversion to paddy fields when the seedlings were planted out, improved seeds and implements, plowing with animals, and rice planting in equidistant checkrows. Similar regulations to improve agriculture were issued by prefectural governments and enforced by fines and an occasional jail sentence. Even so, the program achieved only limited results.[27] During the Russo-Japanese War, seed selection by the brine method was extended from one-half to two-thirds of all rice seed; plowing with draft animals became more common; and the planting out of rice in checkrows to facilitate tillage and weeding rose from one-third to almost half of the planted acreage.[28] It is surprising that a

27 See Takekazu Ogura, ed., *Agricultural Development in Modern Japan* (Tokyo: Fuji, 1963), pp. 159–71. 28 Ibid., p. 305.

practice now so firmly entrenched is of such recent origin. That inefficient or negligent farmers should be punished was generally accepted during the Tokugawa period, but attempts to apply this concept in the twentieth century met with widespread resistance. By 1910, punishments were generally abandoned in favor of encouragement by a system of subsidies and other financial incentives, although the government retained control over a wide range of agricultural matters.

Taken singly, these changes were small, but they were mutually reinforcing. New early-maturing strains of rice and other grains extended the area capable of double cropping, and more responsive varieties made profitable heavier applications of fertilizers and deep plowing. The greater use of commercial fertilizer, mainly Manchurian soybean cake, made possible some reduction in the area of grassland needed for green manure and fallow, thus releasing land for forestry and other direct production. All these changes were further reinforced by the emergence of greater opportunities for profitable farming. For pre-Meiji villagers, farming had been a duty rather than a profitable activity, and the burden of taxes fell so heavily on agriculture that villagers tried to maximize the time that they could devote to more profitable industrial and commercial pursuits. After the Restoration the incidence of direct taxation was still much heavier on agriculture than on industry, but the percentage of agricultural income taken by direct taxes fell from over 20 percent between 1883 and 1887 to just under 10 percent between 1918 and 1922.[29] Although traditional attitudes changed slowly, by World War I, farming had become more professional as developments in technology and marketing created new opportunities and incentives for the use of labor in agriculture at a time when other sources of rural income were beginning to decline.[30]

Agricultural progress in the initial phase of Japan's modern economic growth may not have been as fast as was once thought, nor was it by any means the only source of inputs for economic growth. As we shall see, industrial growth during this phase was mainly the growth of traditional production financed by the traditional industrial sector itself. Nevertheless, Japan did not suffer from the sort of agricultural lag that seems to have restricted economic growth in countries like the Soviet Union or China. Food production kept up with demand until

29 See Tōbata Seiichi and Ōkawa Kazushi, eds., *Nihon no keizai to nōgyō* (Tokyo: Iwanami shoten, 1956), vol. 1, p. 381.
30 See E. S. Crawcour, "Japan, 1868–1920," in *Agricultural Development in Asia*, ed. R. T. Shand (Canberra: Australian National University Press, 1969), pp. 1–24.

1900 and thereafter did not lag far behind. In 1880 an agricultural labor force of 17 million fed a total population of 36 million at a rather low average level of nutrition. In 1920, with an agricultural labor force of just over 14 million, a population of 55 million or more enjoyed modest increases in food consumption per capita, with food imports, mainly from Korea and Manchuria, at no more than 8 percent of total consumption. This balance or near-balance was not achieved solely by improvements in agricultural output; to an important extent it depended on the fact that population growth was moderate and that the per-capita demand for food rose remarkably little.

The experience of other developing countries suggests that as per capita incomes rise from a fairly low level, more than half of the increase is spent on more or better food. In Japan, however, the proportion was much smaller, even though the average levels of nutrition were clearly well below the optimum. Traditional eating habits changed very little, and caloric intake per capita rose only slowly.[31] The reasons for this are not obvious. Estimates of the change in per capita food consumption and national income are not very reliable, and although it seems unlikely that they underestimate the change in food consumption, the rise in national income may be somewhat exaggerated by increasing statistical coverage. It may well be that cultural attitudes encouraged frugality in food consumption, especially by women, and that with increasing urbanization, the need to buy industrial products once produced in the household may have reduced the income that could be spent on food. Most important, however, increasing demands from other sources, especially investment and exports, kept the rise in personal consumption below that of national income per capita, so that its share of gross domestic expenditure fell from about 85 percent in 1880 to 70 percent in 1920. In addition, the greater inequality of personal incomes tended to raise average savings and reduce average consumption as the richer saved while the poorer went short.

The role of agriculture as a source of capital for industrial investment may have been exaggerated in the past by the difficulty of distinguishing agriculture from rural industry and commerce, but the land tax was certainly a vital source of revenue without which the Meiji government could not have survived, let alone have played such a central role in capital formation, the introduction of technology, and

31 See Hiromitsu Kaneda, "Long-Term Changes in Food Consumption Patterns in Japan," in *Agriculture and Economic Growth, Japan's Experience*, ed. Kazushi Ohkawa et al. (Princeton, N.J.: Princeton University Press, 1969), pp. 406–9.

the coordination of economic enterprise. In 1880, taxes on land and rural households provided about 70 percent of all national and local tax revenue. By the eve of the Russo-Japanese War, their share had fallen to one-third as revenues from income, business, and consumption taxes, especially the liquor tax, rose; and by World War I it was below 30 percent.[32] As the government's share of agricultural production fell, however, the share accruing to landlords rose in almost the same proportion, and landlords, as we have seen, had a high propensity to save and invest in both local and national enterprises.

The growth of foreign trade was a key factor in the initial phase of Japan's economic development. In the mid-1880s, total transactions with the outside world represented only 6 percent of all economic activity, but by the Russo-Japanese War they had risen to 20 percent, and by World War I, to 28 percent. In the 1880s over two-thirds of Japan's exports consisted of agricultural products, principally raw silk. By the Russo-Japanese War this proportion had fallen to one-third, whereas homegrown cotton, unable to compete in cost or quality, had been replaced by imports, greatly reducing agriculture's contribution to the balance of payments. Over the whole period, however, agricultural exports played a very valuable role in foreign trade and even during World War I provided a quarter of commodity exports.

In summary, the performance of agriculture during this period, if perhaps not so outstanding as once thought, was adequate. The introduction, dissemination, and sometimes enforcement of better methods of farming and the increasing operation of economic incentives, particularly via landlords, enabled a more efficient use of land and labor with a consequent expansion of output. On the other hand, the adequacy of supply depended also on limited rises in demand and the persistence of traditional patterns of consumption. The broad structural outlines of small-scale farming scarcely changed. Tenancy increased, and landlords and agricultural associations took over some of the functions of the *daikan* and village headmen of earlier times. Eco-

32 Estimates vary. See Kazushi Ohkawa and Henry Rosovsky, "The Role of Agriculture in Modern Japanese Economic Development," *Economic Development and Cultural Change* 9 (October 1960): pt 2, p. 61, where Table 14 shows land tax as a percentage of revenue from four "main taxes" (income tax, land tax, business tax, and customs duty) falling from 85.6 percent in the five years centered on 1890 to 55.8 percent for the five years centered on 1905 and 37.6 percent for the five years centered on 1915. By 1915, however, the four main taxes accounted for only 54.6 percent of the national tax revenue. I have calculated the sum of national, prefectural, and local (*chōson*) land taxes and local household tax as a percentage of all national and local tax revenue. Note that 90 percent of *chōson* were rural villages.

nomic horizons and opportunities may have widened in theory, but for the average farmer it was still a hard life with worse to come in the depressed conditions of the 1920s.

Traditional industry

The policy of the early Meiji leaders was to catch up with the advanced countries of the West by "enriching the country and strengthening the armed forces," and they believed that the way to achieve this was to replace as quickly as possible the "backward" Japanese methods of production with the latest Western technology. Consequently, little thought was given to supporting or improving the existing industrial structure. In the 1870s, attempts to transplant Western production methods were generally unsuccessful, partly because a supporting infrastructure had not yet been built, but perhaps more importantly because methods developed in the Western nations proved unprofitable in Japan where capital equipment was much more expensive relative to labor. The initial policy response to this problem was either to establish modern industries as government enterprises or to reduce the cost of industrial plants to selected firms – broadly speaking the "political merchants" who developed into the zaibatsu – by making it possible for them to raise capital on favorable terms, while assisting with the selection, purchase, and import of machinery and providing technical assistance. The cost of this policy was substantial at a time when other demands were straining fiscal resources to the limit. In the course of Matsukata's fiscal reforms, government enterprises were sold to selected buyers at prices low enough to bring the cost of capital equipment more into line with Japanese conditions.

The recession that followed the Matsukata deflation, however, brought severe hardship to Japan's traditional industry. In 1884 Maeda Masana, a senior official of the Ministry of Agriculture and Commerce who had recently returned from a study tour of Europe, suggested after a thorough survey of Japan's economic grass roots that traditional industry was an indispensable resource; that with support and improvement it was capable not only of providing for rising consumption needs and exports to earn badly needed foreign exchange but also of being gradually developed to a level of productivity comparable to that of Western industry. Industrial modernization along these lines, he submitted, would result in methods suited to Japanese conditions of scarce capital and abundant labor, would involve far less cost than would the direct transplantation of Western factories, and would relieve the economic distress that constantly threatened rural Japan and was particularly acute in the postdeflation recession.[33]

Although not fully convinced by Maeda's arguments, the government did recognize the important role of traditional industry in the economy. Japanese consumer goods were produced in ways that had not changed since the country's opening. The kinds of housing, clothing, processed foods, and household utensils that made up the distinctive Japanese way of life retained their traditional patterns, and traditional industry continued to supply them. In this respect Japan differed from territories such as the Dutch East Indies, where a colonial system producing staple exports and importing many consumer goods had brought about the decline of the indigenous industrial system.

Personal consumption represented 80 percent of Japan's gross national expenditure in the 1880s but fell to 75 percent by the Russo-Japanese War and 72 percent by 1915. Consumption of nonagricultural goods and services,[34] however, was 35 percent of gross national expenditure in the 1880s and actually rose to 38 percent during the Russo-Japanese War and to 43 percent at the start of World War I. These figures show that it was a lag in consumption of agricultural products that kept total personal consumption relatively low. The consumption of nonagricultural goods and services expanded faster than did the economy as a whole. Because there were virtually no imports of these traditional goods, their production expanded as fast as consumption did.

As well as supplying consumer goods, traditional industry contributed to capital formation and exports. A large part of construction, road building, and other public works was carried out using traditional methods by workers employed and organized in traditional ways. Until the 1890s as much as half of Japan's major export item, raw silk, was produced by hand reelers. Handicraft products such as lacquerware, cloisonné, and damascene were prominent among Japanese exports after the opening of foreign trade in 1859. After 1900, Japan exported increasing quantities of pencils and other products that, though new to Japan, were produced by traditional cottage industry methods.

33 Maeda's findings and recommendations were presented in *Kōgyō iken* in 1885. This work with related materials and commentary is published as Andō Yoshio and Yamamoto Hirofumi, eds., *Kōgyō iken hoka Maeda Masana kankei shiryō* (Tokyo: Kōseikan, 1971). See also Soda Osamu, *Maeda Masana* (Tokyo: Yoshikawa kōbunkan, 1973).

34 Calculated as personal consumption less nonprocessed food. For this purpose, rice is regarded as an unprocessed food, even though rice milling was quite a large industry. This is partly balanced by the inclusion of the full cost of processed foods.

Traditional industry was important also as an employer of labor. During Japan's modern economic growth, its agricultural labor force declined, but the total gainfully occupied population rose. Until the 1930s the difference was absorbed almost entirely by the traditional sectors of secondary and tertiary industry. In the process the proportion of the work force in traditional nonagricultural occupations rose from 22 percent between 1882 and 1885 to 30 percent by the Russo-Japanese War, 32 percent by the eve of World War I, and 37 percent by 1920. These figures are conservative, as they assume that all workshops in which more than five persons were employed represented modern industry, whereas in fact many had continued virtually unchanged since before the Meiji Restoration.

In output of manufactures, the importance of traditional industry is hard to quantify because output data do not distinguish between traditional and modern production. According to a rough estimate, the proportion of manufactures produced by traditional means fell from nearly three-quarters in the 1880s to about one-half around the Russo-Japanese War and about one-third by World War I. This estimate of the importance of traditional industry as a producer of manufactures is probably conservative and may well exaggerate the speed with which production methods changed.

Apart from some brewing, oil-pressing, and metallurgical industries using water power and employing twenty or more workers, and city-based decorative craft industries, most traditional industries began as rural, largely part-time cottage industries. Circulating capital, often in the form of materials and sometimes equipment, was provided by merchants (*ton'ya*) who controlled the production process and marketed the output in the major cities. In the post-Restoration transition, "orderly marketing," once supervised by licensed merchant guilds or official marketing boards, largely broke down because of adverse effects on quality, prices, and credit arrangements. Food processing, the cotton industry from ginning to weaving, silk reeling, and some silk weaving were typical of this type of industry.

During the initial phase of Japan's economic growth there were a number of changes. First, some production moved from rural villages to nearby towns or larger cities where household workers or small workshops clustered in areas specializing in a particular trade. During the economic depression that followed the Sino-Japanese War and continued almost uninterrupted until the eve of the Russo-Japanese War, many people moved from villages to towns in search of work. When available, such work was usually of a kind to which these people had been accustomed in the villages and at wages similar to rural rates. Between 1898 and 1918 the urban population almost trebled. Although much of the increase was in tertiary occupations, the growth of urban manufacturing was considerable.

Second, traditional industries were reorganized into trade associations or cooperatives. Early attempts by the Meiji government to coordinate and control the production, financing, and marketing of traditional products through national agencies (*shōhōshi, tsūshōshi*) were soon abandoned in favor of policies that promoted new industries based on the latest technology from abroad. In 1879 the Osaka Chamber of Commerce began to reestablish order in the traditional trades, and at the end of 1880 it reported the formation of 189 trade associations, broadly similar to the pre-Restoration guilds (*nakama*). The following year the Osaka municipal government responded by issuing official regulations for the formation and management of trade associations. These regulations included provisions for registering members, electing officials, and maintaining product quality and commercial ethics, with penalties for offenders under the general supervision of the Osaka Chamber of Commerce. Similar moves were made in Tokyo and Kyoto. In 1884 the Ministry of Agriculture and Commerce issued national guidelines for the formation and management of trade associations. These provided for persons in agricultural, commercial, or industrial occupations to form local nonprofit organizations ostensibly for the members' mutual benefit. Registration and reporting provisions were similar to those of the Osaka municipal ordinance. Once an association had been approved and registered by the prescribed authority on the application of three-quarters or more of those eligible to join, membership by the remainder became compulsory. In Osaka at least, many trade associations so formed were actually the direct successors of guilds or associations that had continued in one form or another since before the Restoration.

In 1897 a new law enforced membership in the Major Export Trade Associations (Jūyō yushutsuhin dōgyō kumiai); and three years later all trades, whether export or otherwise, were required to organize into Major Product Trade Associations (Jūyō bussan dōgyō kumiai). These associations, which embraced the production and marketing of virtually all traditional manufactures, replaced the associations formed under the 1884 guidelines. The new trade associations were intended to maintain product standards, raise productivity, and control excessive competition (although price rigging was expressly forbidden), improve managerial skills, and achieve certain economies of scale. At the same time, like their premodern predecessors, they were a vehicle for the exercise of official control to ensure that free enterprise did not work to the disadvantage of the trade as a whole and that traditional industry developed in a way consistent with the national interest.[35]

Third, although Maeda Masana's gradualist proposals for industrial development based on progressive upgrading of existing industry were not accepted – largely because although they might "enrich the country," they would not immediately "strengthen the armed forces" – they alerted the government to the gains attainable at relatively little cost by improving technical standards and raising productivity in traditional industries.[36] With official encouragement some traditional industries achieved technological advances that enabled them to survive and compete alongside new enterprises based on imported technology. In the silk-reeling industry, for example, attempts to operate the most modern imported machine filatures proved unprofitable in conditions in which cheap experienced labor was plentiful and capital scarce and expensive. Under such conditions hand (*zakuri*) reelers were well able to compete. Hand-reeled silk was inferior in quality to machine-reeled silk, but a series of improvements raised both quality and productivity. Meanwhile, machine filatures were modified to suit Japanese conditions, and their cost fell rapidly. From an astonishingly high ¥1,500 per basin for the filatures imported from France in 1871 to equip the pioneer Tomioka mill, the cost per basin fell to ¥13.5 within a few years. Output per operative also almost doubled in the decade following the installation of the Tomioka plant and almost doubled again by the end of the century. Even so, hand reeling remained competitive, and its output continued to rise until the turn of the century, even though by 1894 filature silk exceeded hand-reeled silk in quantity and had captured the bulk of the export market because of its higher, more even quality. Hand-reeled output showed no tendency to fall until the 1920s when machine production expanded rapidly. In this industry, as in others, imported technology became successful only after it had been adapted to local conditions. In the process, the gap between "acclimatized," largely water-powered machine filatures and improved indigenous hand-reeling technology was narrow enough for each industry to learn from the other. In the absence of great economies of scale and with

35 See Miyamoto Mataji, "Shōkō kumiai," in *Nihon keizaishi jiten*, ed. Keizaishi kenkyūkai (Tokyo: Nihon hyōronsha, 1940), vol. 1, pp. 801–4, which clearly shows the continuity between Japan's modern trade associations and those of the pre-Meiji period. See also Watanabe Shin'ichi, *Nihon no keiei kōzō – Senzen hen* (Tokyo: Yūshōdō, 1971), pp. 53–79.

36 See Soda Osamu, *Chihō sangyō no shisō to undō* (Kyoto: Minerva shobō, 1980).

an abundance of cheap labor, the indigenous technology was thus able to remain viable for over fifty years.[37]

Even in the cotton textile industry, one of the first to be successfully modernized, the indigenous industry survived and developed. Despite imports of cotton yarn and cloth in the early Meiji era, the domestic production of raw cotton and its traditional processing industries continued to flourish until the 1890s, when hand ginning and spinning became unable to compete in either quality or cost with the modern mills by then established in Japan. The traditional cotton-weaving industry, on the other hand, flourished, and the output of narrow-width cloth for Japanese clothing increased fourfold between 1885 and 1910, making this one of the period's high-growth industries. Growth was achieved by improvements in equipment and materials and by greater specialization. Nevertheless the predominantly semirural cottage-industry nature of the trade remained practically unchanged. Even in 1910, 87 percent of looms were hand powered, and of these well over half were in cottages and another third in "factories" with not more than ten weavers.[38] By the 1930s the narrow-width cotton-weaving industry was converting to electric-powered looms but retained its traditional organization and character. The continued viablility of this industry owed much to the survival of the cotton kimono as everyday dress until the Pacific War and to the demand for a great variety of woven and dyed patterns that made long runs and mass production uneconomic.

This same demand for variety aided the survival and expansion of other traditional consumer goods industries such as ceramics, lacquerware, bamboo products, and handmade paper.[39] In addition, new products including matches, straw hats, brushes, Western-style umbrellas, and buttons were also produced by traditional methods, largely for export. Matches, for example, were made by a very labor-intensive putting-out system. The "maker," who financed the industry, often with funds from a local bank, provided the materials and sometimes simple equipment. One or more households shaped pinewood into billets; others split and cut the billets into matchsticks; and still others dipped them to make the heads, while other teams were making matchboxes and pasting labels on them. Finally, yet more

37 See Ōtsuka Katsuo, "Seishigyō ni okeru gijutsu dōnyu" in *Nihon keizai no hatten*, pp. 159–78, and Nakamura, *Senzen-ki Nihon keizai seichō no bunseki*, p. 64.

38 See Nakamura Takafusa, "Zairai men orimonogyō no hatten to suitai – Oboegaki" in *Sūryō keizaishi ronshū*, vol. 2: *Kindai ikō-ki no Nihon keizai – Bakumatsu kara Meiji e*, ed. Shinbo Hiroshi and Yasuba Yasukichi (Tokyo: Nihon keizai shinbunsha, 1979), pp. 219–33.

39 For further examples, see Chihōshi kenkyū kyōgikai, ed., *Nihon sangyōshi taikei*, 7 vols. (Tokyo: Tōkyō daigaku shuppankai, 1960).

teams of household workers packed the matches in the boxes and wrapped them in packets for shipment. The whole process took place within an area small enough for the goods and materials to be transferred from one stage to the next by handcart. One "maker" might employ several hundred people working in their own homes at rates of pay so low that often the whole family needed to work long hours to make a living.

From the 1880s to World War I, the growth of the traditional sector was a vital part of the whole economy's development. Not only was it responsible for the bulk of output growth, but it also nurtured the infant modern sector by providing and maintaining labor, contributing capital, and earning foreign exchange. Several factors account for its growth.[40] First, as we have already noticed, the persistence of traditional patterns of consumption provided a growing demand for traditional products as the population increased and incomes rose. Second, until World War I, traditional industry was the principal beneficiary of the new infrastructure, especially cheaper transport and a modern financial system. Third, the development of modern industry provided cheaper and better materials, like machine-spun cotton yarn, dyes and other chemicals, cardboard, and glass, which lowered costs in traditional industries. Investment in modern infrastructure, industry, and defense, moreover, raised incomes and thus demand for traditional goods and services. Finally, the export markets and the official encouragement of the traditional labor-intensive industries as export producers also stimulated growth. Because of the low labor costs, these industries were able to compete successfully with more highly mechanized producers in the relatively capital-rich advanced industrialized countries, much to their irritation.

Ohkawa and others have credited Japan with being able to maintain growth in both agriculture and industry.[41] It is now clear, however, that Japan's industrial growth before World War I was largely the growth of traditional industry. What appears as the concurrent growth of agriculture and industry was in fact the growth of the traditional sector as a whole. When the modern sector became self-sustaining and established itself as the leader in economic growth around World War I, the growth of the traditional sector, including both agriculture and the traditional industries, slackened as modern

40 See Nakamura Takafusa, "Zairai sangyō no hatten kikō – Meiji Taishō-ki no Nihon ni oite," *Keizai hyōron*, new series, 16 (January 1967): 134–56.

41 See, for example, Kazushi Ohkawa, *Differential Structure and Agriculture: Essays on Dualistic Growth* (Tokyo: Kinokuniya, 1972), pp. 165–81.

technology drew ahead, the sphere in which simple hand production was competitive narrowed, export prices declined, and consumer taste began to change. With the wartime surge in modern industrial development, the complementary relationship between the traditional and modern sectors changed to one of competition for resources, in which all the advantages were on the side of the modern sector. In the postwar recessions, as more and more people were unable to find employment elsewhere, incomes and living standards in the traditional sector fell markedly below those of the modern sector, creating in the 1920s a dual or differential economic structure that was characteristic of the interwar period and persisted well into the high-growth era of the 1960s. The problems of this differential structure were of great significance for both Japan's economic development and its social and political development but are outside the scope of this chapter.

THE MODERN SECTOR, 1885–1913

In late nineteenth-century Japan, manufacturing was a very small part of a modern sector which was itself very small in relation to the whole economy. The new bureaucracy, the army and navy, the education system, modern railways, shipping, and finance provided the bulk of modern employment in the 1880s and even in 1913 employed over half of this sector's labor force. All contributed directly or indirectly to Japan's economic growth. But in the long run it was the development of the modern secondary industries that made it possible to employ a steadily increasing proportion of the work force at levels of productivity far higher than could be achieved with traditional organization and technology, thereby producing a sustained and in fact accelerating increase in overall output. In the late nineteenth century, however, the modern sector, including most modern manufacturing industries, still depended for its existence and growth on resources from the traditional economy and to some extent from abroad.

The order in which modern industries developed in Japan has interested economic theorists. Experience in the older industrial countries of the West suggested a progression from light industries, especially textiles, through mining and metallurgical industries, railways, and the age of steam to heavy engineering, chemicals, and the mass production of motor cars and other appliances. This was thought to be a natural progression, as capital accumulation and technological progress reduced the cost of capital, encouraging the introduction of increasingly capital-intensive methods of production. In Japan, too, this sequence, although compressed into a shorter span of time, was generally similar but had some important differences. We have seen how the development of railways and the merchant marine was able to precede the emergence of the iron and steel industry by relying on imports of rails, girders, rolling stock, ships, and other equipment. Mining developed early largely to supply export markets. Although cotton spinning and some other branches of the textile industry were the first modern manufacturing industries to be profitably established, modern iron and steel mills, shipbuilding, and some other branches of heavy engineering followed so closely as to overlap with them. In the few years that separated the beginnings of light and heavy industry, changes in the relative costs and availability of labor and capital were certainly not great enough to make relatively capital-intensive heavy industries profitable or competitive with imports. On the contrary, those heavy and engineering industries were established at great cost either as state enterprises or with government subsidies, guarantees, and protection. Most did not become economically viable until the World War I boom.

Here we see a major difference between the modern Japanese textile industry and, for example, the iron and steel industry. Both received government encouragement and assistance in one form or another – the textile industry to replace imports and reduce the drain on foreign exchange, and heavy industry to produce in the interests of national security. The former soon adapted to Japan's relative abundance of labor and thereafter became an attractively profitable investment. In the latter, however, the proportions of labor and capital were fixed within narrow limits by the technology, and so their establishment was justified on grounds of national security rather than economic viability.

Enterprises established in the national interest rather than in response to business opportunities tended to be promoted and managed by people with administrative experience and good government contacts rather than by those with sound business backgrounds. This has prompted the view that the typical entrepreneur of the Meiji era was of samurai rather than merchant background and that Japan's traditional business class was conservative and unable to adapt to the competitive world of free enterprise.[42] Whenever the criteria of the marketplace indicated genuine business opportunities, however, businessmen were

42 See, for example, Tsuchiya Takao, *Zaibatsu o kizuita hitobito* (Tokyo: Kōbundō, 1955); and Tsuchiya Takao, *Nihon no keieisha seishin* (Tokyo: Keizai ōraisha, 1959). For a more recent discussion, see Johannes Hirschmeier and Tsunehiko Yui, *The Development of Japanese Business, 1600–1973* (London: Allen & Unwin, 1975).

not slow to exploit them, as they did in the textile industry in the 1890s.

However, investment decisions based on grounds other than free-market considerations are not necessarily less effective or desirable in promoting modern economic growth. Neither economic theory nor experience suggests that the unhampered operation of free-market forces in a situation such as Japan's in the late nineteenth century allocates resources over time in a way that optimizes economic development. The Japanese authorities had no compunction about channeling resources into import-replacement projects designed to conserve foreign exchange, to enhance national security, or otherwise to promote what they saw as the national interest. The development of industries established for such reasons often itself helped create the conditions under which they could eventually be justified in terms of normal business calculations. The relationship between market forces and the pursuit of national objectives is woven into Japan's modern economic development in intricate patterns that need more detailed study.[43]

Light industry

The textile industry was the only light industry to be firmly established on the basis of modern technology and organization before World War I. It consisted overwhelmingly of silk reeling and cotton spinning. Of the two, raw silk was superior in value of output and was far more important as an export commodity.

The modern silk-reeling industry began in the 1870s with the importation of filatures from Europe by the government and a few others. The cost of these filatures was high; the government's three-hundred-basin model plant at Tomioka, for example, was completed in 1872 at a cost of ¥198,000. But because of their high capital cost, poor management, and inexperienced labor, these early filatures could not compete successfully with traditional hand reeling. Not until the development of modified equipment at much less cost did machine reeling become profitable. After the late 1880s this "acclimatized" modern technology spread rapidly, especially in Nagano, Yamanashi, and Gumma prefectures, and by 1894 it produced more and better-quality

43 The many suggestive insights on this topic in the final chapter of William W. Lockwood, *The Economic Development of Japan: Growth and Structural Change 1868–1938* (Princeton, N.J.: Princeton University Press, 1954), have only recently begun to be followed up with as much enthusiasm as they deserve. See Sydney Crawcour, "Japanese Economic Studies in Foreign Countries in the Postwar Period," *Keizai kenkyū* 30 (January 1979): 49–64.

silk than did the traditional hand-reeling industry. The output per basin rose markedly and the production of filature silk continued to expand. After the 1890s the growth of the industry was firmly based on the new technology. Raw silk was already Japan's leading export before the introduction of modern technology, but with the improved quality of filature silk, promoted by producers' associations and checked by a government-sponsored system of inspection, the value of raw silk exports rose from an annual average of ¥17.7 million between 1883 and 1887 to ¥50 million between 1893 and 1897, ¥92.5 million between 1903 and 1907, and ¥206.8 million between 1913 and 1917.[44]

The success of the modern silk-reeling industry can be attributed only indirectly to government initiative. The technology as first introduced by the government was too capital intensive for the indigenous conditions of plentiful labor and scarce capital, but it did inspire local mechanics to produce modified capital-saving equipment. Although the scale increased over time, the optimum remained fairly small so that filatures could enjoy the advantages of being located close to sources of raw materials and local labor. As the industry became concentrated in Nagano Prefecture, however, it increasingly drew its workers from Toyama and other neighboring prefectures. Modern silk reeling was, moreover, well served by financial institutions that had grown up with the traditional hand-reeling industry, and it benefited from the buoyant export demand and elastic supplies of cocoons.[45]

Whereas Japan's raw silk was competitive from the start in international markets, Japan's indigenous cotton yarn could not compete with imports in either price or quality. Cotton yarn and fabric had been Japan's biggest imports throughout the 1870s, amounting in 1880 to ¥13.2 million, or 36 percent of the value of all imports. Faced with a shortage of foreign exchange, the government hoped that a more efficient domestic spinning industry could replace the imported product. At first officials believed, by analogy with silk reeling, that this could be achieved by using Western spinning machinery in small water-powered mills located in the cotton-growing areas and employing hand spinners then being made redundant by competition from imports. The government therefore imported ten, two-thousand-spindle-sets of spinning machinery and sold them on credit to entrepreneurs in various parts of the country. The importation of three more

44 With the growth of other export industries, raw silk's share of total export value fell over this period from 42 percent to 22 percent.

45 See Katsuo Otsuka, "Technological Choice in the Japanese Silk Industry: Implications for Development in LDCs," Working Paper Series no. A-05, mimeographed (Tokyo: International Development Center of Japan, March 1977).

sets was financed with public funds. The Akabane workshops of the Ministry of Industry, commissioned to make another set on a trial basis, eventually produced a copy of imported Platt Brothers equipment, but at twice the landed cost of the original and of such inferior quality as to be unusable. The whole program of introducing two-thousand-spindle mills proved a costly failure involving the expenditure of over ¥1.6 million of public funds between 1880 and 1884, from which virtually nothing was recovered.

Meanwhile, with the encouragement and support of the ubiquitous promotor Shibusawa Eiichi, a group of Kansai businessmen and others, including some outstanding managers with close government connections, raised ¥240,000 to found the Osaka Spinning Company, which began operation with 10,500 mule spindles in 1884. Learning from the earlier mills' mistakes, the new company used imported raw cotton (initially from China) which was cheaper and of somewhat more suitable quality than the domestic was. The mill was therefore located near the port and used steam in place of less reliable water power. No attempt was made to modify the equipment, as the silk-reeling industry had done, but operations were brought into line with indigenous conditions of plentiful labor and scarce capital by the simple but crucial capital-saving device of working two shifts around the clock. Because labor was already used very intensively, the Osaka mill employed roughly four times as many workers per unit of capital as its English or American counterparts did. The company was an immediate success. Within four years of coming into operation, it was paying dividends of 30 percent on a paid-up capital which had by then been increased fivefold to ¥1.2 million. Other businessmen were quick to follow suit. In 1888 the Japan Cotton Spinners' Association was reorganized to exchange information and experience, promote the development of the industry, and coordinate employment policies, with the members agreeing not to hire away one another's workers. Nevertheless, in the boom conditions of the time there were incessant disputes over the poaching of skilled workers.[46]

In the recession of 1890 the association worked to obtain subsidies and other incentives to penetrate overseas markets. The 5 percent export duty on cotton yarn was abolished in 1894, and the import duty on raw cotton was lifted in 1896. Meanwhile, the industry was converting from mules to ring-frame spindles, which were 50 percent more produc-

46 By contrast, in the early days, skilled hands were lent freely to act as instructors in new mills. The change is no doubt connected with the transition of the cotton-spinning industry from a "national interest" to a "profit motive" basis.

tive and could spin finer counts of yarn. The new spindles, however, required finer and longer staple cotton than was available from China, so in 1892 the association entered into an agreement to purchase Indian cotton in Bombay through its trading organ (Nichimen), and the following year negotiated favorable terms with NYK for cotton shipments from Bombay. After 1895 the domestic consumption of cotton yarn began to level off, and exports became the main avenue for further growth. Export growth was retarded by disruption of the Chinese market during the Sino-Japanese War, but in 1897 exports exceeded imports for the first time. The following year, however, a slump in domestic demand, rising costs, and a shortage of finance sharply reduced profits. To some extent the spinning companies had themselves contributed to these difficulties by their practice of paying high dividends while failing to make adequate provision for reserves, but the association prevailed on Minister of Finance Inoue Kaoru to bail them out by arranging export credits on favorable terms and low-interest loans totaling ¥2.371 million (8 percent of the total paid-up capital of all spinning mills at that time). This enabled the cotton spinners to repay loans and finance further expansion at a cost of capital well below the Japanese market rate. Although the recession continued, accompanied by short-time work and concentration through a series of takeovers by the top six firms, with government assistance, exports continued to rise.[47]

The weaving of cotton fabric was largely a cottage industry before World War I. Japanese-made power looms for weaving standard-width piece goods appeared around the turn of the century and increased in number after the Russo-Japanese War. By 1913 about 25,000 such looms, nearly 80 percent of them in weaving sheds operated by the largest spinning mills, produced 345 million yards valued at ¥215 million.

Cheap labor has often been cited as a reason for the success of the Japanese cotton-spinning industry. A high and rising proportion of the mill hands were female – over 80 percent in 1913 compared with about two-thirds in the United Kingdom and less than half in the United States. Most were uneducated teenaged girls recruited from rural areas where the decline of the cottage textile industry was reducing farmers' cash incomes. Although the girls lived under poor conditions virtually unregulated by legislation and worked twelve-hour shifts for cash wages

47 On development of the modern Japanese cotton-spinning industry, see Fujino Shozaburō et al., eds., LTES, vol. 11 (Textiles); Sanpei Takako, *Nihon mengyō hattatsu shi* (Tokyo: Keiō shobō, 1941). On government assistance to the industry, see Tsūshō Sangyōshō, ed., *Shōkō seisaku shi*, vol. 15: *Sen'i kōgyō* (1) (Tokyo: Shōkō seisaku shi kankōkai, 1968), pp. 158–208.

lower than the earnings of a cottage weaver or silk reeler and lower still than those of an Indian cotton mill worker, rural conditions were such that they could be readily recruited by smooth-talking agents prepared to pay a lump sum to the head of the household.[48] Once hired, however, few worked long enough to acquire a useful degree of skill. Despite the efforts of the Japan Cotton Spinners Association and although most of them lived in closely supervised company dormitories, about half absconded within a few months, and only about one in ten stayed for three or more years. The Kanebō Company tried to improve its labor supply by remaining outside the cotton spinners association and offering somewhat better pay and conditions. Although this does not seem to have reduced labor turnover, the association was worried enough to put heavy pressure on Kanebō to join.[49]

Compared with the United Kingdom or the United States, Japanese labor was cheap relative to capital, and the expansion of the cotton-spinning industry depended on using large numbers of workers in round-the-clock operations. It depended also on coordinating production through the cotton spinners association, promoting exports, and offering government assistance, including official warnings to mill owners against paying themselves more generous dividends than sound long-term management warranted. Nevertheless, by international standards, the industry was still small in 1913 when Japan had a total capacity of 2.34 million spindles, as compared with 55.5 million in the United Kingdom and 30.6 million in the United States. Even in the China market, where Japanese exports were heavily concentrated, the value of Lancashire's share was two and a half times that of Japan.[50]

Although cotton and silk were by far the biggest modern light industries, others had begun before World War I. The woolen textile industry began as a government enterprise because demand was overwhelmingly for military or official use and because production costs were too high to make it commercially profitable in the face of competition from imports. Early government policy was no more successful here than in the other examples already described. The first official move

48 A good source of detailed information, though rather questionable in regard to analysis, is by Takamura Naosuke, *Nihon bōsekigyō shi josetsu* (Tokyo: Hanawa shobō, 1971).

49 See Gary R. Saxonhouse, "Country Girls and Communication Among Competitors in the Japanese Cotton-Spinning Industry," in *Japanese Industrialization and Its Social Consequences*, ed. Hugh Patrick (Berkeley and Los Angeles: University of California Press, 1976), pp. 97–125; and Morita Yoshio, *Nihon keieisha dantai hatten shi* (Tokyo: Nikkan rōdō tsūshin, 1958), pp. 37–43.

50 See David S. Landes, "Technological Change and Development in Western Europe, 1750–1914" in *Cambridge Economic History of Europe*, ed. H. J. Habakkuk and M. Postan, vol. 6, pt. 1 (Cambridge, England: Cambridge University Press, 1965), pp. 443, 467–8.

was an unsuccessful attempt to introduce merino sheep as a domestic source of raw material, and in 1877 a government woolen mill was established at Senju to weave imported yarn into serge for uniforms. Not until the 1900s when wool muslin began to be used for everyday Japanese dress was the private woolen industry, with the aid of a 25 percent *ad valorem* import duty, able to compete with imports.[51] Other modern light industries established before World War I include sugar refining, brewing, printing, papermaking, and glassmaking, but in the overall development of Japanese industry in this period, they were of minor importance compared with textiles.

Heavy and engineering industries

Heavy industries like iron and steel, shipbuilding, and engineering emerged at a relatively early stage in Japan's modern industrial development, not because they presented attractive opportunities to investors, but because the government was convinced that national military and economic security required a fair degree of self-sufficiency in those fields. The Japanese government was well aware that the world powers' strength and influence depended on their capacity to produce iron and steel, ships, and munitions, and it was convinced that catching up with the West implied a commitment to the development of these industries.

Iron and high-quality steel had been made in Japan for centuries; indeed, Japanese swords were prized in China and Southeast Asia as early as the sixteenth century. Excellent though it was, however, Japanese steel was produced by small-scale labor-intensive methods totally inadequate for military requirements in the late nineteenth century. Small experimental blast furnaces built by various domains in the 1850s and 1860s used a smelted iron ore with charcoal and produced wrought iron by puddling, a technology already out of date. Neither the Meiji government nor private firms were able to operate these plants profitably, and so their output was negligible.[52] For railways,

51 See Keiichirō Nakagawa and Henry Rosovsky, "The Case of the Dying Kimono: The Influence of Changing Fashions on the Development of the Japanese Woollen Industry," *Business History Review* 37 (Spring–Summer 1963): 64.

52 See Thomas C. Smith, *Political Change and Industrial Development in Japan: Government Enterprise 1868–1880* (Stanford, Calif.: Stanford University Press, 1955). Smith stresses the contribution to Japan's economic development made by the government's industrial undertakings in this period. Their contribution to output, however, was small. Most embodied technology inappropriate to Japan and were not, on the whole, the direct progenitors of modern Japanese industry. They did provide important opportunities for learning by doing, but in most cases the knowledge and experience so gained could have been acquired more easily and at less cost in other ways.

bridges, ships, and munitions, Meiji Japan relied on imported iron and steel. From 1888 to 1893 those imports averaged some 35,000 tons a year, valued at about ¥2 million. Military expenditures increased fourfold during the Sino-Japanese War and, under the ten-year armament plan initiated in 1896, remained high at around 5.3 percent of gross national expenditure, or nearly two and a half times the prewar ratio. With the additional demands of a railway-building boom, steel imports rose between 1898 and 1900 to an annual average of 182,000 tons, valued at over ¥10 million, compared with home production of less than 2,000 tons.

With little prospect of any growth in its steel industry, the Japanese government, itself the largest consumer of steel, had been considering establishing a government steel works since 1880. In 1891 the government put such a bill before the Diet, with an explanatory statement that included the following:

> Steel is the mother of industries and the foundation of national defense. Without a steel industry other industries cannot flourish and the armed services cannot be properly equipped. We all know that a country's prospects can be gauged by the state of its steel industry. If we want to make this country rich and strong we ought to set up a steelworks.

The statement went on to make a case for state intervention on the grounds of substantial external economies. To the private investor, selling imported steel was more profitable and required much less capital than establishing a steelworks in Japan. Nevertheless, because Japan was not short of iron ore, a Japanese steel industry would be able to compete profitably with imports if pig iron were available in sufficient quantities.

> If we put enough effort into exploration, discovery of iron ore is certain. The reason we have not made any discoveries to date is simply that, not having a steelworks, there was no demand for large quantities of pig iron. Thus, while the establishment of a steelworks would promote the development of the iron industry, there is no hope of a steelworks starting unless an iron industry develops. In these circumstances we shall never get a private enterprise steel mill so there is really no alternative but that the state should establish a mill.[53]

Prime Minister Matsukata Masayoshi, better known for selling off government industrial undertakings than for creating them, supported the bill in a speech stressing the defense need for steel and warning of the strategic dangers of relying on imports. He further claimed that

53 Tsūshō sangyōshō, ed., *Shōkō seisaku shi*, vol. 17: *Tekkō* (Tokyo: Shōkō seisaku shi kankōkai, 1970), pp. 70–1.

home-produced steel would be cheaper in the long run and pointed to the drain on foreign exchange reserves associated with the rapidly rising demand for steel.

An uncooperative House of Representatives rejected the bill by a large majority. In the following year a second attempt failed to obtain an appropriation of ¥2.250 million to establish a steel mill under the Ministry of the Navy. A third attempt, this time under the auspices of the Ministry of Agriculture and Commerce, passed the House of Peers but was rejected by the House of Representatives which also slashed naval construction. Not until the Sino-Japanese War had been in progress for six months did the government finally obtain the Diet's approval for an integrated steel mill, at a cost of ¥4.095 million. In 1901 the Yawata Ironworks began operation with a designed capacity of 210,000 tons of steel and planned to rise to 300,000 tons in 1906 and 380,000 tons in 1911.[54] By 1911 the total capital cost had risen to over ¥50 million, and another ¥27 million in state-backed loans had been invested to develop the Hanyenping iron mines in central China.[55] In its first ten years, Yawata accumulated operating losses of ¥9.7 million, but with experience and tariff protection after 1911, the enterprise began to operate at a profit, producing rolled steel competitive with imports. Rolled steel output was, however, far below expectations at 5,000 tons in 1901, 64,000 tons in 1906, and 181,000 tons in 1911. By 1913 it had risen to 216,000 tons, but Japan's total production still met only one-third of its domestic requirements.

The private iron and steel industry produced less than 10 percent of Japan's steel output before the Russo-Japanese War. During that war, however, it made some headway and by 1913 was responsible for about a quarter of the domestic production of pig iron and rolled steel. Whereas a private enterprise steel mill had been unthinkable twenty years earlier, several now emerged without overt subsidies. What made this possible was the assurance of government orders at profitable prices. With the huge increase in money available for defense – the Russo-Japanese War cost ten times as much as did the Sino-Japanese War – costs seemed unimportant to the government compared with the urgent needs of national security.

In an instructive example of state–private cooperation in "national interest" heavy industry, Hokkaidō tankō (Hokkaido Coal Mining)

54 Yawata seitetsusho, ed., *Yawata seitetsusho 50-nen shi* (Tokyo: Yawata seitetsusho, 1950), pp. 62–3.

55 These loans to the Hanyeping (Han-yeh-p'ing) company were the subject of some of the Twenty-one Demands served on the Chinese government in January 1915.

joined with Vickers Armstrong in forming Nippon seikōsho (Nippon Steelworks) to supply ordnance and other equipment to the navy. After the nationalization of their railway lines in 1906, the directors of Hokkaidō tankō found themselves with funds to invest, whereas the navy, frustrated by its experience of intransigent Diets, was looking for ways to satisfy its steel requirements and enhance Japan's self-sufficiency in armaments, by promoting private investment. Through the good offices of successive navy ministers, Admirals Yamamoto Gonnohyōe and Saitō Minoru, the Hokkaidō men came to an arrangement with the commander of the Kure naval base, which in turn interested Vickers Armstrong in the project. By 1913 Nippon seikōsho, with fixed capital of ¥22 million and rated annual capacity of 157,500 tons of steel, was second only to Yawata.

Several mills to make finished steel from ingot and scrap were founded during this period. Some, like Nippon Steel Pipe, Fuji Steel, and Kobe Steel, eventually became major steel manufacturers. All received technical assistance and profitable orders from government agencies. Kobe Steel (originally Kobayashi Steel) owed its success to Kosugi Tatsuzō, a senior engineer of the Kure Naval Arsenal who moved to the firm in 1904, bringing eight of his most promising colleagues with him. The whole group received a year's training at the Vickers steelworks in the United Kingdom before setting up an open-hearth furnace and ancillary plant at Kobe. With assurances of orders from the Kure Naval Arsenal at prices five to six times the prime cost, the project could scarcely fail. Under the navy's policy of raising the Japanese content of its hardware, this and other plants became virtual auxiliaries of the naval arsenals. Sooner or later most came under the aegis of one or another of the major zaibatsu. Coordination of private and public interests was then handled through channels of institutional communication between zaibatsu and government rather than through personal connections.

In 1913, Japan produced 255,000 tons of rolled steel, of which Yawata produced 85 percent, but relied on imports for over half of its pig iron and two-thirds of its rolled steel. Japanese steel production was only one-hundredth that of the United States, and U.S. Steel's Gary, Indiana, mill alone produced five times as much as did the whole Japanese industry. On the eve of World War I, Japan's steel output may have been, in G. C. Allen's words, "of very slight importance,"[56]

56 G. C. Allen, *A Short Economic History of Modern Japan* (London: Allen & Unwin, 1946), p. 74.

but it was more than any country in the world had produced in 1870, a measure of the industry's novelty and of the relative shortness of Japan's lag behind the Western powers.

Shipbuilding, like the steel industry, was closely linked to national security and consisted of state and private enterprises. Of the dockyards inherited by the Meiji government, Yokosuka became a naval dockyard, and Nagasaki passed to Mitsubishi, Hyōgo to Kawasaki, and Ishikawajima, after being closed by the government, to a company promoted by Shibusawa. By World War I, dozens of shipyards had sprung up, but only the naval dockyards at Yokosuka, Kure, and Sasebo and the private yards of Mitsubishi at Nagasaki and Kawasaki at Kobe, were capable of building large modern steamers. Until the Sino-Japanese War, Japanese shipyards were mainly used for repairs and refits. Equipment and technical competence were limited, and materials had to be imported at high prices. The then small domestic fleet of steamships consisted almost entirely of foreign-built vessels of which seventy-three (a total tonnage of 100,000 tons) were imported between 1880 and 1893. Under the major naval expansion plan initiated in 1883, only one naval vessel, the *Hashidate,* was built at the Yokosuka Naval Dockyard. All the rest were ordered from the United Kingdom or France. The Sino-Japanese War clearly showed the inadequacy of Japan's shipbuilding capacity. During the war years, all of the merchant marine's suitable vessels were pressed into service; more than eighty ships (a total tonnage of 160,000 tons) were bought from abroad; and many more were chartered. Most of these ships were steel-hulled steamers of two thousand or more tons. The only civilian shipyard capable of handling even repairs to vessels of this size was Mitsubishi's Nagasaki dockyard.

With a coming confrontation with Russia in mind, the government made strenuous efforts after 1895 to expand the naval fleet, but again all of the larger ships had to be ordered from foreign yards, and only seven torpedo boats were built or assembled in Japan. The Shipbuilding Encouragement Act of 1896 was designed to promote the domestic construction of merchant ships. Under its provisions, steel steamships built by wholly Japanese-owned private shipyards attracted a subsidy of ¥12 per ton for ships of between seven hundred and one thousand tons and ¥20 per ton for those of one thousand or more tons. A further subsidy of ¥5 per horsepower would be paid if the engines were made in Japan. These subsidies, however, scarcely made up for the higher cost of steel plate and other materials. Japanese shipping companies still found foreign shipyards cheaper, far better technically, and more prompt in delivery than were the domestic yards. The Mitsubishi dockyard build the six-thousand-ton *Hitachi Maru* in 1898 with much help from the navy's experts, but it was not until the Navigation Subsidy Act was amended in 1899 to reduce subsidies payable for foreign-built ships to half that for domestically built vessels that Japanese shipyards received enough orders to warrant upgrading their facilities. Between 1899 and 1904, Mitsubishi and Kawasaki built twenty-six steamers of one thousand or more tons, including six of over five thousand tons.

Despite this modest progress, the Russo-Japanese War again found the industry wanting.[57] Once more, nearly the whole Japanese merchant marine was requisitioned for the duration, and imports of merchant ships soared to 314,000 tons. Deliveries of warships from foreign sources were cut off by suppliers anxious to maintain neutrality. Light though Japanese losses were compared with those of the Russian fleet, they included two battleships, two cruisers, and fourteen smaller ships. Under wartime pressure and regardless of cost, the naval dockyards succeeded in building a battleship, an armored cruiser, and two second-class cruisers, and the Mitsubishi and Kawasaki yards, which in 1904 could build nothing bigger than a torpedo boat, built destroyers. Even the naval dockyards, then much better equipped than the private yards were, used very labor-intensive methods. The battle cruisers *Tsukuba* and *Ikoma*, for example, were built by workers operating like waves of shock troops without the aid of large gantry cranes or pneumatic riveters.

As a result of this wartime progress, however, Japan became practically self-sufficient in naval construction. Of the seventy-eight naval vessels totaling 360,000 tons commissioned between 1905 and 1915, all but seven were built in Japan, a quarter of them by private industry. Merchant shipbuilding also advanced. With tariff increases on imported ships from 5 percent *ad valorem* in 1897 to 10 percent in 1906 and 15 percent in 1910, the subsidies, though still of great benefit to the major shipping companies, became a relatively less important source of encouragement to shipbuilders.[58]

Because of both the official recognition of shipbuilding as essential to national defense and naval influence and technical assistance, by

57 The Russo-Japanese War cost ten times as much as did the Sino-Japanese War and stretched the Japanese economy to the limit. Casualties, too, were heavy.

58 Mitsubishi zōsen KK, sōmuka, ed., "Honpō kindai zōsen hogoseisaku no enkaku," reprinted in *Nihon sangyō shiryō taikei*, vol. 5, pp. 729–822.

1914 the industry had, with the aid of subsidies and tariff protection, reached a position from which it could profit from the exceptional opportunities presented by World War I.

The development of the engineering industries generally belongs to the post–World War I period, but their origins date back to the 1880s when military arsenals and the Miyata Small Arms Company began to manufacture rifles in some quantity. We have already described the early progress in the manufacture of marine engines. This was followed by the manufacture of rolling stock, and by the 1890s Japan was producing a growing proportion of the goods wagons and passenger carriages required by its expanding railway network. The first Japanese-built locomotive was assembled in the government's Kobe railway workshops in 1893 under the direction of an English engineer,[59] but this was hardly more than an advanced exercise in technical training. Even in 1912, of Japan's stock of 2,636 locomotives, only 162 were of Japanese manufacture.[60] In textile machinery, the Toyoda Automatic Loom Company produced powered looms in quantity by 1913 in what may have been Japan's first mass-production engineering plant, but almost all spinning machinery was imported before World War I.

The manufacture of electrical equipment began with telegraphic and telephonic equipment. Although government workshops played an important role in introducing the technology, most of the development was by private enterprise. One of the leading firms, Oki Kibatarō's Meikōsha (now Oki denki kōgyō), used profits accumulated during the Sino-Japanese and Russo-Japanese wars to become a competitive producer of telephones, whose price was brought down from ¥55 to ¥10 or even less within fifteen years.[61] The production of electric generators and motors was in the experimental stage and involved a good deal of tinkering until Tokyo Electric in 1905, and then the Shibaura (now Toshiba) works, obtained access to General Electric capital, patents, and technology in return for a share in their companies. Other firms like Nippon Electric (NEC), Mitsubishi Electric, and Fuji Electric later made similar arrangements with major foreign electrical concerns, but for a decade or more after the Russo-Japanese War, General Electric technology dominated the industry. Other

59 Richard Francis Trevithick, brother of Francis Henry, also a locomotive expert with the Japanese railways and a grandson of Richard (1771–1833), whose inventions entitle him to be considered the inventor of the locomotive steam engine.

60 Arisawa Hiromi, ed., *Gendai Nihon sangyō kōza*, vol. 5: *Kikai kōgyō (1)* (Tokyo: Iwanami shoten, 1960), p. 50.

61 Oki Kibatarō denki hensan gakari, ed., *Oki Kibatarō* (Tokyo: Oki Kibatarō denki hensan gakari, 1932), p. 105.

branches of engineering were of little significance before World War I. The value of Japan's machine tool output, a good indicator of the state of its engineering industries, was a mere ¥30,000 in 1914. To put the matter in better perspective, even in 1930 "the entire complex of mining, metallurgy and machinery industries furnished no more than 8% of Japan's national product."[62]

The development of heavy industry and engineering clearly depended on state support, most of which was linked to considerations of national security and defense. The effect of war and preparations for war on Japan's modern economic development has been the subject of some debate. Until World War I the growth of the modern sector was strongly correlated with military expenditure. When military expenditure rose sharply during the Sino-Japanese and Russo-Japanese wars, the modern sector grew rapidly. After each of those wars both the share of military expenditure in gross national expenditure and the share of the modern sector's output in GNP fell somewhat but remained above prewar levels. According to Harry Oshima, "the most important lesson of Meiji public finance is that rapid economic growth and rapid militarization of the economy are fundamentally incompatible."[63] William Lockwood stressed "the continual drain of armaments on Japan's limited capital resources, on her advanced machine skills; and especially on the government budget itself" and suggested that "a small fraction of these sums spent on reducing disease and accident rates in urban industry, for example, would have increased productive efficiency as well as human well-being."[64] In the 1930s and 1940s the heavy and engineering industries were indeed so closely geared to defense that their contribution to the civilian population's living standards was far from obvious. On the other hand, as Kozo Yamamura pointed out, military preparedness was "the principal motivation behind creating and expanding the arsenals and other publicly-financed shipyards and modern factories which acted as highly effective centers for the absorption and dissemination of Western technologies and skills" and provided "at critical junctures" the demand for private firms.[65] Whether in the long run the game was worth the candle is a matter for individual judgment rather than eco-

62 Lockwood, *The Economic Development of Japan*, p. 575.

63 Harry T. Oshima, "Meiji Fiscal Policy and Agricultural Progress" in *The State and Economic Enterprise in Japan: Essays in the Political Economy of Growth*, ed. William W. Lockwood (Princeton, N.J.: Princeton University Press, 1965), p. 381.

64 Lockwood, *The Economic Development of Japan*, p. 577.

65 Kozo Yamamura, "Success Illgotten? The Role of Meiji Militarism in Japan's Technical Progress," *Journal of Economic History* 37 (March 1977): 113.

nomic calculation. Attempts to assess what the effect on national income would have been if military had been replaced by civil investment must fail, if only because military investment was not simply a component of national income but an inseparable part of a whole economic, political, social, and ideological system.

WORLD WAR I

World War I rescued Japan from fiscal and balance-of-payments problems that might otherwise have retarded its economic growth. Victory over Russia cost, along with appallingly high casualties, a direct expenditure of ¥2 billion. The strains of the war affected Japan's economy for nearly a decade. A large part of the war's cost was financed by overseas borrowing that raised foreign indebtedness from less than ¥100 million in 1903 to ¥1.4 billion in 1907. Between 1909 and 1913, deficits in current international payments continued to run at around ¥80 million to ¥90 million annually, precluding an expansionary fiscal policy and prolonging the postwar recession. During this same five years the tax burden per capita, although almost double the pre-1904 level in real terms, did little more than cover military expenditures and service the national debt. But despite these difficulties, output grew at a respectable 3 percent a year, well above the prewar average.

The outbreak of war in 1914 did not bring immediate benefits to Japan. Indeed, the dislocation of the world economy initially added to its difficulties. After 1915, however, the war transformed the economic climate. Although formally engaged on the Allied side, Japan took virtually no part in the hostilities, and so its economy benefited not only from Allied orders for munitions and manufactures but also from the removal of Western competition in both domestic and Asian mainland markets. Between 1914 and 1918, Japan's real gross national product rose by 40 percent, an average annual rate of nearly 9 percent. This growth was accompanied by a massive turnaround in international trade and payments and a spurt in private industrial investment. Because such a high proportion of output went into exports and investment and because productivity in consumption goods industries lagged, gains in personal consumption and average standards of living were much more modest. The distribution of income, too, became more unequal as some investors and speculators made large profits from the boom, whereas those on relatively fixed incomes found their living standards reduced by inflation. As private enterprise in modern industry and commerce, hitherto heavily dependent on government support, suddenly became highly profitable, the modern business establishment (*zaikai*) acquired a new degree of confidence and political influence. The foundation of the Industrial Club of Japan in 1917 by leaders of modern industry headed by representatives of the zaibatsu was symbolic of their new status. When economic conditions returned to normal early in 1920, much of the optimism and confidence of the war years was shown to have been misplaced, but modern industry had made real progress, and the foundations had been laid for self-sustaining industrial growth. This growth continued even in the difficult conditions of the 1920s, whereas change in traditional industries producing consumer goods for the home market was much slower, and the gap between these and modern large-scale industry began to widen.

Foreign trade

In 1913 Japan paid around ¥70 million a year in interest abroad, and partly for this reason, current international payments were running a deficit of about ¥90 million a year. Had this situation continued under the gold standard system in operation at the time, it would have necessitated a fairly severe retrenchment that would have further hampered recovery and led to a period of slower growth. But the export opportunities provided by the war removed this balance-of-payments restraint and permitted an investment boom of unprecedented proportions.

The initial disruption of trade at the outbreak of war caused both exports and imports to fall, but in 1915 receipts from exports and shipping services rose sharply, though imports continued to decline, producing a record current surplus of over ¥200 million. This surplus reached a peak of ¥1 billion in 1917 and totaled ¥3 billion between 1915–1919. Over the same period Japan was a net exporter of long-term capital to the extent of ¥1.5 billion, changing from a debtor nation to a substantial international creditor. Although merchandise exports increased by only a third in volume, world prices rose so high that their value rose over threefold and the value of manufactured exports, mainly textiles, rose sixfold. Asian markets absorbed about half of these exports. There was little change in the geographical distribution of exports until 1919 when European demand collapsed and was replaced by increased sales to the United States. The war years also brought a huge increase in foreign exchange earnings from shipping services. With the Allied merchant fleets suffering heavy losses, freight and charter rates soared to ten or twenty times their 1914 level. Japan's merchant marine expanded from 1.58 million gross registered tons in 1914 to 2.8 million in 1919. Net annual foreign earnings from shipping rose from ¥41 million to a peak of over ¥450 million in 1918.

The financial system could not cope with so large and so sudden a change in international payments at a time when international gold movements were suspended because of the war. The inflationary effects of foreign payments surpluses therefore went unchecked, and the subsequent failure to bring down prices far enough in the postwar years was the main reason that the foreign balances accumulated during the war were run down. Nevertheless, the gains of the war boom were not entirely wasted. Most of the postwar increase in imports went for raw materials, semifinished goods (mainly iron and steel), and machinery to support an expanded manufacturing sector.

Although the output of all sectors increased between 1914 and 1919, the greatest percentage gains (valued at constant 1934–6 prices) were in manufacturing (72 percent) and transport, communications, and power (60 percent). Increases in mining (26 percent) and agriculture (11.5 percent) were much lower.[66] The farm-labor force fell by 1.8 million, but there was a rise of 2.6 million in nonagricultural employment. The mining and manufacturing share of net domestic product in current prices rose from 20 percent to 30 percent but fell back after the war and did not again regain the wartime peak until 1935.[67] Thus, in both output and employment, the share of primary industry fell, but that of the secondary and tertiary industries, especially the modern manufacturing sector, rose during the war.

Agriculture

Improved agricultural productivity, due partly to the diffusion of technical advances introduced in the decade before 1914, was stimulated by increased domestic and export demand for agricultural products that resulted in more than a trebling of prices. Much of the wartime increase in agricultural output was, in fact, due to a 60 percent increase in the output of cocoons to supply the strong United States demand for raw silk. But the steep rise in food prices ultimately proved disadvantageous to farmers when widespread discontent among urban consumers, cul-

66 Ohkawa and Shinohara, eds., *Patterns of Japanese Economic Development*, p. 289 (agriculture), p. 305 (manufactures), and p. 313 (commerce and services). The figure for mining is from LTES, vol. 10, p. 265. 67 LTES, vol. 1, p. 240.

minating in the rice riots of 1918, and political pressure from manufacturers to keep down wage costs forced the government to abandon agricultural protection in favor of increasing imports of cheaper rice and other staple foods from the colonial territories of Korea and Taiwan.

Heavy industry and machinery

It was in industry that change was fastest and most far-reaching. Between 1914 and 1919, manufacturing output increased by 72 percent, with only 42 percent more labor, representing a substantial productivity gain per worker. This was achieved by a large increase in capital investment. Paid-up capital of manufacturing companies increased five- or sixfold, but business was so good that for the leading companies, the rate of profit on paid-up capital rose from around 15 percent to over 50 percent. The highest output growth was in machinery (29 percent per annum), with slower growth in textiles (11 percent), iron and steel (9 percent), and food products (5 percent) and other consumer goods. In the machinery industry, including shipbuilding, vehicles, and machine tools, expansion and technical progress was mainly the work of private industry, whose capacity increased greatly relative to that of government establishments.

Shipbuilding, which had made considerable advances in scale and technology during the Russo-Japanese War, was stimulated by a rise in the price of new ships from ¥120 to a 1918 peak of ¥800 per gross registered ton. The industry increased its work force from 26,000 to 95,000 and its output from eight vessels totaling 40,500 gross registered tons in 1915 to 174 totaling 600,000 gross registered tons in 1918. With prices soaring, the value of output increased from ¥7 million to ¥405 million, but the cost of materials rose sharply too. By 1918, steel plate was fifteen times its 1914 price and in such short supply in April of that year that the major shipbuilders contracted to receive 128,000 tons of American steel in return for an equal deadweight tonnage of ships, and the following month they contracted for a further 123,000 tons of steel in exchange for twice that weight of ships.[68] Demand was so buoyant and profits so large – ships under construction were frequently sold and resold at a huge profit – that even the small, ill-equipped yards that had proliferated during the war yielded good returns. The leading builders greatly raised productivity

68 The United States' embargo on steel exports was one reason for the shortage. These swap deals were exempted from the embargo.

by standardization and improved programming, almost halving construction times. Mitsubishi installed a model-testing tank and other research facilities, and several yards upgraded their technical standards to meet the navy orders' requirements. When demand collapsed at the end of the war, most of the small yards failed, but Mitsubishi, Kawasaki, and three or four other advanced yards were kept going by orders from the navy, which was anxious for these builders to maintain their technical staff and facilities as a national defense resource.[69]

In the manufacture of rolling stock as well, the role of private enterprise increased under the patronage of the Ministry of Railways, which adopted a policy of placing orders with private firms and providing technical assistance where necessary. Confidence in these firms' technical standards was apparently limited, as the ministry's own workshops produced and supplied wheels, axles, bogies, and other parts crucial to safe operation and entrusted little more than coach building and assembly to the private contractors. Locomotives and tenders, however, were fully built by larger specialist firms with technical standards comparable to those of the ministry's own workshops.[70]

During the war, the leading shipbuilding firms, like Mitsubishi and Kawasaki, also expanded their general engineering capacity, building large steam and water turbines for the rapidly growing electric power industry. The output of steam engines, turbines, pumps, and internal combustion engines rose sharply as the major makers expanded their work forces tenfold. By the end of the war Japan was close to self-sufficient in these products. Stimulated by rapid electrification and with technical and managerial assistance from the major firms' American partners, the manufacture of electric motors and equipment was the most advanced branch of the engineering industry, boasting modern machinery, capital-intensive methods, and high standards of quality. As in other branches of engineering, few of the small firms that mushroomed during the war survived the return of overseas competition, but the larger firms that had greatly improved their capacity during the war remained competitive in medium-to-small generators, motors, transformers, and switching gear and even made some headway in the Chinese market.

With so many manufacturers eager to expand during the war, the demand for machine tools was extremely strong, and with imports

69 "Honpō kindai zōsen hogosaku no enkaku," pp. 778–821.
70 "Kikai kōgyō," in *Nihon sangyō shiryō taikei*, vol. 7, p. 33.

reduced to a trickle, domestic producers did their best to fill the gap. Output rose from a very low prewar level to a 1918 peak of nearly seventeen thousand tons, mainly general-purpose lathes but including as well a few turret lathes; planing, milling, and boring machines; radial drills; and gear hobbers. Although the Ikegai Ironworks, one of the oldest and most advanced tool makers, produced good, well-designed precision machinery, much of the domestically produced equipment was of inferior quality. This in turn affected the quality of the goods the equipment was used to produce. Because products of better quality could not be obtained, even indifferent machinery found a ready market, but when imports resumed (with the United States replacing the United Kingdom as the main supplier), the machinery could not be sold. Only the best makers, like Ikegai, were able to survive, owing to orders from the army and navy, which regarded a domestic machine tool industry like shipbuilding as essential to defense purposes.

The most severe wartime shortages were in iron and steel. Private steel-making capacity was still very small in 1914. Even with the expansion of the state steelworks at Yawata after the Russo-Japanese War, Japan produced only one-third of its rolled steel requirements. The price of pig iron skyrocketed from the 1913 average of ¥49 per ton to a maximum of ¥541, steel rod from ¥75 to ¥559, and steel plate from ¥85 to as much as ¥1,285.[71] In January 1916 the government obtained the Diet's approval to double Yawata's output by 1922, at a cost of ¥35 million, but escalating costs and difficulties in obtaining equipment abroad delayed the plan's implementation. By 1919 the plant's output had risen by only about 20 percent. In the wartime sellers' market, however, its operations were highly profitable. In contrast with losses of over ¥11 million accumulated during its first decade of operation, Yawata's wartime profits totaled ¥151 million, more than enough to cover the accumulated losses and the whole capital investment. Leaders of private enterprise, who had long believed that too much of the taxpayers' money had been invested in the state's steel industry, now resented the profits it was making. With the backing of the newly formed Industrial Club of Japan, private iron and steel makers obtained a substantial quid pro quo for dropping their opposition to the state-operated Yawata works, in the form of the Iron and Steel Promotion Act of 1917. Under its provisions, companies with an annual capacity of 35,000 or more tons were eligible to

71 "Honpō kindai zōsen hogoseisaku no enkaku," pp. 809–10.

acquire land on very favorable terms and to import plants and materials free of duty, and individual plants with a capacity of 5,250 or more tons were exempted from business and income taxes. With this encouragement, several small steel mills were set up, many using pig iron from Manchuria and Korea, but the greatest gains were made by large producers such as Nippon Steel's integrated mill in Hokkaido, Mitsubishi's mill in Korea and the Ōkura group and the South Manchurian Railway Company using Manchuria's rich mineral deposits. By 1919, the private enterprise output of pig iron had risen from 80,000 tons to over 500,000 tons, and the output of rolled steel from 52,000 tons to 277,000 tons. This was twice as much pig iron and almost as much steel as Yawata produced at the time, but in the postwar recession, private output fell, whereas that of Yawata continued to rise.[72] Although Japan still produced only half of its rolled steel requirements, with new capacity coming on stream, this proportion was rising, and imports came increasingly from Manchurian and other mainland sources under Japanese control.

Textiles

The demand for textiles, though not as strong as for the products of heavy industry and engineering, was buoyant during the war. Cotton spinners were able to raise their dividends from an average of 13 percent between 1910 and 1913 to an average of 46 percent between 1918 and 1920 on a paid-up capital that had trebled in the interval. Financial expansion was not matched by the expansion of productive capacity. Between 1914 and 1919 the number of spindles in operation rose by about one-third, but output increased by only one-sixth, mainly because high-quality imported equipment and parts were not available. The output per worker, however, rose significantly, as a fourfold wage rise stimulated spinning companies to use their workers more economically.[73] With output barely able to supply strong domestic demand, Japanese spinners were unable to exploit opportunities in the Chinese market and instead invested some of their profits to acquire cotton-spinning capacity in China itself. On the other hand, the spinning companies increased their weaving capacity by 75 percent and their output of cotton cloth by 50 percent. Exports of cotton cloth also rose greatly in value, though much less in quantity.

72 "Honpō seitekkōgyō gaikyō," in *Nihon sangyō shiryō taikei*, vol. 7, pp. 620–1.
73 *Meiji Taishō kokusei sōran*, pp. 610–11.

The silk industry, after suffering from the disruption of its overseas markets at the outbreak of war, enjoyed an unprecedented boom as domestic and United States markets expanded. From a low of ¥700 per one hundred catties in November 1914, the price of raw silk rose to a peak of almost ¥4,000 in January 1920 before plummeting to ¥1,195 in August. Production and exports rose by 60 percent in volume and by far more in value, bringing comparative prosperity to hundreds of thousands of sericulturalists and cottage silk weavers.

From "traditional industry" to "small-scale industry"

In contrast with the industries producing for military or investment demand, those producing for domestic or foreign consumption remained mainly labor-intensive, small in scale, and slower to accept technological innovation. The main change was the application of electric power to traditional production processes. By 1919, 26 percent of plants with five to fourteen workers used electric power, compared with only 7.8 percent in 1914.[74] In organization and style of production, these industries changed little, but their role in the economy, especially their relationship with large modern businesses, was undergoing a transformation. Whereas the traditional industry of the Meiji era had been the mainstay of the economy and its growth had been the necessary complement to the growth of the modern sector, in the post–World War I recession, small-scale industry became very much the poor relation or even the servant of modern business. By that time, small-scale industry included not only traditional consumption-goods industries but also small engineering workshops that had emerged to meet wartime shortages, often as suppliers to larger firms. Those that survived the postwar slump received cast-off equipment and even workers from the larger firms and acted as a reserve of capacity to meet temporary or peak demand.

Although small-scale industries continued to employ the majority of industrial workers, their labor productivity fell far below that of the capital-intensive modern enterprises that responded to the postwar recession by drastically reducing their work forces and more efficiently using those they retained. It was at this time that gaps began to open in wage and profit rates, as between small businesses and leading modern firms. The postwar recession also saw the emergence of differences in the structure of markets for products and factors of produc-

74 LTES, vol. 12, pp. 228–45.

tion that later characterized what has been called the "dual" or "differential" economic structure.[75]

THE ROLE OF THE STATE

No explanation of industrialization and technological change in Japan between 1885 and 1920 would be complete or satisfying without considering the role of the state. Its part in creating the infrastructure of administration, transport and communications, financial institutions, and education was of major importance in providing the environment in which industry and commerce could expand and develop. All sectors of the economy benefited, but throughout the Meiji era, traditional sectors were the greatest beneficiaries, if only because of their aggregate size. We have already discussed the part played by official subsidies, protection (after tariff autonomy was gained), technical assistance, and government demand in the establishment of modern industries like shipping, shipbuilding, and engineering. Let us turn to a consideration of the general impact of the state on the economy.

Fiscal and monetary policy

The Meiji government inherited a taxing power that had put at the disposal of central and local authorities about 20 percent of the national output, a high proportion for a preindustrial country.[76] In the twenty years after the Restoration, the fiscal system was renovated, and the tax base altered and enlarged. Between 1880 and 1920, central and local government income averaged 14 percent of Japan's gross national product, giving the government the power to allocate substantial resources without increasing customary levels of taxation.

Fiscal policy, that is, influencing the economy through the level and structure of central and local budgets, has generally been regarded as important to Japan's economic development in this period. In the 1880s, about half of the government's revenue was raised from agriculture. Although this proportion fell steadily as taxes on consumption, income, and property rose, taxation on the whole before World War I fell more heavily on agriculture and traditional businesses than on the modern sector. Its regressive nature tended to restrict consumption and to promote saving, with positive effects on the rate of growth.

75 Ohkawa, *Differential Structure and Agriculture*, p. 61.

76 Cf. E. Sydney Crawcour, "The Tokugawa Heritage," in *The State and Economic Enterprise in Japan*, p. 31. The figure of 25 to 27 percent given there now seems on the high side.

Military expenditures absorbed the greatest percentage of total government outlays (including capital expenditures), rising from 15 percent in the late 1880s to an average of 34 percent between 1890 and 1900 and 48 percent between 1901 and 1910, before falling back to 41 percent between 1911 and 1920. Whatever its other implications, these expenditures stimulated the growth of the modern sector. Transfer payments,[77] mainly interest on public debt, the second largest budget item, were as high as 15 percent of all government expenditures in the late 1890s and averaged 9 or 10 percent for the remainder of the period. On the whole, these transfers were from lower to higher income groups and so tended to promote income inequality and therefore saving. Over the period as a whole, about 10 percent of all expenditures was for transport and communications.[78] Direct subsidies to industry, though a relatively small budget item, could be quite crucial to particular industries like shipbuilding.

Through monetary policy, governments affected price trends and general business conditions. About half of the period between 1888 and World War I was characterized by the sort of mildly inflationary climate in which business is said to thrive. Budget deficits during the Sino-Japanese War raised the inflation rate to about 10 percent, but with the introduction of the gold standard, prices steadied. The move from silver- to gold-based yen facilitated overseas borrowing, but at the sacrifice of the stimulus to exports that had until then been provided by the steady depreciation of silver. Partly for reasons connected with the move to the gold standard, business conditions were only fair until the Russo-Japanese War, when budget deficits again raised prices, especially of manufactures, despite large foreign borrowings. The war was followed by a period of contractionary fiscal policy designed to maintain the external value of the yen and to facilitate service of the foreign debt. Prices stabilized until the rapid World War I inflation which reflected wartime shortages and the financial system's inability to cope with the surge in foreign exchange holdings. For the period as a whole, fiscal and monetary policy might best be described as moderately benign rather than as a major positive factor in eco-

77 Transfer payments are government expenditures that are not spent on goods and services supplied in the year of payment. Other examples are welfare payments and government pensions. Transfer payments are not included in the national accounts as part of the gross national product.

78 These figures are from Ohkawa and Shinohara, eds., *Patterns of Japanese Economic Development*, pp. 370–4. The figure for transport and communications is derived from Harry T. Oshima, "Meiji Fiscal Policy and Agricultural Progress," in *The State and Economic Enterprise in Japan*, pp. 370–1.

nomic growth. Considering the strains with which policy had to cope, however, this was a creditable performance.

The polity and the market

Did the Japanese government simply provide an infrastructure and a business climate favorable to economic enterprise, leaving investment and production decisions to be determined by market forces? Or were there important areas in which the government effectively preempted those decisions, overriding such considerations as relative factor prices and demand conditions? Is it possible, in other words, that state intervention brought about more growth than would otherwise have occurred?[79]

Some economists oppose state intervention on the grounds that it cannot raise total output above the level that would be produced by the operation of competitive markets. Free competitive markets are not, however, necessarily the best strategy for long-run dynamic growth. Specifically, market forces do not maximize long-run growth when the returns from an investment depend on other developments outside the investor's control. We have already seen that in the 1890s neither an ironworks nor a steel mill in isolation was a profitable investment on market grounds, though both together were profitable. A coal mine might not be profitable without a railway to carry its product to the market, but a railway might not be economical without the development of both the coal mine and other industries along its route. Yet all of these might be highly productive investments as parts of a state-supported development program.

In the advanced industrial countries with which economists were most familiar, these facts were thought to be minor exceptions to the general proposition, and in any case the state could not be expected to see far enough into the future to identify them.[80] Such situations are, however, typical of a backward economy whose development requires introducing many new activities. In a late-developing economy, moreover, they can readily be identified by reference to advanced econo-

79 This question was raised in Chalmers Johnson, *MITI and the Japanese Miracle: The Growth of Industrial Policy, 1925–1975* (Stanford, Calif.: Stanford University Press, 1982), pp. 3–34. See also David E. Williams, "Beyond Political Economy: A Critique of Issues Raised in Chalmers Johnson's *MITI and the Japanese Miracle*," Social and Economic Research on Modern Japan, Occasional Paper no. 35 (Berlin: East Asian Institute, Free University of Berlin, 1983).

80 Those who oppose government intervention in the economy on economic or ideological grounds attribute Japan's economic success to the triumph of free enterprise rather than to effective government policy. See R. P. Sinha, "Unresolved Issues in Japan's Early Economic Development," *Scottish Journal of Political Economy* 16 (June 1969): 141–8.

mies in which a more productive industrial system is already operating. In those circumstances, a government with the will and the means to carry out or coordinate investment in new industries can play an important role. This may, in fact, be the greatest advantage of economic backwardness.[81]

Japan's leaders had the knowledge, the will, and the means to play such a role, and they had no ideological inhibitions about doing so. They had before them a working model, as it were, of an industrial economy acquired by observing Britain, France, Germany, and the United States. This is not, of course, to suggest that the Japanese government's economic measures were systematically designed according to a long-term master plan. Even though the bureaucracy had access to detailed economic information, it made mistakes, such as the early uncritical introduction of Western technology without sufficient regard for Japanese conditions. Much government intervention was piecemeal or opportunistic. After 1890, disbursements were often more influenced by electoral tactics than by development strategy, and government leaders were often at cross-purposes. Nevertheless, the extent of Japan's success seems to indicate the existence of such a wealth of possibilities for constructive intervention that many were realized, despite the less-than-optimal government strategy.

The Japanese government's will to promote economic growth is clear from the political history of the period and needs no elaboration here. Its power to do so derived from its considerable fiscal resources, amplified through control of the Bank of Japan, the Hypothec Bank, the Industrial Bank of Japan, other special banks, and the postal savings funds. By selectively guaranteeing loans and dividends, moreover, the government could influence the investment of private funds. The active role of government in economic life derived also from a tradition of state intervention in pre-Restoration times, when the primacy of the administrative power and the detailed regulation of economic life were taken for granted.[82]

In the older industrial countries of the West, classical economic doctrines postulated the universal pursuit of profit as the "invisible hand" that maximized total outputs. This theory both justified busi-

81 Cf. the title piece in Alexander Gerschenkron, *Economic Backwardness in Historical Perspective: A Book of Essays* (Cambridge, Mass.: Harvard University Press, 1962); and Ronald Dore, *British Factory – Japanese Factory: The Origins of National Diversity in Industrial Relations* (London: Allen & Unwin, 1973), pp. 404–20.

82 Tokugawa political theory assumed that the labor and ingenuity of the people was at the disposal of the administrative power. This view, though greatly modified during the Meiji era, never entirely disappeared and enjoyed a spectacular revival in the 1930s and 1940s.

ness activity and limited the economic role of the state. Although the libertarian ideas of John Stuart Mill and others were introduced to Japan soon after the Restoration, they did not take root. After the 1880s it was the German Historical school, especially Wagner, Stein, and List, that formed the mainstream of academic economic thought and set the tone of the Nihon Shakai Seisaku Gakkai, the professional association to which almost all Japanese economists belonged from the late 1890s until it disbanded in 1924.[83] The German Historical school not only provided a rationale for the state's role in economic development but was more in tune with Japanese nationalist feeling than were the English Classical economists.[84]

In Japan, the concept of the "invisible hand" was never widely accepted; profit beyond what was necessary for a decent livelihood required some other ethical basis, usually a claim of service to the state, a justification that was fully consistent with Confucian thought.[85] Even Shibusawa Eiichi, the champion of private enterprise, said that his aim was "to build modern enterprise with the abacus and the Analects of Confucius."[86] The more successful the entrepreneur was, therefore, the more dependent he would be on the government, not only for material protection and subsidies, but also for validation of his claim to be working for the good of the nation. Failure to obtain this validation could be both socially and financially disastrous, a situation that gave the government great power vis-à-vis the top ranks of modern business leadership.

Early attempts at the direct state operation of modern industries were on the whole unsuccessful and were later dismissed as experimental or for demonstration purposes, although there is little evidence to suggest that this was the original intention. Much more successful were arrangements that gave private concerns, conspicuously the zaibatsu, the responsibility for establishing elements of a modern industrial system with government backing and the assurance that comple-

83 See Sumiya Etsuji, *Nihon keizaigaku shi*, rev. ed. (Kyoto: Minerva shōbō, 1967).

84 "The Germans are fond of saying that the Physiocrats and the school of Adam Smith underrated the importance of national life; that they tended to sacrifice it on the one hand to a selfish individualism and on the other to a limp philanthropic cosmopolitanism. They urge that List did great service in stimulating a feeling of patriotism, which is more generous than that of individualism, and more sturdy and definite than that of cosmopolitanism." [Alfred Marshall, *Principles of Economics*, 8th ed. (London: Macmillan, 1949), p. 634.]

85 Note the contrast with nineteenth-century China where there was a much sharper separation between business and the state. Successful Chinese entrepreneurs could maintain a claim to be serving the state only by investing their profits in enrolling their families in the ranks of the scholar–gentry class from which they could then enter the bureaucracy.

86 Quoted in Johannes Hirschmeier, "Shibusawa Eiichi: Industrial Pioneer," in *The State and Economic Enterprise in Japan*, p. 243.

mentary elements would materialize. While operating in the context of a basically capitalist economy, these private concerns acted in part as agents of a government committed to the success of their enterprise. The relationship was reminiscent of that between Tokugawa domain administrations and merchants who ran industrial and commercial enterprises on the domains' behalf for the profit of both parties. Because the zaibatsu were ready to use their financial strength, ties with government, and managerial resources to adopt new technology in various industries, they were well placed to realize gains from externalities not available to a single firm in a single industry. The zaibatsu's advantage was cumulative and accounts in large measure for their dominance of the modern sector in the interwar period.

State intervention in traditional economic activity was quite different. Traditional handicraft and cottage industries were not, as a rule, critical to national security or prestige. Observation of European industrial economies suggested that except for corner stores, custom-made luxury trades, and other enterprises in which small scale was an advantage, the fate of traditional industries was to decline and eventually disappear. In these areas, government policy was to intervene only to alleviate the social stresses expected to accompany this inevitable decline or to prevent excessive competition from lowering product quality or reducing export prices. In the former policy category fell encouragement of agricultural and industrial cooperatives, credit unions, and trade associations; in the latter, agricultural extension work, inspection stations, and research establishments. The advocacy of cottage industry employment as a source of supplementary cash income for marginal farmers was a premodern legacy persisting well into the twentieth century.[87] Otherwise, the traditional economy was left to the operation of market competition and the effort and initiative of millions of those ordinary men and women for whom William Lockwood had such respect.[88]

The sphere of the free-market economy was quantitatively large, but it would be misleading to infer that free-market competition was therefore the paramount force in Japan's economic development or that the role of administrative action was marginal. Insofar as free-market forces tended to maximize the output of the traditional economy in a static or short-run sense, they increased the resources available for investment in economic development. The more dynamic features of that develop-

87 For details, see Dai Nihon fukugyō shōreikai, ed., *Nihon no fukugyō* (Tokyo: Dai Nihon fukugyō shōreikai, 1911). 88 Lockwood, *The Economic Development of Japan, passim.*

ment, however, were shaped by decisions emerging from consultation and cooperation between government and modern business leaders. The government's policies certainly do not merit unqualified approval. Some resulted in massive waste and unnecessary suffering for both Japanese and the victims of Japanese aggression overseas. If, nevertheless, government intervention and manipulation were an important positive factor in Japan's economic development up to 1920, it is because they did not on the whole counteract the underlying economic conditions and in fact enabled a fuller realization of the economy's development potential than would have been achieved without them.

CHAPTER 3

DEPRESSION, RECOVERY, AND WAR, 1920–1945

INTRODUCTION

The Japanese economy experienced great changes as a result of World War I. With the disappearance of European and American products from Asian and African trade, these extensive markets suddenly became wide open to Japanese products. Export volume and prices shot up, and Japan's industries reveled in an unprecedented boom. A spate of new firms appeared in rapid succession; stock prices soared; and the whole country rang with the sound of hammers at work on new-factory construction. Products like steel, machinery, and chemicals, for which Japan had been dependent on imports, began to be produced domestically. From its status as a debtor nation to the tune of ¥1.1 billion on the eve of the war in 1913, Japan had, by the end of 1920, transformed itself into a creditor nation with a surplus exceeding ¥2 billion. Despite social unrest such as the 1918 rice riots and the intensification of the labor and peasant movements that accompanied the galloping inflation produced by the war boom, the Japanese economy expanded as a result of the war.

When the war ended, however, so did the boom. Because of the renewed export competition and the resumption of imports that had long been suspended while Europe was at war, the international payments balance reverted to a deficit, and holdings of gold and foreign exchange began to diminish. This chapter will trace the path of the Japanese economy from the 1920s to the end of the Pacific War.[1] This period may be divided into three parts: the deflation and depression from the 1920s to 1931, recovery and chemical and heavy industrialization from 1932 to 1937, and the era of war and collapse through 1945.

Table 3.1 indicates the growth rates of real gross national expendi-

1 An excellent study in English is Hugh Patrick's "The Economic Muddle of the 1920s," in *Dilemmas of Growth in Prewar Japan*, ed. James W. Morley (Princeton, N.J.: Princeton University Press, 1971).

TABLE 3.1
Growth rates of real spending and income, 1900–1944

	GNE	Gross domestic fixed capital formation	Private consumption spending	Exports and income from abroad	Imports and income going abroad	Primary industries	Secondary industries	Tertiary industries	GNE deflator
1900–13	1.9	4.8	1.8	8.4	7.2	1.4	6.2	2.2	3.8
1913–19	6.2	8.4	4.7	6.5	5.1	3.3	6.2	7.4	13.6
1919–31	1.6	−0.7	2.2	5.8	5.8	−0.7	4.7	0.7	−2.8
1931–37	6.2	8.3	3.2	12.3	5.2	3.3	7.7	4.9	1.2
1937–44	−1.3	6.2	−6.9	−11.4	−8.5				18.9

Source: Calculated from Ohkawa Kazushi et al., *Kokumin shotoku: Chōki keizai tōkei,* vol. 1 (Tokyo: Tōyō keizai shinpōsha, 1974), pp. 213, 214, 217.

TABLE 3.2
International comparison of real growth rates

	1870–1913 (%)	1913–1938 (%)
United States	4.6[a]	1.1
Great Britain	2.1	0.7
Germany	2.7	1.8
Italy	1.5	1.7
Denmark	3.2	1.9
Norway	2.2	3.0
Sweden	3.0	2.4
Japan	2.4[b]	3.9

[a] From the average for the years from 1869 to 1878 and then to 1913.
[b] From 1887 to 1913.
Source: United States: U.S. Department of Commerce, *Historical Statistics of the United States* (Washington D.C.: U.S. Government Printing Office, 1975). European countries: B. R. Mitchell, *European Historical Statistics* (New York: Macmillan, 1975). Japan: Ohkawa Kazushi et al., *Kokumin shotoku: Chōki keizai tōkei*, vol. 1 (Tokyo: Tōyō keizai shinpōsha, 1974), pp. 213, 214, 217.

tures (GNE) for these periods and the growth rates of real gross output by type of industry. This table shows that during each period there were large differences in the growth rates of GNE and its components and of gross output by type of industry. The rate of price increase varied as well. The principal features of these three periods can be seen in these variations. Table 3.2 presents an international comparison of real GNE growth rates. Japan's rapid growth from the 1950s onward is well known, but its growth rate following World War I was also outstanding by international standards and may be viewed as the prelude to the rapid growth following World War II. It is also possible to regard such growth as the material basis for the policies of military expansionism that led to the Pacific War.[2] Both these contradictory perspectives contain some truth. Hence emerges an additional theme of this chapter: How was rapid growth achieved in this period, and what did Japan obtain as a result?

2 Yamamura Kōzō, "Kikai kōgyō ni okeru seiō gijutsu no dōnyu," in *Washinton taisei to Nichibei kankei*, ed. Hosoya Chihirō and Saito Makoto (Tokyo: Tōkyō daigaku shuppankai, 1978). Yamamura contends that technological progress in the machine tool industry during the 1920s provided the material foundation for the military adventures of the 1930s.

THE ERA OF RECESSIONS

Although prices in the United States and Britain soared to more than twice their prewar levels after World War I, both countries returned to the gold standard without devaluing their currencies against the price of gold. It was thought that reinstituting the gold standard at prewar parity would constitute a "return to normalcy" (in the words of President Warren G. Harding). However, this amounted to adopting a severely deflationary policy that would cut back postwar prices to prewar levels, about half of the current prices. World prices did in fact fall in the 1920s. John Maynard Keynes, author of *Monetary Reform* and *The Economic Consequences of Mr. Churchill,* publicly criticized these policies, but his warnings went unheeded. As is well known, Keynes was also critical of the harsh reparations demands imposed on Germany, but this, too, was ignored. As it turned out, international finance during the 1920s was sustained by the international capital flow, whereby Germany used the capital it received from America to make reparations to England and France, which used the same money to redeem their war debts in the United States. But after the New York stock market crisis in 1929, American capital was withdrawn from Europe, causing a financial strain in Germany that eventually provoked a crisis that brought on world depression.

These events had immediate repercussions in Japan as well. The goal of Japan's economic policy, like that of Britain and the United States, was to return to the gold standard at the prewar price of gold.[3] The Japanese government did not do so until the advent of the world depression in 1929, but during the 1920s the economy was constantly constrained by the worldwide deflation and by the government's goal of returning to the gold standard. Accordingly, the Japanese economy showed a mild deflationary trend after World War I. Moreover, the balance-of-trade deficit persisted. The gold and foreign exchange (specie) holdings that had accumulated during the war declined steadily. For these reasons, Japan's domestic financial policy also shifted toward austerity. This was a period of unprecedented testing for the Japanese economy, which had developed under the influence of inflationary trends since the Meiji period. It was particularly difficult for the new heavy and chemical industries and for capital-weak new firms that had emerged during and after the war. It was also difficult for

3 Ōkurashō zaiseishi hensanshitsu, *Shōwa zaiseishi–Dai 10-kan: kin'yū (I)* (Tokyo: Tōyō keizai shinpōsha, 1955), pp. 155–80.

agriculture, which was troubled by competition from cheap rice imported from Korea and Taiwan and highly susceptible to trends in the New York silk market.

Chronologies of the Japanese economy of the 1920s often refer to this period as one of recurring panics of greater or lesser magnitude.[4] The post–World War I boom turned into a panic with the stock market crash of 1920. The death knell of wartime prosperity had sounded. Domestic funds dried up as monetary austerity was imposed in order to suppress inflation and the mounting outlays for imports that accompanied the shift toward deficit in 1919 in the international payments account. Despite this, the business community continued to expand and speculate boldly. The result was ruin. In only a few months, stock market prices and commodity market prices for rice, raw silk, and cotton yarn collapsed to less than half their former values. There was a stream of trading company, bank, and factory bankruptcies, and economic conditions became chaotic.

The government and the Bank of Japan did their utmost to provide relief. For example, purchasing companies (*kaitorigaisha*) were organized to handle inventory backlogs of raw silk, and a policy of bold lending to depressed industries was established. Losses suffered by smaller zaibatsu like Furukawa, Suzuki, Kuhara, and Masuda, especially hard hit by failures of speculative enterprises during the financial panic, provided new opportunities for the four leading zaibatsu: Mitsui, Mitsubishi, Sumitomo, and Yasuda. Because they maintained sound management policies and did not depend on speculative profits, even during the war boom, the large zaibatsu suffered few losses in the panic. In addition, the leading spinning companies like Kanebō and Tōyōbō had built up large secret reserves during the war, and so they were able to cover the declining prices of their inventories, which were caused by the panic and losses due to customer bankruptcies, thereby maintaining their position unshaken. The dominant position of the four great prewar zaibatsu and the large spinning companies remained firm.

In April 1922, when it appeared that the financial crisis had at last been resolved, a small panic was touched off when a trader (Ishii Sadashichi) went bankrupt after losing heavily on daring rice speculations. At the end of 1922, eleven small banks in western Japan failed in rapid succession. Then, on September 1, 1923, the Tokyo–Yokohama

4 Nihon ginkō chōsakyoku, "Sekai taisen shuryogo ni okeru honpō zaikai dōyōshi," and "Kantō shinsai yori Shōwa 2-nen kin'yū kyōkōni itaru waga zaikai," in *Nihon kin'yūshi shiryō: Meiji Taishō hen*, vol. 22 (Tokyo: Okurasho insatsu kyoku, 1959–60).

region was dealt a crushing blow by a powerful earthquake and the devastating fires that spread in its wake. This crisis was weathered with the help of a government-implemented month-long moratorium on payments in the Kantō area. The Bank of Japan also averted a panic by rediscounting commercial bills that were to have been paid in the area ("earthquake bills.") The Bank of Japan's rediscounts totaled ¥430 million.[5] The devastation wrought by the great earthquake was enormous. According to estimates made at the time, in seventeen prefectures, but primarily in Tokyo, 554,000 out of 2.288 million households lost their homes; 105,000 people lost their lives; 30,000 were injured; and 250,000 lost their jobs. The gross national wealth in 1909 was estimated at ¥86 billion, and losses due to the earthquake were put at between ¥5.5 billion and ¥10 billion.[6] These blows made impossible a return to the gold standard. Exports declined sharply, albeit temporarily, and supplies for reconstruction increased imports. Consequently, the balance of payments went deeply into the red, and the exchange rate fell sharply. Early in 1924 the government raised some foreign exchange by issuing ¥600 million in foreign bonds in Britain and the United States. However, the extraordinarily high interest rate, reflecting Japan's international credit standing at the time, became the target of criticism at home. The reconstruction of the Tokyo–Yokohama area firms that had sustained losses because of the disaster was of course not simple, and the balance sheets of many deteriorated. In 1925, as the postwar business slump continued, Takada shōkai, a large trading company, failed.

A "financial crisis" occurred in March and April of 1927.[7] A large Kobe trading company, Suzuki shōten, which was hard hit by the panic of 1920, had just barely managed to stay in business by borrowing huge sums from the Bank of Taiwan, a colonial bank of issue. In March 1927 the firm found itself unable to settle its loans of ¥67 million. At the time there was a proposal before the Diet calling for the government to dispose of a total of ¥207 million in outstanding earthquake bills and to indemnify the Bank of Japan for losses amounting to ¥100 million. The Bank of Japan was to extend long-term loans to banks holding earthquake bills, and each bank in turn was to have its holders of earthquake bill liabilities redeem their obligations over a period of ten years. While this proposal was being debated, Suzuki shōten's internal condition was revealed, including its relationship with the Bank of Taiwan, and the unsound manage-

5 Tōyō keizai shinpōsha, ed., *Meiji Taishō kokusei sōran* (Tokyo: Tōyō keizai shinpōsha, 1927), pp. 759–60. 6 Nihon ginkō chōsakyoku, "Sekai taisen," p. 876. 7 Ibid., p. 866.

ment of some other banks as well. This set off a run on several banks, resulting in the suspension of operations for many. The earthquake bill proposal was ultimately voted down. In April 1927 when the Privy Council rejected a proposal for an urgent imperial order for the relief of the Bank of Taiwan, the bank temporarily closed down; Suzuki shōten went bankrupt; and the Wakatsuki cabinet collapsed. The bank run had nationwide repercussions. Banks throughout the country were closed on both April 22 and 23. In the meantime, the government announced a twenty-day nationwide payments moratorium. It then decided on a policy for reorganizing the Bank of Taiwan and providing general relief measures for the banks through the Bank of Japan. Calm was thus at last restored. Eleven percent of all bank deposits nationwide were withdrawn during this bank run, and as many as thirty-two banks suspended operations.[8] Among the latter were such presumed bastions of financial soundness as the Fifteenth Bank, a depository for the Imperial Household Ministry (Kunaishō), and the Bank of Ōmi, which had provided extensive credit to the textile industry.

Owing to continuing deflationary declines in commodity prices and in the value of real estate and other financial assets, many business firms continued to operate in the red and to depend on borrowed funds. But the banks supplying these firms with capital were unable to collect on their loans. The deterioration of economic conditions turned into a quickly spreading financial panic.[9] The smaller panics earlier in the decade had occurred for virtually the same reasons as this one, but the failures of such nationally known Japanese firms as the Bank of Taiwan, Suzuki shōten, and the Fifteenth Bank touched off a nationwide crisis. To cope with the situation, the Bank of Japan distributed large quantities of capital. The crisis was resolved, but the return to the gold standard was thereby once again postponed.

One reason that the business conditions of companies and banks deteriorated during this period was that the executives of many small regional banks often were managing other firms as well. After their banks had invested in these companies, their operations stagnated. Finally, these companies went bankrupt and, with them, their creditor banks as well. Concerned about this, the Ministry of Finance amended the Banking Law in March 1927 to prohibit bank managers from simultaneously managing other businesses and stipulated that

8 Ibid., pp. 927–9.
9 Nakamura Takafusa, *Showa kyōkō to keizai seisaku* (Tokyo: Nihon keizai shinbunsha, 1978), pp. 47–51.

any bank with capital of under ¥1 million (¥2 million or less in the large cities) should increase its capital to ¥1 million or merge with another bank within five years. For this reason, the number of banks, which had stood at 1,575 at the end of 1926, fell to 651 by the end of 1932.[10] The banks' business conditions markedly improved as a result of these measures, but at the same time local industries and small businesses also felt the financial pinch.

Because of the prolonged slump that lasted from the postwar crisis of 1920 until the financial panic of 1927, bankruptcies occurred in rapid succession, particularly in the secondary industries that had expanded during the war. Firms that managed to survive were forced to scale down their operations, and many workers lost their jobs. New hires were held down, too. On the other hand, however, the number of small- and medium-sized factories increased. Many workers who lost their jobs set up small factories in order to earn a livelihood. However, these firms were low-income, small urban commercial and service enterprises that absorbed people who could not choose their working conditions and who sought employment simply in order to survive. For this reason, the populations of the large cities continued to increase.[11] The farm villages were in a continuous recession from 1925 onward owing to the worldwide surplus of agricultural commodities and the fall in prices. Farmers were forced to increase their production of silk cocoons in order to maintain their incomes. But this resulted only in a further drop in international prices, and so the farmers were caught in a vicious circle whereby their redoubled efforts to increase production only pushed prices lower.

Again, the only firms that continued stable operations in the midst of this turmoil were the leading textile companies and companies belonging to the big zaibatsu groups such as Mitsui, Mitsubishi, Sumitomo, and Yasuda, which had abundant funds and sound management policies. Some zaibatsu banks were even hard pressed to find ways to use the large influx of deposits from the smaller and weaker banks after the financial panic.[12] The zaibatsu extended their network of influence in the economy by taking over, through stock transfers, the sounder firms owned by companies such as Suzuki shōten or by founding new firms in fields such as rayon and chemicals. Each of the zaibatsu amassed for itself tremendous power in every field of indus-

10 Ōkurashō zaiseishi hensanshitsu, *Shōwa zaiseishi*, pp. 79–117.

11 Takafusa Nakamura, *Economic Growth in Prewar Japan*, trans. Robert A. Feldman (New Haven, Conn.: Yale University Press, 1983), pp. 218, 220.

12 Ikeda Shigeake, *Zaikai kaikō* (Tokyo: Konnichi no mondaisha, 1949), pp. 116–17.

try, from finance and insurance to mining, foreign trade, warehousing, chemicals, paper, metals, and textiles. As a group they reigned supreme over the Japanese industrial world.[13] The power of the zaibatsu at this time probably attained its highest peak since the end of the Meiji period. However, with this notable exception, the outlook for the Japanese economy did not appear bright. Nevertheless, as Table 3.3 shows, the economy, mainly secondary industry, continued to grow in this troubled period. Why?

The fundamental condition for this growth likely resulted from the fact that the economy adjusted the balance of social demand and supply not by quantitative controls but by price fluctuations.[14] As in the example of the vicious circle of expanding cocoon production volume and the falling price of cocoons, it was impossible to regulate the volume of production in agriculture. The core of the manufacturing industry at this time was the production of consumer goods such as raw silk, cotton cloth, sugar, and flour. Competition among the firms in these fields was fierce. Even though temporary cartels were formed, it was difficult to limit production volume and stabilize prices, as the interests of the individual firms did not coincide. Intense competition among the three large firms in the paper industry shows that even in an oligopolistic industry, it was not possible to support prices by restricting production. There were additional examples, too, such as the impact of international dumping of products like ammonium sulphate and matches, or the heavy blow suffered by domestic coal as a result of imports from Manchuria.

Oligopolistic tendencies became conspicuous in a number of industries such as electric power in which firms continued to merge. Cartels were formed autonomously in every industry as a way of dealing with chronic slumps. Thus, during this period, monopolistic economic power rapidly strengthened and the domination of "monopoly capital" became conspicuous. But although it is clear that large firms occupied a high position in Japan's economic world, it cannot be said that they used their power to maintain price supports or price rigidity in the markets. Monopoly prices emerged after the passage of the Important Industries Control Law in 1931 as a means of dealing with the world depression. The law required outsiders to keep cartel agreements and

13 See Takahashi Kamekichi, *Nihon zaibatsu no kaibō* (Tokyo: Chūō kōronsha, 1930).

14 Satō Kazuo, "Senkanki Nihon no makuro keizai to mikuro keizai" in *Senkanki Nihon keizai no kenkyū*, ed. Nakamura Takafusa (Tokyo: Yamakawa shuppansha, 1980), pp. 3–30. Satō's clarification of the function of price fluctuations is applicable to the Japanese economy of this period.

TABLE 3.3

Employed population by industry (thousands of persons)

	1920(A)	1925(A)	1930(A)	1935(A)	1940(A)	1940(B)	Feb. 1944(B)	Dec. 1945(B)
Primary industries	14.388	14.056	14.648	14.450	14.523	14.192	14.028	18.053
Agriculture and forestry	13.855	13.540	14.084	13.871	13.974	13.363	13.155	17.520
Secondary industries	6.274	6.324	6.151	6.811	8.212	8.419	9.951	5.670
Manufacturing	5.071	5.109	4.848	5.498	6.565	6.845	8.089	4.314
Tertiary industries	5.355	6.432	7.331	8.410	7.728	9.403	7.575	6.346
Commerce	3.398	4.260	4.902	5.482	5.000	4.083	1.555	1.794
Totals	27.260	28.105	29.619	31.211	32.500	32.231	32.695	30.069

Source: Figures in columns marked A are annual averages from Umemura Mataji, "Sangyō-betsu koyo no hendō 1880–1940-nen" in Hitotsubashi University Economic Research Institute, *Keizai kenkyū*, April 1973. Figures in columns marked B are estimates from Cabinet Statistics Office, *Kokusei chōsa*, October 1 (for 1940 data); Cabinet Statistics Office, *Shōwa 19-nen jinkō chōsa* (for 1944 data); and *Rinji kokumin tōroku* (for 1945 data). Presented in Arai Kurotake, *Taiheiyō sensōki ni okeru yūgyō jinkō no suitei*, report of the Japan Statistical Association.

reinforced their powers of control. The foregoing shows that economic growth was achieved in conjunction with the expansion of industries, but at the same time, it also indicates why business profits accompanying growth did not necessarily increase as well.

The second main factor in Japan's economic growth was the supply of capital and the protectionist policies toward industry. For example, in 1920 when the silk-reeling industry formed the Imperial Silk Filature Company (Teikoku sanshi kabushiki kaisha) as a cartel to buy up and freeze surplus raw silk in order to support silk prices, the government provided assistance in the form of huge loans.[15] Many large firms borrowed low-interest funds indirectly from the Bank of Japan when facing crises. There were also instances in which the government assisted companies by leasing plants and equipment.[16] In agriculture, a rice law was passed in 1921. The government began buying and selling operations to stabilize rice prices, and it paid out subsidies under a variety of guises.[17] The tariff revision of 1926 substantially raised duties on steel machinery and gave liberal protection to the heavy and chemical industries.[18]

The third main factor was an increase in the government's public investment. Under the slogan of a "positive policy," the Seiyūkai party, in power from 1918 to 1922, vigorously spent public funds on the construction and expansion of railroads, harbors, highways and bridges, riparian improvements, new and expanded educational facilities, and subsidies for the improvement and reclamation of arable land.[19] These policies were an expression of the personal views of Prime Minister Hara Takashi and Finance Minister Takahashi Korekiyo regarding the promotion of regional industries. At the same time they were a means of expanding party power at the regional level. The party's main rival, the Kenseikai (renamed the Minseitō in 1928), stressed fiscal balance and strove to reduce public investment, but when the party came to power in the mid-1920s, public investment spending remained at prior levels owing to the need for post-1923 earthquake reconstruction. Large provincial cities also actively invested in order to modernize. As a result of the impact of public investment, a large drop in the growth rate was avoided.

The fourth factor behind growth was the development of the elec-

15 Nihon ginkō chōsakyoku, "Sekai taisen," pp. 585–8, 598. 16 Ibid., pp. 591–620.

17 Ōuchi Tsutomu, *Nihon nōgyō no zaiseigaku* (Tokyo: Tōkyō daigaku shuppankai, 1950), pp. 116–59.

18 Discussed in detail in Miwa Ryoichi, "1926–nen kanzei kaisei no rekishiteki ichi," in *Nihon shihonshugi: Tenkai to ronri*, ed. Sakasai Takahito et al. (Tokyo: Tōkyō daigaku shuppankai, 1978). 19 Nakamura, *Economic Growth in Prewar Japan*, pp. 157–73.

tric power industry and the effects of its spread.[20] Investment in electric power generation in the mountainous areas and its transmission to regions around Tokyo and Osaka, where demand was great, flourished during this period. Electrochemical industries using this electric power (ammonium sulfate, electric hearth furnace industries, and the like) sprang up, and small factories using electric power expanded. The production of electric machinery, electric cables, light bulbs, and radios naturally increased as well. The development of streetcar networks in the suburbs of the major cities, the opening up of new residential areas, and the attendant stimulus to residential construction also encouraged growth.

In addition, those industries built up during World War I, such as machinery, steel, and chemicals, acquired foreign technology during this decade and eventually moved into full-scale production. Japan, which had once depended on imports for virtually all its machinery, was at last able to achieve self-sufficiency in this area. Second, as the heavy and chemical industries were taking root, heavy industrial belts grew up between Tokyo and Yokohama and between Osaka and Kobe, and a pool of skilled male workers formed in these areas. In order to retain the skills and know-how of these workers within their own organizations and to thwart the budding labor movement, many firms gradually adopted policies such as the lifetime employment system and the seniority pay system, later considered to be the distinguishing features of "Japanese management." The joint labor–management conference system, which was the prototype of the "company labor union," was also a product of this era.

The Japanese economy, which had continued to grow despite these difficulties, was stricken by a severe crisis when the Great Depression suddenly hit in 1929 and the Minseitō cabinet simultaneously lifted the embargo on gold exports at the old parity.[21] Since 1897 the Japanese yen had been valued at 0.75 grams of gold. The rate of exchange against the dollar during this period was ¥100 to $49⅞. In 1916, Japan and the other world powers placed an embargo on gold exports. Although the European powers and the United States lifted their gold embargoes by 1928, Japan alone kept its intact. The nation had an excess of imports over exports (see Figure 3.1); the exchange rate was considerably lower than it had been at the old parity; and gold and foreign exchange reserves steadily decreased. Even in 1929, the yen reached a minimum rate against the dollar in the range of ¥100 to $43.

20 Minami Ryoshin, *Dōryoku kakumei to gijutsu shimpō* (Tokyo: Tōyō keizai shinpōsha, 1976), provides a full-scale study of this question.

21 Nakamura Takafusa, *Shōwa kyōkō to keizai seisaku* (Tokyo: Nihon keizai shinbunsha, 1978).

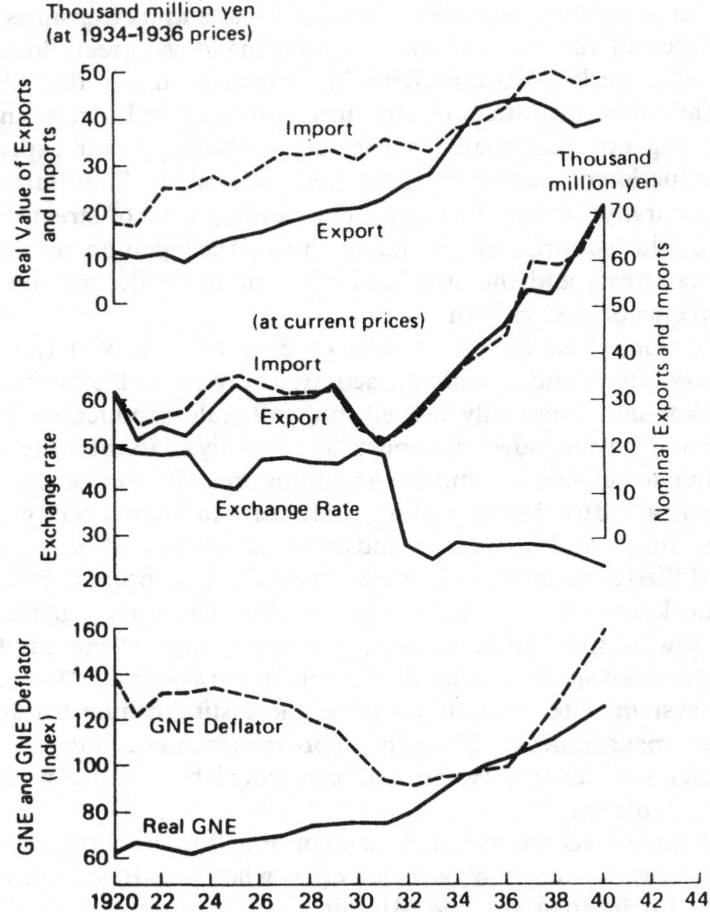

Figure 3.1. Fluctuations in foreign trade, the exchange rate, GNE, and prices. [From Yamazawa Ippei and Yamamoto Yūzō, *Chōki keizai tōkei–14: Bōeki to kokusai shūshi* (Tokyo: Tōyō keizai shinpōsha, 1974).]

Removal of the gold embargo at the old parity would mean a rise in the exchange rate, causing a further increase in the already excessive imports. In order to prevent this, domestic demand would have to fall, and deflationary policies would have to be adopted to pull prices downward. This meant forcing still further hardships on industry. Nevertheless, Inoue Junnosuke, the Finance Minister in the Hamaguchi cabinet, resolutely lifted the gold embargo at the old parity.

Theoretically it would also have been possible to lift the embargo at the so-called new parity, under which the yen's value in gold would have declined in accordance with the market rate of foreign exchange, without damaging business and economic interests.[22] Removal of the embargo at a new parity was hinted at the conclusion of the Genoa Conference of 1922. Ishibashi Tanzan, Takahashi Kamekichi, and other economic journalists, following Keynes's criticism of Winston Churchill, advocated lifting the embargo at this new parity. But there were at least two reasons that Finance Minister Inoue did not choose to do so. The first was his political judgment that a currency devaluation would adversely affect the national prestige. The second reason was his doctrine of "consolidating the business world," according to which deflationary policies should be adopted to promote exports and improve the balance of payments, noncompetitive firms should be eliminated, and the economy's international competitiveness should be strengthened. The Minseitō government took the same course that Churchill had chosen for Great Britain in 1925. Both academic and financial circles supported Inoue's policy and applauded its resoluteness.

While the impact of the American panic of October 1929 was still reverberating throughout the world, the Japanese government lifted the gold embargo at the old parity in January 1930. These two blows struck the Japanese economy simultaneously, and the country was plunged into a severe depression. As the advanced nations began dumping and domestic demand declined, the chemical and heavy industries, which were uncompetitive by international standards, sank and were forced to reduce their work forces. The mining industry, too, confronted with competition from Manchurian coal, dismissed nearly 40 percent of its workers. Although Japan's world-class textile industry was highly competitive, many firms nevertheless chalked up losses. Osaka godōbō, one of the five leading spinning companies, was forced to merge with Tōyō Spinning (Tōyōbō). Even at Kanebō, reputed to be the top firm, a fifty-four-day strike occurred when management proposed a 40 percent wage cut. Every industry formed cartels, striving to reduce output and maintain prices. The government enacted the Important Industries Control Law, which empowered it to compel firms to follow the cartel agreements, and it worked to strengthen the "self-regulation" of industry.[23] Hardest hit, however,

22 Takahashi Kamekichi, *Taishō Shōwa zaikai hendōshi*, vol. 2 (Tokyo: Tōyō keizai shinpōsha, 1954), consistently criticizes Inoue's financial policies from this position.

23 Maeda Yasuyuki, *Shōkō seisakushi Dai 11-kan: Sangyō tōsei* (Tokyo: Tsūshō sangyō kenkyūsha, 1964), pp. 47–76.

were the farm villages, already having been battered by economic slumps throughout the 1920s. The countryside reeled under the sudden drop in the prices of key commodities such as rice and silk cocoons.[24] There were many instances reported of salary payments for village primary schoolteachers being postponed for half a year due to shortfalls in local tax revenues, and of increases in the number of homes that had their electricity cut off. In metropolitan areas the number of unemployed grew, and the majority of recent university graduates were unable to find work.

To cope with this crisis, the Minseitō government did not change its policies. Instead, it continued fiscal and monetary austerity, waited for a recovery from the depression, and attempted to maintain the gold standard. Figure 3.1 shows that even between 1929 and 1931, imports and exports increased steadily in real terms, as did real GNE. In nominal terms, however, there was a marked decline in all three. This demonstrates that the depression was concentrated in a decline in prices, reflecting the special characteristic of the Japanese economy. In 1931, export prices had fallen to 40 percent and the GNE deflator to 73 percent of their respective 1929 levels. As a result, both firms and farm households went into the red, and unemployment grew. Although this pattern was typical of depressions since the nineteenth century, this one was the most severe in Japan's history. Amid the growing social unrest, Prime Minister Hamaguchi Osachi was wounded by a right-wing youth's bullet that claimed his life after he retired from office. Nevertheless, the Minseitō cabinet did not depart from its original policies.

On September 18, 1931, the Manchurian incident occurred. Despite Tokyo's policy of nonexpansion, the Kwantung Army produced a succession of military *faits accomplis* and expanded the battlefront. This put the government in a difficult position. On September 23, immediately after the incident, Great Britain went off the gold standard. Because of the financial crisis in Germany, it had become impossible to recover British funds there. As orders to reclaim funds invested in Britain came pouring in from continental investors threatened by this situation, it had finally become impossible to cope with the volume. From the perspective of the world economy as a whole, the abandonment of the gold standard by Great Britain, the home of the world's gold standard system, marked a shift toward the international managed currency system of the 1930s and afterward. In Japan, speculators, who had already recognized that maintaining the gold standard was impossi-

24 Nakamura, *Shōwa kyōkō to keizai seisaku*, pp. 107–12.

ble, began both to sell yen and to buy dollars in hopes of realizing profits on the forthcoming decline of the yen. The major speculators were actually foreign banks in Japan and wealthy individuals, but the zaibatsu banks, especially the Mitsui and Mitsubishi banks, were considered to be the principal actors at the time. The Mitsui Bank, for example, had been investing in British government securities via the United States because it was difficult to make stable investments in Japan during the depression. When those funds were frozen, the bank bought dollars to cover them, but this was erroneously reported as "dollar buying" speculation.[25]

In the face of these trends, the Minseitō cabinet continued to support the gold standard in accordance with its established policy. The matter turned into an issue that affected the political fate of the Minseitō cabinet. Finance Minister Inoue harshly criticized those purchasing dollars. Mitsui and Mitsubishi, regarded as the main speculators in dollars, thus became the targets of social opprobrium. Because the government and the Bank of Japan tightened monetary conditions by raising the discount rate in order to absorb the speculators' funds, the depression became even more severe. Dollar speculators, particularly the foreign banks, could not readily reverse their course and cancel their dollar buy-orders. As the end-of-December delivery date rapidly approached for the bulk of the foreign-exchange dollars sold, their expected hope of realizing speculative gains grew steadily dimmer. On December 11, the Minseitō cabinet finally collapsed, disagreeing over Home Minister Adachi Kenzō's insistence on a coalition with the Seiyūkai. It is said that a speculator's plot lay behind Adachi's actions, but even today the facts are not clear.

Succeeding to power, the Seiyūkai cabinet of Inukai Tsuyoshi brought Takahashi Korekiyo to the office of finance minister. On December 13, 1931, gold was reembargoed, and payments of specie were suspended. This act proclaimed the end of the gold standard in Japan forever. The relationship of trust and cooperation between Japan's financial circles and those in Britain and the United States gradually cooled afterward. This relationship, cultivated by Japanese financial circles since the Russo-Japanese War of 1905, had made it possible for Japan to raise foreign capital after the Kantō earthquake and to float local bond issues and electric power company bonds repeatedly during the 1920s. But with the Manchurian incident, the founding of Manchukuo, and the outbreak of the Shanghai incident, Thomas La-

25 Ikeda, *Zaikai kaikō*, pp. 135–53.

mont of the Morgan Bank began to take an unfriendly view of Japan.[26] This cooling of international financial relationships meant that when Japan faced a balance-of-payments crisis, it could no longer look abroad for help. However, for several years after Japan's departure from the gold standard, the Japanese economy followed a course of rapid revival and development, and so the balance-of-payments problem became a severe constraint for Japan only after war began with China in 1937.

RECOVERY

With the exception of a six-month interim out of office, Takahashi Korekiyo was at the fiscal and monetary helm as minister of finance from the time Japan left the gold standard in December 1931 until he was felled by an assassin's bullet in February 1936.[27] This was the era of the so-called Takahashi finance. While avoiding abrupt changes, Takahashi gradually relaxed the monetary conditions and promoted industry and foreign trade. In order to do so, he began lowering the discount rate from 1932 onward, reducing it from 6.6 percent to 3.7 percent by July 1933. He took a laissez-faire position on the falling exchange rate. Allowed to settle to its natural equilibrium level, the rate of exchange against the U.S. dollar had dropped from ¥100 to $49⅞ to around $26 by mid-1932 and, after falling below $20 at the end of that year, settled at about $30.80. This was a devaluation of more than 40 percent. Fiscal spending for the military and for rural village relief increased, growing in 1932 by 32 percent over 1931 levels. Central government expenditures declined from ¥1.74 billion in 1929 to ¥1.48 billion in 1931 and then increased to ¥1.95 billion in 1932 and ¥2.25 billion in 1933, after which they were fixed at a level of about ¥2.2 billion. Spending increases were financed with government bonds, but in order not to siphon private funds off the market with a huge government debt issue, a "Bank of Japan acceptance issues" formula was adopted.[28] The Bank of Japan underwrote the bonds when issued, and whenever there was a surplus of funds on the market as fiscal spending proceeded, the Bank of Japan would sell bonds to financial institutions.

26 Mitani Taichirō, "Kokusai kinyū shihon to Ajia no sensō," in *Kindai Nihon Kenkyū*, vol. 2: *Kindai Nihon to Higashi Ajia*, ed. Kindai Nihon kenkyūkai (Tokyo: Yamakawa shuppansha, 1980), pp. 126–7. This study is an outstanding piece of research on the Morgan Trading Company's Thomas W. Lamont.

27 An excellent summary of Takahashi's ideas and policies from the point of view of his contemporaries may be found in Fukai Eigo, *Kaikō 70-nen* (Tokyo: Iwanami shoten, 1941), chap. 21.

28 Ibid., pp. 268–70.

At the heart of the early phase of "Takahashi finance," which lasted until 1933, was a triad of policies consisting of low interest rates, a low exchange rate, and increased fiscal spending. Under these policies the Japanese economy began to recover rapidly. In 1929, at the time the gold embargo was lifted, Takahashi had argued publicly that there was a difference between a nation's economy and that of an individual.[29] Saving and economizing produced increases in individual assets, but for the nation as a whole, they caused a decline in demand and depressed production. Even the money spent at geisha houses became income for the geisha and cooks, and this in turn was respent, increasing demand for the nation as a whole. If gold were disembargoed, fiscal spending squeezed, and public works investment suspended, Takahashi argued, contractors and their employees would lose their jobs first; then as their expenditures declined, the effects would spread to other fields, and both incomes and employment in general would fall, thereby inviting a business slump. Takahashi intuitively understood the "theory of effective demand" subsequently advanced by Keynes, and from that point of view, he criticized lifting the gold embargo at the old parity. As finance minister, Takahashi's policies were based on the concept of promoting effective demand.

These policies were successful. The economy expanded first as a result of the revival of exports and then under the stimulation of increased fiscal spending. According to a survey of the data in Table 3.4 for the years 1932 to 1936, the largest contribution to growth was made by exports. Chiefly responsible for the export increase were textile products such as cotton and rayon fabrics, industries in which depression-induced rationalization – that is, efforts to increase productivity – meshed with the low exchange rate to produce remarkable advances. The rapid increase in Japanese exports during the depression provoked boycotts of Japanese goods in countries such as Britain, India, and the United States. Discriminatory tariffs and import quotas were imposed on Japanese goods, and there were numerous trade disputes.[30] The second-fastest-growing sector after exports was private investment, with both production facilities and residential construction growing at about the same rate. Purchases in government spending were lower than expected. From 1933 onward, Takahashi strove to hold down

29 Takahashi Korekiyo, "Kinshuku seisaku to kinkaikin," in *Zuisōroku,* ed. Takahashi Korekiyo (Tokyo: Chikura shobō, 1936).

30 For the recollections of Inoue Kiyoshi, Okada Gentarō, Tawa Yasuo, and others, see Andō Yoshio, ed., *Shōwa seijikeizaishi e no shōgen,* 3 vols. (Tokyo: Mainichi shinbunsha, 1972), vol. 1, pp. 283–306.

TABLE 3.4

Increases in real gross national expenditure (¥ billions)

	GNE	Personal consumption expenditure	Government operating expenditures	Gross government fixed-capital formation	Gross private fixed-capital formation	Exports and income from abroad	(Less) Imports and income going abroad
1931	13.323	9.754	1.685	0.902	1.058	2.029	2.105
1936	19.338	13.328	2.183	1.427	2.209	4.580	4.389
Amount of increase during this period	6.013	3.574	0.498	0.525	1.151	2.551	2.284
Rate of increase during this period (%)	45.1	36.6	29.6	58.2	108.8	125.7	108.5
			39.5 (combined)				

Source: Calculated from Ohkawa Kazushi et al., *Kokumin shotoku: Chōki keizai tōkei*, vol. 1 (Tokyo: Tōyō keizai shinpōsha, 1974), pp. 214, 218–21.

fiscal spending increases, including military spending, and to reduce the issuing of public bonds. It was once widely believed that the revival of prosperity in the early 1930s was due to increased military spending, but this is incorrect. According to Miwa Ryoichi, the rate of dependence of heavy and chemical industrial output on military demand was at its maximum in 1933 at 9.8 percent and then declined to 7 percent in 1936. For the machinery industry, this rate peaked in 1932 at 28 percent but fell to 18 percent in 1936.[31] Even though the political clout of the military grew stronger, the influence of military spending on the economy was not all that great.

Along with military spending, an important item of fiscal expenditure during this period was the outlay for public works projects for rural village relief ("expenditures to meet the national emergency" – *jikyoku kyōkyūhi*).[32] At the beginning of 1932, rural village relief became a major issue. The assassins of former Finance Minister Inoue Junnosuke, Dan Takuma of the Mitsui zaibatsu, and Prime Minister Inukai Tsuyoshi in the May 15 incident, were farm village youths from Ibaraki Prefecture. In the wake of the bloody May 15 incident, representatives from the peasantry and the provinces submitted a stream of petitions to the Diet. The political parties aligned themselves with their demands. In the summer of 1932 they settled on a plan that called for joint expenditure by the central and regional governments of a total of ¥800 million on rural public works projects creating opportunities for peasants to obtain cash incomes during the three-year period from 1932 to 1934. The plan also provided for low-interest loans of ¥800 million to farm villages over the same period and for the amortization of high-interest obligations. The level of government expenditure on rural relief compares favorably with the increases in military spending during the same period. If the supply of low-interest funds is included as well, the implementation of the plan may even be considered to have had a stimulating effect on the economy, surpassing even that of military spending. The situation of the rural villages gradually improved as the Ministry of Agriculture encouraged the industrial associations movement and the self-reliance movement (*jiriki kōsei undō*).

Policies protecting infant industries were also reinforced. In 1932, tariffs were raised on most chemical and heavy industrial products, particularly pig iron. Considering the roughly 80 percent increase in

31 Miwa Ryoichi, "Takahashi zaiseiki no keizai seisaku," in *Senji Nihon keizai*, ed. Tokyo daigaku shakai kagaku kenkyūjo (Tokyo: Tokyo daigaku shuppankai, 1979), pp. 165, 167.
32 Ibid., pp. 120–2.

TABLE 3.5
The progress of chemical and heavy industrialization

	Index of gross output for manufacturing industries	Share of gross output produced by the steel, nonferrous metals, machinery, and chemical industries (%)
1920	61.4	32.3
1930	100.0	35.0
1936	175.8	45.0
1940	218.2	59.2

Source: Calculated from Shinohara Miyohei, *Kōkōgyō* (Tokyo: Tōyō keizai shinpōsha, 1972), vol. 10, pp. 142, 143.

import prices from 1931 to 1933, caused by the declining exchange rate, it may well be that the chemical and heavy industries found it substantially easier to secure domestic markets for themselves. The shipbuilding and marine transport industries benefited when the government began to pay subsidies in 1932 for the dismantling of old ships and the construction of new ones.[33] Incentives had been granted to the automobile industry since the beginning of the depression, and after 1936 still more substantial protection was added in connection with munitions production. In this way various industries made a steady recovery, seizing on new opportunities for development.

The rapid growth of the rayon industry attracted much attention in industrial circles. By improving their technology, leading firms like Tōyō Rayon, Teijin, and Asahi Bemberg became the world's largest producers of artificial fibers, establishing themselves as a major export industry in the latter half of the 1930s. The technology of such industries as electrical machinery and machine tools, represented by Toshiba and Hitachi, also began to approach world standards and at last became capable of meeting domestic demand. With support from the military, the aircraft industry also raised its level of technology. As Table 3.5 shows, the expansion of chemical and heavy industrial output was remarkable. Its share in the value of the output of manufacturing industries rose by 10 percent from 1931 to 1936 to constitute 45 percent of the total.

Another feature of this period was the emergence of the "new zaibatsu" such as Ayukawa Yoshisuke's Nissan (Japan Industrial Company), Noguchi Shitagau's Nitchitsu (Japan Nitrogen Company), Mori Nobuteru's Shōwa hiryō (Shōwa Fertilizer, later known as Shōwa

33 Ibid., pp. 123–5.

denkō), Nakano Tomonori's Nisso (Japan Soda), Ōkochi Masatoshi's Riken, Inc., and Nakajima Chikuhei's Nakajima hikkōki (Nakajima Aircraft).[34] Nissan controlled firms in mining, automobiles, chemicals, fisheries, records, marine transport, and civil engineering through its holding company. This new zaibatsu grew rapidly by progressively buying up at low prices the stocks of firms whose operations were foundering, improving their performance, and channeling the profits into Nippon sangyō, Nissan's holding company. When Nippon sangyō's stock rose as a result, its capital increased, and these funds were used to expand still further Nissan's sphere of activities. Nippon chisso (Japan Nitrogen Corporation), using electric power obtained from its own hydroelectric generating operations to enter the chemical industry, built a large hydroelectric generating plant in north Korea in the 1920s and produced ammonium sulphate, gunpowder, and methanol with the abundant and cheap electrical power generated there. The cost of Nippon chisso's ammonium sulphate was especially low, making this company one of the strongest firms in Japan at the time. Noguchi Shitagau, the firm's founder, also achieved great success in the rayon industry. Shōwa Fertilizer, which started out as a tiny provincial company, expanded by adopting the process that the Tokyo Industrial Laboratory had developed for manufacturing ammonium sulphate and by linking this process to the development of hydroelectric stations. Nakano Tomonori attained success in the soda industry by presiding over Japan Soda and branching out into related fields. As a Tokyo Imperial University professor, Ōkochi headed up the Institute of Physical and Chemical Research. Devoting his attention to industrial applications of the technology and products developed there, he engaged in a broad range of projects, from piston rings to synthetic sake. Nakajima, a navy officer promoting a domestic airplane industry, turned his hand to producing military aircraft. Toyota had produced automobiles since the 1920s, building on the technology it had developed to manufacture automatic looms.

These new zaibatsu grew by taking advantage of technology that had been accumulating since the 1920s, the economic development that followed the reimposition of the gold embargo, and the stagnation of monetary conditions. The managers of these new zaibatsu had several things in common: They were technical and military men, not management specialists; they developed their firms on the basis of new

34 See Miyake Seiki, *Shinkōkontserun tokuhon* (Tokyo: Shunjusha, 1937); and Wada Hidekichi, *Nissan kontserun tokuhon* (Tokyo: Shunjusha, 1937).

technology; they had few links with the existing zaibatsu and financial institutions; and they had little capital. All of them also started up new industries using state capital. Whereas they were engaged mainly in the chemical and heavy industries and had the capability to produce munitions in wartime, their technology was also useful in peacetime. As such, their firms could easily adapt to postwar economic growth. Because the economy of the 1930s had already produced pioneers like Toyota and Nissan, it also had clear links with the post-1950s economic growth.

Special laws to promote the development of the chemical and heavy industries passed the Diet in rapid succession.[35] Beginning with the Oil Industry Law passed in 1934 and the Automobile Manufacturers' Law in 1936, special laws covering the synthetic oil, iron, machine tools, aircraft-manufacturing, shipbuilding, aluminum and light metals, organic chemicals, and heavy machinery industries had been passed by 1941. Their provisions were generally similar. Government approval was required for the firms' yearly plans via a government licensing system; unified standards and control over manufacturing and distribution were imposed; firms were directed to respond to the requirements of the military and the public interest; and the government could order the expansion and improvement of plants and equipment as well as changes in methods of operation and production plans. These special laws ruled that enterprises incurring losses be compensated according to government decree. The laws also provided other forms of protection, such as exemption from land expropriation, income taxes, and corporate taxes; the granting of bounties and subsidies, special privileges for debenture flotations; and the compulsory amortization of plant and equipment. The protectionist policy embodied in these special laws contributed greatly to the development of the chemical and heavy industries during the war and may be regarded as the genesis of the postwar policy of promoting these industries.

In the meantime, the older established zaibatsu, which had become the targets of social opprobrium, did their best in the early 1930s to avert criticism. The Mitsui zaibatsu, partly because it was the most severely criticized, set up a foundation called the Mitsui hōonkai (Mitsui Repayment of Kindness Association) to perform social work services and forced the resignation of Mitsui bussan's managing director, Yasukawa Shunosuke, who had been criticized for his "aggressive" activities. Mitsubishi and Sumitomo made similar efforts. Frequently

35 Maeda Yasuyuki, *Shōkō seisakushi Dai 11-kan*, pp. 238–50.

likened to the "conversion" (*tenkō*) of Communist Party members, such behavior was called "zaibatsu conversion." The activities of the older zaibatsu were generally conservative in this period, and their influence in the economy as a whole declined. Because fiscal spending increases went to farm villages or to small- and medium-sized enterprises, the expansion of deposits in zaibatsu banks was also slow. After 1933 the Sanwa Bank of Osaka, which had many provincial branches, led in volume of deposits.

But as a consequence of the Shōwa financial crisis, oligopolistic control in individual industries advanced. During the recovery period, huge trusts were formed in the iron and paper industries. In 1933 seven private iron–steel manufacturing firms merged with the government-operated Yawata Iron and Steel Works to form the Nippon seitetsu KK (Japan Steel Company), which controlled 97.5 percent of domestic pig iron production and 51.5 percent of domestic steel ingot production. Before the Shōwa financial crisis, the market had been controlled by means of a cartel centered on the Yawata Iron Works, but as a result of the merger it became possible to control the market through a single giant firm. The same year, Mitsui's Ōji Paper Company, Ōkawa Heizaburō's Fuji Paper Company, and Sakhalin Industries merged to form the Ōji Paper Company, a large trust that controlled 90 percent of newsprint production. Because imports of steel products and machine-made paper were depressed by the low exchange rate, these monopolies ended up dominating their respective domestic markets, and after the war they were broken up by the economic deconcentration policy. During 1932 and 1933, large-scale business mergers were also carried out in rapid succession in banking, beer, and machinery. The functions of cartels were also strengthened. The large electric power companies, hard-pressed during the depression and plagued by the pressure of their loans from financial institutions, acceded to the demands of the zaibatsu banks to form an electric power federation. When prices for goods produced in industries dominated by trusts and cartels increased as a result of these trends, the criticism of these monopolies grew stronger. In 1936 the Important Industries Control Law was amended so as to suppress the activities of the cartels.[36]

In the 1930s, Japan also focused on the economic development of the puppet state Manchukuo and the economic penetration of north China. With support from the government in Tokyo the Kwantung Army, in de facto control of Manchuria, collaborated with the South

36 Ibid., pp. 68–72.

Manchurian Railway Company (Mantetsu) to set up the Mantetsu Economic Research Bureau and the First Economic Construction Plan for Manchukuo. The plan's essential goals, which rested on an ideology critical of a free economy and domestic capitalism, were to prevent "capitalists" from monopolizing profits, to "promote the good of all the people," "to place key economic sectors" under state control, and to develop economic interdependence between Manchuria and Japan.

With regard to currency, the Manchukuo Central Bank was established, and a managed currency (the *yuan*) linked to the Japanese yen at parity was issued.[37] Japan and Manchukuo thus had a shared currency, and the "Japan–Manchukuo Economic Bloc" came into being.[38] This measure was in line with general worldwide trends after the abandonment of the gold standard, that is, the creation of a "sterling bloc" centered on Great Britain and the Commonwealth, and a "dollar bloc" centered on the United States. In industrial development, key industries such as steel, gold mining, coal mining, oil, ammonium sulphate, soda, coal liquefaction, electric power, automobile transport, and air transport were placed under state control. Following the principle of establishing one company per industry, special corporations were created by the Manchukuo government and the South Manchurian Railway, each putting up 30 percent of the capital and the remainder being raised from the general public.[39] The Manchukuo government supervised the personnel and accounting of these special companies, but it also granted them special privileges such as profit subsidies and tax exemptions. Because Manchukuo was originally founded under the slogans of "Denounce capitalism" and "Keep out the zaibatsu," direct investment from metropolitan Japan was excluded. The capital for industrial development was raised through the issue of South Manchurian Railway debentures. Domestic capital was permitted to be used in industries not considered key, but a policy was adopted to discourage the development of industries that competed with domestic Japanese production, such as rice cultivation and cotton spinning.

Because this conception of Manchurian development was based on the anticapitalist ideology of the Kwantung Army and the South Manchurian Railway, the domestic economic community was hostile. The

37 Kobayashi Hideo, "Manshū kinyū kōzō no saihensei katei–1930 nendai zenhanki o chūshin to shite," in *Nihon teikokushugika no Manshū*, ed. Manshūshi kenkyūkai (Tokyo: Ochanomizu shobō, 1972), pp. 151–74. 38 Ibid., pp. 196–206.

39 Hara Akira, "1930 nendai no Manshū keizai tōsei seisaku," in *Nihon teikokushugika no Manshū*, pp. 44–9.

flotation of South Manchurian Railway debentures thus fared poorly. Furthermore, it was impossible for the South Manchurian Railway, whose personnel came mainly from railroad or military backgrounds, to provide the workers necessary for extensive industrial development. This was the Achilles' heel of the South Manchurian Railway Company, which, on the pretext of cooperating in building the new country, was attempting to control the Manchukuo economy. It was also the reason that the company gradually became estranged from the army. After 1933 the Kwantung Army drew up a plan to split the South Manchuria Railway Company into a group of independent affiliates (*kogaisha*), one for each sector. The South Manchurian Railway Company's functions were limited to managing the railroad and acting as a holding company for the affiliate companies. The Kwantung Army also devised a plan to strengthen its control over the affiliate companies. The plan came to naught, but rather than abandon it, the army continued to look for an opportunity to put it into effect.[40]

Driven by a sense of crisis and aware that it might be necessary to comply with the army's plan, the South Manchurian Railway planned to move south of the Great Wall into north China. After 1934 the Kwantung Army cooperated with the North China Garrison army to establish a de facto sphere of influence in north China by cutting it off from Kuomintang control and setting up pro-Japanese political regimes. It also developed plans for obtaining from the area raw materials such as iron ore, coal, and salt, which were in short supply in Manchukuo. The South Manchurian Railway did the research for this project.[41] In 1935 the railway established the Hsingchong ("Revive China") Company as its affiliate. The North China Garrison Army succeeded in establishing a pro-Japanese regime in eastern Hopei and a regime with a certain degree of autonomy from Nanking in Hopei-Chahar. After 1936 the Japanese negotiated with both these regimes for rights to develop their raw material resources, but the effort did not make much progress, owing to opposition from the Chinese. But these practical maneuvers did enable the advance by Japan's big spinning companies into the Tientsin area, particularly after 1936.

The domestic situation in Japan changed radically with the increased power of the military after 1936. On February 26, 1936,

40 Hara Akira, " 'Manshū' ni okeru keizai seijisaku no tenkai–Mantetsu kaisō to Mangyō sōritsū o megutte" in *Nihon keizai seisakushi ron*, ed. Andō Yoshio (Tokyo: Tokyo daigaku shuppankai, 1976), vol. 2, pp. 211–13, 296.

41 Nakamura Takafusa, "Nihon no kahoku keizai kosaku," in *Kindai Nihon kenkyūkai*, vol. 2, pp. 159–204.

Takahashi Korekiyo was killed by a military assassination squad. Under the newly formed Hirota cabinet, which was dominated by the demands of the military, the economy strayed from the path of economic rationality. Since 1934 Takahashi had consolidated the level of fiscal spending, had done his utmost to curb the expansion of military spending, and had tried to reduce the size of government bond issues. These policies seem to have reflected the views of Fukai Eigo, governor of the Bank of Japan and a close partner of Takahashi, who agreed with Keynes's theory of true inflation. According to this theory, if there is a surplus of capital plants and equipment, raw materials, or labor, an expansion of demand will not induce inflation, but if that margin of surplus is lost, inflation will occur. Fukai appears to have believed that Japan had achieved virtual full employment in the latter half of 1935.[42] Takahashi's opposition to an expanded scale of military and fiscal spending was thus based on such thinking.

Finding it impossible to oppose the demands of the military, Finance Minister Baba Eiichi of the Hirota cabinet attempted to cooperate with them. He approved a five-year large-scale armament expansion plan for the army and a six-year plan for the navy.[43] The national budget for fiscal year 1937 was almost 40 percent larger than that of FY 1936. This budget expansion was to be covered by a large tax increase and national bond issues. To facilitate the issue of public bonds, Baba lowered the discount rate and revived a low-interest-rate policy. Business leaders resisted the proposed tax increase, but at the same time they moved to increase imports in anticipation of inflation and a stronger demand for imported raw materials accompanying the expansion in military demand. As a result, the balance of payments was heavily in the red at the end of 1936. At the beginning of the year, the country had to begin shipping gold abroad. Price increases also became noticeable. Baba's policies failed immediately, and after a clash with the Diet in January 1937, the Hirota cabinet was replaced by the Hayashi cabinet. The new finance minister, Yūki Toyotarō, reduced Baba's budget, curtailed the tax increases, and mended relations with business leaders. When the first Konoe cabinet was organized in June 1937, Kaya Okinori and Yoshino Shinji, two leading bureaucrats, took office as minister of finance and minister of commerce and industry.

In the army, Ishiwara Kanji, the planner and executor of the Man-

42 Fukai, *Kaikō 70-nen*, pp. 322–31. See also Yoshino Toshihiko, *Rekidai Nihon ginkō sōsai ron* (Tokyo: Mainichi shinbunsha, 1976), pp. 186–8.

43 Aoki Nobumitsu, *Baba Eiichi den* (Tokyo: Ko Baba Eiichi-shi kinenkai, 1945), pp. 263–4.

churian incident, took the lead in formulating a plan to expand direct military preparations for the expected outbreak of war with the Soviet Union, to expand the chemical and heavy industries, and to establish a firm base for munitions production. This plan's objective was to expand the productive capacity of the Japan–Manchukuo economic bloc, swiftly drawing on the resources of Japan, Manchukuo, and north China. Table 3.6 shows that ¥6.1 billion of the needed capital was to come from domestic Japan and ¥2.4 billion from Manchuria.[44] The army plan, which took approximately one year to draft, was presented to the Konoe cabinet, which was organized with the mission of implementing it. In the summer of 1936, Ishiwara, seeking a review of the plan, had shown the newly completed first draft to a few politicians, including Konoe, and to members of financial circles such as Ikeda Shigeaki, Ayukawa Yoshisuke, and Yūki Toyotarō. He obtained their informal consent to cooperate in implementing the plan. Yūki's appointment as finance minister, Ikeda's appointment as governor of the Bank of Japan during the Hayashi cabinet, and Konoe's subsequent appointment as prime minister all were intended to encourage the realization of this plan.

The Konoe cabinet was unable to use such methods as fiscal and monetary stringency, suppression of domestic demand, reduction of imports, and promotion of exports to eliminate the balance-of-payments deficit. Immediately after taking office, Finance Minister Kaya and Commerce and Industry Minister Yoshino announced three economic principles: "expansion of productive capacity, balance of payments equilibrium, and regulation of the supply and demand for goods." This announcement indicated that their attention would be turned to establishing priorities for commodity imports and expanding productive capacity within the constraints imposed by preserving the balance-of-payments equilibrium. It implied the necessity of implementing direct national controls over commodity imports and capital. Economic controls were thus invoked across the board after the outbreak of the Sino-Japanese War in July 1937, but even if the war had not occurred, it is highly likely that sooner or later controls would have become unavoidable.

In Manchuria, the Manchuria Five-Year Development Plan, based on Ishiwara's first draft, was drawn up and immediately put into effect in 1937. It was thought that to carry out this plan, skilled specialists should manage industrial production. In November 1937 Nissan's

44 Nakamura, *Economic Growth in Prewar Japan*, pp. 268–85.

TABLE 3.6

Production targets in the five-year plan for key industries

	(A) Production targets			(B) Present capacity			(A) as a proportion of (B)		
	Total	Japan	Manchuria	Total	Japan	Manchuria	Total	Japan	Manchuria
Ordinary automobiles (1,000s)	100	90	10	37	37	—	2.7	2.4	—
Machine tools (1,000s)	50	45	5	13	13	—	3.8	3.5	—
Rolled steel (1,000s of tons)	13,000	9,000	4,000	4,850	4,400	45	2.7	2.0	8.9
Oil (1,000s kl)	5,650	3,250	2,400	364	210	154	15.6	15.5	15.6
Coal (1,000s tons)	110,000	72,000	38,000	55,560	42,000	13,560	2.0	1.7	28.0
Aluminum (1,000s tons)	100	70	30	21	21	—	4.8	3.3	—
Magnesium (1,000s tons)	9	9	3	0.5	0.5	—	4.8	3.3	—
Electric power (1,000s kw)	12,750	11,170	1,400	7,210	6,750	460	1.7	1.7	3.0
Shipbuilding (1,000s tons)	930	860	70	500	500	—	1.9	1.7	—

Note: Other than these, the production target for weapons was ¥960 million, a 2.1-fold increase over current capacity, and the target for airplanes was 10,000 (Japan, 7,000; Manchuria, 3,000).

Source: "Jūyō sangyō go-ka-nen keikaku jisshi ni kansuru seisaku taikō (an)," Ministry of the Army, May 29, 1937. Shimada Toshihiko and Inaba Masao, eds., *Gendaishi shiryo*, vol. 8. *Nitchū sensō* (1) (Tokyo: Misuzu shobō, 1964), pp. 730, 746.

Ayukawa Yoshisuke founded Manchurian Heavy Industries (Mangyō). Using Nissan's capital and technology, he gathered all the Manchurian companies in the heavy and chemical industries under its control.[45] The South Manchurian Railway become a holding company concentrating on operating the railroad, and its reorganization was accomplished only after many setbacks.

WAR

In July 1937 Japan plunged into an undeclared war with China. Contrary to expectations that it would be decided quickly, the war stretched on. The nation's economic strength was strained by shortages of key raw materials, particularly oil, and the tightening of economic controls. Economically, the outbreak of the China war was but a continuation of the trajectory along which the country had already been hurled. The Japanese economy was administered with the sole object of meeting the military demand. Ordinary industry and popular livelihood were sacrificed to that end. Although several factors linked to postwar economic growth were developed during this period, the process as a whole was a march to destruction.

The most persistent feature of the war economy was the continual strengthening of economic controls. War with China broke out just after the government accepted the army's plan for heavy and chemical industrialization. There was no alternative but to administer the economy by strengthening controls and by giving priority in allocating limited materials and capital to meet military demand. The necessity for economic controls had been urged by young bureaucrats, military personnel, and even economists since the 1920s.[46] The worldwide depression made clear that the capitalist free economies had come to a standstill. The need to control the economy and to institute planning could be seen from the success of the Soviet Union's five-year plans. The military also contended that World War I had demonstrated that the next war would be a total war requiring the mobilization of the economy as well as the polity. Research on the development of a mobilization structure had in fact been conducted at the Natural Re-

45 See Hara, " 'Manshū' ni okeru keizai seijisaku no tenkai," in *Nihon keizai seisakushi ron*, vol. 2, pp. 209–96.

46 Nagata Tetsuzan, "Kokka sōdōin junbi shisetsu to seishōnen kunren" in *Kokka sōdōin no igi*, ed. Tsujimura Kusuzō (Tokyo: Aoyama shoin, 1925), is a good example of early ideas on mobilization. An outstanding summary of the mobilization scheme focusing on the military may be found in Mikuriya Takashi, "Kokusaku tōgō kikan setchi mondai no shiteki tenkai," in *Kindai Nihon kenkyū*, vol. 1: *Shōwa-ki no gunbu* (Tokyo: Yamakawa shuppansha, 1979), sec. 1.

sources Agency since 1927. Ideological demands for a system of economic control had been tried in Manchukuo after 1932, but at home their realization was limited to the unification of the electric power generation and transmission industry in 1938. Full-scale economic controls in Japan proper were instituted only when other alternatives were discounted.

During the first three months of the China war in 1937, military expenditures came to ¥2.5 billion, an amount virtually equal to the national budget for the year. Faced with a pressing need to check increases in imports and currency expansion, the government passed the Temporary Capital Adjustment Law and the Temporary Export and Import Commodities Law. In March 1938, the Diet enacted the National General Mobilization Law. Under these laws, the government acquired sweeping powers: (1) The establishment of firms, capital increases, bond flotations, and long-term loans came under a licensing system; (2) the government was empowered to issue directives concerning the manufacture, distribution, transfer, use, and consumption of materials connected with imports and exports, particularly their restriction or prohibition; and (3) the government was also empowered to issue directives on the conscription of labor power, the setting of working conditions, the disposition of firms' profits, the use of funds by financial institutions, the administration, use, and expropriation of factories and mines, and the formation of cartels.[47] These measures were invoked one after another as the war situation became more grave.

In October 1937 the Cabinet Planning Board (Kikakuin), charged with comprehensive planning, began operations.[48] Its major responsibilities were to regulate the supply and demand for major commodities necessary for economic activity and to draw up a materials mobilization plan. The required volume of key raw materials imports on which Japan depended – for example, iron and steel, oil, copper, aluminum, raw cotton, wool, and rubber – was calculated as the difference between the combined military, government, and industrial demand and the domestic supply. Within the constraints set by the amount of available foreign exchange, an import plan was drawn up for each commodity, and the commodities were allocated among the army, the navy, and the private sector. These plans were initially made for October to December 1937. From then until the defeat, plans were first prepared every year and then subsequently every quarter. To imple-

47 Maeda, *Shōkō seisakushi Dai 11-kan*, chaps. 2, 3.
48 Mikuriya, "Kokusaku tōgō kikan setchi."

ment the Five-Year Plan for Key Industries, the planning board also prepared the Industrial Capacity Expansion Plan, which it put into effect in 1939.[49]

Japan thus quickly entered a wartime controlled economy. Economic control policies were unavoidable because of the political necessity of raising funds for huge military outlays, ensuring raw materials for the import-dependent chemical and heavy industries, and producing munitions. Japan's foreign trade situation at this time is shown in Table 3.7. After 1938 the aggregate foreign trade balance was in the black. A breakdown of these figures, however, shows that an export surplus was maintained in the yen bloc, in which settlements were made in yen, but in other areas, in which convertible foreign exchange was required, there was a continuous import surplus. For key raw materials such as coal, iron ore, and salt, Japan could be self-sufficient in the yen bloc; but for oil, bauxite, scrap iron, rare metals such as nickel and cobalt, crude rubber, raw cotton, and wool, Japan was compelled to depend on imports from dollar and sterling areas. Efforts to promote further its chemical and heavy industries increased Japan's dependence on the British and American currency areas. The materials mobilization plan, launched at a time of large import surpluses in 1937, was drawn up on the assumption that an estimated ¥3 billion in foreign exchange revenues from 1938 exports would be available, but owing to a slump in the United States and the slack production of cotton textiles for export, the figure was slashed to ¥2.5 billion by midyear. Because priority in the allocation of imported goods was for munitions and for use in expanding productive capacity, the import of materials used for consumer production, such as raw cotton and wool, was cut back. Because of the increasing squeeze on consumer goods as well as poor rice harvests, a rationing system for rice, matches, and sugar was adopted in 1940. Fearing soaring prices, the government fixed prices and initiated price controls. But these new controls only stimulated black market dealings. In order to crack down on such activity, the economic police was established. Allocations of munitions goods were made on the basis of a coupon system, but it was not always easy to obtain the actual goods. Everywhere, complicated controls proliferated.

The Japanese continued to do their utmost to develop the resources of Manchuria and China. The North China Development Corporation

49 See commentary in Nakamura Takafusa and Hara Akira, eds., *Kokka sōdōin*, vol. 1: *Keizai (Gendaishi shiryō 31)* (Tokyo: Misuzu shobō, 1970).

TABLE 3.7

The balance of international trade in the 1930s (¥ millions)

	Totals			Trade with the yen bloc (China, Manchuria, and Kwantung)			Trade with the world outside the yen bloc		
	Exports	Imports	Settlement balance	Exports	Imports	Settlement balance	Exports	Imports	Settlement balance
1931	1.147	1.235	−89	0.221	236	−15	0.926	1.000	−74
1932	1.410	1.431	−21	0.276	206	70	1.134	1.226	−72
1933	1.861	1.919	−56	0.411	281	130	1.450	1.636	−186
1934	2.171	2.283	−111	0.520	311	209	1.652	1.972	−320
1935	2.499	2.472	27	0.575	350	225	1.924	2.122	−198
1936	2.693	2.764	−71	0.658	394	264	2.035	2.370	−335
1937	3.175	3.783	−608	0.791	437	354	2.384	3.346	−962
1938	2.690	2.663	27	1.166	564	602	1.524	2.099	−575
1939	3.576	2.918	658	1.747	683	1.064	1.829	2.235	−406
1940	3.656	3.453	203	1.867	756	1.111	1.789	2.697	−908
1941	2.651	2.899	−248	1.659	855	804	992	2.044	−1.052

Source: Japan Ministry of Finance, Customs clearance statistics, 1931–41.

and the Central China Promotion Corporation set up affiliates in their respective regions to develop natural resources. Coal and iron ore development were given top priority in China, and the Japanese army went as far as to reduce the number of trains transporting local food supplies in order to send coal to Japan. In Manchuria, Manchurian Heavy Industries, headed by Ayukawa Yoshisuke, worked to establish every kind of industry in the region, including automobile production. However, Ayukawa's plan to try to introduce American capital and technology into Manchuria proved overly optimistic. It ignored America's nonrecognition of Manchukuo and the Open Door principle. When his plan finally failed, Ayukawa had to resign.[50]

In July 1939 the United States announced the abrogation of its Treaty of Commerce and Navigation with Japan. In January 1940 the United States became free to restrict exports to Japan as a form of economic sanction. The outbreak of the European war in September 1939 led to expectations that strategic goods imports would become more difficult. From 1939 to 1940, Japan mobilized all the gold and foreign exchange it could and boosted its imports of petroleum products, rare metals, and other strategic goods. The Bank of Japan's gold reserves were nearly depleted.[51] In July 1940, observing Nazi Germany's successful invasion of France and expecting the imminent defeat of Britain, Japan's military drew up plans to invade Singapore and the Dutch East Indies (now Indonesia) to gain access to their abundant supplies of raw materials such as oil, rubber, and tin. Support was growing for the reckless view that the war in China remained unresolved because Britain and the United States were backing the Kuomintang government and that Japan should act in concert with Germany to defeat Britain and force the United States to withdraw from Asia. In September 1940, Japan advanced into northern French Indochina (present-day North Vietnam) and signed a treaty of alliance with Germany and Italy. The United States responded by tightening its export restrictions against Japan and then steadily turned the screws to reduce Japanese economic power.

In 1939, Japan instituted general wage and price controls and established a unified nationwide wage system. The workers in the commerce and service industries were conscripted for compulsory work in munitions production. The companies' dividend rates were restricted, and finance was placed under comprehensive controls as well. Intend-

50 Hara, " 'Manshū' ni okeru keizai seijisaku no tenkai," pp. 248–95.

51 See the explanatory comments in Nakamura and Hara, eds., *Kokka sōdōin*, vol. 1, pp. lxix–lxxii. See also in the same volume, "Ōkyū butsudo keikaku shian" and "Setsumei shiryō."

ing to increase munitions production, the government in the fall of 1940 put forth plans for a New Economic Order parallel to the New Political Structure being organized at the same time.[52] The intent of this plan was to shift firms from a profit basis to a production basis; to separate the owners of capital from the managers of the firms; to designate government officials as managers; to make firms increase their production in accordance with government directives; and to organize cartels called industrial control associations to implement government economic controls such as production quotas and materials allocations. The business community opposed this plan, on the ground that it was a "communist" idea that threatened the fundamental principles of a capitalist economy. A compromise was finally reached, but just barely.

In early 1941 Japanese-American negotiations began. During their stormy course Germany invaded the Soviet Union. In July, Japan advanced into southern French Indochina. In response, the United States froze Japanese assets in America and imposed a total embargo on petroleum exports. The embargo on petroleum, Japan's most critical war matériel, was the biggest trump card the United States held. Japan's army and navy had reserves of 8.4 million kiloliters of petroleum products, an amount that could meet its military demand for no more than two years of fighting. Opinion within the army and navy was dominated by the belligerent view that Japan should go to war with Britain and the United States to obtain raw materials from Southeast Asia rather than give in to external pressure. This mood propelled the country into the Pacific War.[53]

Six months after the beginning of hostilities, Japan occupied a vast area demarcated by a boundary running through Burma, Thailand, the Malay Peninsula, Singapore, Sumatra, Java, Borneo, the Celebes, and the Solomon Islands. Some observers thought that with petroleum supplies safely in hand, the dream of the Greater East Asia Co-Prosperity Sphere had been realized. Many firms moved to invest in the development of mines, rubber, and raw cotton in the region, and some even laid plans for hydroelectric power and aluminum refining. The government drew up the optimistic Plan for the Expansion of Productivity, using "Greater East Asia" as its arena. The plan projected that within fifteen years, production would be expanded from three to five times the cur-

52 See Nakamura Takafusa and Hara Akira, "Keizai shin taisei" in *Nihon seiji gakkai nenpō 1972-nen* (Tokyo: Iwanami shoten, 1972).

53 Nakamura Takafusa, "Sensō keizai to sono hōkai," in *Iwanami kōza, Nihon rekishi*, vol. 21: *Kindai 8* (Tokyo: Iwanami shoten, 1977), pp. 115–16.

TABLE 3.8
Figures on the Pacific War and ocean-going transport

	1941 (December only)	1942	1943	1944	1945
Losses of ship tonnage					
No. of ships	12	202	437	969	639 (271)
No. of tons (1,000s)	56	948	1,793	2,058	1,503 (756)
Ship construction					
No. of ships	4	77	254	699	188
No. of tons (1,000s)	6	265	769	1,700	560
Volume of oceangoing transport					
Planned (A) (1,000s tons)	41,408[a]	40,368	33,397	27,820	9,400
Achieved (B) (1,000s tons)	39,601[a]	39,486	33,047	20,720	7,279
Rate of plan achievement (B/A %)	95.6	97.8	99.0	74.5	77.4
Of amount achieved:					
Japan, Manchuria, and China (1,000s tons)		21,914[b]	29,624	18,151	2,003[c]
Southeast Asia and others (1,000s tons)		862[b]	3,605	2,627	137[c]
Volume of Southeast Asian raw material shipments to Japan					
Oil (1,000s kl)	–	1,428	2,623	1,500	–
Bauxite (1,000s tons)	–	323	792	565[d]	–
Crude rubber (1,000s tons)	–	65	78	68[d]	–
Manganese ore (1,000s tons)	–	71	89	67[d]	–
Totals, including other items (1,000s of tons, except for oil)	–	1,514	1,581	909[d]	–

[a] Totals for Apr. to Dec. 1941.
[b] Jul. to Dec. 1942. [c] Jan. to Mar. 1945.
[d] Figures for 1944 are forecasts.
Source: Nakamura Takafusa, "Sensō keizai to sono hōkai," in *Iwanami kōza, Nihon rekishi, vol. 21: Kindai 8* (Tokyo: Iwanami shoten, 1977), Tables 5, 8, 9.

rent level. The immediate problem, however, was how to fight a war with the raw materials Japan now controlled.

There were no longer any foreign exchange restrictions for raw material imports from the Greater East Asia Co-Prosperity Sphere. Payment was made with Japanese military scrip or with Southeast Asia Development Bank vouchers. Marine transport capacity rather than foreign exchange became the critical bottleneck. The tonnage of Japan's ocean-going capacity at the beginning of the Pacific War was 6.5 million gross tons, of which about 5.5 million gross tons, excluding tankers and repair vessels, could be mobilized (see Table 3.8). It was thought that even if 2.9 million gross tons of army and navy warships were used for combat or military service, 3 million gross tons, including tankers, would be kept in service for freight transport to provide the transport capacity necessary to keep production going at the level called for by the 1941 Materials Mobilization Plan. At the beginning of

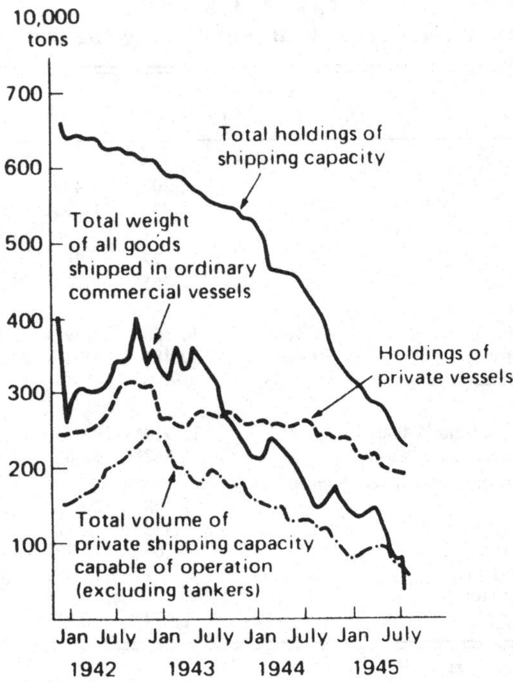

Figure 3.2. Shipping capacity and shipment of goods during World War II. [From Oi Atsushi, *Kaijō goeisen* (Tokyo: Nihon shuppan kyōdō, 1952), appended tables.]

the war, based on estimated annual losses of 800,000 to 1 million tons and estimated annual production of 600,000 tons of new ships, it was forecast that Japan could maintain 3 million gross tons of capacity. This forecast proved excessively optimistic.[54]

In reality, the army and navy vessels were not replaced easily, and losses exceeded expectations. Realizing the importance of shipping, the Japanese government tried to increase shipbuilding output, but marine transport tonnage continued to decline. As Table 3.8 indicates, shipments of Southeast Asian raw materials, in particular, failed to meet expectations. Figure 3.2 shows the decline in shipping capacity as a barometer of fighting strength. Japan's ship tonnage (civilian vessels) for transporting general commodities reached a peak in October 1942 as a result of the cancellation of military vessel requisitioning, but after the battle of the Solomon Islands, its ship tonnage shifted

54 Ibid., pp. 116–17.

into decline. After the latter half of 1943, in particular, it fell steadily because of the all-out American sea and air offensive. Especially notable was the decline of volume shipped, which dropped in conjunction with the ships' falling rate of operation. After the fall of the Marianas in July 1944, the sea lanes to Southeast Asia were blocked, and so it became impossible to procure raw materials anywhere but Japan, Manchuria, and China. In 1945, when food shortages in the homeland reached crisis proportions, the transport of grains and salt from China and Manchukuo became the ultimate mission for shipping, but even that was brought to a standstill by air attacks. In regard to marine transport, Japan had already lost the war in the summer of 1944.[55] Jerome Cohen summarized this situation: "It may be said that in large measure Japan's economy was destroyed twice over, once by cutting off of imports and secondly by air attack."[56]

Domestic production trends until defeat are shown in Table 3.9. Wartime controls clearly expanded Japan's chemical and heavy industrial production and reduced the output for private demand in such industries as textiles. For this reason, production in industries catering to private demand, including agriculture, continued to decline after the latter half of the 1930s. The Japanese were forced to endure extreme hardship. Even within the heavy and chemical industries, the outputs in various sectors achieved maximum levels in different years. Because production priorities focused on aircraft and ships during the Pacific War, the production of materials such as steel and chemicals fell from 1943 onward. Production efforts were concentrated solely on final products such as weaponry, military aircraft, and ships. As a result of extraordinary effort, aircraft production increased from 6,174 planes in 1941 to 26,507 in 1944, and the production of warships grew from 201,000 to 408,000 tons, both peak levels of output.[57] However, the eleventh-hour production effort was unable to turn around the deteriorating war situation.

At the beginning of the Pacific War, the Japanese government was behind in its efforts to organize a wartime economic mobilization, and began only in the fall of 1942. Because Japan's early military successes exceeded expectations, government leaders overlooked the necessity of all-out economic mobilization efforts. When the American counter-

55 See ibid., pp. 123–36.

56 Jerome B. Cohen, *Japan's Economy in War and Reconstruction* (Minneapolis: University of Minnesota Press, 1949), p. 107.

57 According to Okazaki Ayakoto, *Kihon kokuryoku dōtai sōran* (Tokyo: Kokumin keizai kenkyū kyōkai, 1953).

TABLE 3.9
Wartime production indexes (1937 = 100)

	Agriculture production index	Rice	Mining production index	Coal	Manufacturing production index	Steel	Machinery	Chemicals	Textiles	Foods
1936	98	102	92	92	85	87	75	87	88	91
1937	100	100	100	100	100	100	100	100	*100*	100
1938	98	99	106	108	103	115	110	114	83	101
1939	*105*	*104*	112	113	114	123	135	*122*	83	*104*
1940	99	92	*120*	125	119	128	163	120	75	90
1941	95	83	*120*	125	123	132	188	120	60	78
1942	100	101	118	121	120	140	195	100	48	69
1943	96	95	119	*127*	121	*156*	214	87	31	58
1944	76	88	108	120	*124*	146	*252*	80	17	47
1945	59	59	51	74	53	52	107	33	6	32

Source: Agriculture: Production indexes compiled by Ministry of Agriculture and Forestry using 1933–5 as the base period (*Dai 30-ji Nōrinshō tōkeihyō*). Mining and manufacturing: Ministry of International Trade and Industry, *Shōwa 35-nen ki jun kōkōgyō shisū sōran*. (Italicized figures are the maximum values reached by each index during this period.)

attack began, the failure to mobilize adequately became an irretrievable handicap. In any case, once the need for the mass production of aircraft and ships became clear, the Japanese government attempted to "make the impossible possible." For example, in order to increase steel production, the government set up a large number of simple twenty-to-one-hundred-ton-capacity small blast furnaces in Korea, Manchukuo, and China. Their performance was extremely poor, however, and they did not produce the expected results. In order to cope with shortages of metal materials, including scrap iron, the government collected city streetcar rails, the handrails of bridges, and even the bells in Buddhist temples. The textile industry's spinning machinery was scrapped and turned into raw materials for shells. In the wake of shutdowns and cutbacks, many factories in the consumer goods industry were converted into munitions factories. Good results were produced in the shipbuilding industry in 1943 by using a "snowball" method. Shipbuilding volume was expanded by importing iron ore only in the amount needed to build ships, and the ships thus built were then used to import more iron ore. In order to cut down on the volume of ocean shipping, various kinds of production facilities, including blast furnaces, were transferred to China and Manchuria, and the practice of on-the-spot production was adopted, but this effort disappointed expectations.

In the fall of 1943, in order to increase munitions production, especially aircraft, a Ministry of Munitions was established by merging the Cabinet Planning Board and the relevant departments in the Ministry of Commerce and Industry. At the same time a Munitions Companies System was inaugurated. Key firms were designated as "munitions companies"; those in charge of production were given titles as government officials; employees were treated as impressed labor and not allowed to quit their jobs; and the companies were responsible for increasing production in accordance with government instructions.[58] But the government also compensated these firms for losses. In each industry designated, financial institutions took responsibility for supplying the necessary capital.

The labor force presented a difficult problem during the war. Out of a population of slightly under 80 million, 2.4 million had been conscripted into military service by the end of 1941. In August 1945 this number had swelled to 7.2 million. To compensate for the resulting

58 Jūyō sangyō kyōgikai, *Gunjukaishahō kaisetsu* (Tokyo: Teikoku shuppan, 1944). No coherent study of the munitions companies exists.

labor shortage, young men in consumer goods or tertiary industries were conscripted and mobilized to work in factories and mines. After 1944, students from the middle-school level up were employed in munitions production and forced to suspend studies of any kind almost entirely. In the consumer goods industries, especially textiles, and in the tertiary industries, firms either converted to wartime production or went out of business as raw materials and merchandise disappeared. Their machinery and equipment were scrapped for munitions production, and their workers were put to work in factories and mines. The government promoted the forced reorganization of business, and it compelled small- and medium-sized enterprises to convert to munitions production or go out of business, mainly in order to mobilize their workers.[59] The 1944 bulge in the secondary industry work force and the deterioration of the tertiary industry work force, as seen in Table 3.3, were the consequences of such policies.

The quality of daily life suffered. After 1938 it became impossible to obtain cotton and woolen goods. In 1940 necessities such as rice, *miso* (bean paste), and soy sauce were rationed, but these, too, gradually ran short, and food shortages for the urban population became severe in 1943. The standard daily Japanese caloric intake was 2,200 calories, including 70 grams of protein, but the actual daily intake in 1941 was 2,105 calories and 64.7 grams of protein. By January 1944, rations provided a mere 1,405 calories.[60] People tried to stave off starvation by foraging in the farm villages or buying on the black market outside official distribution channels. The government had put limited price controls into effect after the start of the China war for fear of inflation. In 1940 the government began setting official prices for everything, but it was impossible to eradicate illegal transactions. From a 1937 base-year value of 100, the consumer price index rose to 149 in 1940, 208 in 1944, and 254 in May 1945. If black market prices are included, these indexes must be calculated as 161 for 1940 and 358 for 1944.[61] The latter figures are most likely closer to the actual situation.

After 1940 the government officially set wage levels on the basis of type of employment, educational background, age, and number of years of experience. This was done because it was feared that wage–cost increases would cause price increases. Because wage rates were calculated on the basis of official prices, they could never catch up

59 Yui Tsunehiko, *Chūshō kigyō seisaku no shiteki tenkai* (Tokyo: Tōyō keizai shinpōsha, 1964), pp. 342ff.

60 Hōsei daigaku Ōhara shakai mondai kenkyūjo, *Taiheiyō sensōka no rōdōsha jōtai* (Tokyo: Tōyō keizai shinpōsha, 1964), p. 149.

61 Cohen, *Japan's Economy*, p. 356.

with actual consumer price increases. Real wages sank to almost half their prewar level.[62]

By the time of defeat in August 1945, Japan had lost approximately three million lives (more than half were military personnel) and a quarter of its national wealth. The remaining total value of its national wealth was virtually the equivalent of what it had been in 1935. The war reduced the accumulation of the intervening decade to charred and smoldering ruins.[63] It is also true, however, that the conditions for sustaining postwar economic growth were already sprouting among those ruins. The wartime munitions industry provided the prototype for the chemical and heavy industrial sector, which was at the heart of postwar growth. Machine gun factories began to produce sewing machines, and range finder plants began making cameras. Linkages between big factories and small business subcontractors that developed in the munitions industry also became the basis for the postwar subcontracting system. So too the designation of specific financial institutions to finance munitions companies created close relations in which can be found the origins of the postwar "financial groupings" (*kinyū keiretsu*). Administrative guidance by government ministries and the Bank of Japan, often pointed to as a special characteristic of postwar Japan, was also a legacy of the wartime controls. The seniority wage system spread throughout the economy when wage controls were instituted, and enterprise unions were the successors of the Patriotic Industrial Associations (Sangyō hōkōku kai) organized in each firm after the labor unions were broken up. During the war the government purchased rice on a dual-price system, buying cheaply from landlords but paying a higher price when buying directly from producers in order to accelerate increased rice production. This practice had the effect of lowering rental rates, thus clearing the way for the postwar land reform. Even though the recollection of the wartime period is repugnant to those Japanese who lived through it, it was a stage preliminary to rapid postwar growth.

CONCLUSION

Both for the world and for Japan, the period from 1920 to 1945 was an unusually stormy and convulsive era. Looking back on the course that

62 Yamada Junzō, "Senjichū no rōdōsha" in *Gendai Nihon shihonshugi taikei:* vol. 4, *Rōdō*, ed. Aihara Shigeru (Tokyo: Kōbundō, 1958), p. 97.

63 Keizai antei honbu, *Taiheiyō sensō ni yoru wagakuni no higai sōgō hōkokusho* (Tokyo: Keizai antei honbu, 1948).

the Japanese economy pursued during those years, one may point out the following special features relevant to the postwar experience. First, the trend toward chemical and heavy industrialization that began during World War I constantly accelerated. Second, precedents for economic policies aimed at economic growth and full employment had already achieved success in the 1930s. Third, the prototype of postwar Japan's distinctive economic system was molded during the war years, although not necessarily intentionally. These circumstances also explain why Japan was able to achieve remarkably high growth, even by world standards, in the 1920s and 1930s.

However, even from a strictly economic standpoint, the economy of the 1920s and 1930s differed in several respects from that of the post–World War II era. First, politics were in absolute ascendancy over the economy. Examples of this are the removal of the gold embargo at the old parity for reasons of national prestige; the imposition of economic controls in conjunction with the military invasion of China and plans for war with the Soviet Union; and the plunge into the Pacific War without a dispassionate assessment of the nation's economic strength. Second, after the breakdown of the classical principle of laissez-faire, many policies were experimented with on a trial-and-error basis, but no general principle clearly emerged in its place. The failure of Inoue's fiscal policies and the success of Takahashi's are conspicuous examples of this. Third, the economy's extraordinary experience under wartime controls, when all was concentrated on winning the war, reduced the lives of the people to ruins.

CHAPTER 4

THE POSTWAR JAPANESE ECONOMY, 1945–1973

From 1945 to 1973, the Japanese economy maintained an annual growth rate of nearly 10 percent. Because the standards for measuring national income changed during this period, there is no continuous statistical series. However, when the existing data are linked and recalculated, Japan's real GNP shows an annual growth rate of 9.6 percent from 1946 to 1973.[1]

The first decade of this high economic growth was a period of recovery from the economic dislocations brought about by Japan's defeat in World War II. During the war, Japan's maritime transport was cut off by the Allied powers, and it had been difficult to obtain raw materials. In effect, this blockade was continued by postwar restrictions that the American occupying forces imposed on foreign trade, and it was exacerbated by social and economic disorder. Real GNP per capita in 1946 declined to 55 percent of the 1934–6 level as a result, and it did not recover that level until 1953.

The tempo of Japan's postwar recovery from the wartime destruction appears rapid in comparison with that of the countries of Western Europe, because the postwar collapse in Japan was so great, but it actually took the prewar per capita GNP longer to recover in Japan than it did in Europe. In 1951 the per capita national income, based on the prevailing exchange rates, was one-twelfth that of the United States and two-fifths that of West Germany.[2] But once the postwar recovery was complete, Japan maintained an extremely high rate of growth for more than fifteen years. Indeed, the performance of Japan's economy was outstanding compared with that of the other industrial economies.

1 Because of the confusion accompanying Japan's defeat in the war, there was no official estimate of its GNP in 1945. Figures for 1946 to 1955 can be found in Keizai kikakuchō, *Gendai Nihon keizai no tenkai* (Tokyo: Keizai kikakuchō, 1976), p. 578; and for 1955 to 1965 (old SNA) and 1965 to 1973 (new SNA), Tōyō keizai shinpōsha, *Shōwa kokusei sōran* (Tokyo: Tōyō keizai shinpōsha, 1980), p. 99.

2 Keizai kikakuchō chōsakyoku, ed., *Shiryō: Keizai hakusho 25 nen* (Tokyo: Keizai kikakuchō, 1972), p. 9 (chart 2), pp. 11–12.

During this period of rapid economic growth (*kōdō seichō jidai*) (1955 to 1972), Japan was in the process of introducing technological innovations and catching up economically with the West. This period can be divided into two subperiods: from 1955 to 1965 when the economy experienced three major booms (the "Jimmu boom," the "iwato boom," and the "boom that did not feel like one" [*kōkyokan naki keiki*]); and from 1966 to 1972 when the economy grew steadily until the "oil shock" and the onset of "crazy inflation" (*kyōran infure*).

Even after the period of high growth ended in 1973, however, the momentum of the economy continued. By 1975, for example, per capita GNP had reached 62 percent of the United States' and 65.9 percent of West Germany's and had outstripped the levels of Great Britain and Italy.[3] The gap between Japan and the other advanced countries continued to narrow. As a result of its rapid growth, Japan had risen to become one of the world's economic superpowers (*keizai taikoku*).

POSTWAR ECONOMIC REFORM AND RECOVERY

Postwar economic reforms

The transformation of Japan's postwar economy took place against the background of a democratization reform program promoted by the American Occupation forces. These reforms, of course, were not solely the result of the Americans' initiatives but were also shaped by the efforts of Japanese who either cooperated with the Americans or fought with them, in pursuit of their own ideals or agendas. Three economic reforms of particular importance were land reform, dissolution of the zaibatsu, and labor reform.

Land reform. Before land reform, 45.9 percent of Japan's agricultural land was tenanted. Before the war, tenant rent amounted to 5 percent of the national income, and tenancy disputes reached a peak of six thousand in 1935. It had been the policy of the prewar Ministry of Agriculture and Forestry to promote owner-cultivatorship in order to solve the tenancy problem. In the fall of 1945, as an extension of that policy, the Agricultural Land Adjustment Law was revised, limiting landholding to five *chōbu* and requiring that rent be paid in cash.

3 Based on OECD National Accounts (1986); Keizai kikakuchō kokumin shotokuka, *Kokumin shotoku dōkō* (Tokyo: Keizai kikakuchō, 1986).

The American Occupation forces, feeling that this legislation did not go far enough, sent a memorandum on land reform to the Japanese government on December 9, 1945, urging a more extensive change. The so-called second land reform was carried out by the promulgation of the Law for the Special Establishment of Independent Cultivators on October 21, 1946. The law provided for all the land owned by absentee landlords to be purchased by the government; for the land of noncultivating resident landlords to be limited to less than one *chōbu;* for the land of owner-cultivators to be limited to three *chōbu;* and for land purchased by the government to be resold to tenant farmers. Because the real price of the land dropped drastically as the result of inflation, land reform was almost equivalent to confiscation.

During land reform, 1,916 million hectares, or 37.5 percent of the agricultural acreage, changed hands. The land of over 3.7 million landlords was purchased by the government.[4] As a result of the reform, tenanted land was reduced to only 10 percent of agricultural land; the tenants' rent became negotiable; and tenant disputes disappeared. The farmers became more willing to work; the farming villages became more politically stable; and agriculture developed with the help of government price supports and investment in infrastructure. Opportunities for urban employment grew with the rapid growth and reduced the fragmentation of landholdings and agricultural underemployment created by the outflow of people to the countryside immediately after the war.

As a result of land reform, Japanese agriculture after the war became the province of independent farmers. On the other hand, even after the economy moved into its rapid growth phase, the number of farmers with part-time jobs increased, and landholdings remained fragmented. This impeded the improvement of agricultural productivity. In order to solve this problem, many urged increasing the scale of cultivation and encouraging the rental of land. There was a growing demand for a change in the policy of making owner-cultivators central to agriculture (*jisakunō chūshin shugi*), a policy based on the goals of both the Occupation forces and the prewar agrarian reformers in Japan.

Dissolution of the zaibatsu. From the outset the American Occupation intended to dissolve the zaibatsu, which some American officials felt had been complicit in waging Japan's war of territorial conquest. In

4 The basic materials on land reform may be found in Nōsei chōsakai nōchi kaikaku kiroku iinkai, ed., *Nōchi kaikaku tenmatsu gaiyō* (Tokyo, 1951). The standard work in English is by R. P. Dore, *Land Reform in Japan* (London: Oxford University Press, 1959).

October 1945 the Occupation decided to dissolve the head offices (*honsha*) of the zaibatsu holding companies and in April 1946 established a committee to reorganize the holding companies. By June 1947, eighty-three companies had been designated as holding companies. Of these, twenty-eight were reorganized as family holding companies, and the rest were allowed to continue as production enterprises after their stockholdings had been transferred. In the meantime, on July 3, 1947, the Occupation authorities ordered the dissolution of the Mitsui Trading Company and the Mitsubishi Trading Company.[5]

In April 1947 the enactment of the Anti-Monopoly Law, based on American antitrust laws, established Japan's Fair Trade Commission. The following December, the Diet passed the Law for the Elimination of Excessive Economic Concentration, which provided for the dissolution of any company deemed monopolistic. Under these laws, eighteen large firms were dissolved, and their factories were redistributed. The Japan Steel Corporation was split into two firms (Yawata Steel and Fuji Steel); Mitsui Mining was divided into two firms (Mitsui Mining and Kamioka Industries); Mitsubishi Industries was divided into two (Mitsubishi Mining and Taihei Mining); Mitsubishi Heavy Industries was divided into three firms (Eastern Japan Heavy Industries, Central Japan Heavy Industries, and Western Japan Heavy Industries); Tokyo Shibaura Electric divested itself of twenty-seven out of forty-three plants; and Hitachi Manufacturing divested itself of nineteen out of thirty-five plants. As a result of these and other dissolutions, the degree of concentration in the iron and steel, shipbuilding, beer-brewing, papermaking, and other industries was substantially reduced.

Some large enterprises that had dissolved or divided under the economic deconcentration reemerged after the end of the Occupation. The Mitsubishi Trading Company was revived in 1954, the Mitsui Trading Company in 1959, Mitsubishi Heavy Industries in 1964, and the New Japan Steel Corporation in 1970. The zaibatsu's head offices may have disappeared, but the enterprises were reconcentrated into "enterprise groups" (*keiretsu*), centering on banks, through mutual stockholding and financing. Critics often referred to this as the "revival of the zaibatsu."

The dissolution of the zaibatsu and the abolition of concentration permanently affected the economy. The concentration of production, which had been reduced by the antizaibatsu legislation, was further

5 The basic material on dissolving the zaibatsu can be found in Tokushu kaisha seiri iinkai, ed., *Nihon zaibatsu to sono kaitai* (Tokyo, 1951). The standard work in English is by Eleanor M. Hadley, *Antitrust in Japan* (Princeton, N.J.: Princeton University Press, 1959).

diluted as a result of high growth. The competition among enterprises became livelier. Industrial firms not affiliated with the prewar zaibatsu expanded into large enterprises because of opportunities for new entry and enlargement of scale. Among the large postwar firms are many, such as Toyota, Hitachi, and New Japan Steel, that had no relationship to the prewar zaibatsu. The emergence of Kawasaki Steel and Sumitomo Metals as steel makers, the entry of Honda into the passenger car industry, and the rapid growth of Sony and Matsushita suggest that the Japanese industrial organization, on the whole, continued to be competitive. It can be said that this competitive industrial structure developed as a result of the postwar dissolution of the zaibatsu and the abolition of concentration.

Labor reform. At the core of labor reform was the enactment of three labor laws: the Labor Union Law, modeled on the American Wagner Act and promulgated in December 1945, established the right of workers to organize and bargain collectively, exempted labor union activity from civil law, and defined unfair labor practices. The Labor Relations Adjustment Law, promulgated in September 1946, defined the limits of strike behavior and established procedures for the settlement of labor disputes. The Labor Standards Law of April 1947 legislated improved working conditions, such as the prohibition of forced labor, the establishment of an eight-hour working day, the limitation of female and minor employment, and the provision of compensation for work-related injuries. These three laws, but especially the Labor Union Law, stimulated labor union activity.

The labor union movement grew rapidly in the immediate postwar years. Because of the runaway inflation and the general impoverishment of the population, labor disputes were frequent. In 1948 the rate of unionization of the industrial work force (including workers in transport, construction, mining, and manufacturing) was over 50 percent, and the number of enrollees was 6.677 million. In some of the industrial disputes, the labor unions adopted aggressive tactics such as "production control," whereby the workers actually took over the management and control of production.

A general strike organized by the public labor unions was planned for February 1, 1947, but the Occupation authorities prohibited the strike immediately before it was to begin. The confrontation between Occupation policy and the labor movement became more pronounced in July 1948 when the government, in response to a letter from General Douglas MacArthur, promulgated an ordinance that abolished the right of public employees to strike. For a long period thereafter, a struggle for control of the labor union movement ensued between those who considered political issues as primary and those who considered economic issues as primary. As the union movement consolidated on the basis of "enterprise unions" that incorporated all the workers of a firm into a single union, "the principles of Japanese-style unionism," stressing the primacy of economic issues, predominated. In 1955 so-called spring offensives (*shuntō*) began, thereby routinizing the negotiations for wage hikes.

The Occupation and its policies also had an indirect effect on the economy. First, the defeat ended Japan's attempts to increase its economic advantage through war and military means. On the contrary, under the protection of the American "nuclear umbrella," Japan did not need to spend much on defense, and so capital, human resources, and human energy could flow into more efficient activities. Second, under the American Occupation, the Japanese had sustained contact with a foreign country for the first time, and many more Japanese than ever before were able to observe firsthand the high American standard of living and the efficient organizational methods supporting it. Finally, the Occupation brought a change in Japan's elites. New leaders in politics, business, and the bureaucracy turned their energies toward the restoration of a vigorous economy in the midst of postwar confusion.

Postwar economic policy

The postwar leaders were faced with creating a new framework of economic policy responsive to the conditions created by defeat. In part this meant restoring the economy devastated by war; in part it meant bringing postwar inflation under control; and in part it meant establishing the policy principles to be followed in promoting further economic development.

Like all defeated countries in modern times, postwar Japan was beset by deep inflation. Prices had begun to rise during the war even under wartime price controls, and once the war ended, the inflationary pressures grew. Production stagnated but demand, suppressed during wartime, was ready to ignite. Public bonds and other kinds of financial assets had accumulated during the war, and if converted into currency, they could fuel an explosive inflation. To deal with this situation, the government in February 1946 adopted an emergency policy of restricting bank accounts, levying taxes on property, and controlling prices. But these measures merely arrested inflation temporarily,

TABLE 4.1
Price trends (1934–6 average = 1.00)

	Wholesale price index	Annual rate of increase (%)	Consumer Price Index	Annual rate of increase (%)
1946	16.27	–	50.6	–
1950	246.8	97.3	219.9	44.3
1955	343.0	6.8	297.4	6.2
1960	352.1	0.5	328.0	1.9
1965	359.4	0.4	443.2	6.2
1970	399.9	2.2	577.9	5.5
1973	463.3	5.0	719.5	7.5

Source: Keizai kikakuchō, *Gendai Nihon keizai no tenkai* (Tokyo: Keizai kikakuchō, 1976), pp. 616–18.

and from 1946 to 1947, inflation took off. In 1946, wholesale prices were 16.3 times the 1934–6 levels, and by 1950 they were 246.8 times as high (see Table 4.1).

Restoring industrial production was also a major task. The immediate postwar economy was in a state of collapse. The resumption of production was hindered by the disrupted inflow of raw materials from abroad. Until limited private trade was established in August 1947, foreign trade was controlled by the Occupation authorities, and even after that date, the system of public management of trade remained basically unchanged. On the other hand, there was a positive legacy from the wartime economy, that is, capital stock in the heavy and chemical industries and an abundant supply of workers with experience in modern industrial activity. Because it was not possible to rely on imported raw materials, the production bottleneck could be broken only by using domestic coal resources.

Professor Arisawa Hiromi of Tokyo University proposed the so-called priority production method to stimulate industrial production. His plan envisaged first increasing the production of coal by concentrating materials and capital in the coal-mining industry, then using the greater coal output to produce steel, and finally investing the increased steel output in the further increase of coal production. This method of lifting domestic production by its own bootstraps was the government's central policy in 1947–8. In order to implement the priority production method, the Yoshida cabinet established the Reconstruction Finance Bank (Fukkō kin'yū ginkō), lent a large amount of capital to the coal industry, gave substantial price subsidies to the iron and steel industry, and set priorities for materials to key industries.[6] Consequently, in 1947 the output target for coal, 30 million tons, was just barely achieved.

The priority production method is often regarded as a successful example of Japan's interventionist policy in the heavy and chemical industries and it is seen as leading later in the direction of "industrial policy" (*sangyō seisaku*). It certainly was an important stimulus to the resumption of production. Japan had no other way of bringing about the recovery of its economy than using the heavy and chemical industry base it had acquired by the end of the war. As U.S. Secretary of the Army Kenneth Royall noted in January 1948, "It is clear that Japan can not support itself as a nation of shopkeepers and craftsmen and small artisans any more than it can exist as a purely agricultural nation."[7] But it would be a mistake to overestimate the significance of the priority production method. Japan used its existing plant capacity in its chemical and heavy industries but did not intend to expand its scale. Steel production was just 740,000 tons in 1947, no comparison with the 100 million tons produced in the 1970s. The priority production method was in effect a policy of "forced import substitution" developed during a period when the economy was closed to the outside world and raw material imports were curtailed. When the conditions that created it changed, it was abandoned.

Even this degree of industrial recovery would not have been possible if Japan had not been able to retain its chemical and heavy industry base. The initial postwar reparations policy recommended in the Pauley Report of December 1945 was to remove all equipment from Japan's war industry and to reduce drastically its capacity in such defense-related industries as steel, machine tool production, and merchant shipping. As the international situation changed and American economic policy toward Japan shifted away from punitive measures toward economic rehabilitation, these goals were modified.[8] As Secretary of the Army Royall pointed out in his January 1948 speech, if Japan were to achieve political stability and retain its free government, it had to have a healthy independent economy; and furthermore, the United States could not continue to provide indefinitely hundreds of millions of dollars in aid to Japan.

In response to the need to curtail inflation as well as to promote

6 Noted in Kōsai Yutaka, "Fukkōki," *Nihon no sangyō seisaku*, ed. Komiya Ryūtarō (Tokyo: Tōkyō daigaku shuppankai, 1984), pp. 30–4; Kōsai Yutaka, *Kōdō seichō no jidai*, ed. Komiya Ryūtarō et al. (Tokyo: Nihon hyōronsha, 1981), pp. 44–58.

7 Ōkurashō, ed., *Shōwa zaiseishi* (Tokyo: Tōyō keizai shinpōsha, 1982), vol. 20. p. 185.

8 Ibid., p. 440.

Japan's economic recovery and self-sufficiency, the United States dispatched Joseph M. Dodge, a Detroit banker who had planned currency reforms in occupied Germany, to recommend changes in the Japanese government's economic policies. A believer in classic economic liberalism, Dodge recommended a series of policies that he regarded as necessary to establish economic stability that would enable recovery. The major points of the policy that Dodge set forth in March 1949 were (1) balancing a consolidated national budget in order to reduce inflationary pressures; (2) terminating the activities of the Reconstruction Finance Bank, whose loans were uneconomical; (3) decreasing the scope of government intervention in the economy, especially in the form of subsidies and price controls; (4) establishing an exchange rate of ¥360 to $1.00; and (5) returning to international trade through private channels instead of through government trading agencies. These policies continued in force for the next two and a half years, though with decreasing emphasis as the Korean War promoted growth. In the long run, the so-called Dodge line established the principles of balanced budgets, orthodox finance, stabilized prices, and a fixed exchange rate that constituted one side of government policy during the period of high growth.

MACROECONOMIC PERFORMANCE

The period of rapid economic growth was conditioned by macroeconomic conditions such as labor supply, capital accumulation, price trends, income distribution, and the growth of demand. All of these were interrelated in complex ways.

The increase in the labor force

One of the conditions that enabled Japan's rapid economic growth was a smooth and abundant supply of labor. Japan had been overpopulated before the war, and there was a substantial population increase in the immediate postwar years as demobilized soldiers and repatriated inhabitants of Japan's overseas possessions returned home. According to a special census in 1947, the total population was 78.101 million, a marked increase over the 1940 census population (71.933 million) and the 1944 estimated population (74.433 million) (see Table 4.2). In 1947, however, the country was in a state of economic dislocation, and employment was difficult to find. The number of employed had increased by only 846,000 compared with that of 1940, and the total

TABLE 4.2
Changes in population (in thousands)

	Total population	Employed population	Employed in agriculture	Employed in manufacturing	Employed in wholesale and retailing
1940	71,933	32,482	13,557	6,863	4,097
1947	78,101	33,328	16,622	5,439	2,477
1950	83,200	35,625	16,102	5,689	3,963
1955	89,276	39,621	14,890	6,902	5,472
1960	93,419	43,719	13,127	9,544	6,909
1965	98,275	47,633	10,857	11,507	8,563
1970	103,720	52,110	9,333	13,540	10,059
1975	111,940	53,015	6,699	13,158	11,364

Source: Tōyō keizai shinpōsha, *Shōwa kokusei sōran* (Tokyo: Tōyō keizai shinpōsha, 1980), vol. 1, p. 29.

TABLE 4.3
Changes in the labor force

	Worker population (in thousands)	Labor force as percentage of population	Unemployment rate (%)
1948	3,484	64.6	0.7
1950	3,616	65.5	1.2
1955	4,194	70.8	1.8
1960	4,511	69.2	1.1
1965	4,787	65.7	0.8
1970	5,153	65.4	1.2
1973	5,326	64.7	1.3

Source: Tōyō keizai shinpōsha, *Shōwa kokusei sōran* (Tokyo: Tōyō keizai shinpōsha, 1980), vol. 1, p. 58. Statistics are not continuous, and so accurate comparison is difficult.

employment rate (that is, the number of employed divided by the total population) had declined from 45.2 percent to 42.7 percent. The distribution of employment had also changed radically. Whereas the number of workers in manufacturing had declined by 1.400 million and in service industries by 600,000, the number of workers in agriculture had increased by 3 million. As these figures demonstrate, Japan in the immediate postwar period had a surplus of labor and a dearth of employment.

Between 1948 and 1955, however, the working population increased at the high annual rate of 2.6 percent (see Table 4.3). There were two reasons: first, those born in the first half of the 1930s, when the birthrate was high, had reached working age; second, there was an increase in the labor force as a proportion of the population. Although the number of workers had grown substantially, the rate of fully unemployed had also increased. The fact that there was much discussion of a "dual structure" in the labor market (that is, that wage differentials were related to the scale of enterprise) suggests that even in this period there was latitude in the demand for labor.

The annual growth rate of the labor force decreased to 1.3 percent from the period 1955–1965 to the period 1965–1973. By international standards, this was not low. Even though the postwar baby boom increased the size of the working age population, the rate slowed down because (1) the wartime decrease in the birthrate resulted in a decline in the number of new entrants into the labor force between 1955 and 1960; and (2) from 1960 to 1965 many young people continued their education instead of entering the work force. The continuing slowdown in the expansion of the working population in the late 1960s reflected a decline in the birthrate after the end of the baby boom. Meanwhile, because the economy's growth rate continued to be high, the unemployment rate began to drop in the late 1950s. By the early 1960s, wage differentials based on scale of enterprise had narrowed, and for the first time the number of jobs exceeded the number of new graduates. By 1967 the number of job openings exceeded the number of job seekers in the general labor market. The Japanese economy had reached a state of full employment.

As the labor market moved from a surplus of labor to a shortage of labor, economic growth was sustained by a shift of workers among industrial sectors and the substitution of capital inputs for labor inputs. The number of agricultural workers decreased by 1.7 million between 1945 and 1955, by 4 million between 1955 and 1965, and by 4.2 million between 1965 and 1975. By contrast, the number of manufacturing industry workers increased by 4.6 million between 1965 and 1975 (see Table 4.3).

The qualitative changes in the labor supply were as important as the quantitative changes. In prewar Japan, textile industry workers were the heart of the industrial work force, accounting for one-third of the industrial workers. Most typical were the female workers in the cotton-spinning industry who started working in their late teens after graduating from higher elementary school, to augment the family budget, and who quit their jobs in their twenties, to get married. Their working life was short; changes in the work force were frequent; and wages were low. The workers who played the leading role in industrial development from the wartime expansion of the chemical and heavy industries through the period of postwar growth were skilled male workers in the iron and steel and machine industries. They were lifetime employees; they acquired specific skills through on-the-job training; and they contributed positively to small-group production units within the enterprise. They expected improvements in wages and working conditions through seniority and economic growth. Compulsory education was extended from six to nine years, and the rate of those continuing their education increased so that the intellectual quality of the work force also improved.

Savings and capital accumulation

The Pacific War inflicted enormous material damage on Japan, amounting to one-fourth of the national wealth (see Table 4.4). By the end of the war, the national wealth had declined to its 1935 level. In effect, the war nullified any capital accumulation between 1935 and 1945. If we compare productive activities, however, it is clear that there was still some leeway in the economy. Real GNP fell to only half the prewar level. If we look at industries by sector, we can see that although the rate of capacity in the consumer goods industries was damaged because many factories had been converted to war production, by contrast, the damage rate was relatively low in the heavy and chemical industries. The steel and electric power generation industries even emerged from the war with plant capacity above prewar levels (see Table 4.5).

As we have already seen, the first postwar attempt to stimulate industrial production – the priority production method – tried to combine this abundant capital stock with surplus labor. The bottleneck was the difficulty of obtaining raw material imports. After Japan was allowed access to foreign markets, its economic recovery proceeded rapidly. During the recovery period, investment in plant concentrated on repair and renewal. The marginal capital coefficient (i.e., the amount of investment necessary to increase the GNP by 1 percent) remained low.

By 1955, when the level of economic activity had returned to prewar levels, investment in new facilities became necessary, as there had not been much investment during the recovery period. Japan's capital stock was becoming obsolete, weakening the international competitiveness of Japanese industry. After the Korean War rationalization investment began in a number of industries. By the latter half of the 1950s, Japanese industry was moving toward investment in modern produc-

TABLE 4.4

Wartime damage to national wealth (¥1 million at time of defeat)

	Amount of damage	National wealth before damage	Damage rate (%)	National wealth remaining at end of war	National wealth in 1935	Rate of increase (%)[a]
Buildings	22,220	90,435	24.5	68,215	76,275	Δ10.6
Industrial machinery and equipment	7,994	23,346	34.2	15,352	8,501	80.6
Shipping	7,359	9,125	80.6	1,796	3,111	Δ42.3
Electrical and gas equipment	1,618	14,933	10.8	13,313	8,987	48.1
Railroad and rolling stock	1,523	15,415	9.8	13,892	13,364	4.0
Telegraph, telephone, and water supply	659	4,156	15.8	3,497	3,229	8.2
Producer goods	7,864	32,953	23.8	25,089	23,541	6.6
Household property goods	9,558	46,427	20.5	36,869	39,354	Δ6.6
Other	5,483	16,340	33.5	10,857	10,839	4.5
Total	64,278	253,130	25.3	188,852	186,751	1.1

[a]Delta (Δ) indicates decrease.

Source: Keizai antei honbu, *Taiheiyō sensō ni yoru wagakuni higai sōgō hōkukusho* (Tokyo, 1949); Nakayama Ichirō, ed., *Nihon no kokufu kōzō* (Tokyo: Toyō keizai shinpōsha, 1959).

TABLE 4.5
Productive capacity at time of defeat (¥1 million at time of defeat)

	Peak capacity before 1944	Capacity as of August 15, 1945	Percentage remaining	Capacity at end 1941	Rate of increase (%)
Hydroelectric power (1,000s kw)	6,074	6,233	102.6	5,368	116.1
Ordinary iron and steel materials (1,000s tons)	7,998	8,040	100.5	7,506	107.1
Aluminum (tons per month)	11,100	8,350	75.2	7,240	115.3
Machine tools (tons)	190	120	63.1	110	109.1
Petroleum refining (1,000s kl)	3,739	1,443	38.5	2,359	61.2
Soap (1,000s tons)	278	99	35.9	278	54.5
Cotton and staple fiber spinning (million bolts)	13.8	2.8	20.2	13.8	20.2
Cotton textile weaving (1,000s looms)	393	123	31.4	393	31.4
Bicycles (1,000s)	3,600	720	20.0	2,880	25.0

Source: Keizai antei honbu, *Taiheiyō sensō ni yoru wagakuni higai sōgō hōkukusho* (Tokyo, 1949); Nakayama Ichirō, ed., *Nihon no kokufu kōzō* (Tokyo: Tōyō keizai shinpōsha, 1959).

tive facilities. New technologies were introduced, and the face of Japanese industry changed. This was known as the process whereby "investment induced investment" (*tōshi ga tōshi o yobu*). During the latter half of the 1960s, in response to labor shortages, investment in labor-saving technology began, and in the 1970s, investment in antipollution facilities started.

The rate of increase in capital stock was 1 percent to 2 percent higher than the growth rate of the economy as a whole. The reason was that the expansion of plant investment was comparatively low from 1945 to 1955 but rose rapidly after 1955. This high rate of capital formation was financed not from foreign capital but from the increase in domestic savings, particularly individual savings.

The consumption expenditures of the average urban worker household in 1946–7 amounted to more than 100 percent of his or her income. By 1955 that had dropped to 90.8 percent, a level similar to that of the prewar period (the 1934–6 average was 88.3 percent). As economic growth advanced, the propensity to consume continued to decline, and the saving rate increased to twice the prewar rate. After 1955 the Japanese economy was characterized by high saving and high investment.

There are various hypotheses explaining the high rate of household saving. Some argue that because income grew more rapidly than expected, consumption did not keep pace, with the result that savings increased; others point to the population's relative youth; and still others say that because housing and social welfare facilities lagged behind the rest of the economy, people accumulated savings for the future. But the period of high growth was also one in which more people considered themselves as reaching middle-class status, and the high saving rate may be connected to this change in social consciousness.

Personal savings were not invested directly in business but were deposited in bank accounts. In turn, business enterprises financed their investment by borrowing from the banks. Under this system of "indirect finance," there emerged the low rate of self-capitalization among businesses that is so characteristic of the period of rapid growth.

The balance-of-payments ceiling

The most direct limitation on economic growth between 1945 and 1973 was the international balance of payments. From the end of the war until 1955, it was feared that Japan would not be able even to finance basic imports of food and raw materials. Without aid from the United States or the special procurements program during the Korean War, when the American military bought supplies and repaired equipment in Japan, it would not have been possible to achieve balance-of-payments equilibrium during this period (see Table 4.6).

After 1955 the balance-of-payments current account approached equilibrium. However, Japan had adopted a policy of vigorous domestic growth without dependence on foreign capital. Its foreign currency reserves were kept as low as possible, and any reserves that could be spared were used for the growth-oriented expansion of income and imports. At the same time the government also pursued a policy of maintaining the foreign exchange rate at ¥360 to $1.00, set in 1949. As a result, whenever there was a deficit in the balance-of-payments current account, the government had no choice but to decrease the tempo of economic expansion and to reduce imports in order to bring the international balance of payments back into equilibrium. When there were balance-of-payments deficits in 1954, 1957, 1961, and

TABLE 4.6
International balance of payments (in thousands of $)

	Current transactions	Trade balance	Nontrade balance	Transfer balance	Long-term capital balance	Total balance	Foreign exchange reserve
1946–50	726	−958	−340	2,005[a]	−79	726	–
1951–55	525	−1,964	2,211[b]	277	−110	464	738
1956–60	114	466	−103	−248	1	139	1,824
1961–65	−1,358	1,955	−3,038	−275	321	−1,037	2,107
1966–70	6,201	13,626	−6,548	−877	−3,605	4,525	4,399
1971–73	12,285	20,466	−7,131	−1,030	−15,319	2,344	12,246

[a]Including aid. [b]Including special demand.
Source: Tōyō keizai shinpōsha, *Shōwa kokusei sōran* (Tokyo: Tōyō keizai shinpōsha, 1980), vol. 2, pp. 652, 660.

1963, the government adopted a tight money policy, helping the balance of payments to recover relatively quickly.

As the international competitiveness of Japanese industries improved between 1955 and 1965, the balance of the current account came into equilibrium. After 1965, a surplus in the current account grew gradually, and Japan built up its foreign currency reserves. The reason for this was that the price of Japanese export goods remained comparatively stable while inflation was spreading from the United States, then engaged in the Vietnam War, to other advanced industrial nations. This made Japanese products relatively cheap in the world market. In 1970, with a surplus in the current account, the Bank of Japan adopted a defensive tight money policy, and the result was a dramatic increase in Japan's balance-of-payments surplus. In order to cope with this surplus, the yen was revalued in 1971, and in 1973 it was moved to a floating rate.

Price trends

Even after the Dodge stabilization plan had braked the postwar runaway rise in prices, Japan continued to have to contend with inflation. When the Korean War broke out, inflationary trends resumed in 1951 and halted only in 1954 with the adoption of a tight money policy. The immediate postwar inflation had been led by a rise in consumer prices, but the Korean War's inflation was led by an increase in the price of producer goods. As a result of this inflation, the foreign exchange rate, which had been set low in 1949 at the time of the Dodge stabilization, became relatively high. The international balance of payments went out of equilibrium, and the international competitiveness of Japanese industry weakened. In order to deal with these problems within the framework of a fixed exchange rate, Japan thought it necessary to curtail costs in its heavy and chemical industries, and many industries began to invest in rationalizing and modernizing their facilities.

Between 1955 and 1960, prices were relatively stable, but after 1960, a new pattern of inflation appeared – wholesale prices remained stable but consumer prices rose. This pattern occurred as the result of the following mechanism:[9] First, under the system of fixed exchange rates, the economy was managed in such a way that if there were no worldwide inflation, export and wholesale prices would remain stable. Second, even though the wage gap between large and small enterprises was decreasing, owing to the shift from labor oversupply to labor shortage, there was still a gap between them in terms of productivity increases. Productivity rose in the large mass-production enterprises, but labor costs – and hence production costs – rose in labor-intensive small and medium manufacturing and service enterprises. Third, a rise in consumer prices was tolerated as long as it had no impact on wage increases, and hence on the price of export goods.

In other words, although prices were stable in a sector in which the increase in productivity rate was high, prices and costs rose in those in which productivity was low. Increases in consumer prices were usually held down by low wages in sectors in which labor productivity was low, but when full employment eliminated those workers willing to work for low wages, "productivity gap" inflation of the kind described emerged.

In the late 1960s there was a worldwide trend toward inflation. Under these circumstances, as long as a fixed exchange rate prevailed and an attempt was made to avoid an increase in balance-of-payments surpluses, the only way to accelerate the expansion of domestic demand was through fiscal means. In 1969 a tight money policy was adopted to avoid a rise in prices. As we have seen, this only expanded the surplus in the international balance of payments. Consequently, in the early 1970s the government tried to increase the money supply and to expand fiscal expenditures. As a result of these measures, as well as foreign inflation, by the fall of 1973 the wholesale price level in Japan had risen 20 percent

9 The basic work on this subject is by Takasuka Yoshihiro, *Gendai Nihon no bukka mondai*, rev. ed. (Tokyo: Shinhyōron, 1975).

TABLE 4.7
Distribution of national income (as a percentage of national income)

	Employees' income (%)	Self-employed income (%)	Individual property income (%)	Corporation income (%)	Ratio of employer income per capita to employee income per capita (%)
1935	38.0	31.1	23.4	8.7	–
1946	30.7	65.4	3.6	1.1	
1950	41.8	45.6	3.1	9.9	59.4
1955	49.6	37.1	6.8	7.9	57.6
1960	50.2	26.5	9.8	14.3	60.5
1965	56.0	23.4	11.6	10.6	64.8
1970	54.3	20.0	11.7	15.8	68.5

Source: Tōyō keizai shinpōsha, *Shōwa kokusei sōran* (Tokyo: Tōyō keizai shinpōsha, 1980), vol. 1, p. 91. The number of self-employed persons, family employees, and self-employed income per person versus employee income per person is based on Keizai kikakuchō, *Gendai Nihon keizai no tenkai* (Tokyo: Keizai kikakuchō, 1976), p. 599.

higher than it had been a year before. At this point the Organization of Petroleum Exporting Countries (OPEC) raised its prices, plunging Japan into a surge of hyperinflation, or "crazy prices" (*kyōran bukka*). The policy of maintaining a fixed exchange rate helped prevent the development of inflation until the middle 1960s, but it had the opposite effect in the 1970s when there was worldwide inflation and Japanese industry had grown more competitive.

Income distribution

In regard to the distribution of national income (see Table 4.7) immediately after World War II, the income going to individual business owners expanded abnormally, but the shares of national income going to employee income, property income, and corporation income substantially declined. This was because modern industrial production was paralyzed, and many people had become farmers or merchants in order to survive economically. As the postwar economy recovered, the shares of national income going to employee income and corporate income were rapidly restored, but the share of income from property remained low. The reason that property income stayed low was that income from tenant rents had virtually disappeared owing to land reform, and interest, land prices, and housing rents were controlled by the government to check inflation.

In the period of rapid economic growth, employee and corporate income shares steadily increased, and the share of individual business owners dropped below even prewar levels. The increase in corporate income reflected increases in business profit due to high investment and high economic growth. Changes in the occupational structure accounted for the greater income share of employees, who were growing in number, and the decrease in the share for individual business owners, who, along with family employees, were declining in number. But the per capita income of employees, as compared with the per capita income of individual business owners or family employees, shows the gap between them as narrowing.

The distribution of individual income moved toward greater equality. The postwar reforms – land reform, zaibatsu dissolution, and labor reform – all worked toward equality in income distribution. Postwar inflation and impoverishment, together with the 1946 levy of property tax, promoted an "equality of poverty." As the economic recovery progressed, income distribution showed signs of becoming less equal, but by about 1960, with the reduction of wage differentials accompanying full employment, the trend toward equalization of income resumed, especially with respect to wages. During the period of rapid growth, Japan, among all the advanced industrial nations, became the country with the most equal income distribution.[10]

Equality of income distribution was a precondition for the spread of middle-class consciousness among the population. By the 1960s nearly 90 percent of the Japanese people felt that they enjoyed a middle-class standard of living (see Table 4.8). This middle-class consciousness spurred the rapid diffusion of durable consumer goods, a rising rate of children entering universities, a strong desire for home ownership, and a high savings rate, all of which stimulated economic growth. The development of mass-production industries supplying materials needed to make consumer durables increased the demand for labor, accelerated the achievement of full employment, facilitated the movement of the labor force, and stimulated the more equal distribution of income. In turn, these fostered a Japanese-style mass-consumption market economy in which an expanding demand for consumer durables coexisted with a high savings rate. This dynamic logic of industrial society sustained the high growth rate.

10 M. Sawyer, *Income Distribution in OECD Countries* (Paris: OECD, 1976). Tachibanaki Yoshiaki, "Shūnyū bunpai to shotoku bunpu no fubyōdō," *Kikan gendai keizai*, no. 28 (1977): 160–75. Using Sawyer's work, Tachibanaki calculated the Gini coefficient for the distribution of gross (pretax) income as follows: Japan 0.335, Sweden 0.356, West Germany 0.396, American 0.404, and OECD average 0.366.

TABLE 4.8
Increase in middle-class consciousness

	1958 (%)	1964 (%)	*1967* (%)
Upper	0	1	1
Upper middle	3	1	8
Middle	37	50	51
Lower middle	32	31	28
(Subtotal)	(72)	(87)	(87)
Lower	17	9	8
Not clear	11	3	4
Total	100	100	100

Source: Keizai kikakuchō, *Gendai Nihon keizai no tenkai* (Tokyo: Keizai kikakuchō, 1976), p. 207.

TABLE 4.9
Increases in demand items (annual percentage rate)

	1946–50 (%)	1950–55 (%)	1955–60 (%)	1960–65 (%)	1965–70 (%)	1970–75 (%)
Final private consumption	10.2	9.9	7.8	9.0	9.7	6.2
Private housing	{ 1.9	{ 10.2	14.4	17.4	14.0	5.3
Private enterprise plant facilities			22.2	10.8	22.2	1.1
Final government consumption	13.4	2.4	2.6	7.1	5.1	5.6
Public capital formation	Δ 9.2	23.3	12.2	16.2	10.8	6.8
Exports	99.5	13.9	13.0	14.7	15.4	11.8
Imports	25.1	18.1	16.9	13.2	17.1	6.7
Gross national expenditure	9.4	8.9	8.5	10.0	12.3	5.0

Source: Kokumin shotoku tōkei: 1946–55: Keizai kikakuchō, *Gendai Nihon keizai no tenkai* (Tokyo: Keizai kikakuchō, 1976), pp. 578–9. 1955–65, 1965–75: Tōyō keizai shinpōsha, *Shōwa kokusei sōran* (Tokyo: Tōyō keizai shinpōsha, 1980), vol. 1, pp. 99–100. Figures based on old SNA.

The growth of demand

The postwar Japanese economy maintained a rapid growth within the limits imposed by its balance of payments and without relying on foreign capital. Substantial savings, an abundant supply of labor, domestic investment, and consumption demand made this possible. If we look at the GNP from 1946 to 1955 as classified by demand items, the increase in individual consumption is remarkable. Since 1955 the expansion of investment in public facilities has also been striking, and until 1970 exports showed a tendency to rise as well (see Table 4.9).

TABLE 4.10
Household expenses of urban workers

	Engels coefficient	Average propensity to consume (%)
1935	36.4	88.4
1946	66.4	125.9
1950	57.4	98.1
1955	44.5	90.8
1960	38.8	85.1
1965	36.3	83.2
1970	32.4	80.1
1973	30.4	77.8

Source: Tōyō keizai shinpōsha, *Shōwa kokusei sōran* (Tokyo: Tōyō keizai shinpōsha, 1980), vol. 2, p. 358.

The reason for the expansion of consumer demand in the postwar reconstruction was that during the war, Japan's living standards had dropped dramatically, almost to subsistence levels. This stimulated the pressure toward recovery. Once recovery was accomplished, investment in the modernization of plant became more active, and the expansion of consumption was sustained by the diffusion of consumer durables. The process by which mass production developed in Japan was also the process by which it became a mass-consumer society.

In response to industrial development, people changed both their jobs and their residences. From 1955 to 1970 the number of employees increased 15.22 million, from 18.17 to 33.39 million; the cities' population increased from 50 to 75 million, and their percentage of the total population increased from 56.3 to 72.1 percent. The shift toward employment (excluding self-employment) and urbanization went hand in hand.

Consumption levels also doubled during this period. If we look at the consumption content of an urban worker's household budget, we can see that the Engels coefficient dropped from 44.5 percent in 1955 to 32.4 percent in 1970 (see Table 4.10). By contrast, the amount spent on acquiring appliances increased 8.5 times, and cultural and entertainment expenses rose 5.1 times.

In 1957, 7.8 percent of nonagricultural households owned black-and-white television sets, but by 1965 the rate had increased to 95 percent. During the same period, the number of households owning electric or gas refrigerators changed from 2.8 to 68.7 percent, and that for washing machines from 20.1 to 78.1 percent (see Table 4.11).

TABLE 4.11
Diffusion of consumer durable goods (percentage of nonfarming households)

	1957 (%)	1960 (%)	1965 (%)	1970 (%)	1975 (%)
Black-and-white television sets	7.8	44.7	95.0	90.1	49.7
Color television sets	–	–	–	30.4	90.9
Sewing machines	61.9	69.5	83.9	84.5	84.8
Stereo sets	4.0	–	20.1	36.6	55.6
Tape recorders	–	–	20.2	35.3	54.9
Cameras	35.7	45.8	64.8	72.1	82.4
Cars	–	–	10.5[a]	22.6	37.4
Electric or gas refrigerators	2.8	10.1	68.7	92.5	97.3
Washing machines	20.2	40.6	78.1	92.1	97.7
Vacuum cleaners	–	7.7	48.6	75.4	93.7
Air conditioners	–	–	2.6	8.4	21.5

[a]Including light vans.
Source: Tōyō keizai shinpōsha, *Shōwa kokusei sōran* (Tokyo: Tōyō keizai shinpōsha, 1980), vol. 2, pp. 603–4.

The ownership of durable consumer goods continued to rise in the latter half of the 1960s, though consumer preferences shifted toward expensive goods. In 1967, only 2.2 percent of nonagricultural households owned color televisions, but by 1975, 90.9 percent did. The ownership of automobiles also increased from 11 percent in 1967 to 37.4 percent in 1975 and that of air conditioners from 2.6 to 21.5 percent. These durable consumer goods, called by such names as the "three household sacred items" or "three C's," were proof of Japan's emergence as a mass-consumption society. Because most of the Japanese people considered themselves as belonging to the middle class, it was easy for their life-styles to become homogeneous. This encouraged the rapid diffusion of consumer durables, as people tried to keep up with their neighbors.

The major increase in employment that accompanied Japan's industrial development reduced the number of lower-income employees and equalized income distribution. If wages in companies with more than 500 workers are given an index of 100, wages of enterprises with 30 to 99 workers were at an index of only 58.8 in 1955, but by 1965 this had risen to 71. Within enterprises, wage differentials by job category were comparatively low.

As noted earlier, by 1970, among all the advanced countries, Japan enjoyed the most equitable distribution of individual income. Japan's rate of home ownership was lower than in the United States but higher than that in Western Europe. The rate of students continuing their education beyond the compulsory level increased from 47.4 percent in 1955 to 79.4 percent in 1970, and the rate of students entering colleges and universities increased from 17.2 to 24.2 percent (these rates increased by 1975, to 91.9 percent and to 38.4 percent).

THE CHANGING INDUSTRIAL STRUCTURE

The most significant development in the Japanese economy from the end of the war until 1973 was its emergence as one of the world's most advanced industrial powers.

Industrial rationalization plans

Beginning in the early 1950s the government coordinated a series of rationalization plans in Japan's key industries. Whereas the major goal of "priority production" had been to resuscitate the coal and steel industries, the main aim of industrial rationalization was to reduce the costs in these industries. The Korean War stimulated demand in Japan and vitalized Japanese industry, but prices rose sharply, making Japanese goods expensive. The increase in coal and steel prices reduced the international competitiveness of machinery and other industries. Rationalization plans aimed at modernizing plant facilities were undertaken in order to bring down these production costs.

During the first steel rationalization plan, it was anticipated that ¥63 billion would be invested between 1951 and 1954. In fact, actual investment reached ¥120 billion by 1953. Old-style pull-over plants were replaced by strip mills which made the rolling process more efficient. The government launched the development of a major industrial park in Chiba Prefecture on land reclaimed from Tokyo Bay. In 1953 the Kawasaki Steel Company, a new entrant into the industry, opened in the park the most modern integrated steel facility in the world. Located on the waterfront, the production line was a continuous process from the delivery of raw materials to the blast furnace to steel production to rolling. Other, better-established steel-producing firms soon followed suit with the construction of similar facilities. The first rationalization plan substantially modernized the Japanese steel industry.

By contrast, in the coal industry, which realized great profits during the Korean War when excess demand produced coal shortages everywhere, plans to rationalize production through investment in the introduction of advanced mining technology from West Germany and the digging of deep shafts never materialized. Because the quality of Japan's coal deposits was poor, it was not possible to achieve the cost reductions needed to make the industry competitive internationally. In addition, when a lengthy coal strike occurred in the fall of 1952, key industries reduced their reliance on coal as an energy source and shifted to oil and electric power.

Apart from attempts at rationalization in the steel and coal industries, rationalization through technological innovation took place in other industries in the early 1950s. In the electric power industry, hydroelectric power was developed on a large scale, and thermal model plants were imported; in the shipbuilding industry, new methods for the construction of ocean ships were introduced; in the ammonium sulfate industry, production shifted from electrolysis to the gas method; and efforts were made to nurture the synthetic fiber industry.

Just as the priority production method had attempted to restore postwar production by using existing prewar and wartime plants in isolation from the world market, the industrial rationalization plans of the early 1950s tried to lower costs by renewing and modernizing Japan's production facilities and by improving its international competitiveness under a fixed exchange rate. These plans assumed an open world market. Investment in rationalization also helped reduce production costs.

Whereas priority production had been carried out by means of direct government controls, industrial rationalization plans were generally implemented as independent plans carried out by private business enterprises. To be sure, the government intervened in the process, making it a kind of joint venture between the government and key private enterprises, but the government did not use price controls (price subsidies) or commodity controls to achieve its ends. Instead, it relied on other methods. In March 1951 the Japan Development Bank (Nihon kaihatsu ginkō) was established to promote capital accumulation and rapid economic growth. In March 1952 the Enterprises Rationalization Act was passed and the Special Tax Measures Law was amended to assist developing industries. The government had an arsenal of new methods to promote the development of industries specially targeted for rationalization – special tax treatment, subsidy of interest on shipbuilding, loan of government funds through institutions like the development bank, the establishment of the Electrical Power Source Development Company (Dengen kaihatsu KK), the use of import quotas, controls over the import of foreign capital, and "administrative guidance." The popular notion in the 1970s that there was a so-called Japan Incorporated, a close alliance between government and business, with the government directly guiding the activities of private firms, rested largely on impressions of how the Japanese economy operated during this period. But it would be a mistake to regard Japan as a "planned economy" or the government as an "economic general staff" even in this period. Government and business did share information with each other and made their views known to each other, but the final investment decisions were in the hands of the business firms.

The development of technical innovation

Between 1955 and 1965, investment for modernization was in full swing. In the steel industry, the second rationalization plan followed the success of the first rationalization plan. Most noticeably it provided for substantial construction of shoreline mills for pig iron production and the widespread diffusion of strip mills and pure oxygen converters. The first rationalization plan, devised when the industry's base was weak, attempted to reduce production costs and relied on government loans. By contrast, the second plan modernized facilities in order to increase capacity in anticipation of increased demand. Because the industry also expected high profits, it relied less on government funding. Whereas the first rationalization plan required an investment of ¥120 billion, the second plan used an investment of over ¥500 billion. When the second rationalization plan ended, Japan's iron and steel output exceeded that of France, Germany, and Britain, rising to second place behind the United States. In number of hot strip mills, Japan was second only to the United States, and it achieved first place in the efficiency of its pure oxygen converters and in the ratio of coke used to steel ingots produced. In other words, both quantitatively and qualitatively, Japan had become a first-class producer of iron and steel.

Under both priority production and the industrial rationalization plans of the early 1950s, coal had ranked in importance with the iron and steel industry as a key industry. The coal industry, however, failed to overcome its natural disadvantages through rationalization investment. Moreover, labor–management relations within the industry deteriorated, and the supply of coal became less stable. For that reason, energy demand continued to shift from coal to electric power and oil. Japanese industry could develop even faster if it shifted from a high-cost domestic resource to a cheaper foreign resource, namely, petroleum. At this time, new oil fields were being discovered in the Middle East, and the price of crude oil was dropping dramatically. Further savings in energy costs were achieved through the use of high-speed supertankers, which reduced the cost of transporting oil to Japan.

The electric power industry was also changing. Before 1955 the industry had relied primarily on hydroelectric power and only secondarily on thermal power, but then the relationship was reversed, with the primary reliance shifting to thermal power generation. In 1955 when the construction of thermal plants using heavy oil began, hydroelectric power plants produced 7.48 million kilowatts, and the thermal plants produced only 4.1 million, but by 1961, hydroelectric power and thermal power accounted for approximately the same amount, 9.444 million kilowatts and 9.75 million kilowatts, respectively. The scale of thermal plant capacity increased from 58,000 in 1958 to 2.2 million in 1960 and 3.75 million in 1965. The reasons that hydroelectric power declined as the principal source of electrical power were, first, that the number of sites suitable for the construction of hydroelectric plants decreased and, second, that the importation of energy resources was a way of overcoming the limitation of domestic resources.

The shift to new sources of energy also affected the chemical industry. A flourishing carbide industry, relying on hydroelectric power, had supplied carbide for the domestic production of vinyl chloride, acetate, and other chemical products. But in the late 1950s a new petrochemical industry producing polyethylene and polystyrene developed, relying on imported naphtha and the introduction of new naphtha-cracking technology.

Parallel to the technical innovation in producer goods industries, there was also a technical innovation in the production of consumer durables. Mass-production methods were introduced to meet the domestic demand for automobiles and home electric appliances such as television sets and refrigerators, as well as the export of sewing machines, transistor radios, and cameras.[11]

Around 1950 there had been debates about whether Japan should rely for its supply of automobiles on imports or whether it should try to develop a domestic automobile industry under protection. The outcome was the goal of developing a protected domestic automobile industry, and many automobile companies tried to acquire technology through technical tie-ups with foreign automobile manufacturers. In 1955, Toyota, the top producer of automobiles, had a five-year mod-

11 The 1960 *Nenji keizai hōkoku* analyzed the period as "a period in which the machine tools industry led the development of industry." Keizai kikakuchō chōsakyoku, *Shiryō: keizai hakusho 25 nen* (Tokyo: Keizai kikakuchō, 1972), pp. 214–15.

ernization plan with a monthly production target of only three thousand vehicles. But the modernization of its production facilities accelerated, and the scale of production greatly expanded. By around 1960, when Toyota built a compact car plant at Motomachi and Nissan built one at Oppama, each new plant projected a monthly production of ten thousand vehicles. New mass-production equipment such as transfer machines and automatic braces were also introduced.

The mass production of motor vehicles had a major impact on related industries. First, in the iron and steel industry, thin-plate production progressed rapidly. Investment in plant modernization, such as the installation of strip mills, supported the mass production of automobiles. Second, a specialty steel and machine tool industry, whose production volume earlier had been limited by a small market, was presented with new opportunities as the mass production of automobiles grew. The value of the output of machine tools in 1955 was ¥5 billion, but by 1962 it had reached ¥100 billion, twenty times as much, and its international competitiveness was also strong. In 1956 Toyota and related industries began using the now-famous *kanban* method (also known as the "zero inventory method" or "just-in-time production"). Subcontracting firms bought secondhand machinery from parent companies, enabling them to begin mechanization and rationalization, leading to an expansion of the machine tool market.

In the electrical machine industry, conditions were about the same. The improvement in the quality of steel silicon plate provided the basis for mass production. Small- to medium-sized enterprises related to radio and television production also were rationalized and developed into an export industry.

The modernization of Japanese industry relied on the introduction of foreign technology. During the war, Japan had been technologically isolated from the rest of the world, and by the war's end a major technological gap existed. But this gap was soon closed by the massive introduction of technologies from foreign companies. In the early 1950s, technologies were introduced through technical tie-ups with foreign firms in the automobile industry (Nissan and Austin, Isuzu and Hillman), television production (NEC and RCA), and nylon (Tōyō Rayon and DuPont). From the late 1950s and during the 1960s, both the number of technologies imported and the payments for them increased, further improving Japan's technological standards (see Table 4.12).

Because Japan did not encourage direct foreign investment after

TABLE 4.12
Technological imports

	Items imported	Price paid (U.S. dollars)
1949–55	1,141	69 million
1956–60	1,773	281 million
1961–65	4,494	684 million
1966–70	7,589	1.536 billion
1971–75	10,789	3.205 billion

Source: Tōyō keizai shinpōsha, *Shōwa kokusei sōran* (Tokyo: Tōyō keizai shinpōsha, 1980), vol. 1, p. 662.

World War II, this introduction of foreign technology was achieved through technical cooperation without capital tie-ups. The "commercialization of technology" was the only possible way to achieve technological innovation while avoiding foreign control of Japanese business. Many foreign firms were willing to sell their technology because the Japanese market was regarded as too small to be worth developing. The cost of acquiring foreign technology was often quite expensive for individual Japanese firms, but technical innovations enormously increased the productivity of Japanese industry. The Japanese also tried to improve upon the technology that they imported. Often such improvements were made as a new technology was applied to the production process, thereby enhancing Japan's international competitiveness.

The government expanded its policies of nurturing new growth industries such as petrochemicals and machine tools as well as such established basic industries as steel, coal, and shipbuilding. In 1955 the government adopted the Petrochemical Industry Development Policy and in 1956 passed the Temporary Measure for the Promotion of the Machine Tool Industry. The heart of industrial development policy lay in special tax measures and loans from the Japan Development Bank, but other measures were used as well, such as foreign currency allotments, the licensing of foreign capital imports through technical tie-ups, and other forms of administrative guidance.[12] The role played by active competition among enterprises and an energetic entrepreneurial spirit in economic growth was large, and so the effect of government protection and development policies should not be overestimated. Nevertheless, the 1956 law promoting the machine tool industry, for exam-

12 Kōsai, "Fukkōki," pp. 38–42.

ple, was successful in promoting or rationalizing and modernizing the small- and medium-sized machinery producers.

Liberalization of trade, foreign exchange, and capital

Until the 1960s, foreign trade, foreign exchange, and capital movements were under government control, as they had been during wartime. Major resources were scarce, and it was felt that a free market would not achieve an optimal allocation of resources for economic reconstruction. But once the economy had recovered from its postwar dislocation and its involvement in the world market had increased, there was strong foreign pressure on the Japanese, especially from the United States, to liberalize these controls. Foreigners saw import liberalization as a means of increasing their imports, and some Japanese argued that import competition would improve the efficiency of Japanese enterprises.

In June 1960 the government adopted the outline Plan for the Liberalization of Foreign Trade and Foreign Exchange which aimed at raising the liberalization rates from 40 percent (as of March 1960) to 80 percent within three years. The plan was subsequently revised, and by October 1962 the liberalization rate had reached 88 percent (see Table 4.13). In 1963 Japan became an International Monetary Fund (IMF) Article 8 country, which meant that it could no longer place restrictions on foreign exchange, and in 1964 it joined the Organization for Economic Cooperation and Development (OECD), an international consultative body founded in 1961 to promote the liberalization of trade and capital movements. By the beginning of the 1970s, in order to deal with growing surpluses in the international balance of payments, Japan renewed its efforts to liberalize trade.

Japan's participation in the OECD brought the liberalization of capital. In June 1967 the government adopted the Fundamental Plan for Capital Liberalization. The first stage of liberalization took place in July 1967, permitting a 50 percent liberalization in 33 industries and 100 percent in 17 others (including shipbuilding and steel). The second liberalization stage took place in February 1969, when 50 percent liberalization was permitted in 160 categories and 100 percent in 44. The third stage took place in September 1970, and a fourth in August 1971. In April 1971 capital liberalization was applied to the automobile industry, and in 1974, 50 percent liberalization was permitted in electronic computers and 100 percent in real estate.

Japan's adoption of liberalization measures was regarded by foreign

TABLE 4.13
Rate of liberalization (percentages)

1959 (end of Aug.)	26	1961 (end of Dec.)	70
1959 (end of Sept.)	33	1962 (end of Apr.)	33
1960 (end of Apr.)	40	1962 (end of Oct.)	88
1960 (end of July)	42	1963 (end of Apr.)	89
1960 (end of Oct.)	44	1963 (end of Aug.)	92
1961 (end of Apr.)	62	1965 (end of Feb.)	94
1961 (end of July)	65	1966 (end of Oct.)	95
1961 (end of Oct.)	68	1967 (end of Apr.)	97

Note: Months are indicated in which there were changes in the liberalization rate.
Source: Keizai kikakuchō, *Gendai Nihon keizai no tenkai* (Tokyo: Keizai kikakuchō, 1976), p. 146.

critics as being tardy in comparison with liberalization among the Western European countries. In Japan many took the view that the international competitiveness of Japanese industries and enterprises was weak and that liberalization would have an adverse impact on them. Controls on imports and capital were needed to protect infant industries or noncompetitive industries and also employment in the industries affected. When it became clear that liberalization was inevitable, many argued that Japanese industry had to be made more competitive in order to cope with its effects.

The announcement of plans to liberalize foreign trade and foreign exchange in 1960 stimulated investment in new plant facilities, as did the announcement of Prime Minister Ikeda Hayato's Income Doubling Plan, which proposed doubling the national income in the next ten years. The result was an acceleration of the modernization investment boom of the early 1960s. By contrast, the capital liberalization policies of the late 1960s provided one of the main reasons for a rise in the number of company mergers and amalgamations. The most important of these were the amalgamation of Mitsubishi Heavy Industries in 1964, the amalgamation of the Nissan and Prince automobile companies in 1965, the amalgamation of the Nisshō and Iwai trading companies in 1968, the merger of the Yawata and Fuji steel companies in 1970, and the merger of the Daiichi and Nihon Kangyō banks in 1971. Although these mergers may not have promoted modernization in the same way that plant investment did, they did not necessarily harm Japan's international competitive position.

Liberalization, as it turned out, did not hinder high economic growth but, on the contrary, was one of the main factors stimulating and accelerating it. As a result of liberalization, the Japanese economy

TABLE 4.14
Production and exports, classified by heavy and light industries (in ¥1 billion)

	Production	Exports
1951		
Heavy industries	2,570	199
Light industries	2,293	274
1955		
Heavy industries	4,053	330
Light industries	2,956	360
1960		
Heavy industries	11,786	741
Light industries	4,905	572
1965		
Heavy industries	21,624	2,029
Light industries	8,757	756
1970		
Heavy industries	55,772	5,180
Light industries	17,718	1,182
1975		
Heavy industries	98,543	14,059
Light industries	29,372	1,549

Source: Uno Kimio, Input–Output Table in Japan 1951–80, Tsukuba University Department of Social Engineering–Multiple Statistic Data Bank Report no. 14 R2 (November 1983). Industrial numbers: Heavy industry (11 to 22); light industry (4 to 10, 23).

also became more closely linked with the world economy. At the same time, the elimination of controls on foreign exchange, foreign trade, and capital movements reduced the intervention of government in domestic industry and promoted the market economy in Japan.

The expansion of exports

In the mid-1960s many people thought that the period of high growth was coming to an end. The economy was heading toward a recession. There was a wave of large-scale bankruptcies, the most dramatic being the management crisis of the Yamaichi Securities Company, and the Bank of Japan made special loans in order to avoid a financial crisis. But despite this, the economy continued to grow even faster than before, sustained not only by investment in industrial plant and growing consumer demand but also by exports.

Traditionally, textiles had been Japan's principal export industry, whereas its chemical and heavy industries depended on domestic demand. According to Table 4.14, production in heavy industry (met-

TABLE 4.15
Major export items

	1930 ¥1,000	1950 ¥100 million	1960 ¥100 million	1970 ¥100 million	1975 ¥100 million
Synthetic textiles	–	–	116	2,252	3,863
Organic pharmaceuticals		3	45	1,436	3,653
Plastics	–	6	115	1,536	2,958
Iron and steel	8,579	260	1,397	10,237	30,165
Metal products	22,428	93	532	2,569	5,346
Office machines	–	0.4	6	1,186	2,307
Metal-processing machinery	–	5	28	417	1,342
Textile machinery[a]	3,852	68	371	1,172	2,323
Television sets[b]	–		10	1,382	2,326
Radios[b]	–	0.3	521	2,502	3,933
Tape recorders	–	–	34	1,623	1,879
Automobiles[b]	–	2	281	4,815	18,392
Motorbikes[b]	–	0.3[c]	29	1,381	3,430
Ships	5,452	94	1,037	5,075	17,803
Precision instruments	2,727	28	346	2,261	5,420
Watches[d]	1,463	4	13	466	1,360

[a]Including sewing machines. [b]Except parts.
[c]Including three-wheel motor vehicles.
[d]Table clocks and wall clocks.
Source: Ōkurashō, *Nihon bōeki geppyō* (Tokyo: Nihon kanzei kyokai, 1966–76) and *Gaikoku bōeki geppyō* (Tokyo: 1928–30). Sōrifu tōkeikyoku, *Nihon tōkei nenkan* (Tokyo: Mainichi shinbunsha, 1950 – 60).

als, chemicals, machinery, etc.) had overtaken production in light industry (textiles, etc.) by 1955, but light industry exported not only more of its production but also a higher proportion of its production. This reflected the traditional pattern. But after 1960, even though light industry still exported a high percentage of its production, heavy industry exported even more. By 1965 exports as a percentage of total production was the same; by 1965 heavy industry exported a higher proportion of its production than did light industry; and by 1975 heavy industry had far outdistanced light industry. Although heavy industry's dependence on foreign markets increased, light industry withdrew from the export market and relied primarily on domestic demand.

The extraordinary expansion of passenger automobile exports after 1965 was a typical example of this shift. In 1971, Japan exported 1.78 million automobiles, or 63.7 percent more than in the previous year. The export of television sets, tape recorders, and other electronic goods also became more important (see Table 4.15). According to business surveys at the time, many firms entered the 1970s intending

TABLE 4.16
Major import items

	1930 ¥1,000	1950 ¥100 million	1960 ¥100 million	1970 ¥100 million	1975 ¥100 million
Meat[a]	8,871	0.5	51	523	1,962
Seafood	19,023	1.6	15	942	3,554
Wheat	41,509	530	637	1,146	3,315
Corn	3,749	5	292	1,465	3,376
Soy beans	36,664	86	387	1,317	2,795
Sugar	25,972	166	400	1,022	4,992
Wool	73,609	214	955	1,254	1,527
Cotton	362,046	989	1,553	1,695	2,512
Iron ore	18,955	51	769	4,350	6,518
Copper ore	–	0.8	254	1,809	2,399
Raw rubber	17,930	145	638	542	558
Timber	53,078	10	613	5,659	7,768
Coal[b]	34,203	38	508	3,636	10,246
Crude petroleum	89,565	88	1,674	8,048	58,317
Petroleum products		64	487	1,980	4,017
Liquefied petroleum gas	–	–	0.00004	293	2,302
Liquefied natural gas	–	–		83	1,176
Organic pharmaceuticals	–	2.9	182	816	1,437

[a]Including whale. [b]Mostly raw coal.
Source: Ōkurashō, *Nihon bōeki geppyō* (Tokyo: Nihon kanzei kyokai, 1966–76) and *Gaikoku bōeki geppyō* (Tokyo: 1928–30). Sōrifu tōkeikyoku: *Nihon tōkei nenkan* (Tokyo: Mainichi Shinbunsha 1950–60).

to increase their dependence on the export market. Behind this tendency for Japanese industry to increase its exports was the strengthening of its industrial competitiveness caused by the inflation in the United States created by the expansion of the Vietnam War while the exchange rate remained fixed at ¥360 to $1.00. The rapid rise in exports, however, caused economic friction between the two countries, with the result that Japan placed voluntary restrictions on the export of iron and steel in 1968 and textiles in 1971.

Fuel resources continued to be Japan's major imports. According to Table 4.16, the dependence on imported energy sources increased after the 1950s. In 1955 domestic energy sources accounted for 76 percent of the energy supply, and imports accounted for 24 percent; in 1965 domestic sources accounted for only 33.8 percent, and imports made up 66.2 percent; and in 1970 domestic sources had fallen to 16.5 percent, and imports had risen to 83.5 percent.[13] Apart from fuels, the other main import items were food products and mineral resources.

The structure of its foreign trade, then, was one in which Japan

13 Tōyō keizai shinpōsha, *Shōwa kokusei sōran*, p. 391.

exported the products of heavy industry and imported the raw materials to make up for domestic insufficiency. The increase in Japanese exports exceeded that of world trade, and the expansion of imports paralleled the growth rate of the domestic economy. In order to maintain this balance, the Japanese economy had to maintain a growth rate higher than the world average. However, even though in 1970 inflation was spreading worldwide, domestic prices remained relatively stable. Hence, despite Japan's high growth, its surpluses in current account were rising.

In August 1971 President Richard Nixon sought a revaluation of the world's major currencies by ending fixed exchange rates, and by the end of the year the yen was revalued to a rate of ¥308 to $1.00. But this revalued rate did not last for long. In February 1973 Japan shifted to a floating exchange rate, and in the fall of 1973, the Organization of Petroleum Exporting Countries (OPEC) increased the price of crude oil fourfold. These successive shocks had a major impact on the Japanese economy, which depended on the export of heavy industry goods and the import of energy. These shocks marked the end of Japan's period of high growth, but nonetheless, Japanese industry continued to be oriented toward exports, with the result that these problems persisted into the 1980s.

CHARACTERISTICS OF JAPANESE ENTERPRISES

While adjusting to postwar reform, economic rehabilitation, and the onset of high growth, the Japanese economy developed certain characteristics at the microeconomic level that were quite different from those of either the prewar Japanese economy or the Western economies. To be sure, many of these characteristics originated in the prewar period, but they acquired a more definite shape with the postwar reforms and the onset of rapid growth. In regard to management, the raising of capital, labor–management practices, or subcontracting, Japanese firms emphasized long-term relationships. Market and organization influenced each other in complex ways, and a balance was maintained between adaptability and stability in business practices.

Enterprise organization and management

Most Japanese enterprises were joint stock companies, but large enterprises were usually part of an enterprise group (*keiretsu*) whose affiliated enterprises and financial institutions held one another's stocks, thereby avoiding the risk of unfriendly takeover bids by other firms. It was customary for a firm's managers to be chosen from among its long-time employees, who acted in accordance with what they saw as the long-term interests of the enterprise, which they viewed as a group of employees. Japanese enterprises were therefore likely to aim at long-term growth rather than short-term profits, and managers were extremely concerned with market share.

Before the war, the zaibatsu holding companies controlled extensive networks of firms by controlling dominant shares of stock. After the postwar dissolution of the zaibatsu, many former client or affiliate firms and financial institutions organized themselves into enterprise groups (*keiretsu*). Within the *keiretsu*, firms held one another's stock in order to avoid outside takeovers. The amount of stock for sale on the stock market was small, and its value rose remarkably. According to Miyazaki Giichi, in 1970, 57.1 percent of all limited stock companies were controlled by corporations, 20.7 percent by managers, and only 20.5 percent by stockholders.[14] One of the reasons that Japanese business leaders opposed the introduction of foreign capital and were anxious about the liberalization of capital in the late 1960s was that they wished to retain control of their enterprises.

Although this pattern of ownership and management was common in large firms, there were some exceptions. First, many small- and medium-sized enterprises were individually owned. Second, the large enterprises were often controlled by their founder and his family. This was true of the growth industries' leading firms such as Matsushita, Sony, Honda, Toyota, Tōyō kōgyō, Suntory, Kyoto Ceramics (Kyocera), and Daiei. Third, the stock market played an important role in evaluating the firms, as increases in capital investment were influenced by current stock prices. After 1965 in particular, the ratio of equity capital to total assets rose. Even though Japanese enterprises were heavily dependent on borrowing, they had to increase their capitalization as they grew in order to secure loans. Thus in high-growth industries, the possibility of securing loans was enhanced by increased capitalization.

The primacy of indirect financing

During the period of high growth, firms invested more capital than they accumulated internally. But the rate of individual savings was

14 Miyazaki Giichi, *Gendai Nihon no kigyō shūdan* (Tokyo: Nihon keizai shinbunsha, 1976), p. 290.

TABLE 4.17

Flow of funds during rapid economic growth – 1965 (in ¥1 trillion)

	Savings in excess of investment	Deposits	Loans	Securities
Individuals	2.6	2.7	1.1	0.3
Enterprises	1.1	2.1	4.0	0.5[a]
Central government	0.1	–	–	0.2[b]
Public corporations and local governments	1.1	–	0.5	0.8[a]

[a]Issued. [b]Flotation of long-term national bonds.

Source: Tōyō keizai shinpōsha, *Shōwa kokusei sōran* (Tokyo: Tōyō keizai shinpōsha, 1980), vol. 2, p. 116.

high, and the major portion of individual savings was concentrated in bank deposits. Bank loans to individual enterprises served the function of mediating between individual savings and loans to or investment in business enterprises. This type of indirect financing is one of the principal characteristics of this period. Table 4.17 outlines this money flow in 1965.

Obviously, the banks were important to this system of indirect financing. It is sometimes said that the large "city banks" (as commercial banks are called in Japan) stood at the pinnacle of the enterprise groups in the same way that headquarters companies (*honsha*) stood at the pinnacle of the prewar zaibatsu, as they both exercised similar economic power. According to Miyazaki Giichi's "one set hypothesis," because enterprise groups led by banks tried to acquire affiliated enterprises in all industries and to cover the whole range of industries and financial institutions, there was intense investment competition. Others take the view that the banks carried out a profitable "credit rationing" to the firms in the heavy and chemical industries while cooperating with the government's policy of keeping interest rates artificially low.

But even though the city banks were vital to the transfer of savings into investment, that did not mean that they could disregard market forces in distributing capital or that they had discretionary powers in deciding to whom they would lend. First, because there were many city banks, they had to compete to acquire high-quality customers for loans. Second, there were many other financial institutions to which firms could turn for loans besides city banks, for example, long-term credit banks and life insurance companies. Third, as Japan's economic growth accelerated, high-growth enterprises, in particular, built up their own capital reserves through which they could finance themselves. Fourth, after 1965 as the government began to float public bonds, the movement of interest rates was liberalized.

Although the banks cultivated long-term relationships with firms under the system of indirect financing, that does not mean that the banks distributed capital or set interest rates unilaterally as they wished. The mechanisms of a competitive market were still at work, and so the image of the city banks as omnipotent in the business world is misleading.

Labor–management practices

During this period of high growth, labor–management relations were characterized by lifetime employment, seniority-based wages, and company unions. As a rule, enterprises hired new school graduates and gave them on-the-job training. Because enterprises valued personnel skills, workers were hired for a very long term (until retirement age), and wages were based on seniority. Because both labor and management tried to achieve stability in employment, both approached wage settlements with flexibility. The bonus system also helped stabilize employment, by transferring some of the firm's risk to the workers.

The existence of such labor–management practices helped develop the workers' skills and improve productivity by increasing their desire to participate in the production process, thus making high growth possible. This also made labor–management relations relatively stable (see Table 4.18).

Although these labor–management practices prevailed in large enterprises, they were not always followed by medium and small enterprises. Generally, these practices applied to only about 30 percent of all employees, but among the rest of the employed population, job changes were frequent, and the rate of labor organization was low.

According to Table 4.19, by about 1965, as the labor market became tight, medium and small enterprises paid higher wages to younger employees. If they had not, they would not have been able to obtain as many workers as they needed. This meant that the wages for younger workers were determined in a homogeneous external labor market. In the case of older workers, the wage differential grew more pronounced. The reason was that wages in larger enterprises rose because workers had been employed longer and their wages were

TABLE 4.18
Labor unions and labor disputes

Year	Number of unions[a,b]	Number of union members (thousands)[c]	Estimated organization rate (%)[a,d]	Number of disputes[e,f]	Number of participants in disputes (thousands)[e,g]	Number of workdays lost (thousand days)[e,h]
1955	32,012[i]	6,166[i]	37.2	1,345	3,748	3,467
1956	34,073[i]	6,350[i]	34.8	1,330	3,372	4,562
1957	36,084[i]	6,606[i]	34.7	1,680	8,464	5,652
1958	37,823[i]	6,882[i]	33.9	1,864	6,362	6,052
1959	39,303[i]	7,078[i]	31.5	1,709	4,682	6,020
1960	41,561	7,652	32.2	2,222	6,953	4,912
1961	45,096	8,360	34.5	2,483	9,044	6,150
1962	47,812	8,971	34.7	2,287	7,129	5,400
1963	49,796	9,357	34.7	2,016	9,035	2,770
1964	51,457	9,800	35.0	2,422	7,974	3,165
1965	52,879	10,147	34.8	3,051	8,975	5,669
1966	53,985	10,404	34.2	3,687	10,947	2,742
1967	55,321	10,566	34.1	3,024	10,914	1,830
1968	56,535	10,863	34.4	3,882	11,758	2,841
1969	58,812	11,249	35.2	5,283	14,483	3,634
1970	60,954	11,605	35.4	4,551	9,137	3,915
1971	62,428	11,798	34.8	6,861	10,829	6,029
1972	63,718	11,889	34.3	5,808	9,630	5,147
1973	65,448	12,098	33.1	9,459	14,549	4,604

[a]As of end of May. [b]Number of separate labor unions.
[c]Number of labor union members in individual unions.
[d]Number of labor union members as a percentage of number of employees.
[e]Annual statistics.
[f]Including disputes accompanied by strikes.
[g]Number of members in organizations involved in disputes.
[h]Number of working days against the total number of workers participating in strikes and number of workers when plant was closed.
[i]Number of members of separate labor unions.
Source: Rōdōshō, *Rōdō tōkei yōran* (Tokyo: Ōkurashō insatsukyoku, 1965–73).

based on seniority, whereas in small and medium enterprises there was a great deal of labor mobility and no seniority-based scale, and so older workers were more affected by the labor supply.

The large enterprises, of course, did not employ only long-term workers. Around 1960 when the economy grew faster than expected, large enterprises hired a large number of temporary workers, whom they eventually made regular employees. In the 1970s the number of temporary, daily, or part-time employees increased. Subcontractors were also used as a source of labor. Although the labor markets were becoming more and more internalized in large enterprises, the internal and external labor markets still influenced each other.

TABLE 4.19
Wage differentials between large enterprises and small and medium enterprises (enterprises with over 1,000 employees = 100.0)

Age of employees (years)	Enterprises with 100 to 999 employees				
	1954[a]	1961	1965	1970	1975
20 to 24	83.8	93.1	107.3	100.7	98.2
25 to 29	81.1	90.4	107.4	101.7	98.9
30 to 34	76.3	81.6	101.2	98.9	97.7
35 to 39	72.1	74.0	94.3	95.0	94.6
40 to 44 45 to 49	69.5	67.4	85.9	88.7	90.2 85.6
50 to 54 55 to 59	66.8	65.5	78.2	79.0	81.7 76.6
over 60	88.6	87.7	80.9	85.3	80.3
	Enterprises with 10 to 99 employees				
	1954[b]	1961	1965	1970	1975
20 to 24	77.5	89.7	114.1	104.9	98.7
25 to 29	70.5	80.2	109.6	103.8	97.4
30 to 34	65.8	64.3	96.5	96.3	92.9
35 to 39	59.6	54.7	86.2	88.5	85.5
40 to 44 45 to 49	55.0	45.7	74.7	78.5	78.3 73.5
50 to 54 55 to 59	52.4	43.9	65.8	68.2	67.5 65.1
over 60	72.2	65.9	73.2	82.2	72.6

Note: For 1954 and 1961, the differential between "cash salary amount regularly provided" for manufacturing workers; after 1965, the differential between "fixed salary amount" for male workers of all industries investigated. In 1965 and 1970, total number of industries except service industries. In 1961 and 1965, wages in April; after 1970, wages in June.
[a]Enterprises with 100 to 499 employees. [b]Enterprises with 30 to 99 employees.
Source: Rōdōshō, *1954 nen kojinbetsu chingin chōsa; 1961 nen chingin jittai sōgō chōsa. Chingin kōzō kihon tōkei chōsa hōkoku*, 1965, 1970, 1975.

The development of subcontractor enterprises

Another characteristic of this period was the degree to which large enterprises relied on small and medium enterprises as subcontractors. According to a survey in 1976, 82.2 percent of the large manufacturing enterprises relied on outside suppliers, and 58.1 percent of all small and medium manufacturing enterprises had subcontracting relationships with large firms.

It is often said that large firms used subcontractors as a way of adjusting to changes in general business conditions. When business was brisk they used the subcontractors, but when business slowed, the large firms stopped their orders or offered only below-cost prices. In other words, the large firms made their subcontractors completely subservient and exploited their cheap labor and production costs for their own profit. If this were the case, however, it would be difficult to understand why the number of subcontractors increased as the economy grew. According to a survey of subcontractors asked why they had gone into the business, many gave reasons such as "I can concentrate on production without having to worry about making sales efforts" or "The flow of work is stable." Among firms using subcontractors, the principal consideration in selecting a subcontractor was whether or not it possessed special technology or plant facilities.[15]

Subcontracting firms tried to use the technical and managerial skills of the owner continuously and over the long term. They stood between the market and the internal organization of the contracting firm, combining the adaptability of the market with the ability of the large firm to make long-term plans. This created a particularly efficient way of organizing production. In the automobile industry, for example, Toyota's "just-in-time" supply system depended heavily on subcontractors to improve productivity.

ECONOMIC POLICY

Most discussions of government policy focus on "industrial policy" or "industrial targeting," and many maintain that Japan's economy is tightly managed, but such a monolithic picture is not correct. Economic policy is shaped by the interaction of the government bureaucracy, business interests, pressure groups, and the ruling Liberal Democratic Party. It is a mixture of certain basic macroeconomic policies and sectoral or microeconomic policies. Moreover, economic policy is neither fixed nor unchanging over time but has adjusted to changing economic conditions, though not always successfully.

The assumptions of postwar economic policy

In 1955, even after Japan had recovered economically from the war, it still was small and relatively weak economically. National income was low; the international balance of payments was unstable; and overpopulation prevented full employment. The goal of Japan's economic policy was to overcome its status as a small economy and to join the

15 Yutaka Kōsai and Yoshitarō Ogino, *The Contemporary Japanese Economy* (New York: Macmillan, 1984), p. 72.

ranks of the advanced industrial powers; the limitation on its economic policy was that as a small economy, Japan faced a ceiling on its balance of payments. To achieve its goal, Japan had to maximize its growth, enhance its international competitiveness, and achieve full employment. But because Japan was still a minor economy, it had to consider first its balance of payments.

Given its limitations with respect to its balance of payments, the Japanese government sought to avoid changing the existing exchange rate and the inflow of foreign capital. A balance in the current account under fixed prices thus became an important policy target. With respect to financial policy, whenever the balance of payments worsened (in 1954, 1957, 1961, and 1963), finances were tightened. With respect to fiscal policy, the 1949 Fiscal Law mandated sound finance, and public bonds were not issued to raise government funds. With respect to taxation, in 1960 a tax investigation commission recommended that the ratio of tax revenue to national income not exceed 20 percent.[16] "Small government" and a financial policy sensitive to the international balance of payments were the characteristic rules of classical capitalism. Except for the prohibitions on capital movement, the framework of Japan's postwar economic policy was typical of that under the gold standard.

On the other hand, because Japan wanted to catch up with the advanced countries, its economic policy had another side. In 1952, Japan's foreign currency reserves stood at $900 million, rising to $1.8 billion in 1960, but after that they hardly increased at all, reaching only $2 billion in 1967. Meanwhile, Japan's imports had risen threefold, and its money supply had increased by two and a half times. The government adopted a policy of increasing the money supply and expanding the economy as far as the international balance of payments allowed. Because the domestic money supply was not related to foreign exchange reserves, this policy differed from that under the gold standard. Because Japan's foreign exchange reserves were small, it had to pursue a tight money policy in order to manage its foreign exchange funds whenever the international balance of payments moved into a deficit.

In fiscal policy, the national budget was balanced, and every effort was made to maintain "small government" by using part of the natural increase in tax revenues resulting from economic growth to reduce

16 See the 1960 report of the Tax System Investigation Commission (Zaisei chōsakai). For a comment on this, see Komiya Ryūtarō, *Gendai Nihon keizai kenkyū* (Tokyo: Tōkyō daigaku shuppankai, 1975), pp. 107–8.

taxes. At the same time, however, special tax measures, direct government financing, and other sorts of government intervention were used as tools of industrial policy to promote Japan's international competitiveness.[17] In its macroeconomic policy the government followed the principle of balanced budgets, but at the same time in its microeconomic or sectoral policy, it followed government interventionist principles, by providing special tax measures for and fiscal investment in particular industries.

Japan's economic policy during this period, therefore, used two contrasting approaches: a sectoral or microeconomic interventionist policy that assumed Japan was a small economy aimed at catching up with the advanced industrial countries; and orthodox macroeconomic financial and fiscal policies that assumed Japan was a small economy heeding the limitations on its international balance of payments.

Changes in economic policy

By achieving economic growth through industrial modernization, Japan gradually became free of the limitations imposed by its international balance of payments. It was well on the way to changing from a minor into a major economic power. As a result, its microeconomic interventionist policy (at least the protecting and nurturing of particular industries) became more difficult.

Japan's participation in the OECD in the 1960s required that it liberalize its controls over foreign exchange, foreign trade, and capital movements. At the same time, there were not only those who argued that liberalization would improve economic growth, but there were also foreign pressures at work. Liberalization deprived the government of the means to intervene in private enterprise, and interest rates also moved freely in the domestic financial market as the government continued to float government bond issues.

The government naturally hesitated to reduce taxes or give financial assistance to enterprises that were able to compete in international markets. The diversification of the industrial structure, moreover, made it difficult to identify the needy industries. Government finance turned from industry to the improvement of housing facilities and the

17 Scholars do not agree on how to evaluate this industrial policy. For example, see the relevant chapters of Komiya Ryūtarō, *Nihon no sangyō seisaku* (Tokyo: Todai shuppankai, 1984); Komiya Ryūtarō, *Gendai Nihon keizai kenkyū;* Tsuruta Toshimasa, *Sengo Nihon no sangyō seisaku* (Tokyo Nihon keizai shinbunsha, 1982); Ueno Hiroya, *Nihon no keizai seido* (Tokyo: Nihon keizai shinbunsha, 1978); Chalmers Johnson, *MITI and the Japanese Miracle: The Growth of Industrial Policy 1925–1975* (Stanford, Calif.: Stanford University Press, 1982).

TABLE 4.20
Fiscal investment and loan program (¥100 million)

	1955	1960	1965	1970	1975
Housing	415	789	2,259	6,896	19,966
Living environment facilities	230	569	2,010	4,168	15,573
Public welfare facilities	64	109	585	1,017	3,133
Educational facilities	136	214	493	790	2,752
Small and medium enterprises	244	784	2,045	5,523	14,505
Agriculture, forestries, and fisheries	266	439	1,169	1,785	3,795
Subtotal	1,355	2,904	8,561	20,179	59,724
Preservation of national land and restoration after disasters	231	401	506	560	1,100
Roads	110	272	1,284	3,078	7,444
Transportation and communications	366	915	2,250	4,723	11,849
Regional development	255	436	1,124	1,431	3,059
Subtotal	962	2,024	5,164	9,792	23,452
Key industries	471	838	1,262	2,028	2,764
Promotion of exports	210	485	1,219	3,800	7,160
Total	2,998	6,251	16,206	35,799	93,100

Source: Ōkurashō, *Zaisei tōkei* (Tokyo: Ōkurashō insatsukyoku, 1962–).

environment (see Table 4.20), and government intervention in private enterprise became stronger in environmental pollution and labor regulation. In addition, public opinion turned against large mergers or amalgamations.

At the same time, macroeconomic policy, finally freed from the balance-of-payments ceiling, became more flexible. Using the 1965 recession as an opportunity, the government began to raise revenues by issuing public bonds, abandoning in practice the principle of balanced budgets. Under the slogan of "increasing welfare through increasing the tax burden," the government made plans to increase the taxation rate. In 1967 and 1968 efforts were made to return to a balanced budget (i.e., limiting the issue of public bonds and increasing public debt). But the liberation of macroeconomic policy from balance-of-payments restraints reached a peak with the announcement of Prime Minister Tanaka Kakuei's Plan to Reconstruct the Japanese Archipelago in 1972 and with plans to broaden the coverage of social insurance policies in 1973.

After 1968, as Japanese industry became more competitive and world inflation spread, Japan's foreign exchange reserves increased rapidly, climbing from $2 billion in 1967 to $18.3 billion in 1972. Even though Japan enjoyed a positive balance of payments, the Bank of Japan, contrary to previous practice, adopted a tight money policy to keep the domestic economy from overheating, but the positive balance of payments continued to climb, and foreign exchange reserves accumulated. The Bank of Japan then shifted to a looser policy, and between 1970 and 1973 the money supply increased 20 percent a year. In other words, the government returned to the policy it followed in the 1960s of easing the money supply when the balance of payments was in the black. But in the midst of world inflation, increasing the domestic money supply while maintaining fixed exchange rates was bound to create inflation. With the announcement of the Plan for the Reconstruction of the Japanese Archipelago, first land prices and then commodity prices rose. Just before the "oil shock" of 1973, Japan's wholesale prices had increased by more than 20 percent over the previous year, even without an oil price hike.

Even with the adoption of a policy of financial and fiscal expansion, the balance of payments did not stop expanding. Indeed, it was strengthened by the revaluation of the yen in 1971 and the shift to a floating exchange rate in 1973. Had Japan earlier revalued the yen on its own initiative, instead of increasing the money supply, inflation might have been eased, if not avoided. But Japan realized too late that the significance of the balance of payments had changed and so made the wrong policy choice. Instead of revaluing the yen, the government tried to maintain its parity. The freedom of action that the government had acquired with the end of its balance-of-payment constraints was misused, thereby incurring inflation and bringing to an end the period of high growth.

CHAPTER 5

CAPITAL FORMATION IN JAPAN[1]

INTRODUCTION

This chapter analyses the relationship between the input of capital and economic growth in Japan during the past century. The assigned task of exploring the role of investment in Japan necessarily imposes a certain sectoral as well as temporal emphasis. Only relatively little attention will have to be devoted to agriculture, since this sector never became an important recipient of either public or private capital. In Japan, at least, an understanding of the advances created by a rising level of investment deals largely with the growth of modern non-agricultural industry. This also means that (unlike Taira and Yamamura) we must concentrate especially on the history of the twentieth century, when factories, machines, and new social overhead implements reached sizeable dimensions for the first time. Of course, no attempt will be made to slight the crucial transitional years of the Meiji era or even the preceding years of Tokugawa rule, but one should always keep at the forefront the sharp distinction between the hesitant beginnings of economic modernization in the late nineteenth century and its full flowering during the past sixty-odd years.

One further limiting item should be mentioned at the outset. We are concerned with the 'input' of capital – i.e. with the investment rather than the saving side of the equation. How the necessary funds were raised – by individuals, banks, the state, or foreigners – will be treated only as a side issue, but to a considerable extent this matter has been studied by other authors.

Finally, a word or two about the organization of the argument. The chapter is divided into three principal sections. We begin by discuss-

1 We wish to express our gratitude to Nobukiyō Takamatsu for generous help in the preparation of this chapter.

Since the original draft of this chapter was completed, we have published a book in which many of the issues discussed in this chapter are treated in much greater detail: see Kazushi Ohkawa and Henry Rosovsky, *Japanese Economic Growth: Trend Acceleration in the Twentieth Century* (Stanford, Calif., 1973).

ing the pre-modern background of the Japanese economy, focusing on certain broad trends during the Tokugawa era, which lasted from the early 1600s until 1868. This will give the reader a suitable base line from which to judge subsequent events. This is followed by an analysis of capital formation during the Meiji era, which concentrates on approximately the last third of the nineteenth century. In this section the scope expands well beyond capital inputs because of the mixed nature of the economy at that time. The third section deals with the twentieth century and is in two parts. First we examine the evidence concerning investment in greater detail, and secondly we attempt to provide an interpretation of the role of capital in twentieth-century growth.

THE PRE-MODERN BACKGROUND

No country in the history of the world has risen to international prominence as quickly as Japan. One hundred years ago, this insignificant kingdom located in a remote corner of East Asia was of little interest to those concerned with global political or economic affairs. At that time the European powers occupied centre stage, and the United States was just emerging as a major contestant for world power. In Asia – if Russia is considered a European country – only India and China were relatively well known, but neither of these vast countries had an effective voice in international affairs. India was a colony, and China mattered only in the sense that her population and resources appeared attractive to countries with commercial and/or colonial ambitions. This was the situation a century ago, and in most ways this description retained its validity until the beginning of the twentieth century.

Today the scene is radically different. Europe's role has been considerably diminished, and colonialism is largely a thing of the past. Russia and the United States have assumed the position of superpowers; China remains a question mark; most African and Asian countries are independent. But Japan has changed most of all: at present she is one of the major industrial powers of the world. The size of her GNP exceeds that of any other country except the Soviet Union and the United States. Japan leads the world in shipbuilding and is second in steel production. Japanese goods of high and sophisticated value-added content – cars, cameras, computers, etc. – are consumed in large quantities throughout the world. In fact, today the Japanese are considered serious competitors in nearly all levels and types of economic activity, and it took Japan much less than a hundred years to achieve this astonishing transformation.

It must be self-evident that Japan's transformation or modernization was not confined to economics alone. One can no longer call the Japanese remote or of little concern to the rest of the world. In nearly all facets of current life – ranging from mutual-security arrangements to architecture and religion – the Japanese occupy positions of world importance. Perhaps this is especially true because Japan is an Asian and non-white country. Until now, Japan is the only country of non-European origin to have achieved modernization, and those who would like to derive 'lessons' from this event are legion.

The economic transformation of Japan has been the most celebrated aspect of her modern history. As we shall demonstrate, especially for the past sixty years or so this transformation can be conceived in terms of a series of growth phases – or developmental 'waves' – consisting of a spurt and followed by a period of less rapid growth. The greatest growth spurt began after the destruction of the Second World War and the ensuing years of reconstruction and rehabilitation. Frequently this spurt has been called Japan's 'economic miracle', which started in 1952–4 and appears to have ended around 1973. However, there were earlier spurts and earlier waves of growth. During the 1930s the Japanese economy developed at a most impressive pace, which was abruptly interrupted by the events leading up to the Second World War. Similarly, the years between the end of the Russo-Japanese War (1905) and the end of the First World War (1918) witnessed very rapid development, followed by much slower growth during the 1920s. These three spurts, as well as the years in between, all illustrate a similar developmental pattern: growth based on the ever more speedy absorption of modern Western technology. In this process, changes in the rate of *private* investment are especially crucial.

There was, however, one critical phase in Japan's modern economic growth which does not fit into the twentieth-century pattern based on the absorption of Western technology. This is the development of the economy during the years of the Meiji era – roughly from the 1860s until the outbreak of the Russo-Japanese War.[2] Although we will not be primarily concerned with this period of 'initial' modern economic growth, some background is needed to place the later events in proper historical perspective. To appreciate fully how Japan has developed

2 The Meiji era actually began in 1868 and ended in 1912, but from an economic point of view dating based on the reign of an emperor is meaningless.

since the early 1900s it is necessary to describe the economic conditions pertaining at that time. One also has to understand what economic forces created these conditions. In short, we must provide a brief review of Meiji economic history and perhaps even of some of its antecedents.

Where should one begin? The temptation in a review of this type is to go back further and further; it is all too easy to become a victim of what Marc Bloch once referred to as the historian's 'obsession with origins'. By considering the significance of 'AD 1868' or 'Meiji 1', the dimensions of the problem can be made clearer. On one side – pre-1868 – lies the 'traditional' or 'feudal' rule of the Tokugawa, when from the economic point of view it was rather difficult to distinguish Japan from other backward countries in Asia. On the other side of 1868 lies the modern era ushered in by the Restoration of the Meiji emperor, who formally headed a new government dedicated to – among other things – economic growth. These statements are not necessarily incorrect, but they are highly oversimplified. Neither Tokugawa Japan (1603–1868) nor Meiji Japan can be compartmentalized so easily.

Japan was ruled by the Tokugawa family for over two hundred years. These were rich, eventful years from the cultural, economic, and social point of view, and it is impossible to give an adequate overview of this period in a few lines. Yet, in considering Japanese economic growth in this century, is there anything that needs to be said about the Tokugawa shogunate? The answer is Yes, because although Japan remained in a state of relative economic backwardness under Tokugawa rule, her condition – even prior to the Restoration – must not be confused with those countries where economic and other types of backwardness were closely combined.[3] And this situation was a most important asset for future economic development.

That Japan was operating with a relatively backward economy during the seventeenth and eighteenth centuries and most of the nineteenth is not at all difficult to ascertain, even though quantitative evidence is sparse and of poor quality. To begin with, we know that the overwhelming majority of the population at this time were peasants of a rather familiar Asian type. Their output constituted the major share of total product. These peasants cultivated small, often irrigated plots (average size perhaps slightly less than one hectare), and many of them must have been living on the border of subsistence at least during the

3 This was undoubtedly the case in much of Africa and in some parts of Asia.

first half of this period. Production techniques varied from region to region, with the Southwest generally ahead of the Northeast. Broadly speaking, however, it is clear that their agricultural technology was traditional and that yields were well below their potential level even in terms of existing practices. Very little capital equipment was employed by the peasants; the use of organic fertilizers was highly restricted (chemical fertilizers were unknown); and scientific practices such as seed selection and optimum sowing dates were largely unknown. Double-cropping was also employed at well below optimal levels. These observations can be put in general terms. Agricultural technology falls into three clear types: biological, chemical, and mechanical. The Tokugawa years saw some biological and chemical innovations. Significant mechanical improvements, such as the use of machinery, did not occur until after the Second World War.

To cite solid figures for these assertions is nearly impossible, but reasonable guesses are not out of the question. Towards the end of Tokugawa rule – i.e. in the middle of the nineteenth century – roughly 80 per cent of the people were officially classified as peasants. Not all those designated as peasants in the official class structure actually engaged in farming. Some worked in crafts or trade and lived (sometimes illegally) in cities. But most of the peasants must have engaged mainly in cultivation of the soil, and certainly the Tokugawa regime was anxious to see this situation maintained, since taxation of the peasantry was its main source of income. Perhaps, then, the figure of 80 per cent exaggerates the rural nature of Tokugawa Japan. However, even scaling it down to 75 or 70 per cent does not change the picture of a society in which the average inhabitant was an Asian peasant. And the presumption is that in a society of this type the level of income per capita – an *average* concept – is low. Of course, 'low' implies a comparative standard, and to cite actual numbers (usually expressed in US dollars) would only confuse the issue. Following the reasoning of Simon Kuznets, we can simply say that – other things being equal – the greater the share of the entire gainfully employed population employed in agriculture, the lower the level of income per capita.

When one turns to the non-agricultural sectors of the Tokugawa economy it becomes obvious that other things were, in fact, equal. Non-agricultural production consisted of crafts and services. Craft output frequently combined beauty and usefulness; services were often very sophisticated. Nevertheless, these sectors were untouched by the liberating forces of the industrial revolution which made men more productive. Machinery was not in use except in the most unusual circumstances; units of production were small; steam power had not been introduced. In essence, agriculture and non-agriculture resembled one another: both used labour-intensive methods that depended for gains in productivity on the skills of the individual worker. Fixed capital was only a minor element in the production function.

There is no more revealing evidence concerning Tokugawa Japan than her demographic balance and her international contacts. To begin with the latter, we must recall the famous 'closing of the country' (*sakoku*) decree issued in 1637 by the third shogun of the Tokugawa line. The reasons for this drastic step are not entirely clear to this day. Some scholars believe that Shogun Iemitsu feared internal strife fomented by *rōnin* (masterless samurai) and closed the country to prevent these malcontents from securing outside help. Others espouse the more likely explanation that an external threat was the main cause. According to this view, Iemitsu understood the danger of Western expansionism – specifically, of the sword following the cross – in the Philippines and China. He feared that Japan's turn was coming. Whatever the shogun's motives, the 'closing of the country' has to be taken quite literally: no Japanese was permitted to leave Japan, and if someone did so and returned he was put to death. Foreigners were not allowed to visit or to reside in Japan. Only two minor exceptions were made: the Dutch and the Chinese retained extremely limited trading rights at Nagasaki. In order to take advantage of these rights, however, Dutch and Chinese traders lived as virtual prisoners in the far South of the country. The *sakoku* decrees remained in effect for well over two hundred years. They were fully lifted only in the 1860s, when the Tokugawa had reached the last tottering years of what had been an illustrious reign. By then, isolation had become a deeply ingrained tradition, and objection to its abandonment was strong even in the second half of the nineteenth century. Now, however, outside pressure from the major Western powers could no longer be resisted. Commodore Perry and his ships made their point in an unmistakable manner.

What were the consequences of this long self-imposed isolation? These are difficult to trace out unambiguously; yet there is little reason to believe that *sakoku* had only negative effects. To be isolated from empire-building Europeans may have been advantageous; to be left alone may have created sources of inner national strength. All of this is possible; but from the economic point of view, a closed country also meant a necessary condition of relative backwardness – not so obviously in the seventeenth century, when the policy was begun, but very obviously by the time the nineteenth century opened. In the intervening years the Western world – more precisely, Great Britain – had given birth to the industrial revolution. From then on the absence of international contacts meant the availability of only second-best technology and organization; and this remains true today.

Japan's demographic balance before the Meiji Restoration is equally revealing. The first real population census took place only in 1920, but experts agree on the broad magnitudes of earlier figures. In the 1860s, total population was around thirty million. At the start of the Tokugawa era, population is estimated to have been approximately twenty to twenty-five million. These figures convert into the low rates of natural increase typical of less-developed areas before the introduction of modern medical and social advances. Students of Japanese demography have pointed to another phenomenon of equally great interest: between the late seventeenth or early eighteenth centuries and the 1840s – for roughly one hundred and fifty years – the population remained stable; growth began again in the 1840s. The reasons for stability are again not entirely clear, but it has frequently been asserted that infanticide (*mabiki*) was an important means of achieving a zero growth rate. In general, we think that population at this time was a representative variable for the entire economy: change took place, but its pace was slow.

What has been said up to now is only half the story. Some pages earlier we cautioned against confusing Tokugawa Japan with many backward countries today or with some of Japan's near and far neighbors in the nineteenth century. Although unable at that time to avail herself of modern technology and most scientific advances, Japan nevertheless was a vigorous, advanced, and effective traditional society. In many ways it was more advanced than many countries in Africa or Latin America today. This deserves special stress, because there is no denying that we tend inevitably to associate low per capita income with poor organization, corruption, lethargy, and undernourishment. And this gives a false picture of Japan before the Restoration.

A few illustrative details should be helpful. The pre-Restoration governmental structure was effective at both central and local levels. Central government – the capital and the major cities – was under direct Tokugawa control. Local authority was in the hands of Tokugawa vassals. The entire country was divided into about two hundred 'baronies' or 'fiefs', each headed by a lord or *daimyō*. A *daimyō* was responsible for the affairs of his fief, but he was also closely watched by the central authorities, and with sufficient cause his office could be taken away. In return for exercising local authority, *daimyō* received the rights to an income stream originating in their fiefs; its most important form was the privilege of levying a yearly harvest tax, with which they supported themselves and their retainers. Tokugawa administration has frequently been described as 'centralized feudalism', and this is quite accurate. As shogun, the head of the House of Tokugawa was the leading lord of the land: he was the largest individual fiefholder, and his revenues and the number of his retainers exceeded those of all other lords. At the same time, all other lords were – directly or indirectly – vassals of the Tokugawa; this was the 'centralized' part of the feudalism.

The road system of pre-modern Japan was in keeping with the centralized nature of government. Major arteries criss-crossed the country, and both goods and people moved relatively rapidly by nineteenth-century standards. A special word must be added about the institution of *sankin kōtai* (alternate residence), since it has often been linked to the quality of the roads. According to this Tokugawa regulation, the lords had to alternate their place of residence between the national capital (Edo, since renamed Tokyo) and their local capitals. The wives and children of lords had to remain present in Edo all of the time. Normally, the lord and selected retainers spent one year in the capital and one year in the provinces. The idea behind this regulation was simple: hostage families encouraged the lord's good behaviour, and his frequent absences in Edo prevented the creation of a local power base to rival that of the shogun. The resulting movements of people, sometimes in the colourful *daimyō* processions so well depicted by Hiroshige, no doubt contributed to the development of everything connected with travel – roads, inns, restaurants, etc.

Government and roads are part of a broader picture of competence and efficiency. The Japanese knew what they were doing, even though their efforts were circumscribed by very labour-intensive technology. Much of this can be seen by focusing briefly on some of the items used in everyday life under the Tokugawa. Housing was usually well designed and well engineered and satisfied the people's needs. The same can be said of clothing. Indigenous dress was beautiful and functional and was specifically designed to fit harmoniously into the traditional way of doing things. Japanese cuisine performed equally well. It was nutritious, attractive, and somewhat bland; these were exactly the characteristics most desired. Of course the point is not at all that the average Japanese in (say) 1850 was adequately fed, housed, and dressed: probably this was not true. But the point is that the means of satisfying these wants were available within the traditional society;

indeed, when a wider choice became available, traditional means often continued to be preferred.

For a more complete picture of Tokugawa life, other points should also be stressed: the vigour of urban culture inside the large cities (Edo, Kyoto, and Osaka were among the largest cities in the world at that time); the high average standards of education, ensuring that approximately 40 to 50 per cent of all males had benefited from some formal schooling; the official class structure of *bushi* (samurai), farmers, and merchants, which was conservative in intent but which did supply the country with a group of leaders largely of samurai and 'gentry' farmer background. None of these points can be treated in detail, but they all add up to an important premise: in Tokugawa Japan the gap between economic and 'other' backwardness was unusually large, and this made the prospect of modern economic growth all the more promising.

THE MEIJI RESTORATION AND ITS AFTERMATH

The term 'Restoration' refers to January 1868, when the last Tokugawa shogun 'voluntarily' surrendered power and returned the task of governing to the Imperial family, and specifically to the young Emperor Meiji. Without a doubt this was an epochal event in Japanese history, and it can stand comparison with many other great dates in national histories. The Restoration was so crucial that many volumes have been devoted to its interpretation, and there are available any number of social, political, and cultural interpretations. In the general study of 'modernization' – today such a popular subject – the Meiji Restoration is one of the most important and favoured examples. Our own focus, however, must be quite narrow. We shall confine ourselves to outlining the main economic trends from the 1860s to the turn of the century as necessary background information.

Why did a Restoration occur, and why did it occur in 1868? These are questions which undoubtedly will never be answered with precision. Students of the period have suggested many reasons for this change of government: a renewed foreign threat which made continued isolation impossible and called instead for modernization; the presence of a group of discontented lower-ranking samurai from outlying domains who saw their own opportunities for advancement blocked and who wanted power and glory for themselves; a secular economic deterioration as a result of rising expenditures by the Tokugawa (and other domains) without the means further to increase revenues. All of these –

and others – contain much truth, and it is not really necessary for us to delve into this subject more deeply. The main point is that Japanese modernization – economic, political, and social – began, at least symbolically, in 1868 when the Emperor Meiji was restored to the throne.

Despite recent scholarly controversies and revisions, the main features of the era continue to stand out in an unmistakable manner. In considering this period of somewhat over thirty years it is best to divide it into two segments: the years of transition from 1868 to perhaps 1885, and the years of initial modern economic growth beginning in the mid-1880s and ending with the turn of the century. Let us look at each one of these segments in turn.

The years of transition during which the initial shock of Western contact was absorbed were necessarily confused, full of false starts and experimentation. They were more important as years of institutional reform spearheaded by the government than as years of rapid economic growth. (Indeed, the available quantitative information is such that it is most difficult to establish aggregate economic growth rates before the middle of the 1880s.)

A brief look at the major reforms should make their significance obvious. Between 1869 and 1871, for example, the government entirely revamped the old feudal class structure. The official categories of court noble, warrior, peasant, merchant, and outcast were done away with and restructured into two new classes – a small nobility and everyone else. By 1876 the government had also succeeded in pensioning off the former members of the warrior class – previously they had received stipends from Tokugawa or from their domains – at a cost of over 200 million yen. During this time, also, the new government abolished previously existing barriers to internal travel and opened the ports to external visitors. Of great importance also was the agricultural reform which occupied the new leaders during most of the 1870s. The land was formally turned over to the peasants (in feudal times ownership had been officially in the hands of the emperor), but they were now required to pay a heavy land tax to the central and local government. This tax was placed on the assessed valuation of the land (and not, as in the past, on the harvest) and was levied at nationally uniform levels. Currency and banking reforms also occupied the Meiji oligarchy in this period. It introduced order into the system of coinage, and by the end of the 1880s it had succeeded in creating a central bank (the Bank of Japan) and in establishing regulations for a growing private banking system. Other well-known activities of the public sector in this period might also be mentioned: the establishment of model factories, the hiring of foreign experts, and the dispatch of students abroad. All of these activities taken together added up to a most active era of institutional innovation.

During this transition the Japanese economy underwent some severe fluctuations. Until 1876 the situation remained relatively calm, but thereafter great shocks occurred in the form of a severe inflation lasting until 1881, followed by an intense deflation which ended only in 1885. The causes of these events are intricate, but they need not detain us for long. Briefly, throughout the transition years the government lacked sufficient revenue for its ordinary needs. In the latter half of the 1870s, however, these needs were very much magnified by the desire to pension off the warrior class and by the outbreak of the Satsuma rebellion. The government and the banks turned to the printing press, and the resulting inflation – beneficial to no one but the farmers – endangered the stability of the new leadership. Its revenues – especially those relating to the land tax – were fixed, and they were being diminished in real terms by the rising prices. Economic order was restored by Finance Minister Matsukata, but it required four years of severe and officially sponsored deflation.[4]

Modern economic growth in Japan began during the next subperiod, that is to say some time after the middle of the 1880s. Clearly one must not imagine that Japanese industrialization was in any sense an accomplished fact by the time the twentieth century had started, but some very significant steps had been taken in the right direction. The fifteen years following the Matsukata deflation represented a period of virtually uninterrupted development of modern industry. Silk and cotton-spinning were the main achievements of the private sector, while road-building, railways, and public works in general were carried out and encouraged by the government. By 1901 factory output constituted nearly 10 per cent of net national product; gross domestic fixed capital formation was over 10 per cent of GNP; and exports were over 10 per cent of GNP. All these indicators showed sustained increases over the preceding decades.

From our perspective, the most noteworthy element in initial economic growth is its mechanism. As mentioned somewhat earlier, we find it to be rather different from that which obtained in the twentieth century. Ever since the Restoration, the Japanese economy has contained a number of rather well-defined sectors. Usually these have been

4 See Henry Rosovsky, 'Japan's Transition to Modern Economic Growth, 1868–1885', in H. Rosovsky (ed.), *Industrialization in Two Systems* (New York, 1966).

labelled as 'modern' and 'traditional', and sometimes we have added the category 'hybrid'. There is nothing new or surprising about these categories; they are part of all dual-economy analyses. The characteristics of the sectors are equally well known, and they obtain as well in other countries. Modern sectors rely on imported Western technology and organization and employ methods of relatively high capital-intensity. By contrast, traditional production relies on more indigenous technology and organization and on relatively low levels of capital-intensity. Hybrid sectors fall in between, combining (say) modern technique and traditional organization. The Asian peasant cultivating his small field with hand tools is a perfect example of the traditional economy. The large cotton-spinning establishment with its machines and its wage workers is a perfect example of the modern sector.

All of this is very familiar to students of economic development, just as is the fact that modern economic growth is a process by which traditional ways of doing things gradually yield to modern ways. What is perhaps less familiar is the vividness of the contrast between modern and traditional in the Japanese setting. There the traditional economy often has a quaint and (at least for Westerners) an exotic appearance – one need only think of the wonderful Japanese crafts and the range of unusual services – and therefore the dichotomy is more readily identifiable. But in terms of economic analysis this added bit of colour makes little difference.

Four simple propositions applied to modern economic growth in its initial phase.

1. In the absence of large capital imports, and with limited possibilities for redistributing an existing surplus, the initial establishment and subsequent development of the modern economy depended on the accelerated growth of the traditional economy – and also to some extent on the accelerated growth of the hybrid economy.

2. The traditional economy was capable of accelerated growth.

3. However, the growth potential of the traditional economy was limited. When its growth rate began to decline – approximately at the time of the First World War – the initial phase of modern economic growth came to an end.

4. By the time the initial phase came to an end, the dependence of the modern economy on the traditional economy had greatly decreased – although it had not disappeared.

These propositions can be summarized as follows: the opportunities for initial economic modernization hinged on the more rapid growth of peasant agriculture, because this produced most of the needed surpluses for development (public revenues, private investment funds, foreign exchange, and labour force). When traditional agriculture faltered, a different model came into play.

This schematic presentation of nineteenth-century growth is not without its critics. The major problem undoubtedly relates to the rate of growth of traditional agriculture during the Meiji era. At one time it would have been easy to outline the main economic trends. If this is no longer so, it is because of a lively controversy concerning Meiji agricultural growth. This is not the place to cover this dispute in detail: it has been done in many places elsewhere, and all we need to do here is to state our conclusions.[5]

Many authorities seem to agree that Japanese agriculture during the relevant years (from the 1870s to the 1900s) grew at about 1.7 per cent per annum. Some would place this figure slightly lower (some very much lower), and some may select slightly higher figures; but 1.7 per cent seems to us an acceptable modal value. If this rate is approximately correct, it follows that the Meiji era witnessed a considerable acceleration over the older Tokugawa values, for no one has ever suggested that before the 1870s growth was of this magnitude. Undoubtedly Tokugawa agricultural output grew much more slowly than Meiji agricultural output, no matter what the actual rate may have been.

Various reasons can account for the acceleration of agricultural output in Meiji Japan. Of undoubted importance were the development and diffusion of improved agricultural techniques, partly the work of individual farmers and their organizations and partly the result of government sponsorship and research. For example, these activities led to improved seed selection and a wider and more rational use of fertilizers. The improved incentive structure for landowners must also be taken into account. In Tokugawa Japan, the peasant paid a heavy harvest tax, which fluctuated considerably from year to year and frequently depended on the specific short-term financial needs of the lords. Thus there was no guarantee that the agriculturist would be able to retain any of the increased output. Now the situation was entirely different, since the land tax was based on the value of land, and it was pretty well known that the assessments would remain fairly stable. Another element in explaining the acceleration of output is connected to the regional structure of the pre-modern Japanese economy. The

5 See Henry Rosovsky, 'Rumbles in the Rice Fields', *Journal of Asian Studies,* XXVII, 2 (1968). This review article deals mainly with the work of Professor James Nakamura.

agricultural economy of Tokugawa Japan – especially with respect to levels of productivity – was not at all uniform. There existed areas of relatively high and low productivity, and only in part could this be explained by differing qualities of soil or geography. In very broad terms, agriculture was more backward in northeastern Japan than in southwestern Japan. The Restoration provided an opportunity for exploiting these productivity gaps. Before the 1860s the transfer of know-how and technology had been impeded by Tokugawa theory and practice; now it became an aim of the Meiji government to spread useful knowledge throughout the entire country.

This type of expansion, however, has limited possibilities. Output grew in Meiji agriculture owing to the employment of techniques based on increased labour input combined with improvements in conventional inputs – seed, fertilizers, etc. All these were highly divisible and well suited to the peasant unit of production. But this could not go on indefinitely. Eventually, when these types of improvements had been fully exploited, maintaining the growth rate would have required major capital and land improvements. These did not have a significant effect until after the Second World War, and therefore shortly after 1914 the rate of growth of Japanese agriculture started to stagnate.[6]

Why were agriculture and other sectors in similar positions so crucial? This is easy to see when we consider the needs of modern economic growth. Fundamentally it is a matter of 'he who dances must pay the fiddler', at a time when the vast majority of dancers were in traditional occupations. In the beginning their productivity levels were low, but by raising them they could generate the necessary surpluses with which to begin industrialization. And, given the traditional techniques, this could be accomplished without heavy expenditures on fixed investment.

After all, what were the needs of modern economic growth at a time

6 Beginning in 1965, a research group at Hitotsubashi University began publishing a thirteen-volume series of historical statistics: K. Ohkawa, M. Shinohara, and M. Umemura (eds.), *Chōki keizai tōkei* [*Estimates of Long-Term Economic Statistics of Japan since 1868*] (these are the so-called '*LTES*' volumes). Agriculture is dealt with in vol. IX, M. Umemura *et al.*, *Nōringyō* [*Agriculture and Forestry*] (Tokyo, 1966): see especially p. 276. Other available volumes are: I: *Kokumin shotoku* [*National Income*] (1974); II: *Jinkō to rōdōryoku* [*Population and Labour Force*] (1973); III: *Shihon stokku* [*Capital Stock*] (1965); IV: *Shihon keisei* [*Capital Formation*] (1971); VI: *Kojin shōhi shishitsu* [*Personal Consumption Expenditures*] (1967); VII: *Zaisei shishitsu* [*Public Expenditures*] (1966); VIII: *Bukka* [*Prices*] (1965); X: *Kōkōgyō* [*Mining and Manufacturing*] (1972); XII: *Tetsudō to denryōku* [*Railways and Electrical Utilities*] (1965). (Other volumes are planned for Savings and Currency, Textiles, and Regional Economic Statistics.)

Virtually all of the quantitative information used in this chapter is based on those volumes. For the convenience of readers unacquainted with the Japanese language, most of our citations will refer to Ohkawa and Rosovsky, *Japanese Economic Growth*, where the Japanese sources are analysed and described in considerable detail.

when reinvestment by a small sector of modern industry was tiny? and how were those needs met? First of all, Japan needed a growing food supply for a larger population in which the standards of diet were rising. Importing food was relatively expensive and diverted funds from productive investment possibilities. In large measure the increased food supplies were provided by the peasantry. Secondly, the new government required a rising flow of revenues for social overhead and other investment purposes, as well as for administrative modernization. Again the traditional economy played a key role here, through land-tax revenue and as a source of indirect taxation. Thirdly, foreign exchange was vital for the importation of modern producers' durables and to acquire the services of foreign experts. The Meiji economy secured foreign exchange largely through the export of tea and silk, both products closely linked to traditional agriculture. Finally, the Japanese economy needed to effect a labour transfer so as to provide the workers for the expanding modern sectors. These workers came almost entirely from the rural areas, and this transfer did not adversely affect the rate of growth of agricultural output.

Having outlined the mechanism of Meiji economic growth, let us now examine the character of pre-twentieth-century capital inputs. We can accomplish this most easily by attempting to sharpen the contrasts between the nineteenth and twentieth centuries.

By 1900, the proportion of gross fixed domestic investment to gross aggregate product in Japan had probably reached 12 per cent – by no means an insignificant level.[7] Yet the share of modern industry in the economy was very modest. Factory output accounted for some 8 per cent of net domestic product, and the definition of a factory – an establishment with five or more employees – meant that a great deal of handicraft production was included. We know that factory output grew rapidly during the thirty years before 1900 – in 1885 the proportion had been 4 per cent – but we also know that it continued to increase, reaching levels of over 30 per cent after the Second World War.

The output stream emanating from these factories underwent a considerable change during the Meiji era. In 1868, 66 per cent of gross output came from food-processing and kindred activities, and 28 per cent from textile-manufacturing, which was dominated by the silk industry. By 1905, the share of food-processing had dropped to 39 per cent, textiles had risen to 38 per cent – with cotton becoming more

7 It is very difficult to be more precise, because reliable aggregate product figures are not available for the nineteenth century.

important – and chemicals, metals, and machines accounted for 23 per cent. However, it should be added that the representative units were small. At the turn of the century, 68 per cent of the workers in food-processing were engaged in establishments with fewer than fifty employees; for textiles and heavy industry this proportion stood at 37 per cent and 43 per cent respectively.

Once more, a glance at future developments can indicate the magnitude of change to come. Whereas Meiji industrial output was dominated by food processing and textiles produced by rather small units, twentieth-century production – certainly by the 1930s – was dominated by heavier industry and larger units. For example, at the end of the 1930s, chemicals, metals, and machines accounted for about 70 per cent of gross industrial output, and nearly 50 per cent of the labour force in these industries was working in large factories.

The early and limited industrialization of Meiji Japan was supported by a specific pattern of capital formation. It can be described as follows:

1. Public investment generally exceeded the level of private productive investment.
2. Investment in construction outweighed investment in producers' durable equipment.
3. Most of the investments represented the application of traditional techniques and therefore did not embody imported technological progress.

As Figure 5.1 shows, government investments generally exceeded those of the private sector until the First World War. This was undoubtedly due to a combination of two factors. First of all, the government was very active in improving the quantity and quality of social overheads; it was also very active in raising Japan's military capability. Indeed, during the Meiji era one can account for well over half of capital formation on the part of central government by summing up expenditures on public works (especially railways) and military investments. If one adds reconstruction expenditures related to periodic natural disasters such as earthquakes and typhoons, it is possible to account for over 70 per cent of government investment expenditures.

The second explanation of the government's large share in total investment simply relates to the small absolute size of private industry. Figure 5.1 indicates that private investments were gaining on those of the public sector, but during most of the Meiji era the types of industries which made extensive use of expensive capital equipment were still infants – though growing at a lusty pace.

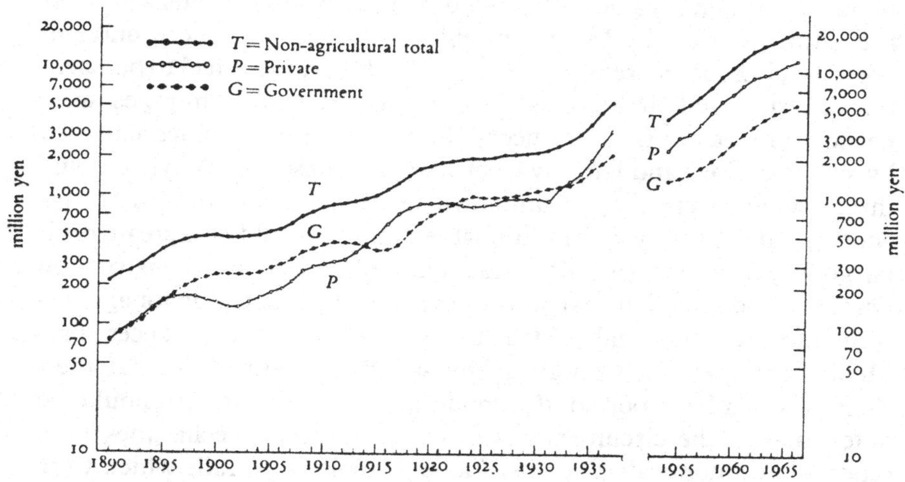

Fig. 5.1. Gross Domestic Fixed Investment (1934–6 prices).
Source: Ohkawa and Rosovsky, *Japanese Economic Growth*, 32.

At this time also – especially if we concentrate on productive investment – construction was the main form of national investment. This generalization is valid through the first decade of the twentieth century; at some time between 1911 and 1917, a sharp break occurred in the compositions of domestic capital formation, and from that time onward private producers' durable equipment absorbed the greatest share of resources.

In large measure the leading role of construction was merely a reflection of the overall primacy of public investments and their nature at this time. Road-building, port improvements, government buildings, etc. – all construction activities with high capital-output ratios – accounted for over two-thirds of public capital formation. Even in the private sector, investments were relatively equally divided between construction and durable equipment until the time of the First World War, when the latter category suddenly assumed a new level of significance. Factory and commercial construction, and also – before the nationalizations of the early twentieth century – private railway construction, represented expenditures that were nearly as great as those on machinery and equipment.

The last aspect of the Meiji investment pattern is, perhaps, the most unusual. In Japan at this time, capital goods were produced by two rather distinct methods: one can be called 'traditional' and the other 'modern'. When it came to the building of railways or waterworks, or the acquisition of producers' durables, all sorts of modern and imported techniques were necessarily involved. Roadbeds had to be scientifically surveyed and graded; steam pumps and iron pipes were needed for waterworks; producers' durables meant machines activated by steam engines and later by electricity. All these were ways of doing things which were largely unknown in Meiji Japan. But there was another side to the coin. Traditional techniques could also create capital goods, as in the case of residential and commercial construction (largely wooden structures), irrigation and land reclamation for agriculture, and even road and bridge construction. In these instances, pre-Meiji techniques of a highly labour-intensive nature retained their usefulness and supported the modernization process. It should be noted that in the circumstances of the times, these techniques were especially economical. They used labour, tools, and skills which were readily available; they did not require much capital or new skills which were relatively expensive.

According to this classification, in Meiji Japan roughly one-half of the capital goods were produced by traditional techniques. This was a unique characteristic of early Japanese industrialization, because in post-Meiji years the proportion of traditional investments declined sharply while, simultaneously, many of the older ways in (say) house- and road-building were abandoned in favour of imported methods. However, while it lasted, Japan provided a good example of what Joan Robinson has called 'walking on two legs'.

Perhaps we can now summarize the situation obtaining in the last third of the nineteenth century. Initial modern economic growth was in large measure based on the achievements of a traditional economy. This was the first step towards the accomplishment of industrialization. It was now time to take the second and much bigger step – perhaps one could call it the leap toward a semi-developed state – and for that we turn to an analysis of the period from 1900 to the present.

TWENTIETH-CENTURY JAPAN: THE ECONOMICS OF TREND ACCELERATION

The historical path of investment

We begin the analysis of the twentieth century by outlining some of the major quantitative aspects of investment. The primary focus will be on the rate of growth of private non-agricultural capital formation

($\Delta I/I$).[8] This emphasis has a number of justifications. Most important, our intention is to argue (in an ensuing section) that private investment was the key dynamic element for rapid economic growth in this century. Secondly, the amplitude of private $\Delta I/I$ moves with great clarity. Finally, the measurement of private $\Delta I/I$ is direct and comparatively simple, and therefore statistically more accurate than competing measures.[9]

Quantitative analysis of Japanese capital formation covers a period of nearly one hundred years, from the present back to the 1870s. For this long period, the pattern has been remarkable stable. It consists of a steeply rising trend combined with wave-like movements of the growth rate. An investment wave or long swing consists of a period of relatively rapid growth of capital formation followed by a number of years of lower growth.

Taking the broadest possible time span, it is possible to speak of three and one-half swings. The first consists of very high growth rates until the middle of the 1890s, followed by about six years of much slower capital formation. As Table 5.1 shows, a second upswing begins somewhat hesitantly during the Russo-Japanese War and falters a bit between 1909 and 1912, but then the expansion carries through the First World War. The latter half of this swing comprises the rather low investment growth rates prevailing throughout the 1920s. Then, beginning in the 1930s and continuing until the impact of the coming war made itself felt directly, a sharp investment spurt is in evidence. This has to be considered a 'half-swing', because the period between the late 1930s and the early 1950s – some fifteen years – includes the destructive effects of the Second World War, the occupation, and the initial rehabilitation of Japan's economy. Normal economic analysis for this time span would make little sense; statistics are unavailable, and a great variety of distortions effectively prevent the fitting of these years into a consideration of long-run development. However, after the Second World War the familiar pattern appears again. Private investment expands at near-record rates somewhat beyond the 1950s; this upsurge is followed by considerably slower investment growth through 1966, when our period of analysis ends.

8 To be more precise, gross domestic fixed private capital formation, excluding residential dwellings.

9 Both total product and capital stock measures entail greater statistical problems. In the former case, there are difficulties in estimating the output of tertiary production and the output of the handicraft sector. In the latter case, problems of valuation and depreciation create many obstacles.

TABLE 5.1
Private non-agricultural investment: Annual rates of growth (per cent) at constant prices

	Growth rate		Growth rate		Growth rate
1901	−7.2(T)	1918	8.9	1935	20.3
1902	2.7	1919	6.3	1936	31.4
1903	14.5	1920	−0.4	1937	20.2(P)
1904	9.8	1921	−2.5		
1905	12.0	1922	−8.5		
1906	9.7	1923	−9.5		
1907	14.0	1924	−9.8	1956	12.1(T)
1908	19.3	1925	−4.2	1957	15.1
1909	6.1	1926	1.2	1958	25.3
1910	5.4	1927	8.0	1959	26.4
1911	6.1	1928	−2.1	1960	18.6
1912	2.6	1929	−4.7	1961	17.6
1913	9.1	1930	−2.0	1962	18.3(P)
1914	18.9	1931	5.0(T)	1963	9.0
1915	24.0	1932	12.0	1964	6.0
1916	23.9	1933	11.4	1965	11.4
1917	19.3(P)	1934	13.9	1966	16.0

Note: Investment in residential construction is excluded. Growth rates are based on series smoothed by a seven-year moving average before the Second World War. 'Constant prices': 1934–6 prices before the Second World War; 1960 prices after the Second World War.
Source: K. Ohkawa and H. Rosovsky, *Japanese Economic Growth* (Stanford, Calif., 1973), 33.

While a general identification of these long investment swings is a pretty simple matter, the selection of actual turning points (peaks and troughs) is inevitably more complicated and debatable. For the twentieth century, we suggest the following dating:

	T	P	T
Swing I	1901	1917	1931
Swing II	1931	1937	
Swing III	1956	1962	1966

Perhaps some of these dates could be shifted a year in either direction, but this would not affect the conclusions. In any event, peaks and troughs are based on moving averages, and each individual year stands for the centre point of a band of seven (pre-war) or five (post-war) years. What should be unambiguous, especially after an inspection of Table 5.1, is that before and after each turning point (T or P) the annual rates of growth of private investment maintain – for a long time – very different levels.

Let us, however, take note of three specific problems of interpretation relating to the selection of turning points.

1. In our periodization, 1901–17 is treated as a single upswing even though the smoothed growth rate of private capital formation falters from 1909 to 1912. Had the First World War not provided a strong stimulus to entrepreneurs during the decade 1909–19 – and we must always keep in mind that these are time series smoothed by a seven-year moving average – it is entirely possible to say that 1909–12 would have developed into a fully fledged downswing. As it is, we prefer to consider the period as a unified step forward containing a small stumble. There is no 'right' or 'wrong' in this sort of conclusion; it is largely a matter of taste.

2. The post-war investment spurt is dated as beginning in 1956. This decision contains a measure of arbitrariness and is related to the aftermath of defeat in the Second World War. Nearly all authorities agree that around 1952–4 the Japanese economy returned to 'normalcy': the allied occupation had ended, and most indicators – capital–output ratio, employment, food production, etc. – were showing expected long-run levels. We accept this date, and since moving averages are employed we begin in 1956, which is the earliest available entry.

3. Lastly, a word about the 1966 turning point. A new investment spurt may have begun at that time; alternatively, one may eventually wish to treat 1962–6 as a 'stumble' analogous to the earlier experience of 1909–12. In any event, the data are as yet too sparse for making a long-range historical judgement.

Of the three spurts contained in the data, the second (1931–7) and third (1956–62) are much more powerful than the first (1901–17). In fact, the average level of annual growth rates of private non-agricultural investment was higher in each successive spurt.

One should also note the relationship between public and private capital formation. It is clear from Figure 5.1 that the gap between these types of investment changes in accordance with the historical periodization: it narrows during upswings and widens during downswings. In other words, whenever the Japanese economy experienced its most rapid secular expansions, private investment expanded more rapidly than public investment, and the reverse was true when the economy contracted.

The changing composition of investment

Although investment spurts have recurred regularly in Japanese economic growth, their composition has changed, reflecting the increas-

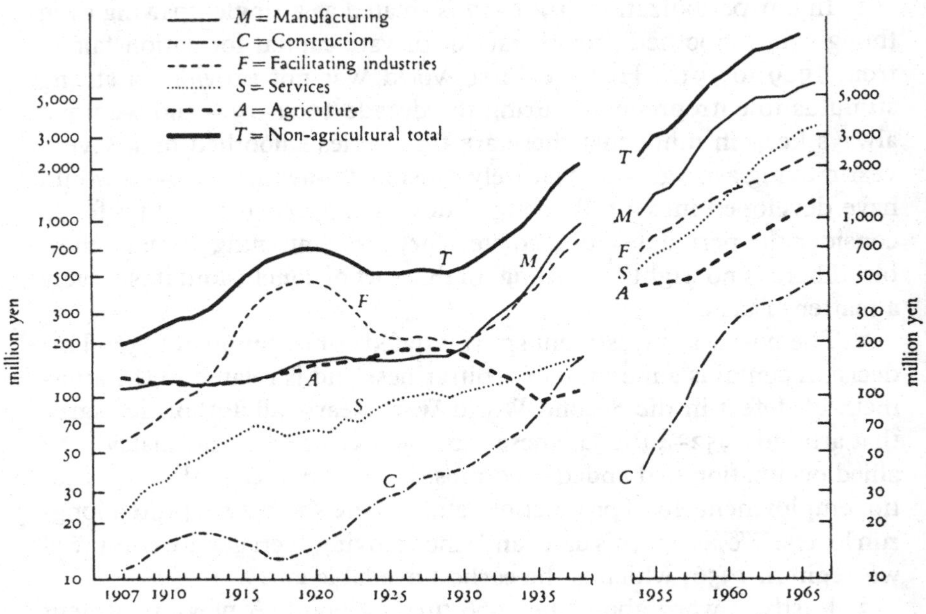

Fig. 5.2. Composition of Private Investment (1934–6 prices).
Source: Table 5.2.

ing maturity of the industrial structure. Visual evidence is provided in Figure 5.2, where private capital formation has been divided into major industrial components: agriculture, manufacturing (including mining), construction, facilitating industries, and services.

The first investment spurt of this century was due most of all to the rapid increase of investments in private facilitating industries, which include transportation, communications, and public utilities. At the beginning of the twentieth century, total non-agricultural private capital formation in constant prices averaged approximately 200 million yen per annum (see Table 5.2). By the end of the First World War, this had risen to an average of over 600 million yen per annum. The level of investment flow rose by some 400 million yen, out of which 350 million yen were accounted for by facilitating industries.

During the second investment spurt the lead was taken by manufacturing industries, with facilitating industries a close second. In the early 1930s, private capital formation averaged 600 million yen per annum; towards the end of that decade, yearly totals were in the neighbourhood of 1,800 million yen. The average annual flow had

TABLE 5.2
Average private non-agricultural investment by industries: selected years (million yen, 1934–6 prices)

	Manufacturing	*Construction*	*Facilitating industries*	*Services*[a]	*Total*
1907[b]	111	11	57	22	201
1917	135	13	402	69	619
1931	232	46	228	113	619
1937	820	143	682	161	1,806
1956	1,504	70	889	709	3,172
1962	4,830	336	1,680	2,065	8,911
1966	5,812	478	2,376	3,382	12,048

Note: Seven-year averages before Second World War; five-year averages after Second World War.
[a] Excludes residential construction.
[b] Investment by industrial sectors cannot be carried back further than 1907.
Source: Ohkawa and Rosovsky, *Japanese Economic Growth*, 154.

risen by 1,200 million yen, of which some 800 million yen originated in manufacturing, and 700 million in facilitating industries.

The post-war investment spurt (1956–62) produced sharp increases in capital-formation levels for all industries: a threefold increase in the total and in manufacturing and services, fivefold in construction, and twofold in facilitating industries – all accomplished in six years. However, when the weights of the industrial sectors are considered, it becomes apparent that manufacturing played an even stronger leading role than in the 1930s: it accounted for close to 60 per cent of the increases. Furthermore, capital formation in the service industries became a significant factor for the first time: its contribution (25 per cent) was larger than that of facilitating industries (14 per cent).[10]

Although these data classify investment by industrial origin, they can equally well confirm the growing significance of durable equipment as opposed to construction. All industries engage in construction activities, but the proportion of this kind of investment is greatest for

10 Having identified the industries whose growth was most responsible for twentieth-century investment spurts, it would now be logical to discuss the experiences of individual industries. Unfortunately the data for this type of analysis are unavailable. The only exception applies to the period 1955–61. For this period, the Economic Planning Agency has provided figures which indicate an average annual real rate of growth of capital formation in manufacturing of 34.4 per cent. The individual rates are as follows: metal products, 50.4 per cent; transport machinery, 44.4 per cent; other machinery, 49.4 per cent; petroleum and coal products, 38.3 per cent; chemical products, 23.7 per cent; ceramics, 25.7 per cent; food and tobacco, 20.1 per cent; textiles, 13.7 per cent; other industries (timber, pulp and paper, printing, hides, rubber), 20.1 per cent.

facilitating activities; it represents a much smaller part of manufacturing expenditures.

Finally, a brief look at the changing composition of investment during the two downswings. Clearly the periods in question were very different. In the former – 1917–31 – the average flow of private capital formation remained unchanged for well over a decade. In the latter – 1962–6 – private capital formation continued to rise, though at much lower rates. Nevertheless there are important similarities. With the exception of the decline in private investment in facilitating industries for 1917–31, all industries continued to raise their levels of investment. But a strong growth leader is missing. Compared to the preceding spurts, the growth rates are not only lower but also more nearly at similar levels for the various components.

The growth pattern

The years from 1901 to 1966 constitute an identifiable historical unit – or, to use a term previously employed, a growth phase[11] – because during this long period certain important characteristics of Japanese economic growth have persisted. In other words, this period established a specific growth pattern whose principal features we must attempt to outline.

1. During the sixty-odd years with which we are concerned, the trend rate of growth of aggregate product has been very rapid, as indicated by the average annual growth rates shown in Table 5.3.[12] The expansion can be described as 'very rapid' because among the fifteen to twenty countries that have established a long-term record of modern economic growth, only the United States and Canada (and perhaps Sweden and the Soviet Union) have turned in achievements of similar magnitudes. Thus, in the overall distribution of historical growth rates, a conservative estimate of Japan's performance would place her in the top quartile.

2. An inspection of the figures in Table 5.3 also shows that Japan's trend rate of growth of aggregate product has been accelerating during the period of analysis. Average growth rates, according to our period-

11 These ideas were initially developed in Kazushi Ohkawa and Henry Rosovsky, 'A Century of Japanese Economic Growth', in W. W. Lockwood (ed.), *The State and Economic Enterprise in Japan* (Princeton, 1965), and the same authors' 'Postwar Japanese Economic Growth in Historical Perspective: A Second Look', in L. Klein and K. Ohkawa (eds.), *Economic Growth: The Japanese Experience since the Meiji Era* (New Haven, Conn., 1968).

12 The GDP figures which form the basis of these growth rates are still subject to future revision, especially in the case of tertiary production.

TABLE 5.3
GNP: Average annual rates of growth during long swings (smoothed series at constant prices; per cent)

	Period	*GNP*[a]
(1)	1897 (Peak)–1901 (Trough)	1.96
(2)	1901 (T)–1917 (P)	2.88
(2′)	1912–1917	4.56
(3)	1917 (P)–1931 (T)	2.75
(4)	1931 (T)–1937 (P)	5.71
(5)	1937 (P)–1956 (T)	1.83
(6)	1956 (T)–1962 (P)	10.72
(7)	1962–1969	11.91

Note: All series smoothed by a seven-year moving average before the Second World War, and by a five-year moving average thereafter, except for 1969, which represents a three-year centred average. Pre-war data in 1934–6 prices. Postwar data in lines 5 and 6 in 1960 prices; line 7 has been tentatively converted to 1960 prices by using the aggregate deflator. The values for 1937 (1934–6 prices) and 1956 (1960 prices) have been linked using the aggregate deflator for gross national expenditures: this was 321.6 in 1955 (1934–6 = 1).

[a] Average compound growth rates between successive trough and peak years of the smoothed series.

Source: Ohkawa and Rosovsky, *Japanese Economic Growth*, 25.

ization of the time series, alternate between periods of comparatively more rapid and less rapid growth, but the trend rate is clearly rising all the time: the economy developed more speedily in the 1930s than in the early part of the century, and the sharpest acceleration occurred after the Second World War.

3. The more than sixty years between 1901 and 1966 have been subdivided into segments of unequal length, and each one of these segments represents an upswing or a downswing of a long swing. Long swings have been an enduring feature of Japanese growth, and they have been especially prominent in the rate of growth of private and total capital formation. Since 1901 there have been three periods of especially rapid growth of capital formation – 1901–17, 1931–7, and 1956–62 – and these have been designated as 'investment spurts' or upswings. The remaining years – 1917–31 and 1962–6 – were periods of much slower investment growth and have been designated as downswings.

4. Long swings in the rate of growth of capital formation and aggregate product have had, between 1901 and 1966, certain system-

TABLE 5.4
Investment ratio (I/Y) and related terms (per cent)

	I/Y: *total*	*I/Y:* *private non-agricultural*	*K/Y:* *private non-agricultural*
1907	12.75	5.68	1.29
1917	16.46	11.78	1.39
1931	15.13	6.47	1.83
1937	20.53	12.00	1.74
1956	29.74	17.38	1.88
1962	36.42	23.66	1.59
1964	35.68	21.98	1.61

I, gross domestic fixed investment; *Y*, gross domestic product; *K*, gross fixed capital stock.
Note: Smoothed series. Figures for 1907, 1956, and 1962 are five-year moving averages; those for 1917, 1931, and 1937 are seven-year moving averages; and those for 1964 are three-year averages.
Source: Ohkawa and Rosovsky, *Japanese Economic Growth*, 47 and 148.

atic associations with some other standard measures of economic performance.

(*a*) From the figures cited previously, we already know that capital formation grew more rapidly than output, and therefore during the years under review the trend of *I/Y* (the investment ratio) rose substantially. However, the rise of this ratio was closely associated with investment spurts: when the rate of growth of capital formation spurted, the investment proportion went up sharply; when capital formation grew at more deliberate speeds, *I/Y* remained relatively stable, as Table 5.4 shows. The stability of *I/Y* during downswings – when a sharp decline might have been expected – is related to a persistent 'leader–follower' relationship between public and private investment. When the rate of expansion lies above the long-run trend line, private investment grows more rapidly than public investment. The reverse is the case when output growth is below trend values. This pattern can be observed in the changing proportions of private and public investment (see Fig. 5.1).

(*b*) The proportion of total domestic savings to total product (*S/Y*) presents essentially the same pattern as the development of *I/Y*. As a trend, the domestic savings proportion rose steeply during this century, and the path of increase closely resembled that of the investment proportion: when capital–formation and output growth rates were in

TABLE 5.5
Composition of domestic savings (per cent)

	Gross aggregate ratio[a]	*Net ratio*[b]	*Proportion of private to total domestic savings*[c]
1908	15.6	7.9	23.7
1917	32.6	22.4	57.8
1924	15.6	5.3	−14.5
1931	15.7	6.7	24.5
1937	24.5	16.3	50.4
1956	27.7	20.4	47.6
1962	33.9	25.6	45.9
1966	36.0	26.7	48.3

Note: Smoothed series. Figures for 1908, 1956, and 1962, and 1966 are five-year moving averages; figures for 1917, 1924, and 1931 are seven-year averages; and figures for 1937 are three-year averages.
[a] National savings/GNP.
[b] Net savings/NNP.
[c] Corporate savings are included.
Source: Ohkawa and Rosovsky, *Japanese Economic Growth*, 167.

an upswing, domestic saving rates went up sharply; by contrast, saving rates declined during downswings. The figures in Table 5.5 tell the story.

(*c*) The relationship between long swings and the private non-agricultural capital–output ratio (K/Y) is somewhat complicated, and the historical pattern is most readily discernible in Table 5.4. These movements combine the divergent influences of trends and swings. During an upswing or investment spurt, the values of K/Y generally declined. In a trend sense, however, K/Y gradually increased from the beginning of this century until the first half of the 1930s. From then until the beginning of the 1960s, the values of K/Y generally declined.

(*d*) The trend and swing association of the relative income shares of capital (α) and labour (β) are also systematic. The trends of both shares were rather steady in this century. For example, the values of α during the entire pre-war period ranged from a low of 33.7 per cent in 1924 to a high of 50.2 per cent in 1917. However, during investment upswings it was characteristic for α to rise and for β to decline, and the opposite was true for downswings. A very typical case was the expansion that peaked in 1917. From the beginning of the century until that year, α rose quite steadily from values in the neighbourhood of 40 per cent to above 50 per cent. During the 1920s, when the economy contracted, the average level of α was below 35 per cent.[13]

(*e*) The movements of K/Y and α also suggest certain systematic alterations in the expected rate of return on capital (r). Since $\alpha = Kr/Y$, during investment upswings the rate of return on capital must tend to rise, since K/Y rises less rapidly or declines while the income share of capital increases. During investment downswings, a reverse tendency must have existed. For trend values, we may assume that r was relatively steady.

5. Another growth characteristic of this period is the steady and uninterrupted rise in the capital-intensity (K/L) of production of the non-primary private sector. The figures are as follows (in terms of average annual growth rates):[14]

For	1908–17, $G(K) - G(L) =$	4.27 per cent
	1917–31	3.25
	1931–8	2.69
	1955–61	4.67
	1962–4	8.44

Were it not for the unusually low rate of growth during the 1930s, one would conclude that $G(K/L)$ exhibits both trend acceleration and a close association with the investment spurt. In fact, this was undoubtedly the case; the failure of a strong upturn of $G(K/L)$ from 1931 to 1938 was obviously due to the abnormally heavy weight of military investments. If these were to be included, we can safely assume that the average growth rate of capital-intensity would have been well in excess of 4.5 per cent per annum.[15]

6. Elsewhere we have characterized the Japanese economy of this period as being affected by a special type of dual economy called 'differential structure'. A dual economy implies the presence of two sectors – one traditional and the other modern – operating with different methods, techniques, and incentives. Differential structure includes the additional attribute of a growing gap between the modern and traditional sectors, and this can be most conveniently expressed in terms of relative partial productivity (Y/L) and wage levels. As a

13 See Ohkawa and Rosovsky, *Japanese Economic Growth*, basic statistical Table 18, pp. 328–9.
14 *Ibid.*, Table 3.1, p. 47.
15 See K. Boulding and N. Sun, 'The Effects of Military Expenditures upon the Economic Growth of Japan' (mimeographed: Tokyo, 1967).

TABLE 5.6
Wage differentials for selected years

	Wa/Wm (per cent)
1905	67.4
1910	68.3
1915	71.9
1919	83.3
1925	79.7
1931	48.9
1935	47.9
1939	71.3
1954	36.5
1960	40.4
1965	51.1

Wa, wages of male daily-contract workers in agriculture; *Wm*, wages of regular male workers in manufacturing.
Note: Smoothed series: five-year moving averages (except 1965, three-year average).
Source: Ohkawa and Rosovsky, *Japanese Economic Growth*, 126

representative example for the modern sector, one can use manufacturing, with its imported and increasingly capital-intensive methods of production. As representative of the traditional sector, one can take agriculture, which at this time retained many indigenous features: small units, labour-intensive methods, etc. What happened to the relative positions of these two sectors in the twentieth century can be seen in Tables 5.6 and 5.7.

From the point of view of the partial productivity of labour, the gap between agriculture and non-agriculture widened both before the Second World War and again between 1956 and 1964. This is reflected in the movements of the ratio of agricultural to non-agricultural wages. It sustains two distinct levels, until the 1920s agricultural wages – though lower – did not suffer relatively. Since the 1930s, however, we can easily see the effect of the so-called differential structure.

7. Finally, two characteristics of Japan's export growth pattern should be noted. During the entire period under review, the average annual rate of growth of exports (in constant prices) exceeded that of GNP. This can be seen in Table 5.8, where exports occupy an ever larger share of

TABLE 5.7
Productivity differentials for selected years, 1897–1937 (yen, 1934–6 prices) and 1956–64 (hundred yen, 1960 prices)

	Y/L Total	Y/L Non-agricultural	Y/L Agricultural
1897	231	464	120
1901	243	466	129
1917	404	711	171
1931	534	863	199
1937	850	1,069	229
1956	2,480	3,293	1,155
1962	4,607	5,880	1,584
1964	5,044	6,846	1,695

L, labour force; *Y*, output (gross of depreciation).
Note: Smoothed series: five-year averages centred on the indicated year.
Source: Ohkawa and Rosovsky, *Japanese Economic Growth*, 36.

aggregate demand – with only a brief interruption during the Second World War. Furthermore, as shown in the same table, the prices of exports declined, relative to domestic prices, during the entire period.

AN INTERPRETATION

The main historical facts have been presented, and our last task will be to suggest how they might be interpreted. We are primarily interested in saying something about the overall significance of capital inputs in Japanese modern economic growth during the twentieth century. Specifically, we should like, if possible, to shed some light both on the rapidity of Japanese growth from 1900 to the present and also on what we have called trend acceleration. These are complicated issues, and within the confines of even a long chapter it is out of the question to deal with them in depth. Nevertheless, it would be even less satisfactory to ignore these issues, which are of wide interest.

We may begin by going back once more to the recurring swings in private investment. In terms of formal economic reasoning, they can be 'explained' without undue difficulty. Let us make four behavioural assumptions (based on standard economic theory):

1. that private investment was the main agent of economic modernization as the carrier of new and largely imported technology;

TABLE 5.8
Exports: Prices and proportion of aggregate demand indexes of relative prices

	Exports	*General expenditures prices*	*Exports/Aggregate demand (per cent)*
1906	100.0	100.0	5.5
1912	69.5	120.5	7.7
1917	74.7	165.4	10.8
1924	70.6	250.0	–
1931	41.7	191.6	13.0
1938	43.5	249.8	17.0
1953	100.0	100.0	–
1955	86.3	105.1	9.4
1960	79.9	118.5	10.6
1965	57.9	149.1	12.6

Note: The original price indexes are three-year averages for the pre-war and single years for the post-war period. Individual indexes have been expressed as ratios of the general price index, and then converted to 1906 and 1953 comparison bases.
Source: Ohkawa and Rosovsky, *Japanese Economic Growth*, 179 and 143.

2. that the level of private investment is determined by profit expectations;

3. that a simple aggregate production function of the type $G(Y) = G(R) + \alpha G(K) + \beta G(L)$ can describe the main trend of output growth for the private modern sector. $G(R)$ (R being the residual) refers to the rate of growth of technical and organizational progress (as is well known, this production function assumes the existence of neutral and disembodied technological progress);

4. that there exists a personal savings function of the type $S_t = A + bY_t + cY_{t-1}$. This simply says that the savings ratio depends on a constant term, the level of income, and the rate of growth of income.

The historical record shows that the duration of upswings and downswings varied considerably, and there is no doubt that *ad hoc* phenomena such as wars and a changing international political and economic climate played key roles in determining certain turning points. And yet these observed long swings do have significant common characteristics. Coupled with our standard assumptions, they can suggest a formal explanation.

It is most convenient to start with an investment spurt which can be outlined first as a simple or theoretical case; then we can turn to a less simple and more true-to-life version. In the simple case we rigorously retain the specifications of the production function in which α is held constant. Even with this restriction, the rate of return on capital (r) could rise owing to a fall in K/Y attributable to technological and organizational progress and rising demand. A rise in r would mean a greater amount of capital formation as well as a shift towards more capital-intensive production for private modern output. S/Y would also increase with a time lag – in accordance with the previously assumed savings function.

The simple case has been mentioned only to show that technological progress and demand alone could give rise to an investment spurt. But it is a much too simple-minded and unrealistic formulation. We have shown that α rises in the upswing, and this must have been so for two reasons: first, technological progress may be not neutral (as assumed by our long-run production function) but biased in favour of capital, especially in the upswing; secondly, there may be a wage lag behind increases in the partial productivity of labour. Both reasons would raise the rate of return on capital and intensify the investment spurt.

Whether technical change in Japan has or has not been biased – and in which direction – is a most difficult empirical problem. No one can render a valid historical judgement, and one can safely continue to think in terms of neutrality. At the same time it is clear that in Japan the wage lag was present, especially in earlier upswings, and that both technological influences (via K/Y) and lagging wages raised the rate of return on capital in the modern sector. Both were present at the same time, and they interacted with one another: this is the essence of the less simple and more empirical case.

Lagging wages or a flexible supply of labour are related to the differential structure. By a flexible supply of labour we mean simply that a small increase in modern wages produces a relatively large increase in the labour supply. The labour supply was flexible because of the productivity differentials which characterized the Japanese economy, and flexibility was additionally supported by a growing population and the comparatively small labour requirements of the modern sector.[16]

The end of the upswing and the ensuing downswing are harder to systematize because there are only two downturns in the record, each

16 That these requirements were comparatively small is demonstrated by the fact that the absolute size of the gainfully employed labour force in agriculture remained stable until the Second World War. After the war it started to decrease, but even at present around 15 per cent of Japan's labour force is still gainfully employed in the primary sector.

of which is strongly affected by different external events. Still, the common features stand out. Towards the end of the upswing, the expected rate of return on capital falls owing to a rise in K/Y caused by a slowdown in the rate of growth of technological progress, which has to be explained by considering specific historical circumstances. (Admittedly, all of the foregoing is stated in very 'ideal-typical' terms.)[17] At the same time, the labour supply will – temporarily – become less flexible as the pool of transferable workers shrinks. All these factors combine to pull down the growth of private capital formation, and during the downswing $\Delta I/I$ and $G(R)$ maintain lower average levels, while to some extent government activity helps to sustain the aggregate investment proportion (I/Y) at a new plateau. After some time, the rate of return on capital will rise again when – because of a renewed wave of technological or organizational opportunities – K/Y begins to decline, and another private investment spurt will have started.[18]

We come now to the heart of the matter: the relationship between long swings in the rate of growth of private capital formation and the trend acceleration of aggregate output. What happened during upswings or investment spurts has already been described: the very rapid expansion of private investment, declining capital–output ratios (especially in the leading expansion industries),[19] and a rising share of private as opposed to public capital formation. In addition, each investment spurt features an identifiable set of growth industries. Foods and textiles accounted for more than half of the growth of manufacturing between 1901 and 1917; in the 1930s, chemicals, metals, and machinery contributed over 60 per cent;[20] during the 1950s and 1960s one would have to assign leading roles to electronics and cars.

17 Clearly, market conditions which would affect the capacity level of operations could lead to similar results.

18 However, we have noticed that a lag of varying duration may be present. Three points can be made in connection with this apparent discrepancy. First, our observations are based on five- or seven-year moving averages, and therefore a specific turning point must be thought of as a rather broad band of years. Secondly, investment spurts are here considered in the aggregate, but they begin in specific industries, and the mechanism which we describe applies especially to the leading industries. Thirdly, external factors – changes in demand, foreign markets, etc. – could precede, and set the conditions for, an investment spurt.

19 It has already been shown that the post-war decline of the aggregate capital–output ratio (K/Y) was steeper than at any previous time. Sectoral capital–output ratios are available mostly for the postwar period. They indicate the most marked declines in manufacturing, at rates about nine times as rapid as the average for the entire economy. (In agriculture, the capital–output ratio actually increased.) Within manufacturing, the most impressive declines occurred in the machinery, petroleum, and chemical sectors.

20 See Y. Shionoya, 'Patterns of Industrial Development', in Klein and Ohkawa (eds.), *Economic Growth*.

Taken together, all these factors establish the strong presumption for viewing investment spurts as periods of innovational changes – i.e. periods during which technological and organizational progress was imported and introduced at especially rapid rates. Subject to the severe limitations of the previously used production function, this is apparently confirmed by the changing growth pattern of the residual. The measured residual invariably grew more rapidly during investment spurts, and never more rapidly than after the Second World War.[21]

The framework of the production function also suggests a relationship between the input of capital, the residual, and trend acceleration. A stable 'equilibrium' growth path for the private modern sector in the twentieth century can be described by the equation $G(R) = (1 - \alpha)[G(K) - G(L)]$. This equilibrium growth path is simply the production function used previously, where K/Y and α are taken as constants – which was in fact approximately true for the trends. Therefore, in this historical long run, we can reasonably assume a steady relationship between the growth of the residual (technological and organizational progress) and the rate of growth of capital-intensity. Of course, the equilibrium growth path also contains all the necessary ingredients of trend acceleration if – as was indeed the case – the rate of growth of K/L keeps rising over time. But that leaves open the central question: Why is a higher rate of growth of K/L associated with a higher rate of residual growth?

Relationships between $G(R)$ and $G(K/L)$ are not meant to be interpreted as simple causalities. On the contrary, to gain a realistic historical picture of this relationship requires the supposition of complicated interactions. By way of conclusion we should like to offer a few speculations concerning these interactions.

Periodic spurts in private investment of long duration must have had both a supply-production and demand effect. On the supply side, an investment spurt resulted in more rapid capital accumulation, a higher level of capital-intensity, and more output. It would also be reasonable to suppose that new investment, which served as a carrier for imported technology on which Japan depended, contributed towards raising $G(R)$. This is the most direct and simple explanation.

21 Our own research indicates that the aggregate residual grew over four times more rapidly following the Second World War, in comparison with the 1930s. Residuals grew most rapidly in manufacturing and facilitating industries. See Ohkawa and Rosovsky, *Japanese Economic Growth*, chaps. 3 and 4. For a quite similar perspective, see Edward F. Denison and William K. Chung, *How Japan's Economy Grew So Fast* (Washington, 1976).

Investment spurts also affected demand because we can assume that the increases in output raised the level and rate of growth of per capita income, especially in an economy in which underemployment was a persistent characteristic; and the rate of growth of per capita income can also affect $G(R)$. To explain the reasoning behind this last assertion requires a much broader view of economic processes.

That Japan was a borrower of Western technology is a well-established fact. Furthermore, in acquiring foreign machinery and know-how Japan was not, in general, limited by the availability of suitable items. In a follower country there always existed room for introducing improvements of foreign origin, and this is why one can take the rate of growth of technological opportunities as given or as externally determined. There is, however, a very different side to this issue. Technology is developed in the most advanced countries, and it conforms most closely to the factor proportions and skills available in the United States or Western Europe. Almost by definition this makes technological emulation a most difficult task for a less-developed country like Japan, in which capital was relatively scarce and labour relatively plentiful. Thus, despite the manifold opportunities for borrowing, there existed also a set of limiting factors which we shall call the level of 'social capability' – those factors which constitute a country's ability to import or engage in technological and organizational progress.

A higher rate of growth of per capita income may raise social capability in two major ways. First, it would improve human capital (better schools, improved diet, etc.), thereby making labour more suitable for work with advanced methods. Second, rising per capita income would also widen the market, thereby improving the possibilities of exploiting economies of scale.[22]

This then is what we mean by the 'interaction' between $G(R)$ and $G(K/L)$. In the simple case one can move from increases in K to a higher level of R. But R can rise because income has risen, and this can lead to a higher level of K/L.

In this chapter we have, for obvious reasons, concentrated on the role of capital. One should not, however, overlook the importance of institutional developments in raising Japan's social capability to import increasing quantities of productive technology. Each investment

22 The inclusion of foreign trade reinforces these arguments. Possibilities of exporting obviously raise the level of aggregate demand and improve the chances of obtaining economies of scale. On the supply side, the case for the direct or simple explanation is especially applicable as seen in the relative secular decline of export prices. After all, Japanese exports, since 1900, consisted almost entirely of modern manufactures – i.e. those products that benefited most from imported technology.

spurt brought forth new institutions which enhanced this process. Between 1901 and 1917 there arose both the zaibatsu and permanent employment. Combines of the zaibatsu type created early and lasting opportunities for taking advantage of economies associated with large-scale, worldwide operations. Permanent employment led to a labour force which had no incentive to resist even labour-displacing innovations. During the 1930s an alliance between the zaibatsu and government, which centred on military needs, led to the development of heavy industries subsidized by public funds. After the Second World War, the newly created Ministry of International Trade and Industry and the new activities of private banks were both critical factors in furthering the rapid absorption of American and West German technology. Undoubtedly these institutions all contributed to a secular increase in the level of social capability. Furthermore, we believe that these advances were additive: an advance created in one era did not lose its effectiveness in later years. All these are aspects of Japan's trend acceleration in the twentieth century which deserve closer study.

CHAPTER 6

FACTORY LABOUR AND THE INDUSTRIAL REVOLUTION IN JAPAN[1]

INTRODUCTION

An industrial revolution transforms a traditional society into an industrial one. The primary agent in this process is the factory system, which organizes capital and labour on a scale unheard of in traditional society, on the basis of technology and behaviour that are difficult for 'traditional man' to understand. By the logic of traditional social organization and according to the outlook of traditional man, the human dimension of a typical work place under the factory system is mysterious and fearsome: that is, a large number of workers, far exceeding the population of a typical traditional village, are organized into a work force in which tasks follow the dictates of the technologically determined division of labour but hang together at the same time in an interdependent framework administered by management. In other words, workers are divided and ruled by managers who derive their authority from technology and the market. Whether this new social structure, though limited to the workplace, is a boon or peril to traditional man depends very much upon the style and pace of industrialization. Eventually traditional man is transformed into 'industrial man', as he sheds the traditional outlook and work habits and acquires new personal qualities that enable him to manoeuvre rationally in the class structure of an industrial society. These concurrent transformations, societal and personal, are often fraught with lags and frictions requiring facilitating or regulatory interventions by the state. This chapter sets out to trace these developments in the course of Japanese industrialization. It covers such major aspects of the factory system as the hiring, training, structuring, and rewarding of the work force, the fashioning of principles, rules, and procedures of industrial relations, and the use of state power to regulate and resolve conflicts between workers and managers.

The abbreviations and definitions used in the footnotes of this chapter are found on page 293.

1 The author wishes to acknowledge financial support from the East Asian Studies Center of Stanford University, which has made this study possible.

Japan made substantial progress in industrialization during the seven decades between the Meiji Restoration of 1868 and the Second World War, although even at the end of this period Japan was at best a semi-industrialized society. The fiasco of the Pacific war initiated by Japan herself demonstrated the dynastic and atavistic backwardness of her values and the uncontrollable irrationality of her institutional processes. Nevertheless, her transformation into a semi-industrial society was a historical reality of great significance. Although this transformation was not thorough enough to produce even a nineteenth-century equivalent of European liberalism, it at least represented a more or less unique case of industrial revolution in which a non-Western traditional society had managed to absorb the impact of Western industrialism without losing its own national identity or historical continuity. Because of the peculiar circumstances which governed Japan's participation in the worldwide spread of industrialism and the uniqueness of the cultural base on which she erected her industrial system, the expansion of her factory system and the formation of her industrial labour force produced many unusual features unknown in Western labour history.

While the topics of this chapter are limited to the factory sector of the Japanese economy, it is useful to take an aggregative view of Japan's economic growth before the factory sector is extracted from it for an intensive observation and analysis. Unlike post-war Japan's spectacular rate of economic growth, averaging about 10 per cent per annum (stopped by the oil shortage of 1973 and the ensuing 'stagflation'), economic growth in pre-war Japan was a rather leisurely affair. The most careful estimates ever made on Japan's long-term economic performance indicate that between 1887 and 1938 (on the basis of five-year averages centred at the indicated dates) the gross national product in constant prices increased at 3.16 per cent per annum in the aggregate and at 1.94 per cent per capita (the difference being the rate of population growth, 1.22 per cent).[2] The pace of economic growth represented by these figures is certainly moderate, even compared with the performance of average underdeveloped countries after the Second World War. But, historically, Japan's pre-war economic growth is still commendable by the standards that today's developed countries reached at comparable stages of development.

The moderate nature of Japan's pre-war growth comes to the fore when the growth of factors of production is considered along with the

2 *ELTES*, 1, 'National Income', 16.

aggregate income growth. During the same period, between 1887 and 1938, Japan's labour force increased at 0.8 per cent per annum, while her gross capital stock increased at 3.6 per cent excluding residential stock (or at 2.6 per cent including residential stock).[3] On the basis of these rates of increase in capital and labour, and with the help of an assumption about the relative shares of factors in output – such as, for example, 40 per cent for capital and 60 per cent for labour – it can be calculated that the growth of factors of production alone would have brought about the growth of the gross national product at 1.80 per cent per annum excluding residential stock, or 1.40 per cent including residential stock.[4] Thus, the total growth rate of the gross national product (3.16 per cent) was far higher than what was possible owing solely to the sheer quantitative growth of factors of production. This 'residual' growth rate, under the stated assumption about the relative shares, amounts to 43 per cent of the total growth rate excluding residential stock, or 56 per cent including residential stock. Different relative shares of factors would naturally produce different values of the residual rate, but it is clear that within conceivable limits of the relative shares the residual would still be quite substantial. What accounts for the residual is a complex issue, as it signifies everything other than the growth of labour or capital as measured in the usual quantitative manner (the number of gainfully employed persons, and the value of all capital goods in constant prices). Therefore this at least suggests that qualitative aspects of Japan's socio-economic changes ('modernization' is a convenient catch-all term for these changes) were far more important than the mere increases in aggregates associated with capital accumulation and the growth of the work force. These qualitative changes certainly include changes in economic structure, such as the relative expansion of industry and the widening of markets for all kinds of goods and services, as well as improvements in the efficiency of factor use in each sector of the economy.

Now, to turn to the rise and expansion of the factory sector, it is

3 Computed from *ELTES*, III, 'Capital Stock', Table 1, pp. 148–50. Since *ELTES*, II, 'Population and the Labour Force', was not available at the time of writing, the labour-force growth rate in the text was computed from data in Kazushi Ohkawa *et al.*, *The Growth Rate of the Japanese Economy since 1878* (Tokyo, 1958), chap. 5, part II.

4 The formula for this calculation is as follows:

$$G(Y) = aG(K) + (1 - a)G(N) + G(R)$$

which states that the growth of income (Y) is the sum of the weighted growth rates of capital (K) and of labour (N), the weights being relative shares of capital (a) and of labour ($1 - a$). When $G(Y)$ is not equal to this sum, a residual growth rate ($G(R)$) has to be recognized to balance the equation. For a thorough inquiry into the size of the residual in Japan, see Kazushi Ohkawa and Henry Rosovsky, *Japanese Economic Growth* (Stanford, Calif., 1973).

generally accepted that in the early 1870s more than 80 per cent of the gainfully occupied population was in agriculture and less than 5 per cent in manufacturing.[5] The percentage for the factory labour force was infinitesimal. By 1940, the proportion of employment in agriculture had dropped below 50 per cent, enabling Japan at last to look like a non-agricultural society. At the same time, the proportion of employment in manufacturing rose to more than 20 per cent by 1940, but it was only during the 1930s that factories had begun to absorb more than 50 per cent of manufacturing employment.[6] Even so, the 'factory' was generously defined as a manufacturing establishment employing five or more operatives. In hindsight, the incursion of the factory system into pre-war Japan seems rather benign, absorbing only 12 or 13 per cent of the labour force at the end of seventy years of industrialization. Although this fact attests to the resilience and viability of non-factory manufacturing processes in the course of industrialization, as well as to the productivity of all sectors other than manufacturing, the growth of the factory labour force was phenomenal – from a few thousand in the 1870s to nearly four million in 1940, representing roughly a thousandfold increase over seventy years. The wedge relentlessly driven into the Japanese economy by the factory system during this period was the source of several major economic, political, and social convulsions, often shaking Japanese society to its foundations, as will be reviewed in this chapter.

A warning of a methodological nature may be noted in passing. In view of the small proportion of Japan's labour force in factory employment throughout the pre-war period, one may be tempted to conclude that Japan should have been in a state of 'unlimited supplies of labour', in Arthur Lewis's phrase, for her modern sector and that the recruitment of factory labour should have posed no problem at all. Had Japanese employers emerged with the foresight, courage, and calculation that generations of economists have attributed to the hypothetical entrepreneur, they would no doubt have succeeded in taking advantage of the demographic and economic conditions of Meiji Japan and thus ensured themselves unlimited supplies of labour through an appropriate manipulation of pay and working conditions. However, the Meiji employers were just as much a part of the society's traditional backwardness as all other Japanese. The problems related to the hiring, training, organization, and retention of a work force were as

5 Henry Rosovsky, 'Japan's Transition to Economic Growth, 1868–1885', in H. Rosovsky (ed.), *Industrialization in Two Systems* (New York, 1966), 93.
6 Computed with the help of tables in *NRUS*, x, 154–65.

formidable to them as capital flotation, factory construction, and technical choice. Although capital was scarce, at least its use posed no problems once they obtained it. But hiring labour was just the beginning of problems of work-force management. In this sense, labour could have been a serious constraint on the rationality of technical choice, the scale of production, and ultimately the general rate of economic growth. Appropriate control over the size, skill, and quality of the work force as required by the expanding, and often fluctuating, output were acquired only after much trial and error. The great pains suffered by workers, employers, and society at large in order to generate an expanding, committed labour force for Japan's factory sector, as detailed in the subsequent pages, should serve as a warning against a cavalier acceptance of the hypothesis that labour is no problem when industrialization takes place in the setting of traditional backwardness.

THE PRECONDITIONS FOR FACTORY LABOUR, 1850–1890

One prerequisite for the expansion of factory employment is that employers and workers understand their relationship as trading work for wages. To borrow Polanyi's felicitous phrase, labour and land must become 'fictitious commodities' bought and sold in the market. But a transaction that treated land or labour as if they were no different from ordinary commodities was alien to the social organization and economic relations of feudal Japan, and the transformation of feudal into capitalist employment relations was a protracted and complicated process. Although the subject of this chapter is factory labour, changes in the use of labour in agriculture prior to Japan's industrialization are useful as an indicator of how feudal institutions were changing toward capitalist resource allocations and employment relations.

From servitude to wage labour in agriculture

T. C. Smith describes the development of rural employment relations in feudal Japan as a progressive loosening of the bond between master and servant. It became easier for a servant (*hōkōnin*) to redeem his freedom. Smith notes three types of *hōkōnin* in this respect. 'Least free of the three types was a *hōkōnin* given to someone by his family for an indefinite period in return for a loan. He served as a kind of security on the loan and was compelled to work for the person with no compensation but his keep until the loan was repaid.'[7] However, the loan was usually too large for the borrower to repay, and the *hōkōnin* had no chance to redeem his freedom. The second type in Smith's classification was the *hōkōnin* who, like the first, was put in service for a loan but whose wages were computed and charged against the loan, so that when the loan was repaid the amount actually paid was smaller than what was due by the amount of accrued wages. The third type was the *hōkōnin* whose labour and period of service were reckoned in such a way as to write off the debt completely by the end of the loan period.[8]

So long as labour services were subsidiary to the transaction of loans, employment relations as transactions in wage labour were a remote possibility. However, the development of commercial agriculture gradually changed the situation. The worker customarily still received a lump sum at the beginning of the employment period. But its character changed from a loan to a partial advance payment of wages. The emergence of *hiwari-hōkōnin* (service reckoned on a daily basis), which was already in practice in the early nineteenth century, is a case in point. An employment 'contract' dated 1829 in the Osaka area specifies two years' service on the basis of twenty days per month and stipulates a certain sum of money as a 'wage immediately payable' (*sokkyūgin*).[9] The contract is signed by the *hōkōnin*'s father, the *hōkōnin* himself (aged thirty-three at the time), and two 'guarantors', in that order. It may be emphasized that the *hōkōnin* was not the principal party to the contract, although it was his labour service that was contracted. The contract was accompanied by an affidavit by his father and guarantors stating that in default of the specified service by the *hōkōnin* they would send a substitute or return the advance payment. Records surviving with another family in this area indicate that the number of *hiwari-hōkōnin* consistently fluctuated with the state of farm work between 1838 and 1868.[10]

Furthermore, according to the records of a leading peasant family in the Prefecture of Yamagata, wage-earning servants contracted for three to twelve months (*kyūdori-hōkōnin* or *nenki-hōkōnin*), and servants hired by the day are found together with Smith's second type as

7 T. C. Smith, *The Agrarian Origins of Modern Japan* (Stanford, Calif., 1959), 112.
8 *Ibid.*, 113–14.
9 Toshio Furushima, 'Bakumatsuki no nōgyō hiyō rōdōsha' ['Paid Labour in the Late Edo Period'], in Takamasa Ichikawa *et al.*, *Hōken shakai kaitaiki no koyō rōdō* [*Paid Labour during the Period of Disintegration of Feudal Society*] (Tokyo, 1961), 184. 10 *Ibid.*, 180–1.

early as in 1777. For 1824, however, the debt-linked servants are no longer listed.[11] These examples, together with those mentioned in the preceding paragraph, indicate that many types of *hōkōnin* coexisted for a long time, and there was no neat succession of one type to another over time. But in terms of shifting importance, one can speak of an evolution in employment relations during the feudal period – that is, of an increasing number of shorter-term, debt-free servants, and ultimately of day labourers.

By the early 1870s, a substantial proportion of Japan's rural inhabitants had come to depend for livelihood on day labour (*hiyatoi*). In six villages in the Murayama area, Yamagata, this proportion rose to 12 per cent.[12] A close inspection of the data indicates that the *hiyatoi* in the early 1870s were largely peasants who no longer possessed enough land to fully occupy themselves. Many of them had lost their land completely.[13]

The surveys of agrarian conditions undertaken in 1890 in various prefectures (*nōji chōsa*) clearly indicated that employment relations in agriculture were no longer independent of expanding labour markets for rural and urban industries.[14] Four types of agricultural employment were noted in the survey for Osaka: daily, monthly, semi-annual, and long-term. The first two types of employment strictly depended upon the demand for labour during the busy seasons. The semi-annual employment applied to domestic servants. The long-term employment (*nenki yatoi*), usually from a period of five to seven years, was no doubt a direct descendant of the *nenki-bōkō* of the previous age. But no indication was found concerning the indebtedness of the *nenki* worker.[15] Farming, sericulture, and other by-employments in the countryside competed for the same labour. Weaving, silk-reeling, and cotton-spinning absorbed increasing numbers of women and girls from the farm households. Mining, industry, and construction drew away large numbers of men and boys from the villages. For example, the villages near Osaka lost their workers to Osaka's urban industries and replaced them by workers brought over from other parts of Japan through middlemen in the labour market. This geographical reshuffling of the labour force was not always smooth. Consequently, complaints about a labour shortage were often heard among the richer farmers.

11 Nobuo Watanabe, 'Shōgyōteki nōgyō ni okeru koyō rōdō' ['Paid Labour in Commercial Agriculture'], in Ichikawa *et al.*, *Paid Labour*, 54–7. 12 *Ibid.*, 81.
13 *Ibid.*, 80–103. 14 *NRUS*, 1, 25–36. 15 *Ibid.*, 26–7.

Labour services in weaving

One of the oldest branches of manufacturing is weaving, which during the feudal period was an important by-employment of the peasant households. The hub of the fabric industry was the merchant-employer (clothier – *orimoto*), who put out work to weavers working in their homes. The clothier undertook major preparatory and finishing processes within his factory and trained weavers who would later work under the putting-out arrangement. The clothier also employed adult weavers, mostly women, to work on the looms set up in his factory. The development of the factory system and wage labour in the textile industry meant the expansion of the numbers of directly employed adult weavers. During the feudal period and through much of the Meiji Era, working for the clothier as an apprentice or a weaver was invariably called '*hōko*' and the worker '*hōkōnin*'.

During the feudal period, it was usual for a peasant family to state in the service contract, as a reason for supplying a *hōkōnin*, that they were hard pressed with the tax burden, implying that *hōkō* was resorted to as a means of raising money for paying taxes. Among the eighty-three remnants of old employment contracts in the possession of two cotton clothiers in the Prefecture of Aichi, two contracts dated 1879 and 1884 indicate that the *hōkōnin* were sent into service precisely for this reason.[16] This kind of tax burden, which originated in the feudal lord's desire to keep the peasantry tied to the land – is no longer mentioned in contracts effected after 1887. The content of the typical contract followed a pattern that was characteristic of feudal employment relations. It specified that the purpose of service was learning how to weave, that the employer would supply clothing twice a year, that the employment period would be extended by the same number of days as were lost through the *hōkōnin*'s illness (if such were to occur), and that the *hōkōnin* and her family would return the cost of her keep, fees for her training, and the loan, principal, and interest, in case she should leave prior to the expiration of her contract. The service contract was signed by the *hōkōnin*, her parent or guardian, and a few guarantors.

Among ninety-four service contracts surviving from the period of 1849 to 1866 at a fabric factory in the Prefecture of Tochigi, a leading centre of fabrics, twenty-seven were renewals by the same workers.[17]

16 Hideo Hayashi, 'Bisai ni okeru meiji kōhanki no koyō rōdō' ['Paid Labour in Western Aichi during the Late Meiji Era'] in Ichikawa *et al.*, *Paid Labour*, 235–7.

17 Takamasa Ichikawa, 'Nōson kōgyō ni okeru koyō rōdō' ['Paid Labour in Rural Industries'], in Ichikawa *et al.*, *Paid Labour*, 129–46.

For thirteen of these workers, the records indicate that each of them started as a young apprentice for a term of service well beyond five years and, after one or two renewals with successively shorter terms of service, ended up as a weaver hired by the day or by piece. Several long-term *hōkōnin* returned home to take work put out by the clothier who had trained them. This leaves unexplained how so many other *hōkōnin*, older skilled weavers, had come to be employed by the clothier in question, or where other apprentices trained by him had gone. Perhaps many apprentices trained by this clothier became domestic weavers or *hōkōnin* for other clothiers, while he also used the existing pool of weavers (trained by other clothiers) for obtaining his own short-term *hōkōnin*. Thus, there was evidently something akin to a labour market in this area. Another interesting feature of the ninety-four surviving contracts under discussion is that they are for a wide variety of employment periods. Excepting four unclear cases, the remaining ninety are distributed as follows: thirty-seven for more than three years (fifteen of which are for five to six years), thirty-five for less than three years (of which twenty-one are for one to two years), and eighteen for day work or piece work. Many of the weavers contracted for day or piece work are free of the loans which characterize the other *hōkōnin*, and their wages are higher than those of others. Nevertheless, the *hōkōnin* was not yet a wage-earner. The unusual strength of the putting-out system in the fabric industry had long resisted the full proletarianization of the weavers. And although the custom of calling the employee '*hōkōnin*' tended to disappear in the 1880s, the terms of employment contracts largely remained the same as when she was a *hōkōnin*.[18] The terminology of the factory system was adopted in the fabric industry as in other industries during the 1890s.

The labour market for the raw silk industry

The production of raw silk was an offshoot of agriculture. Factory-like establishments were fewer in silk-reeling than in weaving during the feudal period. After the Meiji Restoration, owing in part to the government encouragement, there was a remarkable increase in the factory production of raw silk. Because of the rapid transition to the factory system, labour recruitment in the raw silk industry was at first fairly free of the traditional procedure of recruiting *hōkōnin;* but it was not

18 *Ibid.*, 151.

long before a reaction set in due to a tightening labour market. Employers discovered that a 'feudalistic' control of their workers was easier and more profitable than following the dictates of the labour market.

The Meiji Government in the early 1870s encouraged the modernization of raw silk production by introducing Western technology through model factories.[19] Particularly impressive was the silk filature at Tomioka, modelled on French silk-reeling techniques. The operatives trained in the Tomioka Filature were then employed by private mills in other parts of Japan to start operation of newly imported silk-reeling machines. A private company, the Ono-gumi, had already experimented with less-machinized Italian techniques in a mill built in Tsukiji, Tokyo, in 1871. The Ono-gumi had also financed silk factories adopting these techniques in the Nagano area. The Nagano silk manufacturers were also the first to try French techniques after the superiority of the Tomioka Filature was demonstrated. Still, among more than three thousand silk factories employing ten or more workers in 1893, those using the traditional techniques (*zakuri*) amounted to nearly one-fourth.[20] Nor do these figures capture the total picture of the silk industry, since non-factory establishments were of equal importance in this industry, though less so than in fabrics. According to data for three relatively advanced counties (*gun*) of the Prefecture of Gunma, technologically inferior to Nagano but far above the average for a silk-producing area using Japanese techniques, there were only twenty 'machinized' filatures among the 24,193 silk-reeling establishments in 1890, and the putting-out system was widespread.[21] This structure was more representative of the Japanese raw silk industry as a whole. The broad non-factory base of the raw silk industry implies that there were large numbers of non-factory workers experienced in silk-reeling whom the expanding factories could draw upon.

In the 1880s these workers were locally recruited and were paid wages according to a peculiar combination of piece and time work.[22] But the quality of silk thread reeled was also important. Therefore, wages were eventually quoted as daily rates differentiated into several steps according to the amount of cocoons used and the quality of silk

19 T. C. Smith, *Political Change and Industrial Development in Japan: Government Enterprise, 1868–1880* (Stanford, Calif., 1955), chap. 6. See also *NRUS*, 1, 136–47.

20 Mikio Sumiya, *Nihon chinrōdōshi ron* [*A Tract on the History of Wage Labour in Japan*] (Tokyo, 1955), 156.

21 Computed from the agrarian survey for the prefecture of Gunma, *NRUS*, 1, 158–60.

22 Sumiya, *Tract on the History of Wage Labour*, 152–74; and Mitsuhaya Kajinishi *et al.*, *Seishi rōdōsha no rekishi* [*A History of Workers in the Raw Silk Industry*] (Tokyo, 1955), chap. 1.

thread reeled. But once a worker was placed in a certain step indicating her skill level, she enjoyed the wages appropriate to the step irrespective of the quantity of her work, which naturally varied from day to day, principally owing to factors not directly under her control. The identity of personal status and wage rank (*tōkyūbetsu chingin*) was a general characteristic of wage administration in Japanese factories in the 1880s.

In contrast to later developments in employment relations in the silk industry, it is significant that the workers in the silk factories of the 1880s were local commuters and that many of them were married women. The 'dormitory system', which became almost synonymous with the factory system in textiles after 1890, did not exist during the 1880s. When lodging was needed near factories, workers found it on their own. Also, many of the workers at the time of hiring were already skilled in the sense that they had reeled silk at home. The women of the farm households engaged in sericulture often worked in the factories which bought their cocoons. Since the factory method of reeling was not yet decisively superior to household reeling, there was no urgency for farm families to send their women and children to the factories. Factory employment was a 'secondary' occupation (*kakei hojo teki rōdō*) in the true sense of the word. And since no mention was made of loans in the employment contracts in the raw silk industry of the 1880s, it may be supposed that the element of coercion over a worker by her employer was minimal. The working day was generally fourteen hours long. This was the normal length of a working day in peasant households, and workers did not object to it in the factories. However, when employers tried to lengthen the working day by half an hour in Kōfu, Yamanashi, in 1886, workers considered it unacceptable. A few spontaneous strikes not only restored the customary working day but shortened it by half an hour in some factories.[23] The fluid and relaxed employment relations in the raw silk industry would lead one to believe that a free labour market – with no disadvantages to the workers, remarkably enough – had finally emerged in rural Japan. Workers and their families were free of debt and of prior commitment to a fixed period of service as a condition of employment. The workers were free to leave any time they wanted to. Yet this kind of labour market frustrated and annoyed silk employers, since they did not know how to expand output and make profits while operating within such a tight labour market. The employers'

23 Kajinishi *et al.*, *op. cit.*, 36–44. See also *NRUS*, 1, 155–8.

feudalistic reaction set the stage for the next development in Japanese employment relations.

The metal and engineering industries

In contrast to the predominantly female labour force of the textile industries, workers employed in metalworking and engineering factories were predominantly skilled adult males. They were originally traditional artisans but were drawn into factory employment when the government promoted metalworking and engineering industries.

After the visit of Commodore Perry in 1853, the Shogunate and provinces had reacted to the impact of the West largely through their military reflexes. These military and industrial efforts by the feudal governments were bequeathed to the Meiji Government as a substantial list of capital assets and industrial plants.[24] The Meiji Government itself added more but was forced to liquidate all non-military enterprises because of operational losses which caused tremendous treasury drains. Most of these enterprises were sold to private interests by 1885. The liquidation was completed when the Tomioka Silk Filature was transferred to Mitsui in 1893. Nevertheless, so far as the metal and engineering industries were concerned, throughout the Meiji Era (1868–1912) the government was employing far more workers than private factories in similar lines.

Unlike weaving and silk-reeling, these government factories had two major problems due to their technology and size. Their scale was enormous by Meiji Japan's standards, creating a grave organizational problem. To this the government responded with traditional techniques of feudal administration. The other problem, far more serious, was to find the proper quantity of skilled labour to work with imported technology. The problems of organization and skills may be illustrated by the experience of government-operated shipyards at Yokosuka and Nagasaki. Although the Nagasaki shipyard passed to Mitsubishi in 1884, these problems did not disappear with the change to private ownership.[25]

24 Smith, *Political Change and Industrial Development*, chap. 1.

25 The rest of this section draws upon Hiroshi Hazama, *Nihon rōmu kanrishi kenkyū* [*Studies in the History of Work-Force Management*] (Tokyo, 1964), chap. 4; *NRKN*, 1; *NRUS*, 1, 97–118. For analyses and discussions of labour conditions in the government-owned heavy industries, see Sumiya, *Tract on the History of Wage Labour*, 208–39, and Masao Endo, 'Meiji shoki ni okeru rōdōsha no jōtai' ['The Conditions of Workers during the Early Meiji Era'], in M. Sumiya *et al.*, *Meiji zenki no rōdō mondai* [*Labour Problems in the Early Meiji Era*] (Tokyo, 1960), 43–95.

The construction of the Yokosuka Shipyard was started in 1865 by the Shogunate and taken over by the Meiji Government. Initially, there were forty-five French engineers and mechanics; their number decreased to twenty-five by 1876, and to one or two by 1885. The activities at the shipyard covered the whole range from iron-smelting to the building and rigging of iron ships. The workers were essentially paid labour. Yet the work-force structure consistently followed the feudal pattern. In 1868 there were fifty-three Japanese officials and clerks and 705 Japanese workers. The officials and clerks were samurai, and the workers artisans or common labourers. There were 575 artisans, of whom sixty-five formed the privileged core (*kakae shokkō*), supported by 113 regular workers (*jōyatoi*) and 397 helpers (*shokkō tetsudai*). In addition, there were fifty-four common labourers. For launching and sailing ships, a similarly structured small group of seventy-six workers was maintained. The difference in status between leading and ordinary artisans followed the feudal pattern in which a small number of artisans (*okakae shokunin*) served the feudal lord directly and held power over the rest of the craft community in the castle town. At first, there were no Japanese engineers or mechanics. The sole function of the Japanese officials and clerks was to manage the work force. The technical organization and supervision of work were left to the Frenchmen. The skills were essentially traditional or adapted from what was then available in Japan, but the French engineers organized them into a system of interrelated processes for making modern products with modern techniques (tools, machines, materials, etc.). Thus the problem that lay ahead of the Yokosuka management was to transform this peculiar duality of modern technology and feudal social relations into a viable system which was Japanese both socially and technically.

Although traditional crafts were adapted to the requirements of modern shipbuilding to a remarkable extent, it was necessary to obtain a corps of Japanese engineers and technicians who could understand modern technology and take over the shipyard operation upon the departure of the French. The Shogunate had inaugurated two training schools, for engineers (*gishi*) and technicians (*gite*) respectively. Although discontinued for a while after the Meiji Restoration, these schools were later reopened under new names. Originally, engineering candidates were selected from among young samurai in Edo and Yokohama; the candidates for technicians were selected from among commoners in or near Yokosuka. In 1876, there were thirty-seven trainees in the 'engineering school' (now called *seisoku gakkō*), and more than fifty in the 'technical school' (called *hensoku gakkō*). The samurai–

commoner division was no longer honoured. Young samurai who desired to 'rise in the world through industrial work' also enrolled in the 'technical school', and the presence of samurai in their midst seemed to stimulate the commoner–trainees enormously, so that the performance of all the trainees rose substantially.[26] The ordinary workers who did not go through the training schools learned their skills on the job from senior workers. They were a new breed of apprentices (*minarai shokkō* – trainees on the job). Since internal training alone fell far short of requirements, many were hired from the labour market. The fifteenth of each month was the day of hiring at the gate. Applicants had to be at least fifteen years old, and they were sent to different shops within the shipyard according to their qualifications and the labour needs of each shop. Simple tests were given to evaluate the skills of the experienced workers or the aptitude of novices, and each shop enjoyed substantial autonomy in hiring, training, assigning, promoting, retiring, or dismissing workers. In 1872, the working day in the summer was from 6:30 a.m. to 5:30 p.m., with an hour of lunch break; it was from 7.0 a.m. to 5.0 p.m. in the winter. There were no rest days except on a few traditional festive occasions.

After hiring, training, and assigning workers, one faced the problem of how to keep them as long as they were needed. The employment relations at the Yokosuka Shipyard were essentially 'capitalist'. Even before 1868, workers voluntarily applied for jobs and quit freely without fearing feudal sanctions. Because of competition from new factories after 1868, however, the Yokosuka authorities began to experiment on the method of retaining workers. In the late 1870s, the manual workers at Yokosuka were in three classes: regular craftsmen (*jōyatai*), daily employed craftsmen (*hiyatoi shokkō*), and common labourers (*jōninsoku*). The workers admitted to 'regular' status had to promise to stay for a given number of years (varying according to the worker's age), in return for certain amenities. In addition, the regular workers were exempted from military service. Further exemptions were made during the 1880s, but these were largely changes in job titles and manipulations of related allowances and privileges. The frequency of these experiments reflected both the resourcefulness of the Yokosuka management and the difficulty of reducing labour turnover and stabilizing the work force.

A stable work force is meaningless, however, if management cannot

26 This information is from a report by François L. Verny (1837–1908), who built the Yokosuka Shipyard and supervised it until 1876. See Kunitaro Takahashi, *Oyatoi gaikokujin–gunji* [*Foreign Employees – Armed Services*] (Tokyo, 1968), 119.

use it efficiently. During the Meiji Era, management was largely ignorant concerning daily work performance on the factory floor. Effective work-force supervision was beyond their management techniques, since the feudalistic mentality of Meiji Japan barred interactions between management and workers except for commands and obedience from a distance. One curious result of this status difference and communication barrier was the high degree of autonomy enjoyed by the workers, who clustered around leaders of their own choice and formed informal groups to organize and execute work. The Yokosuka Shipyard authorities reluctantly recognized this fact and tried to co-opt the worker groups into the managerial structure. In 1882, confessing that the availability of manpower kept factory supervision at a minimum, and fearing (for no valid reason) that pilfering and other wasteful uses of materials might result from lack of supervision, they proposed to create 'worker gangs' (*shokkō kumiai*) headed by gang leaders (*gochō*) appointed from among senior operatives. A gang included five to twenty workers, and each shop manager (*kōbachō*) was directed to organize his workers into such gangs. Gangs were then exhorted to display the *esprit de corps* through collective achievement. Each gang, when its work was slack, was expected to spontaneously help busy gangs. The gang leaders within a shop were directed to meet daily to discuss measures for coordination and mutual help. Each leader had responsibility for misdemeanours by his gang members if he failed to detect them early and report them to the shop manager for corrective action.

However, there is no evidence to suggest that the worker gangs ever worked in the way the Yokosuka management had intended. Informal worker groups had already existed and functioned as the basic operational units without management's meddling in their daily activities. By co-opting them into the formal structure and trying to mould them in some fashion by appointing leaders and setting down rules, the Yokosuka management may even have damaged the effectiveness of informal control and discipline among workers under their own arrangements. For example, at the Nagasaki Shipyard, which passed to Mitsubishi in 1884, the evolution of work-force management was not characterized by the formal rules of the official Yokosuka Shipyard. Until work rules were elaborated for the first time in 1890, work-force management at Nagasaki was frankly admitted to be a system by 'craft masters' pushes and pulls' (*oyakata suiban hō*). The craft masters (formally '*kogashira*' in the managerial structure, informally '*oyakata*' among workers) recruited, trained, rewarded, and disciplined their workers at the Nagasaki Shipyard. The situation was about the same at

Yokosuka, but the bureaucratic officials appointed to manage the shipyard cared more about structural neatness than about getting work done. Nevertheless, it is interesting that the naval bureaucracy of autocratic Meiji Japan, by its own admission, had to depend, for the daily work of iron-smelting and shipbuilding, upon the ingenuity and spontaneity of the craftsmen it looked down upon.

More generally, the social process leading to the emergence of a labour market was accompanied by government efforts at fashioning modern rules for Japanese life. A new state, still backward by the international standards of the day, was finally brought into being by the Imperial Constitution of 1889, which brought in its train the Civil Code (1890), the Commercial Code (1890 and drastically revised later), and many other laws and regulations designed for a capitalist system. The Civil Code, for example, envisaged capitalist employment relations by declaring the relationship between employer and worker to be a private contract freely entered into by the parties concerned. In anticipation of the worst cases that might arise under the pretext of a contract (like indentured labour or slavery dressed up as a voluntary agreement), the Civil Code prohibited employment contracts of more than five years and in such cases explicitly enabled either party to dissolve such contracts unilaterally at three months' notice. In most cases, employment relationships could be terminated by either party with notice equal to one-half of the accounting period for wage computation and payment. In emergencies, the contract could be dissolved immediately, though the injured party could contest the legitimacy of the 'emergency' and sue the other party for damages.

FACTORY LABOUR, 1890–1910

Large-scale factory production in the private sector spread rapidly in the late 1880s and the 1890s, led by the cotton textile industry. The factory scales in silk-reeling and weaving also expanded, though not to anything like the extent of cotton textiles. The metal and engineering industries were expanding faster than all textiles, but the latter still had a preponderance of factory employment (65 per cent in 1890 and 55 per cent in 1920). Textiles, metalworking, and engineering together maintained a roughly stable proportion of employment (around 70 per cent) through the decades before the Second World War. The prime characteristics of the labour market until about 1920 were the labour shortage in textiles and the backwardness of work-force management in the metal and engineering works. On account of these extraordinary circumstances, capitalist employment relations, either as an ideal or as a reality, had no chance to emerge.

Labour shortage in textiles

During its early years, the Meiji Government encouraged cotton-spinning by both direct investment and favourable credit to entrepreneurs. The mills were generally small, with 2,000 spindles at most, and were usually operated by water power. They used domestically produced cotton. This period of government encouragement (*shōrei jidai*) came to an end in the early 1880s, however, because of widespread bankruptcies stemming from excessive production costs, insufficiency and irregularity of raw materials, and the difficulties of marketing. These cotton-spinning mills also suffered from managerial difficulties on account of their character as workhouses (*jusanjo*) for the declassés created by the Meiji Restoration. But the failure was the father of innovation. Eiichi Shibusawa, one of the most celebrated 'community-centred' entrepreneurs of the Meiji Era, travelled in England and noted that most cotton-spinning mills had at least 10,000 spindles, five times as many as in the average Japanese mill. He then organized the Osaka Cotton Textile Company and in 1883 began the operation of the first large-scale modern cotton textile factory in the history of Japan.[27] This mill initially had 10,500 spindles, and, in a few years more than 60,000. It used steam power and was located in the heart of urban Osaka. Its initial work force in 1883 was under three hundred workers, of whom 80 per cent were women and girls. By 1891 the Osaka Cotton Textile Company was employing nearly four thousand workers, of whom more than three thousand were women and girls. Stimulated by its success, many new mills arose in the late 1880s, and soon the cotton textile industry was heavily concentrated in Osaka.

Between 1887 and 1893, the number of cotton-spinning mills in Japan increased from nineteen to forty and the number of workers from 2,330 to 25,448 persons. Ordinarily one would not associate this situation with intense employer competition for labour. The large urban centres like Tokyo and Osaka could easily have supplied the required number of workers to these textile factories. But the average number of workers needed for starting the operation of a mill was very

27 Taichi Kinukawa, *Honpō menshi bōseki shi* [*The History of Japanese Cotton Textiles*], 7 vols. (Tokyo, 1937), II, chap. 12. See also Johannes Hirschmeier, 'Shibusawa Eiichi: Industrial Pioneer', in W. W. Lockwood (ed.), *The State and Economic Enterprise in Japan* (Princeton, 1965), chap. 5.

large, and it was difficult to assemble several hundred workers on short notice. Worse still, the new mills wanted workers who could tend the machines immediately. In the absence of advance work-force training, the only source of labour was workers employed by the established mills. Thus each new mill invariably 'stole' workers from older mills at least in numbers large enough to start its operation and train new recruits. Employer competition for labour eventually became general. Each firm, new or old, raided all other firms for experienced workers whenever possible, although while training large numbers of workers at the same time. Under the circumstances, workers themselves quickly learned to turn the state of the labour market to their advantage. The textile workers in the Osaka area frequently changed their jobs, sometimes for no other reason than a desire to see different places. The acute labour shortage turned the employer–worker relationship upside down: the employer had to kneel and beg for help, while the worker stood aloof and pondered the offer.[28]

Labour turnover in cotton textiles was very high during the 1890s. An annual hiring or dismissal rate of 100 to 120 per cent of the work force was common in many factories. At first, a considerable proportion of this labour turnover was voluntary job mobility on the part of the workers. Later, when labour-market intermediation became a flourishing business, much of the turnover was brought about by middlemen's machinations. But during the 1880s and early 1890s – before this complication arose – the fluid labour market was on the whole advantageous to the worker, though it was a woe to the employer. Unfortunately, popular opinion was not ready to accept job mobility as a normal feature of modern life. On the employment relations in cotton textiles during the days of government encouragement, a historian has observed approvingly: 'The wages were low and the period of employment was long. The workers found it a great shame to leave their jobs for whatever reasons. The employment relations were much like the lord–retainer relations of the feudal period.'[29] In the space of a little more than ten years, the traditional values seemed to have collapsed among the workers in cotton textiles. Public officials were alarmed by the new state of the labour market and, with their feudalist ethics, regarded the mobile workers as 'deserters' (*tōsō*

28 Keizo Fujibayashi, 'Meiji nijūnendai ni okeru waga bōsekigyō rōdōsha no idō genshō ni tsuite' ['The Mobility of Workers in Japanese Cotton Textiles in the Mid-Meiji Era'], in Sumiya *et al.*, *Labour Problems in the Early Meiji Era*, 137–76.

29 Kinukawa, *History of Japanese Cotton Textiles*, III, 179.

shokkō). Employers, too, considered many possible measures to reduce labour turnover.

The employers' first response was a dormitory for factory workers. By erecting a fence around the dormitory and the factory and guarding the gates day and night, it seemed an easy matter to keep the workers from moving to other employers. In this way, the factory dormitory ceased to be a housing facility and took on different characteristics. Kazuo Okochi observes: 'The girl recruits were as a rule lodged in factory dormitories, which often had more in common with a prison than a welfare institution.'[30] The dormitory, to put it differently, was a storehouse for the human factor of production. The factory was run for twenty-four hours a day on two shifts, for the day and night, each working twelve hours. However, when there were absences, some workers were bound to their machines day and night until their replacements were found. The dormitory rooms ranged from ten to twenty *jō* in area (one *jō*, or one *tatami*, equals three by six feet), accommodating girls at the rate of one per *jō*, or two girls to every three *jō* in better places. It was like covering the entire floor of an unfurnished Western apartment with mattresses and accommodating lodgers at the rate of one person per mattress. Taking a walk outside the dormitory compound was a privilege granted only to those who were so faithful and diligent that the management did not fear their desertion. The same criteria applied to outings on Sundays or holidays. The area outside the dormitory compound was constantly patrolled by the factory's private police force. When attempted deserters were discovered (though many did succeed in deserting despite the careful policing), they were physically punished: slapped, kicked, or beaten. Subject to the whims of the dormitory management, the offenders were sometimes stripped of all their clothes and led stark naked around the dormitory halls carrying signs describing their offences. The predominant concern of the dormitory management was to keep workers from deserting and to ensure a maximum flow of work to the factory. There were also boarding houses operated under special contracts with factories (*shitei geshuku*). The owners made easy loans to their boarders and foreclosed their pay with the co-operation of the factory management. Many of these boarding-house owners were members of well-known gangster groups and had no scruples about scheming for exploiting the mill workers who were defenceless

30 Kazuo Okochi, *Labor in Modern Japan* (Tokyo, 1958), 15. See also Wakizō Hosoi, *Jokō aishi* [*A Tragic History of Female Factory Workers*] (Tokyo, 1925), chaps. 7 and 8.

in the face of cold-blooded violence. The boarding-house owners were even more efficient in forcing workers to work and in keeping track of them than the dormitory management.

Three factors were responsible for turning the dormitory into a prison: (1) a fixed term of employment (three to five years), (2) the employers' preference for workers from faraway places, and (3) labour-market middlemen.

As the labour shortage had become more acute, employers in the Osaka area in 1892 agreed to regulate employer competition for labour by a variety of measures, including a fixed term of employment uniformly imposed on textile workers. Toward the end of the 1890s, in all but a few factories, a promise to stay on the job for three to five years was exacted from each worker when he or she was hired.[31] New workers from faraway places, before they knew whether or not they were fit for factory work, were thus 'sentenced' to a term of servitude within the factory–dormitory complex.

The employers' preference for workers from faraway places was a calculated policy. The cotton textile employers' association, *Dainippon Menshi Bōseki rengōkai,* in its 1898 report on the labour conditions in the industry compared the benefits and costs of hiring from local and distant areas.[32] It was observed that workers from faraway places tended to put up with the rigour of factory work and to honour the terms of employment more readily than local workers. The report noted that fifty mills had already extended their hiring areas to a radius of hundreds of *ri* (one *ri* equals roughly 4 km). Regional variations in workers' reputations were also carefully analysed. Workers from Osaka, where four-fifths of the cotton-spinning mills were concentrated, were said to be lazy, footloose, devoid of perseverance, and full of grievances. On the other hand, workers from Hiroshima (to take one favourite example) were lauded for their extreme perseverance, if at times they were slow in learning new skills. About half of the mills engaged in long-distance hiring mentioned Hiroshima as one of their major sources of labour. The Tokyo factory of the Kanegafuchi Cotton Textile Company, for example, at first recruited from Osaka, Aichi, and Niigata, but by 1894 it concentrated on Hiroshima.[33]

The third factor that turned factory dormitories into prisons was the employers' dependence on labour-market intermediaries for obtaining

31 Gennosuke Yokoyama, *Nihon no kasō shakai* [*The Lower-Class Society of Japan*] (Tokyo, 1898), 200–1; Sumiya, *Tract on the History of Wage Labour,* 196–202; Hosoi, *A Tragic History,* chap. 4. 32 *NRUS*, 1, 255–90. 33 *Ibid.*, 125–6.

workers from faraway places.[34] The middlemen, interested only in the profit that the 'sale' of workers to factories brought to them, did not care about the well-being of their recruits so long as a minimum of willingness to try a factory job was observed. They used all kinds of tricks, not excluding outright lies, to talk country women and girls into taking factory jobs. Guided by considerations of the ease of persuasion, degree of credulity and need for money among peasant households, the labour-market middlemen focused their attention on the unsophisticated and poverty-stricken peasants in backward areas. A pittance of advance payment accompanied by some gifts, kind words, and a glowing picture of life, work, and pay in factories easily moved these poor inhabitants of the hinterland. Having 'bought' the workers at an exorbitant price, the factory tried to hold on to them as long as possible. The dormitory overseers saw to it that girls were kept at all costs. In this connection, it may be useful to remember that labour-market intermediation has always been a flourishing, if contemptible, business in Japan. Around the turn of the century, when total dependence on men was women's supreme virtue and any kind of independent dealings by women were frowned upon, it was customary that men – fathers, brothers, relatives, friends, or even strangers in acceptable guise – should stand as guarantors when women were involved in business contracts whether for sale of property or for employment. The social inferiority of women was abused in many aspects of Japanese life. Women had no place except essentially as servants in the very households where they were wives and mothers. Girls and unmarried women were 'sold' (that is, put in long-term service in return for a loan) to brothels or for domestic service. Labour-market intermediation for factory girls was only one aspect of a value system and social organization that held women in a grossly inferior position as objects fit for traffic.

Since there were monetary incentives involved, anyone with wits and guts could become a labour-market middleman. The male employees of a textile firm, who pirated workers from other firms, would soon put their skills to their own advantage as independent operators. Sometimes they obtained better positions in other firms by supplying a group of operatives whom they decoyed out of their former work place. Everywhere, the kidnapping of girls became something of a

34 For the state of this peculiar phenomenon before and around 1900, see Kashiro Saito, *La Protection ouvrière au Japon* (Paris, 1900); Ernest Foxwell, 'The Protection of Labour in Japan', *Economic Journal*, XI (1901), 106–124; and *Shokkō jijō*, vol. 1. For its subsequent development, *NRUS*, 1, 290–7; and Hosoi, *A Tragic History*, chap. 3.

national sport. Labour-market middlemen even ambushed girls at railway stations, diverting them to different employers than those to whom they were originally going. Outlaws, gamblers, pimps, and hooligans in the towns were naturally extremely skillful labour-market intermediaries. The houses of ill repute were their principal customers. They also operated many cheap inns and boarding houses. Textile firms also employed these gangsters to guard the dormitories and to hijack workers from other firms. These middlemen saw little difference between factory employment and brothel service. Their labour-market manipulations included handing girls on from one middleman to another, leading to the large-scale degradation of factory girls. Kidnapping occurred everywhere, in shops, street-corners, playgrounds, and village squares. Ironically, Japan's progress in industrial urbanization threatened to bring about a reign of terror for women and girls throughout the country.

Because of the indiscriminate recruitment, many of the girls brought to factories by the labour-market middlemen were unfit for factory work. Nearly one-half of the recruits dropped out in the first six months; about half of the rest failed to reach the end of the contractual period; eventually 20 to 30 per cent of the initial cohort fulfilled the contracts.[35] The survivors usually re-contracted with the same employer or became regular participants in the textile labour market for several more years. The typical work force of a cotton textile factory around the turn of the century was 80 per cent female. Of these female workers, 60 per cent were aged twenty or under.[36] Though the minimum age varied from factory to factory, about 10 to 20 per cent of all the female workers were fourteen years old or younger. More than half the female workers were accommodated in dormitories. But the commuters were not 'free' by any means. They had to give the same promise of a specified period's faithful work as dormitory inmates and had a fraction of their pay deducted as a surety. Many of them were boarders in the boarding houses which subcontracted dormitory functions under special arrangements. Yet labour turnover was still very high. In 1900, in one factory near Osaka, 1,112 male and 4,524 female workers were carried over from the previous year.[37] During the year, this factory dismissed 1,877 male workers and hired 1,323. The corresponding figures for female workers were 5,824 and 4,762 respectively. The nor-

35 Computed from data reported by the cotton textile employers' association (mentioned above): *NRUS*, I, 259–60. See also *Shokkō jijō*, I, 66–8. 36 *Shokkō jijō*, I, 5–18. 37 *Ibid.*, 69.

mal dormitory population of this factory at the time was not revealed, but what happened to it in 1900 was reported as follows:

Dismissals:	400 persons
Desertions:	2,800
Discharges for illness:	225
Deaths:	31
Total:	3,456

If it is assumed that 60 per cent of the female workers of this factory at the beginning of 1900 were dormitory inmates, the total number of discharges can be said to have exceeded the dormitory population by 30 per cent. This was about the same as the turnover rate for the factory in question.

Another point of interest shown by the above figures is that the rate of illness and death per year in the dormitory population was 9 per cent. Deaths alone exceeded 1 per cent. By comparison, during the period of 1899 and 1903, the death rates of all Japanese girls in the age group of ten to nineteen ranged between 3.8 and 9.3 per thousand.[38] In 1909, in six northern prefectures (Niigata and others) of Japan known as sources of factory workers, there were 14,834 persons who emigrated for factory work and 5,358 persons who returned. Of the latter, 1,233 persons (23 per cent) were already ill, or fell critically ill after they returned, or died of illness at home. Deaths alone accounted for 5 per cent of those who returned from factory work.[39] As the health hazards of factory work should have been greater in 1900 than in 1909, one should add several dozens of deaths to those who died in the particular factory dormitory in 1900 as mentioned above to give a more complete picture of the fate of factory girls. It is known only that this factory was the Hyogo mill of some textile company, but it may have been the Hyogo branch of the Kanegafuchi Cotton Textile Company, one of the most progressive textile companies in work-force management at that time. Labour conditions in other companies must have been far worse. Indeed, well before 1900 there was a popular belief that factory girls were particularly liable to illness and death, and death was the factory girl's familiar neighbour in everyday life. One former factory girl interviewed by the officials of the Ministry of Agriculture and Commerce said that in her factory she saw people die

38 Japan, Prime Minister's Office, *Nihon teikoku tōkei zensho* [*Statistical Collection for the Empire of Japan*] (Tokyo, 1928), 23.

39 Computed from data in the official explanation of the need for the Factory Law: *NRUS*, III, 209–19.

of illness or accident at the rate of one person per month.[40] Another girl, asked how many had died in the dormitory where she stayed, said 'a considerable number' (*zuibun aru*). At the same time, factory managements failed to treat those dead in a way that would alleviate the fear and sorrow of their workers. One of the former operatives of a certain textile factory, who jumped the fence one night under cover of storm and darkness, recalled that her horror at the casual burials given to dead workers by her former employer had made her brave the dangers of desertion. But then, life in Meiji Japan was short, brutish, and miserable for most people. During the period from 1891 to 1913, life expectancy at birth was only forty-five years; and at the age of ten it was only forty-eight.[41] Far from being a forerunner of modernization, industrialism in Japan was a concentrated and condensed version of the general misery.

As for labour conditions in weaving and silk-reeling, a brief note suffices. During the period from 1890 to 1920, these indigenous industries shared fully in the general expansion of the Japanese economy, employing a large proportion of industrial labour. Large-scale factories were rare, however. The smallest modern cotton textile factories would easily have ranked among their largest. On the other hand, factory employment was larger in weaving or silk-reeling than in cotton-spinning. In 1909, there were 103,000 workers in cotton-spinning as against 155,000 in weaving and 192,000 in silk-reeling.[42] But the recruitment areas of these industries were not as extensive as in the case of cotton textiles and were largely limited to towns and villages within the prefectures where the factories were located, extending to neighbouring prefectures in certain cases.[43] Nevertheless, employer competition for labour and long-distance hiring brought into being the evils of labour-market intermediaries and factory dormitories. The working conditions and dormitory facilities were even poorer in silk and weaving than in cotton textiles. But the silk factories were closed during the winter, and the contracts were negotiated annually during the slack season. The working day was longer than in cotton textiles, ranging from twelve to seventeen hours, though the daily wages were slightly higher. There was some night work, but it was not

40 This and other episodes in this paragraph are from *Shokkō jijō*, III, 166–92. For other incidents, see Hosoi, *A Tragic History*, chap 11.

41 Prime Minister's Office, *Statistical Collection for the Empire of Japan*, 23–4.

42 Japan, Ministry of Commerce and Industry, *Kojō tōkei hyō* [*Factory Statistics*], I (Tokyo, 1909).

43 *Shokkō jijō*, I, 177–88 and 240–68. See also Kajinishi *et al.*, *History of Workers in the Raw Silk Industry*, chap. 2.

universal as in cotton textiles. The statistics for length of employment in 205 factories in the Prefecture of Nagano around the turn of the century indicate that 34 per cent of workers had worked one year or less, while 29 per cent had worked three years or more.[44] Similar data for sixteen cotton textile factories in Osaka indicate that 48 per cent had worked one year or less and 21 per cent three years or more.[45] Thus, despite annual contracts and less favourable working conditions, the silk industry enjoyed a higher degree of worker retention than cotton textiles.

In the weaving industry during the period of Japan's 'take-off' in the 1890s, tradition still dominated work and life. The aggregate output of fabrics increased, but this was due principally to the multiplication of household workshops together with the widening of the merchant employers' marketing network. The traditional practice of taking in apprentices (*denshūjosei*) was continued in many weaving establishments. The initial loans and the promises of steady work for a period of years were still prevalent. The intrusion of the labour-market middlemen was accommodated by contracts between them and the parents of prospective workers, delegating to the middlemen all power and responsibility for negotiating with employers on the workers' behalf. The typical contract was couched in language which implied the unconditional subservience of the worker to her employer. But both parties knew that the words were only rhetoric, so that no litigation ever arose over the terms of the contract.[46]

Managerial backwardness in the metal and engineering industries

Until the First World War, Japan's metal and engineering industries were in a primitive state. As late as 1909, there was more employment in government-owned factories than in private enterprises, though the expansion of the private sector during the First World War remedied this situation. In 1920, therefore, employment in the private sector outweighed that in the public sector by a ratio of three to one. During the Meiji Era, with the exception of basic metals, heavy machinery, and shipbuilding, small-scale workshops dominated the metal and engineering industries. The industrial revolution in these industries was small, but it was a social revolution – it provided an outlet for the manual aptitude of the Japanese and obliterated the status and privilege of the traditional artisans. The Meiji Government abolished the

44 *Shokkō jijō*, 1, 187. 45 *Ibid.*, 70. 46 *Ibid.*, 244–68.

traditional craft guilds which had controlled access to manual trades, and under the stimulus of imported consumer goods, the variety of products that could be made or repaired in household workshops increased. In the mind of the public, the proud artisans were grouped together with all these domestic workers (*shokōgyōsha*) without allowing for their specialized skills and tradition. With the increased commercialization of the economy, the traditional crafts and new manual trades came under the control of merchant employers. Metalworkers (blacksmiths, casters, cutlers, pattern-makers, turners, and so on) went to work in factories or operated their workshops under subcontracting arrangements. Some of them expanded their workshops into small-scale factories, reducing the journeymen and apprentices to the position of hired hands. Thus the socio-economic forces inside and outside the craft community conspired to cheapen the social standing of the traditional crafts.[47]

The traditional apprenticeship, where it survived, was a grossly outmoded training technique. The apprentice was considered no better than a household servant. The master often lacked formal education and was not capable of explaining his trade systematically to his apprentice. Only the exceptional masters welcomed their youngsters' pursuit of formal education. Watching hands rather than reading books was their way of learning skills. In fact, before the Second World War – but especially before 1914 – acquiring skills was a kind of occult art akin to a personal religious experience. An objective analysis or explanation was considered vulgar. The skill was transmitted from master to apprentice through many years of close relationship and co-operation in all aspects of life and work. The union of minds (*ishin denshin*) was the basic principle of skill training. Of course, young men found this type of training highly frustrating, and the attrition rate among apprentices was very high. Remarkably, some youngsters did survive the period of frustration and uncertainty in traditional apprenticeship. These, together with craftsmen coming up from factory apprenticeships, become periodical additions to the supply of skilled workers for the metal and engineering industries. From among them, new craft masters emerged running their own workshops or supervising work teams in factories. They then took their turn in training the next generations of craftsmen.

In the factory, skill training was casual up until the end of the First World War, owing to a general backwardness of work-force manage-

47 Yokoyama, *The Lower-Class Society of Japan*, part II; and *NRUS*, II, 241–87.

ment. Young workers in the age group susceptible to training (those in their teens) increased from less than 10 per cent of factory employment before 1890 to nearly 20 per cent on the eve of the First World War, in the metal and engineering industries.[48] Many of these young workers were in the process of learning skills, but in a majority of factories they were 'apprentices' (called *minaraisei* or *shūgyōsei*) only in name. They were not given the formal courses or work schedules necessary for systematic skill acquisition. Around 1900, there were two types of apprenticeship in the factory.[49] One was a variant of traditional apprenticeship in which a craft master came to work in the factory with his journeymen and apprentices and continued the workshop type of training. The other kind of training was a variant of on-the-job training which, it was hoped, would be acquired by youngsters while they were working in the midst of craftsmen as their helpers. No formal instruction was given to the young workers. They swept the floor, cleaned machines and tools, made tea, and ran errands for the craftsmen. If luck was with them, they received a few moments of guidance from this or that craftsman. The concept of a 'trade' tended to disappear from factory work. It was broken down into a series of specific tasks, and by knowing how to do one or another task, a worker could style himself a craftsman. By learning one task here and another there, alert workers were able to learn the whole 'trade'.

The absence of systematic skill training in Japanese factories before the First World War reflected the dearth of managerial talent required to organize, maintain, reward, and motivate a large number of workers as a single unit within the factory. An easy way around this impasse was to call in groups of craftsmen from outside and to form a work force via subcontracting relationships with these groups within the factory. The Japanese shipyards have been particularly adept at using such subcontracting groups. Adaptation of this type of decentralized work-force management was the method which the Yokosuka Shipyard formalized, owing to circumstances previously described. It was an arrangement under which group leaders were appointed, from among the workers hired by the factory, according to age, length of service, skill, or any other quality that would enable them to command the other workers' respect. They were then given a wide range of employer-like privileges, i.e. power and responsibility for managing their groups within broad guidelines laid down by the factory manage-

48 Inferred from Endo, 'Conditions of Workers', 56–7, for the 1880s; *Shokkō jijō*, II, 5–7, for around 1900; and Ministry of Commerce and Industry, *Factory Statistics*, 1914.

49 *Shokkō jijō*, II, 36–8.

ment. While the degree of autonomy of the group varied from factory to factory, this was the principal method of work-force management in Japanese factories before the First World War.

The group leader [called variously *kogashira, kumichō, gochō* (where the title of *kumichō* was not used), *joyaku, sewayaku,* etc.] hired, fired, and trained his underlings within broad limits in response to the fluctuating demand for labour in the factory. The management's function concerning the work force was thus reduced to keeping accounts of wage payments. The group leader was the *de facto* employer so far as the ordinary workers were concerned. He was seen as the *oyabun* or *oyakata* (parental role), while the workers perceived themselves as the *kobun* or *kokata* (filial role). In this way, the role structure in the factory was closely aligned with the prevailing social patterns and ethics. The factory was like a large village composed of many workshops and each workshop was a kind of extended family anchored to the principle, ethos, and structure of the Japanese family. To society at large, the factory *oyakata*'s reputation was equivalent to that of a workshop-owner or craft master. Once his social standing was so fixed, he became the first point of contact for any worker seeking a job in the factory. The subdividing of the factory into workshops closely aligned to the general pattern of social organization reduced workers' fears and misgivings about the imposing size, strange appearance, and impersonal character of the factory. A worker was a member of his *oyakata-kokata* group, not an employee of the factory. Unlike the latter-day workers of Japan, a Meiji craftsman would rarely name the factory as his employer, nor would he derive any particular pride from mentioning its name. His pride was in his trade and in belonging to the circle of a respectable *oyakata*. The Meiji labour market for skilled metalworkers was a nexus of such social groups. Workers moved among factories by utilizing the network of references among the well-known *oyakata*.[50] The coveted goal for any worker was to establish himself as an *oyakata* with his own workshop and *kokata*.

The mobility of craftsmen during the Meiji Era was high, but it was less a strategy for economic gains than a cult or a step in the lives of craftsmen. When direct personal experience was practically the sole method for learning a trade, an aspiring journeyman had to travel widely in order to increase his knowledge of the world and to improve his skills so that he could be a respectable *oyakata* at a later stage.

50 Mikio Sumiya, *Nihon rōdō undōshi* [*A History of the Labour Movement in Japan*] (Tokyo, 1966), 51.

Since travelling was accepted as something fashionable, it was also practised by many workers as a cult without any other purpose. By practising it, however, the mobile workers became agents of technological diffusion because of their wide exposure to techniques and opportunities in different places. Therefore the mobile workers were generally considered more skillful and knowledgeable than those who stayed with the same employers for a long time. A report on the Nagasaki Shipyard explicitly recognized that workers who had travelled widely were often more skilled than workers who were trained and retained by the Shipyard.[51]

During the Meiji Era, the status of wage-earner was generally regarded as temporary. With age and experience, one hoped to rise to a supervisory position in the factory or to become a craft master on his own, with a concomitant rise in social standing. Because of this incomplete proletarianization of factory labour, the trade-union movement that arose among metalworkers toward the end of the nineteenth century proved to be far from a movement of wage-earners primarily interested in job security, wage increases, or improved working conditions. After having withdrawn legal status from all kinds of feudal guilds, the Meiji Government soon realized that free enterprise and occupational mobility tended to result in excessive competition in certain trades, coupled with a reduction in product quality. In 1885, the government therefore began to encourage the formation of trade associations (*dōgyō kumiai*) according to official guidelines defined in a series of regulations. A trade eligible for the formation of an association was broadly defined as a gainful activity in agriculture, industry, or commerce. Craft associations, organized within the legal framework for *dōgyō kumiai,* were particularly successful among building trades. They regulated individualistic competition among members, endeavoured to secure favourable and uniform pay scales, policed the quality and standards of work, and contributed toward their members' moral uplift and educational development.[52] Since these were also some of the activities that trade unions would pursue, it seemed an easy matter to turn craft associations into craft unions. However, this process did not prove to be as simple as that.

The earliest attempt to organize a craft union was Dōmei Shinkō Gumi promoted in 1889 by craftsmen employed in the Ishikawajima Shipyard, the Army Arsenal, and other public and private engineering

51 *NRKN,* I, 109.
52 *NRUS,* II, 241–2. See also Yoshio Morita, *Wagakuni no shihonka dantai* [*Industrialists' Associations in Japan*] (Tokyo, 1926), 25–35.

works in the Tokyo area. In addition to carrying on the activities of a trade union, the Dōmei Shinkō Gumi hoped to accumulate funds to build its own co-operative factory in order to employ its members and to train apprentices for the craft. This last hope was frustrated owing to an improper management of funds, and the union itself subsequently collapsed.[53]

The first trade union worthy of the name in Japanese labour history was Tekkō Kumiai (Metalworkers' Union), organized in December 1897 in Tokyo under the auspices of the Rōdō Kumiai Kiseikai (Society for the Promotion of Trade Unions).[54] Many of the workers related to the former Dōmei Shinkō Gumi joined the new Metalworkers' Union. The greatest attraction of the new union was its mutual-assistance scheme to pay benefits to dues-paying members in cases of work injury, sickness, and death. The union also organized co-operative stores. But the union's activities never reached the point of collective bargaining with any employer. In three years its failure was evident; the union rose and fell with the success and failure of its mutual-assistance scheme. The union had aspired to be a trade union but disappeared before it showed any signs of developing into one. There were many reasons for its failure. The main reason was that workers were not ready for a trade-union movement. The assistance scheme was an incentive for workers to join the union, but they wanted the benefits without paying for the costs. For example, although the union claimed a membership exceeding 5,000 in forty-two locals at its zenith three years after its organization, the dues-paying members were only one-fifth of the total membership. In addition, police harassment was constant, culminating in the Japanese Diet's hurried passing of a Public Peace Police Law in 1900. Although workers' organizations as such were not outlawed and the Metalworkers' Union was not officially dismantled, the trade-union movement could no longer exist under the regulations stipulated in the Public Peace Police Law. After 1907, no more was heard of the Metalworkers' Union.

The membership of the Metalworkers' Union largely consisted of craftsmen in supervisory positions and their close associates in various factories. Given the shortage of skilled workers in Japanese factories

53 Sumiya, *History of the Labour Movement*, 18. Benji Yamazaki, *Nihon shōhi kumiai undoshi* [*A History of Consumers' Co-operatives in Japan*] (Tokyo, 1932), 18.

54 For personalities involved in this movement, see Hyman Kublin, *Meiji rōdō undōshi no hitokoma* [*An Aspect of the History of the Meiji Labour Movement*] (Tokyo, 1959); and the same author's *Asian Revolutionary: The Life of Sen Katayama* (Princeton, 1964).

during this period and the high voluntary job mobility, job protection was not an issue for most metalworkers. Thus the principal factor which built and sustained labour movements in other countries, namely job scarcity, was absent in Meiji Japan. Furthermore, the shortening of the working day, which gave rise to a social movement at an early stage in other countries, was not among the objectives of the Japanese labour movement. Around the turn of the century, the working day ranged from ten to twelve hours, including a lunch break of thirty minutes or less, or sometimes none at all.[55] However, there were conflicting tendencies concerning the amount of work. Compared with the experience of Yokosuka and Nagasaki in the early Meiji years, the working day had become longer by an hour or more everywhere by 1900. But unlike the earlier period, two days of rest per month had become common. At a few factories, there were three days of rest. At the Nagasaki Shipyard and the Shibaura Engineering Works, weekly rest in the Western fashion was provided for. At the same time, given the autonomy of the *oyakata*-led worker groups, the intensity of work was no doubt adjusted to the level considered appropriate by them. Wages in the metal trades were fifty to eighty per cent higher than unskilled wages in cities or villages. However, the household economy was in difficulty, for the metalworkers' life style, with a heavy emphasis on the excellence of manual performance and magnanimity of heart, put a low value on careful pecuniary calculations such as savings and expenditure planning.[56] Under the circumstances, it was quite consistent with the reality of work and life that the Metalworkers' Union was more active in the organization of co-operative stores and mutual assistance than in fighting for economic ends within the factory. About thirty co-operative stores were built by locals of the Metalworkers' Union, and many continued to prosper independently of the union.

The Society for the Promotion of Trade Unions was also equally enthusiastic about the promotion of co-operatives of all kinds. In addition to co-operative stores, the Society proposed co-operative factories, housing co-operatives, and credit unions. These proposals were not realized, with the exception of one co-operative factory which enjoyed a brilliant, but short-lived, success. An affiliate of the Society, Kōgyō Dantai Dōmeikai (Federation of Industrial Organizations – a misleading title for workers' organizations) was a case in point. It was

55 *Shokkō jijō*, II, 14.

56 This certainly offers an extreme contrast to Japanese workers' propensity to save after the Second World War. But see, for example, *Shokkō jijō*, II, 19–20.

an association of metalworkers, drawing its membership, numbering 800, from the Army and Navy arsenals located in many parts of Japan and Formosa. In 1900, the Federation established a co-operative factory in Koishikawa, Tokyo, for the production of machines and tools. As might be expected of a co-operative venture of craft masters, the factory was keenly interested in enforcing rigourous apprenticeship. Heartened by the financial success of the factory, however, the members retired their original subscriptions, assuming that profits alone would ensure the continuation of the factory. It then terminated its status as a co-operative as of 1906 and continued to operate as a private business for a while longer, under the ownership and management of key figures in the Federation.[57]

There were other unsuccessful attempts at trade-union organization around the turn of the century. The basic reason for the failure of trade-union movements at this time was that the skilled workers, if they happened to be working for wages at a particular time, hardly saw themselves as permanent members of the wage-earning class. They envisaged their future as workshop-masters on their own account. Self-employment, not paid employment, was the idea, and it was reasonably within reach for many workers. The early trade-union movement would have fared better had the unions styled themselves craft associations. Indeed, a trade-union leader himself, Sen Katayama (1860–1933), spoke about sawyers' and plasterers' associations as examples of successful organizations of workers.[58] In the meantime, quite independently of the success or failure of the trade-union movement, the individual privilege and prestige of the *oyakata* in the factory continued unimpaired. Some of the *oyakata* had acquired extensive influence over other *oyakata* and their underlings as a consequence of informal socio-political forces within the factory and community. The leading *oyakata* collected around themselves large groups of followers and took advantage of management's passivity in order to secure preferential treatment (i.e. better jobs, overtime, subcontracting, etc.). It was reported that some of these influential *oyakata* came to work leading large entourages, numbering tens or hundreds depending upon the factory size.[59] The workers who were not members of the powerful groups were saddled with the worst jobs and had little chance for better work or higher pay. Occasionally, their dissatisfaction erupted in disputes, quarrels, and

57 Yamazaki, *History of Consumers' Co-operatives*, 46–53.
58 Sen Katayama, 'Labor Problem Old and New', *Far East*, October 1897 (reprinted in *NRUS*, II, 255–63); and *The Labour Movement in Japan* (Chicago, 1918), chaps. 1 and 2.
59 *Shokkō jijō*, III, 169–70.

even physical violence. It also showed up in quick labour turnover, high absenteeism, mass sabotage, and other outlets for grievances. The sudden increase in industrial conflicts which took place after the Sino-Japanese War (1894–5) was attributed in part to these ordinary workers' complaints about the disproportionate power and privilege of some *oyakata*. Ironically, the factory-owner, who was the true employer, was spared these complaints thanks to the protective layer of *oyakata* who faced and settled the disputes with the workers. With time, this factory life changed as well as society as a whole. After the Russo-Japanese War (1904–5), the ordinary workers rose up against the factory management, and the *oyakata* workers acted merely as intermediaries between workers and management. These direct conflicts between management and workers indicate a change in the status and power of the *oyakata* and in work-force management.[60] This change will be reviewed in the next section.

Looking over the industrial scene of Meiji Japan, one feels that the adjustment of employment relations to the emerging industrialism was a difficult, often painful, process. Despite the belief of many Japanese to the contrary, the virtuous tradition anchored to the employer's absolute, though ideally benevolent, authority and reciprocated by the employee's good-natured and unconditional loyalty was not workable in large factories. But employers generally rejected a labour market based on wage incentives and the freedom of occupational choice as valid alternatives to traditional Japanese life. The prevailing labour shortage intensified their reactionary longing for the past pattern of employment relations, creating cruel despots in textile mills or effete feudal lords of a classic type in metal and engineering works. Dangers implicit in traditional authoritarianism spelled personal catastrophe for factory girls in textiles. Although the craft communities in the metal and engineering industries represented an ingenious interim synthesis of traditional life style and industrialization, they were a tremendous drag on efficiency and technological progress. The labour market at the time favoured the workers, but they were no more committed to market behaviour than were employers. Labour-market participation was only temporary, and early withdrawal into domestic life or self-employment was characteristic. Workers who remained in the market beyond a certain time were regarded as gross failures and

60 See Yokoyama's observations reported in *Shinkōron* [*New Review*], September 1910 (reprinted in *NRUS*, III, 11–16).

were denied social status. In autocratic Meiji Japan the poor had no suffrage, and workers, as long as they depended on wages, had no chance to earn enough to vote. In the meantime, employment relations in the factory sank into chaos, inefficiency, and indignity.

THE EMERGENCE OF JAPANESE-STYLE MANAGEMENT

A contract is meaningless unless both parties can read and understand its terms; nor can it be equitable unless both parties are on an equal footing in negotiating its terms. The worker in particular is at a grave disadvantage unless he is free and knowledgeable about the rights and obligations stipulated or implied in the contract he concludes with his employer. These qualities, however, depend upon education. Regrettably, one must recognize that Meiji workers were deficient in the qualities that would have made them the equals of their employers. Although the Meiji Government's sense of law and order easily turned into the oppression of the masses, atomistic but equitable contractual relations were recognized as the line of least resistance in the modernization of employment relations, as evidenced in the Civil Code. In addition, the Meiji Government did other things relating to industrialization and labour conditions, of which two most relevant to the issue at hand were universal elementary education, and measures to redress power imbalances between employer and worker. The latter finally took the form of the Factory Law of 1911 and its associated rules and regulations.

The Meiji Government's objectives in modernizing Japan were summarized in two slogans: '*bummei kaika*' ('civilization and enlightenment'), and '*fukoku kyōhei*' ('a rich country and a strong army'). The first slogan was comprehensive enough to gain support or acknowledgement from all classes. The second slogan, in the course of time, created a dilemma. Capitalism and private enterprise seemed eminently capable of delivering the goods to enrich the country. But a strong army needed sturdy and intelligent soldiers. Since youths tended to be overworked in their early years, their physical fitness for military service was very low. Factory girls grew up under circumstances hazardous to mind, health, and morals. Later, as wretched wives and mothers, they failed to rear their sons to be good soldiers. There was therefore a serious conflict between *fukoku* and *kyōhei*, which was resolved only when private business learned how to maximize profit while strengthening workers' health and intelligence. The Meiji Government's response to the conflict was the Factory Law, which business at first instinctively rejected. Faced with unusual firmness on the part of the government, business leaders then changed tactics by stalling the legislation and improving their conduct in the hope of obviating the legislative intervention. But in the course of time, business discovered that greater output and profit were not irreconcilable with better working conditions. Out of this discovery emerged a Japanese-style management, major features of which are now well known in the sociology of the Japanese factory.[61]

Elementary education

At the beginning the Meiji Government entertained a grand dream about education.[62] The objective was universal literacy at short notice. According to the educational system instituted in 1872, the whole country was divided into eight university districts, each of which was in turn subdivided into thirty-two secondary-school districts, with 210 elementary schools for each secondary school. Elementary education had two cycles with four years in each, the first cycle being compulsory. Secondary education also had two cycles, of three years each. Finally, fourteen years of elementary and secondary education were to be crowned with four years of university. Various levels of special and technical schools were also envisaged, though not emphasized, for those who would not qualify for the course leading to university. This grand scheme was a great failure from the start. Since the government had no resources, the cost of elementary education had to be partly borne by the localities and families of the school-going children. To poor farmers, compulsory education appeared as an encouragement to the children to loaf in school when they could be helping on the farm. In some poorer parts of Japan there were a number of riots against compulsory education, in which hundreds of school buildings were destroyed.

Eventually, the government learned the lesson and experimented with more realistic principles and methods of education. Educational policy was very much in flux in the 1870s and 1880s. The Matsukata deflation of the 1880s reduced school attendance. The new school ordinances in 1886, the Imperial Constitution of 1889, and the Imperial Rescript on Education of 1890 finally stabilized the purpose and organization of education in Japan. The rapid economic expansion of the 1890s helped ease the economic burden of education for the govern-

61 R. P. Dore, *British Factory – Japanese Factory* (Berkeley, Calif., 1973), part III.
62 Herbert Passin, *Society and Education in Japan* (New York, 1965), chap. 4.

ment as well as for the common households of Japan. The Japanese school system during the first twenty years of the Meiji period was particularly deficient with respect to vocational and professional training. Remedies began with public subsidies to vocational schools in 1892 and became firmly established with the ordinance for vocational and professional schools issued in 1899.[63] The period of compulsory elementary education was extended to six years in 1907, while the second cycle of elementary education was cut to two years.

The spread of education and the emergence of an educated populace were a slow, often frustrating process. Only a modest accomplishment was made during the Meiji Era. At the end of the Edo period, according to Dore, the school attendance rate may have been 40 per cent for boys and 10 per cent for girls.[64] Allowing for the secular rise in school attendance which occurred during the Edo period, one may say that the literate were at most 30 per cent of the working-age population at the end of the Edo period. During the Meiji Era, the educational level of the Japanese population rose slowly, even haltingly, during its earlier years. In 1910, only 41 per cent of males and 23 per cent of females in Japan's working-age population had finished elementary or higher education.[65] If one-half of the rest were 'literate', the literacy rate of the working-age population in 1910 would be about 70 per cent. The rise in the literacy rate from 30 per cent to 70 per cent during the Meiji Era may appear to be an impressive accomplishment, but the qualitative content discounts the quantitative indicator.[66]

To the distress of many Japanese, the educational effectiveness of the time spent in school or in learning in general is reduced by the difficulty of the written language.[67] Western historians often identify

63 Japan, Ministry of Education, *Jitsugyō kyōiku gojūnenshi* [*Fifty Years of Vocational Education*] (Tokyo, 1934); Mamoru Sato *et al.*, *Totei kyōiku no kenkyū* [*Studies in Apprenticeship*] (Tokyo, 1962), part I.

64 R. P. Dore, *Education in Tokugawa Japan* (London, 1965), 321.

65 Kazushi Ohkawa, 'Nihon keizai no seisan bunpai 1905–1963' ['Production and Distribution in the Japanese Economy, 1905–1963'], *Keizai kenkyū* [*Economic Review*], XIX, 2 (April 1968), 136.

66 For further details, see Koji Taira, 'Education and Literacy in Meiji Japan: An Interpretation', *Explorations in Economic History*, VIII, 4 (July 1971), 371–94.

67 Inazo Nitobe, *Japan* (New York, 1931), 239–44. The 'curious fact' which Nitobe mentions in this connection is extremely illuminating: 'the blind man can be better educated than his more fortunate brothers who are endowed with good sight; for the former, by acquiring the forty-seven letters of the [*kana*] syllabary, through the Braille system, can read history, geography, or anything written in that system; whereas he who has eyesight cannot read the daily papers unless he has mastered at least 2000 characters' (p. 242). For literacy tests administered to military conscripts, see Taketoshi Yamamoto, 'Meiji kōki no riterashi chōsa' ['Literacy Survey in the Late Meiji Era'], *Hitotsubashi ronsō* [*Hitotsubashi Review*], LXI, 3 (March 1969), 345–55.

literacy by the ability to sign one's name and have attempted to trace the development of literacy at the pre-industrial stage of Western economies through marriage contracts signed by the marriage partners. This convenient yardstick of literacy is useless in Japan because the ability to write the specific symbols representing one's name does not imply that the person understands all the ideographs required for effective communication in daily life. There are two sets of forty-seven phonetic symbols each (*kana*) which in principle can be used to spell any word in Japanese. But a knowledge of these symbols alone does not constitute literacy in the Japanese culture: even the daily newspapers would be beyond the ability of anyone with that level of literacy. It is doubtful that the full four years of elementary education during the Meiji Era provided people with the ability to handle the number of ideographs necessary for effective communication. Several hundreds of these symbols would have been a bare minimum. On many occasions, thousands were necessary.

Due to the historical accident of cultural borrowing from China, ignorance was perpetuated in Japan by a barrier more formidable than in other countries. In 1894, deploring the absence of a labour movement in Japan, one of the first trade-union organizers, Fusataro Takano, pointed to ignorance as its principal cause. Without education, the working people lacked the motivation for a better life. Without this motivation, he concluded, there would be no labour movement.[68] A few years later, he was happily surprised to discover that his call for organization did reach thousands of workers. But it turned out to be a short-lived triumph, for the movement collapsed in a few years. Takano's letter to workers urging them to organize – *Shokkō shokun ni yosu* (*To My Friends Who are Workers*) – was brilliant and heart-warming, written in excellent literary Japanese, as different from spoken Japanese as Shakespeare is from modern English. It employed more than five thousand different characters (*kana* and *kanji*), many of which required more than fifteen strokes to write.[69] A majority of today's university students, educated in simplified writing and more familiar with loan-words from Western languages than with those from Chinese, would fail to understand Takano's letter; the workers in 1897 would have been even more helpless. One reason for the failure of the labour movement to capture more workers and to sustain itself may thus very well have been the unwieldiness of written Japanese. There-

68 Takano's article in *American Federationist*, 1, 8 (October 1894) (reprinted in *NRUS*, 1, 396–400). 69 *NRUS*, 1, 403–5.

fore, when the police suppressed public speech, mass rallies, group recreations, etc., workers' loss of control over the spread of ideas was almost total. The barrier to effective literacy created, on the one hand, a small group of radical intellectuals – the intelligentsia – who monopolized theory and, on the other, the lagging masses whose social values and economic behaviour perforce remained traditional and unimaginative. Workers' dissatisfaction and frustration at times exploded in a variety of collective protests; but ideals, principles, and logic, which alone can turn discontent and protest into a sustained social movement, were notably absent among workers of Meiji Japan.

Under these circumstances, it is not surprising that only 15 per cent of male and 8 per cent of female workers in six cotton textile factories in Osaka in 1898 had completed four years of compulsory elementary education. Those showing no signs of education amounted to 29 per cent of male and 42 per cent of female workers in these factories.[70] The rest were considered 'slightly educated', meaning that although they fell short of the standard of full elementary education they were not completely illiterate either. About this time, workers in an engineering works in Osaka showed a higher level of education; 25 per cent of them were graduates of elementary or higher schools.[71] Workers at the Nagasaki Shipyard were much better educated, nearly half of them having finished elementary or higher levels of education. Among the least educated were workers in cement factories. In one of these, female workers were 100 per cent illiterate – not even 'slightly educated'. Even among the males, total illiteracy amounted to 80 per cent in this factory. Workers in raw silk factories were comparable to those in cotton textiles, while workers in the fabric industry were inferior to the latter. The glass and match factories were the worst sweat-shops, exploiting workers from the most poverty-stricken and least educated segment of the population.

Deplorable though it was, the quality of factory workers described above was no worse than that of the general population. In 1905, only 30 per cent of men and 12 per cent of women in the working-age population were graduates of elementary or higher schools. By 1910, these proportions had increased to 41 per cent and 23 per cent respectively.[72] These were rather rapid changes for a period of five years. For the same reason, the level of formal education of the general population in the years before 1900 would have been far worse than in 1905 –

70 Data in this paragraph, unless otherwise noted, are from various volumes of *Shokkō jijō*.
71 According to a survey of the Osaka Education Society: *NRUS*, x, 170–1.
72 Ohkawa, 'Production and Distribution', 136.

perhaps as bad as that of factory workers quoted earlier. In contrast, a Home Ministry study of 344 factory workers in Tokyo in 1912 showed that of 312 married male workers nearly 75 per cent had at least completed elementary education, while 41 per cent of their wives had done so. Those who had 'no education' were only 7 per cent of the men and 33 per cent of the wives.[73] The workers of 1912 were thus far better educated than workers of 1900.

One may infer that factory workers of the 1910s were on the whole more knowledgeable and more self-assured than those of the 1890s. Despite this improvement over time, however, the perspective of factory workers at the end of the Meiji Era was still imprisoned in a negative self-image. In 1912, among the aforementioned 344 factory workers in Tokyo, those who claimed that they had become factory workers out of their own preference or volition were barely 10 per cent of the workers interviewed. Diverse involuntary factors, which suggest that one would have not taken a factory job had there been other choices, accounted for two-thirds of the stated motives or reasons for becoming factory workers. These factors were revealed by answers like 'having lost other jobs', 'compelled by family poverty', and 'persuaded by parents and friends'. Conviction, dignity, and pride were hardly visible among the answers given by these workers. On the eve of the First World War, Japanese workers had not yet acquired the fierce class-consciousness of European workers or the rugged individualism of Americans. Given the workers' passivity, employers were in a privileged position to experiment on various methods of work-force management for the avowed goal of profit maximization. Indeed, after the Russo-Japanese War (1904–5), an increasing number of employers initiated such experiments in search of better approaches in work-force management.

Cotton textiles[74]

The employers' problem, when reduced to its essence, was simply how to attract and hold the quantity and quality of labour required for production and how to motivate the work force to perform in ways that would maximize their profits. When employers became aware

73 Japan, Ministry of Home Affairs, *Saimin chōsa tōkeihyō tekiyō* [*Statistical Abstracts on the Survey of the Poor*] (Tokyo, 1912). See also *NRUS*, III, 85–101.

74 For data and sources, see Koji Taira, *Economic Development and the Labor Market in Japan* (New York, 1970), chap. 5. In addition, see Hazama, *Studies in the History of Work-Force Management*, chap. 3; *NRKN*, II, part I; and *NRUS*, III, 111–76.

that the 'know-how' of work-force management was considerably variable and subject to choice rather than being fixed in a single set of traditional behaviour patterns, they were beginning to acquire the much-needed analytical and rational outlook which later led to the improvement of work-force management. Certainly, such an outlook was not to be generated overnight. It also depended on education. After the turn of the century, however, the management of Japanese business was increasingly transferred to a new generation of businessmen and managers who were highly educated in Japan and abroad. The modernization of management therefore started at the top and trickled down to the factory level.

The largest and most attractive employer for educated persons during the Meiji Era was the civil service. Due to large salary differentials between the civil service and private business, private business was not attractive to university graduates. The degree of attractiveness of the civil service was particularly high before 1890. When he entered Mitsui in 1891, Hikojiro Nakamigawa (1854–1901), one of the most highly educated persons of his day, initiated a managerial revolution by doubling the salaries of the directors by a profit-sharing device and raising those of managerial personnel in varying degrees all down the line. The effect of this reform was an influx of educated manpower into Mitsui concerns, demonstrating the obvious truth that the higher the pay, the larger and better the supply of labour. One reform led to another. Some years passed, and tension arose among salaried managers on the question of equitable salary scales. There had now developed wide income differentials between the directors (*jūyaku*) and the directors of departments or branch offices (*buchō* or *shitenchō*). The source of this gap was the distribution of 10 to 20 per cent of the net profit to the *jūyaku* class in the form of bonuses, which was a legacy of Nakamigawa's reform. In the early years of the twentieth century, Shigeaki Ikeda (1867–1950), who later rose to the highest position in the Mitsui zaibatsu, led a protest against the meagre rewards accorded to young executives. A further equalization of pay occurred, spreading the benefits of the House of Mitsui over a larger number of persons.

As salaried managers in time moved up to business directorships, the demand from below for greater equality and rationality was increasingly realized. As managing director of the Fuji Spinning Company in 1906, Toyoji Wada (1861–1924) – once one of Nakamigawa's lieutenants – reduced the directors' bonuses from the customary 15 per cent to 5 per cent of the net profit, using the other 10 per cent for bonuses, pensions, and benefits for the other managers, staff employees, and factory operatives. Another business leader who grew up under Nakamigawa's influence, Sanji Mutō (1867–1934), became an evangelist for modern management and demonstrated his ideals through the Kanegafuchi Cotton Textile Company, with which he stayed for thirty years beginning in 1894.[75]

Examples of efforts observed in cotton textile firms after the Russo-Japanese War (1904–5) may now be summarized. There were three interrelated problems: absenteeism, labour turnover, and recruitment. The traditional technique of handling the problem of absenteeism was to attribute it to workers' sloth and to resort to punitive measures. The factory dormitory was particularly conducive to managerial despotism. The reluctant workers were hunted out and subjected to physical torture. Accrued wages were often confiscated. Medical facilities, the pride of Japanese textile firms in later years, were first brought into being for the necessity of checking upon the feigned illness of dormitory workers and of those who ended their day's work before the closing time. The modernization of work-force management was marked by a transition from punishment to inducement.

The first step in a constructive approach to the improvement of work-force management was to ascertain and analyse relevant data. Research and analysis were the first habits that management had to acquire before it could hope to do something useful about the organization and utilization of the work force. Upon researching their own records, some cotton textile firms discovered that the ups and downs in absenteeism within each month were found to be related to the method of wage consumption prevalent in those days. At a spinning mill in Osaka, for example, the work records were closed on the twentieth day of each month, and the wages accrued during the month ending on this day were paid on the fifth of the next month. The daily attendance records showed that attendance fell drastically after the twentieth day, reached the bottom on the twenty-third, increased irregularly until the fifth of the following month, then fell drastically again until the ninth, after which attendance steadily improved until the twentieth. Some firms therefore made every day a payday for a certain group of workers, so that, given the rate of absenteeism following payday, there would at least be a stable, predictable level of absenteeism. More popular were a variety of bonuses, paid on an individual as well as on a group basis. Payments in addition to the regular daily

75 For a brief biographical review of these modernizers of management, see Koji Taira, 'Factory Legislation and Management Modernization during Japan's Industrialization, 1886–1916', *Business History Review*, XLIV, 1 (Spring 1970), 84–109.

wages were made to individuals or groups of individuals who worked without absence for a whole month. The bonus sometimes took the form of exemption from boarding charges for workers housed in the factory dormitory. Another form was a remittance of additional cash directly to the homes of the workers in the hope that parents might become instrumental in encouraging their children to cultivate regular work habits. A group bonus was also used; one form of it was to improve the facilities of the dormitory rooms for commendable groups of workers, so that they could share in an increase in comfort as the fruit of group effort.

In addition to the day-to-day instability of the work force, there was also the problem of high labour turnover. In some mills, labour turnover was seasonal, the difference between the peak of the work force (March and April) and the trough (August) often amounting to 30 per cent of the annual average. Given the regularity of the fluctuation, however, one counter-measure was to employ two groups of workers, so that when one group was falling below the normal level of work requirements, the other group could be called in to fill the gap. Temporary workers were often hired from the neighbouring communities. There were some ingenious and elaborate measures. One large establishment hired a number of girls of twelve to fourteen years of age, housed them in dormitories, taught them factory work part of the time after school, and used them as supplementary workers to fill vacancies due to seasonality or absenteeism. A few mills had a training course for the wives and daughters of the salaried employees for similar purposes. There were also attempts to reduce labour turnover by differential awards for long and steady work records. These rewards were various in form but were always related to, or scaled upwards by, the length of service – e.g. periodic investments, bonuses, profit-sharing, company-paid recreational trips, advantages in company-sponsored lotteries, and company contributions to workers' savings. According to one example, the last device worked in this fashion: a worker was required to save 10 per cent of his wages from time to time at a rate of interest equal to 4.5 per cent per annum, and at the end of a year of steady work he received an extra payment equal to 35 per cent of the sum of the principal saved and interest earned. The worker's desire for recognition and prestige was also manipulated by measures like public announcements of merits (*hyōshōsei*), e.g. the fulfilment of a contractual period, unusual frugality as demonstrated in savings or remittances to parents, and so on.

Despite these efforts by the cotton textile firms, however, the length of service did not improve very much. In 1915, data on factory girls in Osaka indicated that 48.5 per cent of them were employed for less than a year and 18.4 per cent for three or more years. This situation was almost identical with what had prevailed in the industry fifteen years earlier.

The recruitment of labour for textile mills was the most difficult problem in work-force management. The problem of recruitment described previously could have been abolished by shifting the source of labour to nearby urban workers by raising wages enough to attract them. Textile mills did not consider this to be a major solution for their problems. Girls from the distant hinterland were preferable, but this source of supply was dwindling fast because even the poorest farm households wanted their daughters to survive and grow up to be good wives and mothers. It was not unusual for factory girls to return home sick or disabled for the rest of their lives. Many died away from home. It was common for girls to learn nothing during the period of factory employment that prepared them for their family and community roles later. For this reason, local communities one after another joined silent revolts against factory employment. This was known to the textile mills as the 'drying-up' of recruitment areas, which led to further increases in recruitment expenses. One obvious step for easing the labour supply to factories was the reform of living conditions within the factory dormitory. These had to be improved so that the period of employment would cease to be just one large hole in the personal and cultural development of young girls. Major textile firms did carry out such reforms. Educational, recreational, and cultural facilities were installed, and the hours of work were shortened, while holidays were increased to allow girls to utilize the new environmental amenities.

Then there was the problem of labour-market intermediaries. After many years of dependence on middlemen, some firms began to set up personnel departments in order to administer the procedure of recruitment, selection, hiring, and training of workers. Guidelines were set for hiring standards in terms of health, education, and aptitude. Recruitment methods were worked out as a step in the whole series of measures for rational work-force management. A new type of recruitment, which was approximated in varying degrees in different firms, was embodied in the notion of a 'recruitment territory', in which the firm's resident representative maintained direct contacts with the local families and kept a close watch over demographic developments in the area. The firm consciously co-ordinated its labour requirements within the demographic dynamics of the 'territory', so that as older workers withdrew from factory employment after several years of service, vacancies were filled by younger ones recruited from the area. When the growth of the firm required more labour than the area could supply, the firm used more capital per worker instead of enlarging the recruitment territory, which would surely have started 'colonial wars' with other firms. Since the security of the recruitment territory depended upon the working and living conditions of employees, the firm made continuous efforts to improve them at a rate that would enable it to maintain friendly relations with people in the recruitment territory. Concomitantly, therefore, public-relations activities were stepped up. It was generally believed that two sick girls from a given area would wipe it out as a recruitment territory. Given the strength of the local resistance, textile firms were compelled to devise better methods of work-force management and greater safety in factory life. Of course, one should not be too sanguine about the extent of the rationalization of work-force management in cotton textiles at the end of the Meiji Era. When the First World War brought about an unprecedented boom in Japan, the pattern of the 1890s returned to the textile labour market. It took the relative stability of labour requirements during the 1920s and sustained legislative efforts to produce a tolerable level of order in the textile industry's labour market and employment relations.

Nevetheless, there is no doubt that the quality of labour as well as the cultural level of textile workers improved greatly after 1910. To mention but one of the best-known cases in point, a substantial tome of 400 pages, entitled *Jokō aishi* [*The Tragic History of Female Factory Workers*], was published in 1925 by an ordinary factory hand, Wakizō Hosoi. Raised in a broken family and having lost his mother at the age of seven, Wakizō Hosoi (1896–1925) entered the world of work before he finished elementary school. Starting as an apprentice weaver at the age of twelve, Hosoi worked in the weaving departments of different cotton textile companies until his death in 1925, only a month after the first publication of *Jokō aishi*. He lost many jobs because of his trade-union activities, but his skills as a weaver and mechanic ensured him a series of brief spells of employment as long as employers failed to notice his name on the black list.

Jokō aishi was the fullest possible description of technology, management, life, and work in cotton textiles that had ever been attempted. As a work that contains detailed information on labour conditions in an important branch of Japanese industry, *Jokō aishi* takes its place in the stream of classics of labour history such as *Nihon no kasō shakai* [*The Lower-Class Society of Japan*] (1898), by Gennosuke Yokoyama, and *Shokkō jijō* [*The Conditions of Factory Labor*] (1903), prepared by the Ministry of Agriculture and Commerce.[76] But *Jokō aishi* is not only a classic from today's point of view. At the time of its publication, it was a sensation. By capturing the attention and arousing the conscience of the whole nation, it contributed in no small measure to a cultural enrichment of society and a further modernization of factory life. The weak and sorrowful found an understanding companion in *Jokō aishi*. The brave and active were stimulated to action in search of social justice. The rich and powerful were reminded that the society they controlled was devoid of humanity. Since Hosoi's death shortly after the publication of *Jokō aishi*, royalties from the book have been paid to an association called Hosoi Wakizō Ishikai (The Friends of Wakizō Hosoi), and used for the promotion of the labour movement and social work among textile workers.

Metalworking and engineering

The first task in the rationalization of work-force management in metalworking and engineering was the transfer of the *oyakata* functions to the firm, while changing the *oyakata* into a first-line supervisor akin to the foreman in the Western factory. There were two crucial questions in this process: (1) who – the employer or the *oyakata* – should enjoy the loyalty of workers, and (2) how workers should be trained. The contest between *oyakata* and employer over worker loyalty was a real power struggle which at times erupted into violent personal confrontations. In most cases, compromises were worked out much like the Meiji Restoration: just as the feudal lords handed their people over to the Emperor, the *oyakata* gave up their workers to the firm for its direct management. But as the ex-lords were assured of position, prestige, and income, the *oyakata* were offered a variety of comforts and inducements such as a status in the management structure, permanent tenure, higher pay, and regular increments. This comparison is more than heuristic; the Meiji Restoration, which was at first little different from a palace coup, permeated Japanese society and, at the end of the Meiji Era, began to touch the factory floor. The logic of the socio-political process was surprisingly identical at all levels of Japanese society. The principal instrument of reform was always a compromise. On the factory floor, there were technical and

76 When these classics were reprinted after the Second World War, they received notes of introduction or recommendation from prominent scholars as follows: Yokoyama from Yasoji Kazahaya, *Shokkō jijō* from Takao Tsuchiya, and Hosoi from Kazuo Okochi.

social reasons that made these compromises not only desirable but inevitable. At the stage of socio-economic modernization that characterized Japan at the end of the Meiji Era, the *oyakata* were after all the only people available for an effective management of workers in practical activities in the factory. Managers and engineers, university-educated and with privileged family backgrounds, scarcely knew how to mix with workers who were largely from the lower classes, with inferior education and different values about life and work. Managers and engineers had the basic scientific knowledge about broad outlines and designs of factory work; but they lacked skill or experience in the details of actual tasks in production. Since the status differences between management and workers were too great to bridge without intermediaries, someone like an *oyakata* was indispensable.[77]

A typically Japanese institutional reform which transformed the *oyakata* system into the employer's direct management took place at the Nagasaki Shipyard.[78] Two types of training were devised for different levels of skills and functions. By the First World War, these were firmly established and were consciously perceived as indispensable elements in the modernization of work-force management. One was a vocational school (Mitsubishi kōgyō yobi gakkō) which gave three years of education and training to boys with elementary or higher education. The graduates of this school were then assigned to the *oyakata* at the shipyard as their assistants. These young workers, who were called *shūgyōsei* (student workers), were required to attend formal courses in the training school for four or more years. With several years of practical experience after this, they were promoted to the position of *oyakata*. The second type of training was a type of apprenticeship called *minaraikō* (training on the job). Young workers aged twelve years or older were assigned to different shops and worker groups for unskilled tasks, receiving training for certain skills at the same time. The *minarai* period was five years. During this period, the *minarai* spent a few hours each day on formal course work in the vocational school mentioned above. Upon completion of the *minarai* period, these young workers joined the ranks of ordinary workers (*futsū shokkō*).

77 S. B. Levine, 'Labor Market and Collective Bargaining in Japan', in W. W. Lockwood (ed.), *The State and Economic Enterprise in Japan* (Princeton, 1965), chap. 14. See also Ryu Nibuya, 'Nenkō seido no kaiko to tenbō' ['Reflections upon *Nenkō seido*'], *Nihon rōdō kyōkai zasshi* [*Monthly Journal of the Japan Institute of Labour*], VI, 12 (December 1964). The latest, most comprehensive study of the history of industrial relations and work-force management in Japan's heavy industry is Tsutomu Hyodo, *Nihon ni okeru rōshi-kankei no tenkai* [*The Development of Industrial Relations in Japan*] (Tokyo, 1971).

78 A report of the Mitsubishi Holding Company (1914), *NRUS*, III, 17–29 and 119–24; *NRKN*, II, 16–19 and 166–9.

The Mitsubishi Vocational School was inaugurated in 1899 with forty-two students. The enrolment fluctuated from year to year and remained most of the time well below 200 students, as against the planned capacity of 400. If at least five more years of practical experience were needed on top of the seven years of the full course of training before the graduates became mature enough to take over the *oyakata*'s functions, it would seem that the new *oyakata* from this source began to appear in 1912. This suggests that the process of replacing the traditional *oyakata* was a protracted battle. To make matters worse, the attrition rate at every stage of the trainees' program was very high. Only a quarter of students admitted in a given year stayed in school until they were graduated. Although more than 90 per cent of the graduates went to the Nagasaki Shipyard as 'student workers', half of them resigned in five years, during the first ten years of this programme (1902 to 1912). Therefore, roughly one-tenth of the original cohort of students admitted to the vocational school ever reached the *oyakata* level. At this rate, the new *oyakata* would have numbered fewer than 200 in the middle of the 1920s, when the Nagasaki work force comprised 12,000 men. The *minarai* had reached 15 per cent of the work force of the Nagasaki Shipyard by 1910. If one-fifth of the recruits for *minarai* had stayed on to become ordinary workers and if there had been no further attrition, it should have taken ten years for the internally trained workers to reach one-half of the work force at Nagasaki. But given the cult of travelling journeymen, the commitment rate should have been lower. Of course, these calculations are merely heuristic, but they suggest that the efforts at the modernization of the work force which were started in the 1900s began to show some effects only in the 1920s. In the meantime, the traditional *oyakata* remained in large numbers and continued to play a vital role in the firm's work-force policy.

Upon a closer look, the Nagasaki Shipyard's policy for replacing traditional *oyakata* was much more benign than is implied in the preceding paragraphs. The admissions policy at the vocational school preferred the children and relatives of the shipyard workers, while the *oyakata* recruited and selected the *minarai*. Between 1903 and 1912, 17 per cent of the vocational-school students were related to shipyard workers. Since the sons and relatives of the *oyakata* shared this privilege, when the older *oyakata* gave up their positions and retired they were in part doing so in favour of their sons and relatives. While formal control over personnel administration was centralized through a series of institutional reforms, the *oyakata* were still at the critical junctions between management and ordinary workers, holding the power to recommend action in all matters affecting the well-being of the workers.

During 1908–10 other institutional reforms appeared in rapid succession at the Nagasaki Shipyard. The customary practice of subletting work to the *oyakata* was abolished; hiring standards were specified and upgraded; piece-work and premium-wage systems were adopted; relief and assistance schemes were strengthened or newly established for injury, sickness, disablement, death, unemployment, retirement, and other inconveniences of workers. Within the framework of industrial bureaucracy under management's direct control, the *oyakata* were assured of their proper functions as employees of the firm. Indeed, given the size and sophistication of the structure, the complexity of work rules, the refinement of wage payment, the variety of incentives and benefits to workers, and the pace of change in all aspects of life and work, independent worker groups led by the *oyakata* under subcontracting arrangements would have failed to maximize the benefits which the shipyard made available to workers.

The example of the Nagasaki Shipyard was repeated in the experience of many other firms in varying forms and degrees. In a nutshell, management's direct grasp of the work force transferred to management three functions of the traditional *oyakata:* training, pay, and the provision of job and income security. An experienced observer of the industrial scene of Meiji Japan noted in 1910 that the traditional *oyakata* had disappeared from many engineering works and that their place was taken by younger supervisory personnel while the whole work force was brought under the firm's direct management.[79] Where firms found it difficult to have formal training schools independently as in Nagasaki, they jointly financed training schools for their workers.[80] Eventually, firms discovered the power of wages as a factor in keeping or losing their workers. Under the impact of an acute labour shortage during the First World War, large firms raised wages faster than the market, reversing the trend in which wages in large firms had lagged behind market wages before the war.[81] However, it was only after the mid-1920s that wages in large firms began to show a decisive superiority over market wages, partly aided by the downward pressure

79 Yokoyama (1910), *NRUS*, III, 12.

80 For example, the Tōkyō-fu shokkō gakkō (Tokyo Prefectural Vocational School) was jointly utilized by the Ishikawajima Shipyard, the Shibaura Engineering Works, and others (Hazama, *Studies in the History of Work-Force Management*, 458).

81 Konosuke Odaka, 'A History of Money Wages in the Northern Kyūshū Industrial Area, 1898–1939', *Hitotsubashi Journal of Economics*, VIII, 2 (February 1968).

on wages in smaller firms in the course of deepening depression. As for income security, employers learned a lesson from the popularity of the Metalworkers' Union for its mutual-assistance scheme. At the same time, public and private research was turning up evidence on the physical hazards of industrial work, and not a few industrial conflicts had their origins in the workers' desire for safer working conditions.[82] Thus, after the Russo-Japanese War firms began to set up various compensation and benefit schemes, while the enactment of factory legislation at the state level was considered only a matter of time.

Factory legislation[83]

In the 1880s, the government repeatedly consulted representatives of industry and commerce on the draft statutes on labour. The consensus was hard to obtain, and these early attempts were duly abandoned. Nevertheless, the Bureau of Industry of the Ministry of Agriculture and Commerce continued to explore new avenues of thoughts and methods, while accumulating data on the conditions of industry and labour. In 1896, prefectural governors were sounded out as to the desirability of legislation for the 'protection and regulation' of factory labour. Twenty out of forty-six prefectures turned in their opinions, and fifteen of them roughly favoured the idea. The Minister of Agriculture and Commerce then appointed a council, consisting of representatives of industry and of the academic world, to discuss economic and industrial problems, including the question of factory legislation. It was called the Supreme Council on Agriculture, Commerce, and Industry (Nōshōkō Kōtō Kaigi), and it met in three sessions to discuss the question of factory law. A draft factory law emerged from the conferences of this council. The cabinet crisis in 1898 destroyed the chances for the draft to reach the floor of the Diet.

A draft factory law actually reached the floor of the Diet in 1910, but the government voluntarily withdrew the bill. Further revisions were made, and copies of a new draft were sent to various ministries, prefectural governments, chambers of commerce and industry, textile

82 See a report on accidents and health hazards at the Tokyo Artillery Factory, in *NRUS*, I, 348–53.

83 Iwao F. Ayusawa, *A History of Labor in Modern Japan* (Honolulu, 1966), chaps. 3 and 4; Japan, Ministry of International Trade and Industry, *Shōkō seisakushi* [*A History of Commercial and Industrial Policies*], 25 vols. (Tokyo, 1962), VIII; *NRUS*, III, 178–256; Yasoji Kazahaya, *Nihon shakai seisakushi* [*A History of Social Policy in Japan*], 2 vols. (Tokyo, 1951), I, chaps. 3, 4, and 5; R. P. Dore, 'The Modernizer as a Special Case: Japanese Factory Legislation, 1882–1911', *Comparative Studies in Society and History*, XI, 4 (October 1969), 443–50.

manufacturers' associations, other industrial associations, and the Association for Social Policy, an academic organization which had recently come into being. In March 1910, a special commission called the Commission for Inquiry into Production (Seisan Chōsakai) was appointed by an Imperial Ordinance to examine the draft factory law. The draft that emerged from the Commission was approved by the Cabinet Council of Ministers (Kakugi) and sent to the Diet in 1911. The House of Commons quickly acted upon the bill and, within a month, passed it on to the House of Peers with certain modifications. The Upper House passed the bill within three weeks. The Factory Law was enacted on 20 March 1911; but as was usually the case with the pre-war legislative process in Japan, no date for the implementation of the Factory Law was specified in the Law itself.

The Factory Law proper was a short document of twenty-five articles and stipulated a minimum set of standards for employment, covering manufacturing establishments employing fifteen or more operatives (later amended to cover those employing ten or more) or establishments using processes of work dangerous to health. It prohibited the employment of persons below the age of twelve, the use of operatives between the ages of twelve and fifteen or of female operatives regardless of age for more than twelve hours a day, and night work for minors or women between 10.0 p.m. and 4.0 a.m. The law required at least two rest days per month for minors and women, at least four rest days per month for night-shift workers, and at least a thirty-minute rest period per day where a day's work exceeded ten hours. The law prohibited the employment of workers under fifteen years of age on certain dangerous or disagreeable jobs and obligated the factory-owner to support disabled workers and their families. Factory-owners who violated the provisions of the law or who did not co-operate with the factory inspectors were subject to fines.

For the specification of some vital matters the Factory Law depended upon the Imperial Ordinance for the Implementation of the Law, which was finally issued in August 1916 to put the law into effect beginning in September of that year. The ordinance elaborated the provisions of the Factory Law. It specified the frequency and methods of wage payment, though wage determination was largely left to free bargaining between the parties concerned. Each factory had to maintain the register of workers employed. Wages were to be paid in legal tender at least once a month. When the employer took charge of workers' deposits, he had to obtain the prior approval of the prefectural governor. No employment contract was allowed which obligated the worker in advance to compensate the employer for a possible breach of the contract or for damage to property.

Matters related to recruitment, hiring, and dismissal were elaborated to some extent. For example, where school-age youths were employed, the employer had to guarantee their continued schooling. Young workers and women employees who were discharged at the employer's discretion were entitled to return to their homes. In addition, certain formalities were prescribed for employing apprentices. Fines were stipulated for violations of the law and the ordinance as well as for fraudulent practices in the recruitment of workers by either employer or recruiter. Additional rules for the implementation of the Factory Law were simultaneously issued as a Ministerial Order of the Ministry of Agriculture and Commerce.

Unfortunately, two exceptions – on hours of work and night work – were written into the Factory Law for the duration of fifteen years. The first exception had to do with Article 3, which limited a day's work to twelve hours. The Minister of State was allowed to permit the extension of the working day by two more hours in certain industries. The other, more important, exception was to Article 4, which prohibited the night work of young workers or women. These exceptions were granted to factories where the production process required continuous work and where workers were organized in two or more shifts. The workers in the night shift, who were more numerous in the textile industries, fluctuated between 15 and 25 per cent of all workers in factories covered by the law during its first six years (1916–22). In the textile industries, it was the large concerns that took advantage of the night-shift exception: smaller ones did not have that much work to do. The number of workers in factories where the working day was allowed to exceed twelve hours was about one-tenth of 1 per cent of all the workers in the factories covered.

Other state actions relating to the labour market and employment relations during the inter-war period may now be quickly noted. The Factory Law was revised in 1926. By this time, a few important pieces of legislation had been enacted. In 1921, the Employment Exchange Law was enacted and set up public employment offices in several parts of the country to render services gratis and to subsidize job-seekers with transportation expenses, keeping an eye on the activities of private labour recruiters at the same time. In the following year the Health Insurance Law was enacted, to be implemented in 1927. In 1923, there were laws to define minimum ages for factory workers and seamen. Among the administrative ordinances issued during this period, the most important from the point of view of the labour market were the Ordinance to Regulate Labour Recruitment (1924) and the Rules to Regulate Private Labour Exchange Businesses (1925).

The revisions of the Code of Factory Law in 1926 postponed the life of the escape clauses on the use of women for night shifts for three more years (until 1929). An important innovation was added to the Code, however – two weeks' advance notice for the termination of employment when initiated by the employer or two weeks' pay in the case of an immediate dismissal. The benefits payable to the worker or his family were all upgraded substantially. Certain benefits which overlapped with the Health Insurance Scheme were transferred entirely to the jurisdiction of the latter. Modifications of certain provisions of the Code continued throughout the inter-war period, owing to the necessity for adjustments with other statutes. In 1931, the Law to Aid Injured Workers was passed to take care of workers not covered under the Factory Law or the Health Insurance Law. These were the workers employed in civil engineering, construction, quarries, transportation, docks, and warehouses. Because these industries were organized on the basis of complex subcontracting arrangements, there was a technical difficulty in pinning responsibility on any employer. The state therefore agreed to underwrite benefits paid, and primary responsibility was placed on the principal contractor for the workers in his employ and for those employed by his subcontractors. In 1936, the Law for Funding Retirement Allowances and Payments was enacted, requiring factories and mines employing more than fifty workers to pay allowances to retiring or dismissed workers. It may be useful to summarize the non-wage benefits provided for by the Code of Factory Law before and after 1926.

	1916–26	1926–40
1. Compensation for work injury		
i. Medical care	Facility or cost	Facility or cost
ii. Sickness benefit	50% of daily wage up to 3 months, $\frac{1}{3}$ of daily wage thereafter	60% of daily wage up to 180 days, 40% of daily wage thereafter
iii. Disability benefit		
a. Unable to care for self	170 days' wages	540 days' wages
b. Unable to work	150 days' wages	360 days' wages
c. Unable to do previous work	100 days' wages	180 days' wages
d. Temporary, able to return to previous work	30 days' wages	40 days' wages
iv. Death benefit	170 days' wages	360 days' wages
v. Funeral allowance	10 yen or more	30 days' wages but not less than 30 yen
vi. Terminal medical benefit after 3 years of medical care	170 days' wages	540 days' wages

2. Travel expenses for young workers, women, and disabled workers	Obligatory	Obligatory
3. Dismissal allowance	Not obligatory	Obligatory
4. Health insurance premium	Not obligatory	Cost equally shared with employee, 3% of pay
5. Retirement allowance	Not obligatory	Obligatory, partly on a contributory basis

The thirties were the period of Japan's real industrialization. In manufacturing employment, the weight of textiles declined from more than 50 per cent in 1930 to about 25 per cent in 1940. The weight of 'heavy and chemical' industries rose from 25 per cent to 55 per cent during the decade. The coincidence of progress in social policy and heavy industrialization during the 1930s gave rise to an industrial relations system that was to develop more fully after the Second World War. In any age, however, it is only the least efficient employers who stay close to the legal minimum standards. Major firms had become far more 'paternalistic' than was implied in the above discussion of the Factory Law.

The impact of the labour movement[84]

The influence of the labour movement on the progress of social policy and work-force management has never been officially acknowledged, but one suspects that during the inter-war period the government and employers modernized industrial relations partly as a way of keeping trade unions at a distance. The labour movement was cautiously revived in 1912 by Bunji Suzuki (1885–1946), and his Yūaikai (Friendly Society) expanded rapidly during the First World War. In 1921, Yūaikai became Sōdōmei (General Federation of Trade Unions). Trade union membership reached 234,000 persons in 1925 and increased to 384,300 in 1930, attaining the inter-war peak of 420,600 in 1936. Although it never amounted to more than 8 per cent of all paid workers in Japan, its distribution varied from industry to industry – more than 80 per cent unionization in gas and electricity, about 30 per cent in transportation and communications, and a little more than 25 per cent in metalworking and engineering.[85] During the early years of the International Labour Organization, the Japanese government refused to recognize the right of trade unions to elect and send their representative to the International Labour Conference. Labour fought hard and succeeded in secur-

84 For further details, see Koji Taira, 'Labor Markets, Unions, and Employers in Interwar Japan', in Adolf Sturmthal and James G. Scoville (eds.), *The International Labor Movement in Transition* (Urbana, Illinois, 1973), 149–77. 85 Computed from data in *NRUS*, x, 426–7.

ing this right, starting to exercise it in 1924. Although the Japanese government continued its policy of non-recognition of trade unions in domestic industrial relations, it honoured – though selectively – the international conventions on labour standards in which the Japanese labour representative participated.

With the end of the First World War, massive unemployment appeared for the first time on the Japanese industrial scene. Workers protested, and strikes became a familiar feature of Japanese life during the 1920s and 1930s. Throughout Japanese society there was unmistakable enthusiasm for democracy, modern life, and ideological freedom, which found expression in diverse forms and activities. Under the pressure of popular demand, the government enacted universal manhood suffrage in 1925, enabling the whole adult male population, rich and poor, to vote. On the other hand, political leaders felt that too much democracy was bad for the country and cracked down on communists, anarchists, and suspects of like persuasions through the Public Peace Maintenance Law of 1926 (*Chian Iji Hō*). At the same time, the government and employers became more paternalistic in work places. The repression of progressive activities in national politics, combined with the provision of amenities in firms, corroded the labour movement, which in 1939–40 voluntarily dissolved itself and handed over workers to Sampō, the nationalist 'Movement in Service for the Country'. The unofficial war with China, started in 1937, developed into the total Pacific War in 1941, leading to the collapse of Imperial Japan in the atomic holocaust of 1945.

CONCLUSION

By the standards of the 1860s, when servants, labourers, and artisans were mostly illiterate, the factory workers of the 1930s were incomparably better educated and more sophisticated. All of them, save a small fraction (4 per cent in 1936),[86] had completed six years of elementary education, and many of them (two-thirds of male workers and one-third of female workers in 1936) had received at least two additional years of education. At the same time, the average worker in the 1930s was three times better off than the average Japanese of the 1860s. Unlike the commoners of the 1860s, the adult males of the 1930s had a share in government, though the effectiveness of the popular suffrage

86 Japan, Prime Minister's Office, *Rōdō tōkei jitchi chōsa hōkoku* [*Report on the Survey of Labour Statistics*] (Tokyo, 1936).

was debatable in many cases. Furthermore, in contrast to the hereditary status system of the 1860s, modern Japan had erected no barrier to social mobility, although there was much to be desired about the distribution of opportunities. In the mid-1930s, Japan had not yet acquired the sense of equality before God or law, but there was a homespun notion of equality before the Emperor. As the subjects of His Majesty, the Japanese equally took part in the political process, and in his name, they received fair trials at courts of law. But lacking the support of individual freedom and the sanctity of contracts between individuals, Japanese 'equality' before the Emperor quickly turned into unreserved loyalty to him, equally shared by all. In place of the individual pursuit of happiness in a growing economy, the Japanese bound themselves together and shared the discipline and toil for a better future which never became a reality. When Japan mobilized for the Second World War, even the freedom of occupational choice was obliterated, and finally 'all traces of individuality were submerged in service to the country' (*messhi hōkō*). Thus, with Japan's decision to enter the war, the history of Japanese workers had run full circle, from *hōkō* to *hōkō* – that is, from servitude to servitude.

The following abbreviations are used in the notes:

ELTES Kazushi Ohkawa, Miyohei Shinohara, and Mataji Umemura (eds.), *Chōki keizai tōkei suikei to bunseki*, or *Estimates of Long-Term Economic Statistics of Japan since 1868*, 13 vols. (Tokyo, 1966– : see above, p. 504 note 6).

NRKN Rōmu Kanri Shiryō Hensankai [Society for the Compilation of Historical Materials on Work-Force Management], *Nihon rōmu kanri nenshi* [*The Chronicle of Work-Force Management*], 2 vols. (Tokyo, 1962).

NRUS Rōdō Undō Shiryō Iinkai [Committee on Historical Materials on the Labour Movement], *Nihon rōdō undō shiryō* [*Historical Materials on the Labour Movement in Japan*], 11 vols. (Tokyo, 1959– : 6 vols. published by 1968).

Shokkō jijō Japan, Ministry of Agriculture and Commerce, *Shokkō jijō* [*The Conditions of Factory Labour*], ed. T. Tsuchiya, 3 vols. (Tokyo, 1947: first published 1903).

CHAPTER 7

ENTREPRENEURSHIP, OWNERSHIP, AND MANAGEMENT IN JAPAN

INTRODUCTION

Because of its rapidity, sustained achievement, and initial low per capita income, the process of Japanese industrialization is a fascinating subject of study for economists and economic historians. An increasing number of Western students of Japan, after nearly two post-war decades of concerted work with their Japanese colleagues, are providing us with a substantial amount of quantitative evidence on the performance of the Japanese economy during the past hundred years. This evidence has been examined and re-examined, and we now have extremely useful sets of analyses and yet more refined data which compare favourably with those made for any other nation.

While these studies on Japan – analogous to those of Deane and Cole and others on England – were being made, another set of equally important questions for economic historians trying to understand Japan's industrialization suffered relative neglect. I refer to the set of questions which can be loosely classified under the heading of 'entrepreneurship and management in historical perspective'. More specifically, this is the whole spectrum of questions relating to the rise, recruitment, and composition of entrepreneurship; ownership and control; and the management of industrial firms in the process of Japan's industrialization and modernization.

During the past several years, increasing attention has been paid to these questions by Japanese and Western students alike. But the literature on these aspects of Japanese economic history is either inaccessible or fragmentary, or both. The inaccessibility is mostly due to the fact that the literature is available only in Japanese. Studies of Japanese entrepreneurship and management are fragmentary because each study deals in turn with a limited aspect of one of these questions or with only a sub-period of time, without providing a historical perspective and a cohesive analysis of all related issues.

The relative neglect suffered by this aspect of Japan's industrialization is not difficult to explain. One of the major reasons is undoubtedly that a majority of Japanese economic historians have been Marxists and have had little interest in analysing the functions of entrepreneurship and the evolution of the managerial system within a capitalist economy. They have their answers. Several Western students who attempted before the Second World War to examine entrepreneurship and management questions became, perhaps unconsciously, merely transmitters of the Marxist view at worst, and at best they made the Japanese literature more palatable to Western readers. There were few exceptions.

Two important factors tended to perpetuate this uninspiring state of research. One was the severe linguistic barrier which made original research by Western scholars extremely difficult; and any competent research on Japanese entrepreneurship and the managerial system necessitates a wide use of Japanese sources. The other factor was the basic approach of Western students in analysing Japanese entrepreneurship and management. Because Japan was the only nation in Asia to industrialize, the Western student sought out what he thought to be unique in that country. Earlier Western students were predisposed to find what contrasted the Japanese case with the Chinese and the Western cases. When this approach was grafted on to the Japanese literature, which long lacked a comparative perspective, the end results were often explanations and descriptions which rarely provided anything more useful than the undefined 'spirit of samurai' and a tiresome emphasis on Confucian ethics.

This unsatisfactory state of affairs has changed rather dramatically since the end of the Second World War. Both the quantity and the quality of Japanese and Western studies in entrepreneurship and the managerial system have undergone significant changes. Along with the economists who are essentially interested in various quantitative analyses of Japanese growth, economic historians and others interested in entrepreneurship and the managerial system began to provide more searching, cohesive, and comparative analyses of these neglected aspects of the Japanese success story. Though a large part of the contribution is still being made in Japanese, the depth of understanding and the level of analyses achieved by Western scholars, especially during the past decade, have indeed been remarkable.

What appeared out of these pre-war and post-war endeavours is by now a widely accepted view – which we could perhaps call an 'orthodox' interpretation – of Japanese entrepreneurship, ownership, and control of industrial firms, and the Japanese managerial system. This, in effect, is a major thesis, well supported by leading students of these aspects of Japanese industrialization and modernization, and one which provides a persuasive set of explanations for Japan's singular accomplishment.

Thus, a major task of this chapter is to attempt to capture the salient tenets of the 'orthodoxy' in as concise a form as possible. Parts of this chapter therefore recapitulate certain basic arguments, and this I hope will be useful to those not specializing in Japanese economic history. Also, an equally important task of this chapter is to attempt to present several recent suggestions for the revision of this orthodoxy. These reflect new sets of questions now being asked of established interpretations, and they also indicate the increased interest in questions relating to entrepreneurship, ownership, and control in Japanese economic growth. The new suggestions range from differences in emphasis to a relatively clear-cut challenge to the orthodoxy. As research in the area continues, these new suggestions may prove to be a difference in emphasis and may cause parts of the orthodoxy to be re-written, or they may force a basic revision of the orthodoxy. In dealing with such large and multi-faceted questions as entrepreneurship and management, and in attempting to summarize what is already a large volume of literature appearing in Japanese and in Western languages, this chapter cannot hope to cover all aspects of these large topics. For instance, the discussions on the managerial system and on the years after the Second World War are only outlines of what is required of fuller treatments.[1]

It should be pointed out before proceeding that the term 'entrepreneur' is used loosely in this chapter. Entrepreneurs are a group of individuals who precipitate changes in the method and manner of producing goods, and the group can include government officials, business leaders, bankers, and any other individual who is instrumental in effecting such changes. Also, even when I implicitly touch upon better-known general frameworks of analyses such as Gerschenkron's or Schumpeter's, or upon economic theory in general, I subsume these in the writing as they will be obvious to the reader.

1 Faced with subjects which could easily be expanded to several times the length of this chapter, I choose to emphasize those aspects which are not sufficiently dealt with in English and which are of interest to persons not specializing in Japanese economic history. Some sections of the chapter, as described in the text, are brief and only highlight uniquely Japanese or selected important aspects. Interested readers are referred to the Bibliography.

Throughout this chapter, Japanese names appear with surnames last, following Western usage.

THE RISE AND COMPOSITION OF JAPANESE ENTREPRENEURSHIP

Immediately following the Meiji Restoration of 1868, the government began vigorously to encourage industrialization by building pilot plants, hiring foreign experts, and granting various types of subsidies. Energetic and determined private entrepreneurs also appeared. By the turn of the century, it was obvious that Japan had successfully undertaken the important first step toward industrialization. Who supplied this initial entrepreneurial leadership, and why?

A large number of articles and books (mostly in Japanese) which attempted to answer this question appeared before the end of the Second World War. The answer, evolving as a common denominator out of this literature, is a thesis which stresses the uniqueness of Japanese entrepreneurship as a product of Japan's cultural and historical heritages, and one which emphasizes the overriding significance of the lateness of Japan's entry into industrialization, in explaining the composition and motivations of the Japanese entrepreneurs. The essence of this thesis can be summarized as follows.

During the Tokugawa period, class distinctions between the samurai (the warriors) and the *heimin* (commoners consisting of peasants, merchants, and artisans) were formally established, and the barriers became increasingly rigid. The education, aspirations, and *Weltanschauung* in general of the samurai class and those of the *heimin* class differed significantly. Samurai, the moral and political elite of the Tokugawa society, were indoctrinated in Confucian ethics, which stressed dedication to duty and selfless devotion to the established order and authority. The prime virtue and obligation of the samurai class was to provide leadership in whatever task was assigned to them for the good of the total polity. The commoners, on the other hand, lacked – or rather were not required to possess – the samurai virtues; rather they were to obey, to be thrifty and to produce – virtues more fitting to their ordained station in life. The samurai leadership was not immediately challenged after the Restoration because it was the Shōgunate which was discredited by the events of 1868 and not the samurai class.

Thus, following the Restoration, the new government was manned by the samurai, who were expected to provide the leadership. The international circumstances of the mid nineteenth century only strengthened the samurai's relative position, as Japan hastened to 'enrich the nation and build a strong army' in order to ward off possible incursions by foreign powers on the Japanese sovereignty. This was the basic framework of analysis which was sufficient, for example, for Tsuchiya, who believed that 'in the case of Japan' it was 'inevitable' for the samurai to become entrepreneurs.[2]

The pre-war Japanese thesis argued that the samurai were destined to lead, while the *chōnin* (merchants) – the logical contenders for the entrepreneurship, if European histories are any guide – were expected to follow the samurai leadership and did so.[3] The merchant class was found to be passive, cautious, and conservative. In Sansom's words, they were 'too narrow, they had thrived under protection, and with a few exceptions they fell back on huckstering, while ambitious samurai of low and middle rank became bankers, merchants and manufacturers'.[4] Also, the *chōnin,* in addition to their unsuitability for innovative leadership, were thought to be financially incapable of assuming the role of entrepreneurship, as they had been ruined by the forced loans and general economic dislocation of the late Tokugawa period. Even the largest house, the House of Mitsui, was tottering. Thus, it was argued that they had neither the innovative leadership nor the capital necessary to venture into modern industry.

This, then was the basic premise, and evidence to support the dominance of samurai-entrepreneurs was marshalled by two generations of Japanese economic historians. They richly documented the role of the former samurai as bureaucrat-entrepreneurs, as innovative industrialists, and as patriotic bankers. This literature stressed the importance of government-funded industrial undertakings as the path-breakers of Japanese industrialization.[5] The government-operated ventures, in-

2 Takao Tsuchiya, who wrote nearly a dozen volumes on related topics, put forth his view repeatedly with little or no variation. One of his books, from which the above quotation was taken, expressed his theme (which he has been expanding since the 1930s) as follows:

> In the case of Japan, the feudalistic samurai or their sons shouldered the leadership role of the Meiji entrepreneurs. Unlike any other nation, the development of capitalism was guided by bureaucrats who were samurai and by business leaders who were also of samurai origin . . . Thus, the Meiji entrepreneurs were strongly motivated by the semi-feudal spirit of *shikon shōsai*. This, of course, was inevitable.

Takao Tsuchiya, *Gendai nihon keizaishi kōwa* [*Lectures on the Economic History of Modern Japan*] (Tokyo, 1958), 53.

3 George B. Sansom wrote: 'It was these men [samurai], and not the bourgeois, who laid the foundation of a capitalist structure and at the same time developed a political system that bore little resemblance to those which came into force in the advanced industrial countries of Western Europe under the influence of a powerful money class.' Sansom, *The Western World and Japan* (New York, 1951), 110–11.

4 George B. Sansom, *Japan: A Short Cultural History* (New York, 1943), 509.

5 One of the earliest and most influential works in this body of literature is Yasuzō Horie, *Nihon shihonshugi no seiritsu* [*The Formation of Japanese Capitalism*] (Tokyo, 1938). Horie's English articles – 'An Outline of the Rise of Capitalism in Japan', *Kyoto University Economic Review,*

deed, extended to numerous industries including silk filatures, shipyards, glass, cement, sugar-refining, paper, printing, minting, weaponry, and mining.

Examples of samurai-bureaucrats and samurai-entrepreneurs in establishing modern banking and the cotton textile industry are useful in capturing the main thesis of this pre-war literature. These writers credit the establishment of the modern banking system – an important step toward industrialization – well-nigh completely to samurai-bureaucrats and samurai-bankers. The pre-war literature argued as follows. The government, first showing its concern in providing sufficient credits to the economy, unsuccessfully attempted to launch the Commerce Bureau and then the Trade Bureau during the first few years of its existence. But after failing in these ventures, it succeeded in building four Western-type banks by the first Banking Act of 1872, and soon afterwards 153 banks based on the law of 1876. The first four depended on the capital supplied by large merchant houses, but it was the government which forced unwilling merchants to establish these banks. The 153 banks, which became the real foundation of Japanese modern banking, relied both on the initiative of the former samurai and on their capital in the form of commutation bonds which they received in exchange for their lost economic and social privileges.

The cotton textile industry has been cited by numerous writers as the prime example of government entrepreneurship. To develop the industry, the government established and operated pilot plants which trained workers and introduced new technology. The government also imported ten sets of spindles, 2,000 units each, and sold them mostly to samurai-turned-entrepreneurs on ten-year credit. These activities and subsidies provided by the government, it was argued, meant that the government assumed the initial risks of new ventures and played a major role in laying the foundation for the industry which by the end of the century had grown to lead Japanese industrialization.

These and numerous other examples of government-samurai entrepreneurship only make the well-known point that the economic development of Japan came from above, and this was 'inevitable' given the socio-economic heritages of Japan and the lateness of her entry to industrialization. To make the same point, the life of Eiichi Shibusawa – the Meiji entrepreneur *par excellence* in the pre-war literature – has been

XI (1936), and 'The Government and Industry in the Early Years of Meiji Era', *Kyoto University Economic Review,* XIV (1939) – have often been quoted by Western writers.

told many times, and to devote a few paragraphs to him here is perhaps necessary to convey the image of the Meiji entrepreneur as seen by those early writers.

Shibusawa (1840–1931), the son of a rich farmer, became a low-ranking samurai at the end of the Tokugawa era, when he entered the service of the last Shōgun. He soon gained the confidence of the Shōgun and was even selected to accompany the Shōgun's brother to Paris, in 1867, as financial manager. After the fall of the Shōgunate, he found it equally easy to advance in the new Meiji government hierarchy, and he attained the second highest position in the Ministry of Finance before he left the post as a protest against militaristic and bureaucratic policies.

As a private individual, Shibusawa took the initiative in many 'modern', i.e. Western, ventures. He was a key promoter of the First National Bank (Daiichi Ginkō) in 1872 and was its first president. Again, as he had done in the case of the bank, he persuaded rich merchant houses to build the first large Western paper mill in Japan and was also instrumental in founding the giant – by the standard of the day – Osaka Cotton Spinning Company, which was to lead the cotton textile industry in the years to come. The list of his achievements is impressive.

What stood out in Shibusawa in the eyes of pre-war writers was his constant concern for the good of the nation – his efforts to strengthen the Japanese economy by reducing imports and increasing exports, and his role in advocating the necessity of carrying out Japanese industrialization based on the ethical doctrines of Confucianism. His voluminous writings and numerous speeches were a mine of quotable phrases and epigrams for those early economic historians intent on finding evidence to support the view that he was an ideal type of entrepreneur, evidence needed for their general thesis of Japan's rigid success. Shibusawa constantly wished to elevate the social status of business leaders, and to do this, he demanded that these men possess the samurai spirit and 'the Japanese spirit' (*yamatodamashii*), which honoured integrity, justice, magnanimity, chivalry, and courtesy. The first duty of the entrepreneur was to the public, and in discharging this duty the Japanese business elite could gain the respect of their fellow-countrymen and of the West. In short, the Meiji entrepreneurs were to conduct their affairs 'with the abacus and the Analects of Confucius'.[6]

6 Eiichi Shibusawa, *Rongo to soroban* [*The Analects and the Abacus*] (Tokyo, 1928), 304. Takao Tsuchiya's views on Shibusawa, representative of writers of his generation, are found in his *Nippon shihonsugi no keieishiteki kenkyū* [*A Business History Study of Japanese Capitalism*] (To-

The main thesis of these pre-war writers, who saw in Shibusawa an ideal entrepreneur, is clear. The government, along with active programmes to provide social overhead capital (for example, capital investment in telegraph and communications equipment), actively introduced Western technology, provided subsidies, and by the other means at its command promoted economic development from above. The government was manned by samurai bureaucrats who assumed the leadership role taken by the samurai in the pre-Restoration era. It provided the energizing force for the economy even when it had to pull and push unwilling merchant houses and commoners. In industrialization, government initiative was direct and pervasive, and modern banks too were initiated by the government and made possible because of the capital provided by samurai. Tsuchiya, compiling a list of leading Meiji entrepreneurs, found the samurai and the samurai spirit dominating the industrializing efforts during the Meiji years.[7] The main virtue of this pre-war thesis was that it seemed to offer a unique explanation for the rapidity of Japanese growth in terms of her culture, history, and traditions. This also was a general thesis which explained why the lateness of Japan's entry to industrialization was an important cause of her rapid achievement, and why Japan alone in Asia was able to accomplish the feat. Then, beginning about 1950, Japanese entrepreneurship began to receive the renewed attention of Western students. It was natural that the post-war interest in Japan as a case of successful industrialization should include studies of her entrepreneurship. These studies on Japanese entrepreneurship, however, were essentially a refined version of the pre-war thesis described above. Refinements came in the Schumpeterian framework, with comparative insights and often with generally higher standards of scholarship.

That these post-war writings were only refinements is obvious in their basic view of Japanese entrepreneurship. One writer called the Meiji entrepreneurs 'community-centered' and found them to lie 'somewhere between the innovating and profit-maximizing Schumpeterian entrepreneurs and bureaucrats' whose 'motivation is quasi-tribal, to further the ends of the community; the individual seeks to grow, not so much in reflection of his wealth, a private good, as in the

kyo, 1954), 189. Johannes Hirschmeier, *The Origins of Entrepreneurship in Meiji Japan* (Cambridge, Mass., 1964), 167–75, and his 'Shibusawa Eiichi: Industrial Pioneer', in W. W. Lockwood (ed.), *The State and Economic Enterprise in Japan* (Princeton, 1965), 209–47, are useful, as Hirschmeier made full use of pre-war Japanese sources.

7 This is the major thesis of Tsuchiya's *Business History Study of Japanese Capitalism*.

prestige of the cohesive unit, a social good'.[8] Nearly ten years later, another author expressed the same view a little more directly:

An important characteristic of the samurai mentality was a sense of public consciousness, a concern for public welfare, and a strong nationalistic spirit. These attitudes were a product of the Bushidō tradition and Confucian philosophy. This spirit undoubtedly spurred those who shared samurai values to rise to meet national challenges at the time of the great crisis of the need for modernization.[9]

Perhaps the consensus of the post-war literature in English is best summarized by Hirschmeier, who contributed a significant book on the subject. He wrote:

The uniqueness of the Meiji experience is that the samurai were declassed by compeers who were extremely anxious to activate the best qualities of that elite class, and succeeded in doing so. Thus the samurai were able to generate a good deal of entrepreneurial dynamism and eventually provided the modern entrepreneurial elite with a new status image, based on the old vibrant 'spirit of samurai'.[10]

The Meiji entrepreneurs were seen as possessors of the samurai spirit, and in fact Hirschmeier and other post-war writers found, as had Tsuchiya before the war, that former samurai comprised the dominant part of Meiji business leaders. As had Tsuchiya, Hirschmeier too found Eiichi Shibusawa to be the Meiji entrepreneur *par excellence*, because 'in his career as a government official, banker, and industrialist, and in his life philosophy, we find reflected most of the basic characteristics of the Meiji elite'.[11]

The social origins of entrepreneurs and their motivations explained to their satisfaction, these post-war writers proceeded to find (as pre-war writers had found) the dominance of the samurai government in the process of industrialization, both in banking and in industry. Post-war writers' observations on banking differed only in the degree in which they emphasized the importance of the samurai's role in the establishment of modern banking. These post-war writers, represented in Hirschmeier's words below, in essence repeated the pre-war view by saying that 'The rush of the samurai to found banks stands out in striking contrast to the attitudes of the wealthy merchant houses, which had to be forced to establish the first four national banks in 1872. Correspondingly, in the early phase the merchants fell far be-

8 Gustav Ranis, 'The Community-Centered Entrepreneur in Japanese Development', *Explorations in Entrepreneurial History*, XIII (1955), 81.

9 Michael Y. Yoshino, *Japan's Managerial System* (Cambridge, Mass., 1968), 50.

10 Hirschmeier, *Origins of Entrepreneurship*, 68. 11 *Ibid.*, 209.

hind the samurai as contributors of capital to the whole banking system.'[12] And in support of their view, the post-war writers often cited the following breakdown by class of the contribution made to the total capital of the banks in 1879: *kazoku* (nobility and former *daimyō*), 44.1 per cent; samurai, 31.9; merchants, 14.6; farmers, 3.5; artisans, 0.1; and others, 5.6.[13] The argument was straightforward: the nobility and samurai contributed initiative and three-fourths of the capital to found the first successful modern banks.

In discussing industrial development in general, the post-war writers, especially those Western writers who depended heavily on Japanese studies of a generation ago, followed the pre-war view in stressing the importance of the roles of the government and the samurai. Their evaluation gained depth, but their views ranged from mere restatements of the pre-war literature to carefully guarded and refined versions of the earlier assessments of the roles of the government and the samurai. But, as the few samples below show, these writings nevertheless were cut out of the same cloth from which the pre-war writers fashioned their views. T. C. Smith appraised the role of the government by saying that

> The government mills had served as models for private enterprise, working out technical difficulties and problems of plant organization. But equally if not more important was the financial assistance government extended to private enterprises after 1878. It seems clear that without government help of both kinds, private capital would have been no more successful than it had been in the decade before.[14]

Also representative is the view expressed by Bronfenbrenner on the contribution of samurai and an assessment of *chōnin* in industrialization. He observed, like many Japanese scholars before him, that 'the *chōnin* were technologically conservative and generally unwilling to embark on innovation, or indeed on production (as distinguished from trade and finance), until the way had been shown by foreigners or by the Japanese government. For this reason, they were outstripped early in the Meiji period by rival entrepreneurs of samurai origin.'[15] The

12 *Ibid.*, 58. Hirschmeier, who made an extensive use of Japanese literature, again summarizes the pre-war Japanese view on this point.

13 For example, this figure has been quoted by Toshihiko Katō, *Hompō ginkōshi-ron* [*A History of Banking in Japan*] (Tokyo, 1957), 33, and in Takao Tsuchiya, *Chihō ginkō shōshi* [*A Brief History of Local Banks*] (Tokyo, 1961), 27. The original source is the Ministry of Finance, *Ginkō-kyoku dai niji hōkoku* [*The Second Report of the Banking Bureau*] (Tokyo, 1880), 129.

14 Thomas C. Smith, *Political Change and Industrial Development in Japan: Government Enterprise, 1868–1880* (Stanford, Calif., 1955), 63. However, Smith, unlike several other authors, is careful to exclude silk-reeling from this statement.

15 Martin Bronfenbrenner, 'Some Lessons of Japan's Economic Development, 1853–1938', *Pacific Affairs*, XXXIV, I (Spring 1961), 14.

echoes of the pre-war literature are evident. What Moulton had to say in 1931 differed little in content:

The government has, in fact, performed in a large way the function of the entrepreneurs. We have already noted that because of old traditions and conditions, there were few experienced business entrepreneurs in Japan in the early part of the Meiji era and virtually no accumulation of capital, and that under these circumstances the government performed a very important function in setting the pace for private enterprise and furnishing funds required for development of economic resources.[16]

How accurate is this view? It is correct, I believe, to say that a re-evaluation of this view had begun to call into question its fundamental premises. The emerging revision cannot yet be called a counter-thesis, but when these recent challenges to the established view are considered in their entirety, they appear to require a synthesis with the existing interpretation of Meiji entrepreneurship.

The challenge comes from many fronts. The new perspective argues in essence, however, that the roles of the government and the samurai have been overemphasized to a degree which seriously misinterprets the nature of Japanese entrepreneurship in the Meiji era. That is, the new perspective argues that the Meiji government did not initiate but rather aided the first steps, and in a manner much more analogous to that observed in the industrialization of the Western European nations during comparable stages of industrialization. This also means, as a corollary, that it was entrepreneurs and capitalists of various social origins who began the industrialization of Japan. An added advantage claimed for the new perspective is that it will enable us to evaluate the importance of the role of the Meiji government in performing the role which is more commonly associated with a government during the early stages of industrialization – the establishment of infrastructure and institutions to enhance industrialization.

The implicit theory of those who support the 'orthodox' view of the Meiji entrepreneur is, in effect, that

1. almost all of the leading Meiji business leaders were samurai or quasi-samurai;

2. the *Weltanschauung* of the samurai class is distinct from that of other classes because of the long tradition of the 'spirit of the samurai', which was cultivated and preserved by their education and mode of living: the spirit of the samurai, in the final analysis, was the ability to

16 Harold G. Moulton, *Japan: An Economic and Financial Appraisal* (Washington, 1931), 337.

sacrifice self-interest, be it for one's feudal lord or for the 'enrichment of the nation'; thus,

3. most of the leading Meiji entrepreneurs possessed *shikon shōsai* (spirit of the samurai, ability of the merchant) and were 'community-centered'.

The danger of this type of theorizing, however, is made evident when a closer scrutiny is made of the leading entrepreneurs of the Meiji years. To emphasize or to assume the meaningfulness of class distinction is the common and necessary weakness of the orthodox view. Those entrepreneurs often classified as 'of samurai origin' by writers from Tsuchiya to Hirschmeier reveal, upon closer examination of their respective biographies, that in many cases their class origins were at least doubtful and that they were often samurai only in name. Examples can be cited readily. Zenjiro Yasuda, 'the King of bankers', was technically a samurai, but his education and the pattern of his daily life differed little from those of peasants.[17] Yataro Iwasaki, the builder of the Mitsubishi Zaibatsu,[18] came from generations of peasant-merchants. He bought a *gōshi* (country samurai) share so that he could obtain a job with a *han* (domain) bureaucracy.[19] Rempei Kondō and Ryōhei Toyokawa, both of whom helped Iwasaki to build the Mitsubishi Zaibatsu, and who were leading businessmen in their own right, were commoners who became marginal samurai. The former was the son of a *han*-doctor who was given a quasi-samurai status, and the latter was the son of a country samurai who later became a *han*-doctor.[20] The great manager of the House of Sumitomo, Saihei Hirose, who had worked as an errand boy since the age of eleven, is known to have come 'from the farm': i.e., he

17 For a detailed account of Yasuda's life, see Kozo Yamamura, 'A Re-examination of Entrepreneurship in Meiji Japan (1868–1912)', *Economic History Review*, 2nd ser., XXI, I (April 1968), 144–58.

18 '*Zaibatsu*' literally means a financial clique. Many economists have defined it, and the following three characteristics are usually attributed to pre-war zaibatsu: (1) a semi-feudal character, in that centralized control rests in a zaibatsu family, which extends its power through strategically arranged marriages and other personal knight-vassal types of relationships; (2) well-knit, tightly controlled relationships among the affiliated firms by means of holding companies, interlocking directorships, and mutual stock-holdings; and (3) extremely great financial power in the form of commercial credit, which is used as the central leverage to extend control in all industries. As will be shown, not all these characteristics become evident until after the First World War. For further discussion on the nature of zaibatsu, see: Kozo Yamamura, 'Zaibatsu, Prewar and Zaibatsu, Postwar', *Journal of Asian Studies*, XXIII, 4 (August 1964), 539–54.

19 For a fuller account of Iwasaki's life, see Kozo Yamamura, 'The Founding of Mitsubishi: A Case Study in Japanese Business History', *Business History Review*, XII, 2 (Summer 1967), 141–60.

20 Kazuo Suchiro, *Kondō Rempei den oyobi ikō* [*The Life and Writings of Rempei Kondō*] (Tokyo, 1926); and Kumakichi Uzaki, *Toyokawa Ryōhei* [*The Life of Ryōhei Toyokawa*] (Tokyo, 1922).

was either of peasant or, at most, of *gōshi* origin.[21] Rizaemon Minomura, who almost single-handedly rebuilt the House of Mitsui, is known 'to have come from nowhere' and to have worked as a child. Tsuchiya ventured his opinion that Minomura's father was a *rōnin*, a masterless samurai.[22] Sōichiro Asano, who was called a 'demon of business' for his ruthless activities in the cement and shipping industries, was selling cloth at the age of fifteen, when 'he would have been going through a ceremony of *genpuku* [to mark his attainment of manhood] had he been a samurai'.[23]

These men, and others such as Tomiji Hirano, Takeo Yamabe, and Keiichiro Kawabe, were in fact *chōnin* or at best marginal samurai.[24] Coming from 'very poor families in which there was only one *kimono* for each person',[25] they rose to become leading entrepreneurs through their willingness to work 'for days without sleep'[26] and other qualities similar to those found in Iwasaki and Yasuda. In short, biographies of these men show that they simply were not the kind of samurai who, with the 'spirit of samurai' and a knowledge of Confucian ethics, dedicated themselves to great causes.[27] Noteworthy also in this context is a recent study which found that over three-fourths of a sample of 189 early Meiji entrepreneurs came from the commoner classes, and most of these commoner-entrepreneurs were drawn from the upper economic and social strata.[28]

Perhaps a more important point to be made is that the distinction between the samurai class and the *chōnin* class is of highly questionable validity. That the distinction had become unimportant by the late Tokugawa period has been noted often. Horie observed that 'many samurai had been reduced to supplementing their income by earning

21 Hidemitsu Shiroyanagi, *Sumitomo monogatari* [*The Story of Sumitomo*] (Tokyo, 1931), 183–7.

22 Tsuchiya, *Business History Study of Japanese Capitalism*, 174.

23 Takao Tsuchiya, *Zaibatsu o kizuita hitobito* [*The Zaibatsu-Builders*] (Tokyo, 1955), 210.

24 Biographical accounts of these men are found in Kōkichi Mitani [*Motoki Shōzō and Tomiji Hirano*] (Tokyo, 1913); Tōyō Textile Company, *Tōyō Bōseki 70-nenshi* [*Seventy Years of the Tōyō Textile Company*] (Tokyo, 1953); Tsuchiya, *The Zaibatsu-Builders*, 77–8.

25 Tsuchiya, *The Zaibatsu-Builders*, 78. 26 Mitani, *Detailed Biographies*, 229.

27 In contrast to the view on the samurai class that is popularly held, especially among Japanese writers, Lockwood went as far as to say that

> It is incorrect to contrast the Japanese samurai and the Chinese scholar official class as a whole, and to find here a key to the divergency of the two countries after 1868. Many samurai were as inert and obscurantist as the typical Chinese mandarin in the face of the western challenge. As a class they were more idle, more ignorant, more arrogant. Most of them sank into obscurity once their caste privileges were cancelled.

W. W. Lockwood, 'Japan's Response to the West: The Contrast with China', *World Politics*, IX, 1 (October 1956), 45–6.

28 James C. Abegglen and Hiroshi Mannari, 'Leaders of Modern Japan: Social Origins and Mobility', *Economic Development and Cultural Change*, IX (October 1960), 109–34.

wages or by trading',[29] and Yui wrote that 'at the end of the Tokugawa period, one finds rich peasants and small-scale entrepreneurs in villages who begin to have thoughts and education akin to those of the samurai class, and class distinction became negligible'.[30] Many writers, Western and Japanese alike, would agree with the view that class distinctions had become, as Hirschmeier himself put it, 'blurred'[31] by the late Tokugawa period.

The importance of re-evaluating the current view lies in the fact that it encourages inaccurate evaluations of historical facts, which in turn are used to support the orthodoxy. A case in point is provided by the interpretations of the development of modern banking referred to earlier. Many authors, as we have seen, have long maintained that modern banking in Japan was developed by the samurai class under the guidance of the government. These sources also reiterated that the *chōnin* had to be pressured by the government and the samurai class to join in the establishment of the banks. Recently, empirical studies have shown that such a view is untenable.[32] Rather, the foundation of modern banking in Japan was laid in 1876 when the Banking Act of 1872 was amended to allow profitable banking operations for the first time. All earlier attempts by the government had failed, but once the profitability of modern banking was assured, banks were immediately established in large numbers. When close examinations of annual reports and bank histories are made, the only possible conclusion is that the initiative in establishing and operating these banks came from merchants and rich peasants who saw an opportunity for profit, rather than from the samurai class who might have wished to serve the cause of the modernization of Japan.

The observation that the success of modern banking in Japan must be attributed to the samurai class cannot be supported. The major 'evidence' that the samurai class contributed over three-quarters of the initial capital is inadequate. The fact is that the samurai contributed the commutation bonds they had just received to the establishment of these banks more for lack of alternatives than for any more positive reasons.

29 Horie, *Formation of Japanese Capitalism*, 83.

30 Tsunchiko Yui, 'On *the Origins of Entrepreneurship in Meiji Japan* by J. Hirschmeier', *Japan Business History Review*, I (1966), 105–6.

31 Hirschmeier, *Origins of Entrepreneurship*, 47. His exact words are: 'The last decade of the Tokugawa period had done much to blur class distinctions with respect to education, patterns of thinking, and economic activity.'

32 The points made in this and the following paragraphs are based on Kozo Yamamura, 'The Role of the Samurai in the Development of Modern Banking in Japan', *Journal of Economic History*, XXVII, 2 (June 1967), 198–220, and several recent Japanese studies cited in that article.

While the participation of samurai in new banks was thus passive, the commoner class participated actively in the majority of new banks by supplying the necessary cash (20 per cent of the initial capital) and the entrepreneurial energy in the form of directors and initiators in obtaining charters. Even the nominal control of banks by the samurai as majority shareholders shifted, in most cases, to the hands of commoners a few years after the establishment of these banks. Hugh T. Patrick, who has studied Japanese financial institutions, and who does not subscribe to the earlier view of the 'community-centered' entrepreneurs, aptly summarized the new view when he wrote that 'it was mainly through the initiative of profit-minded individuals that most Japanese financial institutions were born'.[33]

More generally, how accurate is the prevailing view which stresses the importance of the roles of the government and the samurai in the development industries? Can the oft-cited examples of government entrepreneurship be supported by facts and figures? Let us closely examine a few cases of the most frequently cited examples of the effectiveness of the government's – and therefore samurai's – contribution in the early phases of industrialization.

We can begin with the case of the Tomioka filature, one of the first government-owned and government-operated plants and the one which has been cited constantly as the best example of the entrepreneurial role of the Meiji government. Despite the stated objective of the government – that it financed the plant in order to help develop the silk industry – a close examination reveals how one could be misled in interpreting the role of the government, and therefore the role of the *chōnin,* if one takes such policy statements at face value. The records reveal that the plant officials consistently refused permission to aspiring entrepreneurs to see the machines and plant organization. For example, Furushima found that 'the filature plant at Tomioka did not allow access to those who wished to examine the machines at the plants so that they could copy the machines'.[34] Existing records also show that a newly organized company called Rokkō-sha had to learn the workings of the plant's boiler from a fireman of the boiler and that a would-be silk-reeler obtained access to the plant with the special aid of a cook at the plant.[35]

33 Hugh T. Patrick, 'Japan, 1868–1914', in Rondo Cameron (ed.), *Banking in the Early Stages of Industrialization: A Study in Comparative Economic History* (New York, 1967), 249.

34 Toshio Furushima, *Sangyō-shi* [*A History of Industry*] (Tokyo, 1966), 237. He also writes: 'These delegates [sent from Matsushiro in Nagano prefecture] were denied permission to see the plant, and the same applied also to those from Okaya [also in Nagano prefecture] who came to see the plant.' 35 *Ibid.*, 236.

These actions of the plant officials are baffling when considered in the light of the declared goal of the government. But it is not difficult to understand these actions when we learn that 'these bureaucrats were more concerned with writing good reports to the Ministry which could influence their own advancement. Also, they were often ignorant of financial and technical matters.'[36] Understandably, they were afraid of exposing their own inefficiency, which could hinder their promotion. In fact, according to a study made by Kensō Hayami, the plant had much to hide, as it failed to live up to its billing as a 'model plant of silk-reeling'. The officials paid 'high prices for large quantities of cocoons, as they possessed no skill in bargaining; they were also plagued with a high turnover of female labour, which caused a shortage of skilled employees, and by unwise decisions in the selection of the plant sites'.[37]

Hayami found the performance of the Tomioka filature extremely poor. When filatures were grouped into the six categories of superior, average, and inferior filatures using Western machines and superior, average, and inferior filatures using hand-operated machines, Hayami found that for a given scale of operation (450 employees each working 288 days per year) the yield of filature per yen of cocoon was lowest for the Tomioka filature. The Tomioka's yield was 21.42 *momme*, while all other categories of plants showed a yield of some 36–42 *momme*. Also the yield of filature per hand per day was the lowest for the Tomioka filature – slightly lower than 17 yen for the inferior plant using hand-operated machines. The figure for non-government machine-operated plants was as high as 26 yen. When it was operated on this 450-employee, 288-day scale – which was chosen for the Tomioka filature's technical requirements – Hayami found that the government plant lost 55,268 yen annually while all the others made profits ranging from 486 yen to 12,214 yen.[38]

More importantly, 'the rapid increase in the number of silk-reeling machines during the period 1878–86 was based on wooden machines which were not reproduced from the Tomioka model'.[39] The industry grew through the use of Italian and traditional models, either hand-operated or driven by water power, rather than by the engine-operated French model which the Tomioka plant used. The Italian model was introduced and popularized by the merchant house of Ono in Nagano,

36 Shumpei Okada (ed.), *Meiji-shoki no zaisei kinyū seisaku* [*Fiscal and Monetary Policies of the Early Meiji Period*] (Tokyo, 1964), 250–1. 37 *Ibid.*, 253.
38 For a table including more detailed information and data, see *Ibid.*, 252.
39 Furushima, *History of Industry*, 235.

Fukushima, and Chikuma[40] prefectures, in which the industry grew most rapidly. Furthermore, Furushima noted that while Gumma prefecture supplied the largest number of apprentice-employees to the Tomioka plant in Fukushima (708 out of a total of 3,472), Gumma prefecture lagged in the development of the industry. Obviously the oft-stated benefit expected from the government plants – the training of future textile workers who would in turn work in privately built plants or establish more plants – was not obtained in the case of the Tomioka filature. This caused Furushima to observe that 'little relationship exists between the Tomioka filature and the growth of the industry'.[41]

As noted earlier, the ten sets of 2,000-spindle units imported by the government from England and sold on a ten-year credit basis to ten private individuals in 1880 have been cited frequently as a typical example of the Meiji government's role in stimulating the development of the cotton textile industry in Japan.[42] Even in this case, a close examination of the records reveals facts which many writers on Japanese economic development have failed to note or have chosen to ignore. Of the ten entrepreneurs, a few failed shortly after the operation of spindles began, while others remained in struggling and obscure establishments. The only successful case was that of Denhichi Itō, who went on from his 2,000 spindles to establish a leading cotton textile company. A study of his biography and company history, however, casts serious doubts on the importance of the government contribution to his success.

Inventive and mechanically adept, Itō had a long-standing interest in cotton-spinning.[43] He had been exposed to his cousin's interest in cotton-weaving and had heard the news of imported cotton-spinning 'machines' used by Satsuma-*han*. It is evident that by 1870 Itō had made up his mind to pursue cotton-spinning. A few of the major factors in his decision can be seen readily. First, Itō's *sake-kabu* (guild

40 Now a part of Fukushima prefecture. 41 *Ibid.*, 236.

42 John E. Orchard, for example, wrote (in his *Japan's Economic Position* [New York, 1930], 93) that

> Dissatisfied at this rate of progress, the government in 1879 began to encourage the spinning industry more actively and more directly. Orders for spinning machinery were placed abroad and model government mills of 2,000 spindles each were established in Aichi and Tochigi Prefectures. In the next five or six years, similar mills were established in the prefecture of Hiroshima, Nara, Hyōgo, Okayama, Mie, Yamanashi, Shizuoka, Miyagi, Osaka, and Nagasaki. These mills were later handed over to private enterprises and those located more favorably have increased in size and become the nuclei of large companies of the present day.

43 The major sources on Itō's case are: Taiichi Kinukawa (ed.), *Itō Denhichi Ō* [*The Venerable Denhichi Itō*] (Tokyo, 1936), and Tōyō Textile Company, *Seventy Years*.

rights to *sake*-making) were abolished by the new government, and his village monopoly had begun to be threatened by increasing competition. Second, his cousin indicated that he was willing to help Itō's new venture financially. Last, but perhaps most important, the more Itō investigated the industry, the more he was fascinated by the mechanical aspects of the industry compared to the tradition-bound area of *sake*-making. One could, as has been done too frequently, quote Itō's biographer as to why Itō entered cotton-spinning: 'to stop the flood of foreign cotton goods' to Japan.[44] I am confident that for those who read Itō's biographies, this possibility is akin to imputing to early settlers in the American West the desire to spread the virtues of freedom of religion.

During the next several years, Itō visited the Sakai Bōseki-sho (Sakai Spinning and Weaving Plant, a former Satsuma-*han* plant which had just been taken over by the Meiji government), and in 1875 he and his cousin somehow managed to acquire a hand-operated American spinning machine. They studied it until it was 'completely mutilated'. By the late 1870s, Itō had reached the stage of designing his plant and was casting about for appropriate machines, as he already had financial resources, his own plus those of his cousin and other relatives. It was at this point that the government announced its plan to sell the ten sets of 2,000-spindle units on ten-year credit without interest. Itō applied immediately; and his application was successful, despite stiff competition from a group of samurai from the same Mie prefecture. His long-standing interest in the industry apparently was sufficient to overcome the officials' usual preference for samurai who were in need of a new livelihood. However, immediately after this success, his cousin suddenly decided to withdraw his financial backing. Although the reasons for this were not stated explicitly, it is evident from the carefully expressed resentment of Itō that his cousin found traditional weaving more to his liking than risking capital on foreign machines. To fill this gap, Itō managed, with considerable difficulty, to persuade a few friends to supply capital. A sum of 30,000 yen was raised, of which Itō contributed 55 per cent.

Itō's life for the next several years was a biographer's dream and Itō's nightmare. Itō and his son struggled through the designing and supervising of the building of the plant and the installation. 'During this period, Itō's life was hard. He worked with his employees and so

44 Kinukawa, *The Venerable Denhichi Itō*, 16.

did his family. He often forgot to eat and went without sleep.'[45] Technical and financial problems beset Itō from the beginning. The machines were larger than had been expected, and the plant had to be redesigned. A sum of 65,000 yen, more than twice that originally anticipated, had to be spent. This meant that, with minimum operating expenses of 10,000 yen, Itō was deeply in debt without even counting the 22,416 yen of government credit for spindles. His house had to be second-mortgaged and loans from friends and relatives increased rapidly; on occasion he had to sell his family's clothing to pay the wages.

Once the spindles began operation in 1883, it was evident that his problems had just begun. A 2,000-spindle unit was not economical in terms of making efficient use of inputs, labour, and ancillary machines. The river site selected on the advice of a government official yielded only one-third of the expected power, and to supplement this Itō had to buy a 25-h.p. steam engine at the cost of 4,078 yen, of which 4,000 yen was borrowed and 78 yen came out of the already meagre operating fund.

At the height of these disappointments, Itō died. This was in September 1883, at a time when he was writing to the government that 'the credit could be repaid if another 100 years were allowed'.[46] Itō's son, also named Denhichi Itō, then 34 years old, carried on for the next few years with no visible success. In 1886, he listed four major causes for his difficulties:

1. The initial capital requirement was far larger than anticipated and critically affected all aspects of operation from the beginning.

2. The 2,000-spindle unit was highly uneconomical because of its 'imbalance' for efficient uses of labour, inputs, and ancillary machines, thus affecting the unit cost or even the quality of the product.

3. Little guidance in the operating of imported spindles was available, and operations had to be executed on a costly trial-and-error basis.

4. For various reasons, the use of water power, which had been recommended by the government, was a mistake. Also, the site selected on the advice of government officials was insufficient to operate 1,000 spindles, even in seasons of maximum water supply.[47]

Convinced that there was no hope for the 2,000-spindle unit, and seeing the successful example of the entirely privately financed and

45 Tōyō Textile Company, *Seventy Years*, 49.

46 Kinukawa, *The Venerable Denhichi Itō*, 126. The six letters written by Itō to the government asking for postponement of payment spell out his difficulties in painful detail: *ibid.*, 91–134.

47 *Ibid.*, 76–7.

operated Osaka Cotton Textile Company (Osaka Bōseki) – which had a dividend rate of 18 per cent in 1885 – Itō's son decided to increase the number of spindles to 10,000, the scale of Osaka Cotton Textiles. To achieve this, he needed 170,000 yen. Itō himself could contribute in the form of the physical assets and inventories of his failing plant. For the remainder, he had to rely on public subscription; but, given the record of Itō's plant, there were no subscribers to the shares. Fortunately for Itō, however, the governor of the prefecture, who had known Itō's father because of his long struggles in the venture, introduced Itō to Shibusawa Eiichi, then the president of the First National Bank (Daiichi Ginkō). Shibusawa instructed his branch office in Mie, where Itō's plant was located, to purchase a portion of the shares. After this show of confidence by the largest bank in Japan, the remaining shares were fully subscribed by the public within a brief period. The total capital was increased to 220,000 yen shortly afterwards, and Itō's Mie Cotton Textiles began operation in November 1886. From then on, the company history of Mie Cotton Textiles was one of continued success. It absorbed seven smaller firms before 1914, when Mie Cotton Textiles merged with Osaka Cotton Textiles to create the giant Tōyō Cotton Textiles. At the time of the merger, the Mie's paid-in capital stood at 7,768,450 yen, and it owned eleven plants and 306,376 spindles.[48]

Even in the case of the most successful of the ten recipients of government credit, it is difficult to conclude that the government had built a foundation for the large Mie Cotton Textiles, let alone to support the inference carelessly made by some writers that those ten sets of 2,000-spindle units somehow became the foundation of the Japanese cotton textile industry. We should recall that even in Itō's case the venture became successful only after Itō's son decided to follow the example of the successful, entirely private Osaka Cotton Textile Company and to completely abandon the uneconomical 2,000-spindle plant, the use of water power, and the site, all recommended by the government. The major ingredients in the success of the Mie Cotton Textile Company were the tenacity and drive of the men involved and the capital which became available in the form of subscribed shares. If the importance of the government contribution is to be stressed, one should recall that for this assistance Itō paid 55,000 yen and went through years of agonizing struggle.

In addition to these well known and frequently cited examples in the

48 Tōyō Textile Company, *Seventy Years*, 145–6.

silk and cotton textile industries, the case of Tōsaburō Suzuki in sugar-refining is also a very revealing one. Because I believe that this case represents many Meiji *chōnin*-entrepreneurs who succeeded in establishing a firm in a 'Western' industry without the help of an influential banker, without the guidance of foreign experts, and with no direct help from the government, I shall sketch its bare outlines.[49]

Although an adopted son of a poor candy merchant, Suzuki did not want to 'end his life as a small merchant'. He was extremely ambitious, in the American 'get-rich-quick' sense of the term. Always on the lookout for new money-making schemes, he speculated in tea but was unsuccessful because of his meagre capital. He worked tirelessly in his small candy business but was reminded constantly that wealth could be gained only by beginning some new business. Although he did not yet know what that new business might be, he resolved to save as much and as fast as he could. A large amount of capital, he had decided, was necessary for success. For the next five years, he worked almost to the point of ruining his health. The hard work, along with extreme self-denial, increased his savings from 260 yen to 1,300 yen.

During the next five years, he became increasingly curious about the manufacture of what the Japanese call ice-sugar, or crystalline sugar; this interest deepened into a large commitment of time and effort. This was a natural evolution of events stemming from his daily use of brown sugar and inferior 'cloudy' ice-sugar, which was then imported mostly from China.

Suzuki's initial efforts were discouraging. His search yielded no books on sugar crystallization, and he found that only a few merchants on the island of Shikoku were producing 'cloudy' ice-sugar, refined by the traditional method. In 1877, modern refining was virtually unknown in Japan, and refined sugar was imported from Hawaii, Russia, and Europe. In 1878, the government imported the first machines from France, but they failed to produce sugar though they were operated in Hokkaidō, where European-type beets were grown. Machines repeatedly exploded when operated by the inexperienced Japanese.

49 The major sources used for this section are: Gorō Suzuki, *Suzuki Tōsaburō den: Kindai nihon sangyō no senku* [A Biography of Tōsaburō Suzuki, A Pioneer of Modern Japanese Industry] (Tokyo, 1956); Gorō Suzuki, *Reimei nihon no ichi kaitakusha: Chichi Suzuki Tōsaburō Suzuki Tōsaburō no isshō* [*A Pioneer of Japan's Dawn: The Life of My Father, Tōsaburō Suzuki*] (Tokyo, 1939); Dainihon Seitō KK, *Nittō saikin 25-nenshi* [*A History of the Japan Sugar Refining Company during the Past Twenty-Five Years*] (Tokyo, 1924); Dainihon Seitō KK, *Nittō 65-nenshi* [*Sixty-five Years of the Japan Sugar Refining Company*] (Tokyo, 1906). The first two are useful, though written by Suzuki's son, as he conscientiously attempted to maintain an objective tone. There are also many brief writings on Suzuki in relation to his inventions and his political career.

This was about the extent of the government's efforts until 1883, when two German experts arrived to operate the machines. Private groups, including a company called Hōraisha, had also imported machines from England and attempted to operate them, but all attempts were unsuccessful. The unrewarding efforts Suzuki made in 1887–8 were understandable when seen in this light. He, in effect, was attempting to start modern sugar-refining in a country which still practised the method it had been using since 1723, when the first sugar was refined from sugar cane imported from Okinawa.

From 1878 to 1882, Suzuki continued to experiment against the strenuous objections of his family. Since he had neither training nor scientific knowledge, his experiments consisted of boiling and cooling various sugar solutions under numerous combinations of heat, duration, and quantity. At one point, he used the ash of human bones, misinterpreting the advice of a local druggist who had recommended the use of a catalyst. This attempt failed to yield ice-sugar, though it produced sufficient stench to bring in the local police. An ordinary man would have given up, but Suzuki persisted.

It was in early 1883, when he was away at a university in Tokyo to learn more about possible catalysts, that ice-sugar was produced almost by accident. By a series of fortunate coincidences, the family unintentionally heated one sugar solution which Suzuki had left in an airtight container. It was then cooled over the period of Suzuki's absence. The quantity of ice-sugar yielded was small and not entirely pure; but Suzuki, now knowing the basic process of crystallization, plunged into a new series of experiments. He continued to improve the yield and purity during the next eleven months in a large furnace he built, and by the end of 1883 he finally succeeded in producing pure ice-sugar at a cost which would allow profitable marketing.

A merchant in Tokyo agreed to sell Suzuki's ice-sugar. The business was excellent from the beginning, and Suzuki soon wished to expand his output. The immediate problem he faced was capital. His savings spent, and his expenditures for new equipment not yet amortized by the profits of his current business, he tried his circle of friends, but to no avail. His guarantee of a return of 10 per cent failed to interest possible investors, who could earn more by making safe loans. Desperate, Suzuki decided to try a relative stranger, a retired second-hand-kimono dealer who was reputed to be wealthy. To Suzuki's surprise, the dealer agreed to lend him 2,000 yen.

But Suzuki was the kind of man who constantly thought of the next step before the first was completed. He now made the decision to relocate his business in Tokyo, for two reasons. The first was to increase his sales and profits by reducing transportation costs to Tokyo and by obtaining his inputs at lower cost. The second, equally important, was his new desire to refine his sugar according to Western methods. By this time Suzuki was confident of successfully competing against the imported Chinese ice-sugar and brown sugar. He now wanted to tackle modern refining itself.

This meant that he needed a large amount of capital to relocate and to begin refining. Suzuki had, however, little difficulty in persuading the kimono dealer – who had seen the results of his first investment – to invest another several thousand yen. For additional funds, Suzuki tried his sole agent in Tokyo, but the latter flatly refused any loan on the ground that earlier private attempts and 'even the government had failed' in sugar-refining. This was a bitter disappointment for Suzuki. He wanted to relocate in Tokyo but had to abandon the idea because of a lack of finances. With the capital provided by the kimono dealer, Suzuki built a second oven to increase his business. Though Suzuki's net profit was only 3.5 yen for the first six months of 1885, because of the costs of expansion and interest, the expansion paid off by the end of the year, and he showed a net profit of 3,000 yen for the last half of 1885. Throughout 1886 and 1887 sales of Suzuki's ice-sugar increased. The annual profit began to exceed 10,000 yen, and he completely eliminated his Chinese competition. His biggest problem during these two years was the constant attempts of others to copy his process.

A decisive moment came in April 1888 when his father, who had vigorously opposed his plans, died. With his accumulated and projected earnings, and with no one to object to the move, Suzuki decided to relocate. The new plant in Tokyo was completed early in 1889, and it proved much more profitable than he had anticipated. New ovens, which eliminated all the weaknesses of the former mud ovens, performed far better than had been expected. Savings owing to reduced costs of transportation and raw material were added to his profits. Following this success, Suzuki began to concentrate on refining. He worked all day at the new ice-sugar plant, and in the evenings he read – often till dawn – all the available scientific writings on the subject. He visited chemists and engineers and learned to read blueprints. He took copious notes from foreign books which were read to him by university students. This time he did not wish to waste several years for lack of a systematic and scientific approach.

Finally, Suzuki visited the Hokkaidō sugar plant before he embarked on a new large investment. This was the factory which had originally been begun by the government and was now operated by a group of former samurai. The operation Suzuki saw was badly run and hardly profitable; but there Suzuki confirmed what he had learned and made mental improvements on what he saw. He then began to build refining machines. To do this, he had to build a machine-tool shop of his own, since no one was able to produce what he needed. By June 1890, Suzuki succeeded in producing the first sugar-refining machines in Japan. The costs were huge and took all the reserved his successful ice-sugar plant could provide. For the next ten months, Suzuki had to improve the machines to increase the yield ratio of sugar to a profitable level, and this was accomplished by April 1891. Suzuki was now ready to conquer the refined-sugar market of Japan which imported 93 per cent of its needs.[50]

In lieu of more cases to prove the point I wish to make, let me merely add the following. The oft-cited government-owned glass factory was actually begun as a private firm, and success came only after the government sold the plant back to private entrepreneurs. Again, a careful reading of the five-volume history of the giant Oji Paper Company shows that it was merchant capital and entrepreneurship which made this firm a success in spite of occasional competition and interference from government officials. Even in shipbuilding, shipping, and electricity, a long list of cases can be compiled to demonstrate that the contribution of the government and the samurai class has indeed been overemphasized at the cost of an accurate appraisal of the role of merchant capital and entrepreneurship.

In the new perspective, the former *chōnin* and other non-samurai individuals play a much more important role as entrepreneurs and capitalists in Japan's industrialization than has been previously granted. For those students who have held the long-standing view, this is perhaps difficult to accept, and the difficulty is easily understandable. In a framework which stressed the leadership role performed by the government and the former samurai class in Japan's rapid industrialization,

50 Hirschmeier notes that 'he decided to produce refined sugar because of his concern that all refined sugar was imported' (*Origins of Entrepreneurship*, 267). This is an uncritical acceptance of Gōrō Suzuki's view (expressed in his *A Pioneer of Japan's Dawn*, 80). Although Suzuki expressed such a view in 1899, in a pamphlet which he wrote commemorating an increase in the capital of his company, I am inclined to believe this either was written for public consumption or else reflected what he himself had come to believe by this time. In 1885, when he began to plan for refining, his goal, I believe, was simply to obtain cheaper domestically produced raw material for his ice-sugar, and he was confident that he could successfully challenge his foreign competition as he had done with the Chinese sugar (Tōsaburō Suzuki, 'Nihon tōgyo ron' ['A Treatise on the Sugar Industry in Japan'], published in the daily *Tōyō Keizai Shimpō* [*Oriental Economic News*] on 15 June 1899, and reproduced *in toto* in Gōrō Suzuki, *A Pioneer of Japan's Dawn*, 194–204).

the former *chōnin* with their supposed lack of initiative had to be relegated to a minor position. This framework was readily acceptable to many students of Japan, since it provided them with a ready explanation of the rapid industrialization of Japan as a typical case of growth 'induced' from above, and because it accommodated a simple extrapolation of the behaviour and role of the Tokugawa *chōnin,* who are supposed to have lacked 'high ideals' or the 'spirit of samurai'.

Paraphrasing Keynes, if we are not to be enslaved by the theories of yesterday, all facts must be accommodated within a new framework. The facts of the cases we have examined above appear to suggest that Landes was quite right when he wrote:

> In promoting economic growth, government spending is just one of several devices for mobilizing and allocating resources. For backward countries especially, it is linked closely as we have seen to import of capital from abroad, the one complementing the other. When one examines the Japanese experience in this light, one is less impressed by the contribution of the state; one expects it to be higher to compensate for the lack of funds from outside. And one is struck by the high proportion of investment accounted for by private enterprise.[51]

Also, as Landes noted, the new perspective is not inconsistent with Rosovsky's findings that the government was responsible for an important share of gross domestic fixed capital. On the contrary, the new perspective adds strength to Rosovsky's view of the early Meiji years as a transition phase, in which the government provided the environment for rapid economic growth, and supports Crawcour's recent emphasis on the role of government as a builder of the infrastructure necessary for economic development.[52] These views of my colleagues and such observations as the one that the Japanese relied 'far less than Europeans on the skills, knowledge, and enterprise of foreigners' begin to fall into place in the framework of the new perspective. The Itōs and Suzukis who provided the sustaining force for rapid economic growth need not and cannot be neglected as we realize the necessity of a renewed evaluation of this Asian success story.

51 David S. Landes, 'Japan and Europe: Contrasts in Industrialization', in W. W. Lockwood (ed.), *The State and Economic Enterprise in Japan,* 101–2.

52 Rosovsky would consider the 'institutional reform and financial policies' of the government 'during the years of transition (1868–1885)' to be of more long-run significance than the fact that the government 'operated factories, subsidized certain industries, imported technicians', etc. (Henry Rosovsky, 'Japan's Transition to Economic Growth, 1868–1885' in H. Rosovsky (ed.), *Industrialization in Two Systems* (New York, 1966), 133. See also Sydney Crawcour, 'The Tokugawa Period and Japan's Preparation for Modern Economic Growth', paper given at the 1967 meeting of the American Historical Association in Montreal; and Hugh T. Patrick, 'Lessons for Underdeveloped Countries from the Japanese Experience of Economic Growth', *Indian Economic Journal,* X (October 1961).

By the beginning of the new century, when the cotton textile industry was rapidly expanding, both the demand and supply of entrepreneurs – now gradually coming to include the executive-level personnel of the more rapidly expanding among the larger firms – underwent a visible change. Larger and more complex firms demanded a set of abilities akin to those required of corporate executives as we envision them today, rather than those personal qualities of successful managers of merchant houses or of zaibatsu-founders such as Iwasaki and Yasuda. Firms sought their top-level executives and managerial staff at the newly expanding universities and colleges. That the firms began to find their entrepreneurial recruits in the schools reflects the importance of education in Japanese society. As has been demonstrated by Dore, Jansen, and others,[53] learning historically commanded deep respect among the Japanese, and newly emerging schools, especially a few elite universities, were now looked upon as the source of the most able. Firms naturally relied, as did the bureaucracy, on this efficient filter of abilities. And the ability to learn, and mostly from books, was precisely the talent needed for a nation which was busily learning in all phases, but especially in industrial ones, from the West. Dependence on the universities was well-nigh complete by this time, and thus Dore was able to write: 'By the first decade of this century an individual's life chances were determined not so much by his family status in itself as by the income and amenities attaching to his father's occupational position – the pattern of occupational mobility became not so very different from that of western societies.'[54] This fact should not be underrated, inasmuch as it indicates the rapid adaptability of the Japanese in meeting the demands of a new age.

This transition can be seen quite well in the House of Mitsui. The last of the old-style *bantō*, Rizaemon Minomura, was a *chōnin*'s son with no formal education.[55] He was shrewd in the best tradition of the Tokugawa commercial world and adept at gaining favours from political leaders who were in a position to dispense substantial financial rewards. Thus, during the politically and economically turbulent years of the late Tokugawa and early Meiji periods, Minomura's talents were great assets to the House of Mitsui, which, on the eve of Restoration, was none too secure. But the new industrial age, with its

53 Ronald P. Dore, 'Mobility, Equality, and Individuation in Modern Japan', in R. P. Dore (ed.), *Aspects of Social Change in Modern Japan* (Princeton, 1967); and Marius B. Jansen, 'Tokugawa and Modern Japan', in J. W. Hall (ed.), *Studies in the Institutional History of Early Modern Japan* (Princeton, 1968).

54 Dore, 'Mobility, Equality, and Individuation', 114.

55 Takao Tsuchiya, *Nihon no seishō* [*Japan's Political Merchants*] (Tokyo, 1956).

more impersonal and complex requirements, was beyond his understanding and ability. When he died, Mitsui was facing numerous difficulties; compared to Mitsubishi it was slow to make the transition needed in building an industrial empire, and its bank was in grave difficulties because of large amounts of loans made, largely to high government officials, with little or no collateral.

Hikojiro Nakamigawa, who took over Minomura's position at Mitsui, was a product of the new age.[56] A graduate of Keiō University, he had taught at a college and had lived for three years in England. He was progressive and injected the economic rationality of the industrial age into Mitsui's management. The temporary frictions he caused were to be expected. To the chagrin of Buddhists all over the nation, he forced Higashi Honganji, one of the largest temples, to pay back its overdue loans immediately, thus compelling the abbot of the temple to launch a nationwide campaign to raise the money. He next required collateral for loans to high government officials, in order to maintain sound banking practices on Western standards. Well supported by able lieutenants, most of whom were college graduates, he acquired the government-owned Tomioka filature, won control of the Oji paper firm, and took over the Kanegafuchi Cotton Textile Company. When Nakamigawa gained control, even the money-losing Kanegafuchi was made profitable and was soon the most efficient textile mill in Japan.

The transition of Mitsui was dramatic; but in most other firms the same change from merchant business leaders to college-educated industrial entrepreneurs took place, though less dramatically and more gradually. It had to, if the firms were to survive and prosper. For each merchant house which failed at the beginning of Meiji, such as the house of Ono, scores of large and small firms made the transition successfully. And this pattern of using colleges and universities as the sources of business leaders became gradually more entrenched as Japanese industrialization continued. Dore wrote:

> At any rate the existence of the trend [of placing emphasis on learning] is not hard to document. Of a sample of business leaders in a directory of 1915, only 15 per cent had been to a university. The figure was 83 per cent for a similar sample from the 1955 edition. In the latter year 48 per cent of the sample had spent all their working lives in salaried employment, compared with only 5 per cent in the earlier sample.[57]

56 Tsuchiya, *The Zaibatsu-Builders;* and Hidemitsu Shiroyanagi, *Nakamigawa Hikojiro den* [*A Biography of Hikojiro Nakamigawa*] (Tokyo, 1950).
57 Dore, 'Mobility, Equality, and Individuation', 118.

In making a study of the inter-class mobility of Japanese elites, Abegglen and Mannari found that in the late 1950s the top-level business leaders' 'grandfathers were of two groups for the most part, merchants from an urban setting perhaps, and small businessmen and landowners from rural backgrounds, with movement to urban white-collar and business positions in the next generation'.[58] We can assume that the men examined by these writers were born about 1900 on the average, and it might be assumed that their fathers were born about 1870, while their grandfathers would have been born about 1840.

Leaving further observations on Japanese entrepreneurship in more recent times to the last section of this chapter, we might conclude here with the following caveat. Given the weight of the literature supporting the orthodox view, I am not contending here that the foregoing discussions and the limited evidence are sufficient to disprove the long-held view. Rather, the main aim of this section is to present those observations and evidence which are helpful in gaining a more complete, and I hope a more accurate, understanding of Japanese entrepreneurship. For some, the descriptions of the cases of Itō and Suzuki may have been too detailed, and the view expressed on the roles of the government and the samurai may have been too forceful. But these must be understood as attempts to counterbalance the accumulated evidence marshalled on behalf of the orthodox view.

Those who are familiar with the pre-war literature can easily recall Tomoatsu Godai, a samurai who became an industrial pioneer in many fields; Takashi Masuda, a former samurai entrepreneur who was a leader in mining and in international trade; and a dozen other former samurai entrepreneurs including Goichi Nakano, Heigoro Shoda, and Taizo Abe.[59] The once-giant Fifteenth National Bank, which played an important role in financing the first privately owned railways in Japan, among other industrial ventures was established by former *daimyō* and nobility who provided entrepreneurship and capital.[60] A long list of significant contributions made by the government toward industrialization can also be easily compiled. It is an academic truism that the evidence gathered and the observations made by earlier generations of economic historians can no more be ignored than the evidence presented in this chapter.

An eminent British historian has written that 'the facts are really not at all like fish on the fishmonger's slab. They are like fish swimming in

58 Abegglen and Mannari, 'Leaders of Modern Japan', 120.

59 Hirschmeier, *Origins of Entrepreneurship*, 246–86. 60 Patrick, 'Japan, 1868–1914', 283.

a vast and sometimes inaccessible ocean; and what the historian catches will depend partly on chance, but mainly on what part of the ocean he chooses to fish in and what tackle he chooses to use – those two factors being, of course, determined by the kind of fish he wants to catch.'[61] The fish we catch may appear to fit badly into the established scheme of classification which we hold dear, but when the ocean is searched more thoroughly and a new classification scheme is fully worked out, I am confident that all the fish will find their places, resulting in an increased knowledge of the sea.

OWNERSHIP AND CONTROL

A small number of industrial undertakings during the late Tokugawa period were owned and operated by the Bakufu or *han* (domains). Wide-ranging commercial activities of large merchant houses were exclusively controlled by the respective families. *Bantō,* the chief managers, usually conducted the day-to-day business of these merchant houses, and in a few instances strong *bantō* made important entrepreneurial decisions. However, as a rule they were hired managers. The Meiji Restoration did not change this pattern immediately. The government plants were owned and operated by the government and managed by samurai-turned-bureaucrats. The ownership and control of merchant houses remained as before, and the emerging fortunes of Iwasaki, Yasuda, Asano, Furukawa, and other zaibatsu were strictly owned and controlled by the strong-willed founders. In fact, the law establishing *kabushiki kaisha* (share-issuing incorporated legal persons) was not enacted until 1890.

Though Japanese economic historians have not agreed as to when the first firm with share capital in the modern sense came into existence – in fact if not in name – one finds that a forerunner of the *kabushiki kaisha* had already appeared within a few years of the Restoration.[62] Mostly to supply credits and also to aid trading firms engaged in international trade, the government in 1869 established eight *kawase kaisha* on a share-capital basis in port cities. '*Kawase kaisha*' literally means 'bills-of-exchange companies', but this was meant to be a translation of the English word 'bank', for which there existed no exact equivalent in Japanese. *Kawase kaisha* had the 'characteristics of

61 E. H. Carr, *What is History?* (New York, 1967), 26.

62 Meiji Zaiseishi Hensankai [Editorial Committee of the Meiji Financial History], *Meiji zaiseishi* [*Meiji Financial History*], 15 vols. (Tokyo, 1904–5), XII, 328.

banks and were authorized to issue their own notes'.[63] The capital for these *kawase kaisha* was supplied by wealthy merchants, rich farmers, and money-exchangers who had established large houses during the late Tokugawa period, and by the government, which nearly matched the capital supplied from these private sources. Excessive and unwise control and interference by the government, and the generally unfavourable economic conditions of the time caused these *kawase kaisha* to fail, save one in Yokohama.[64]

While the government financed its industrial undertakings, attempted to establish *kawase kaisha,* and enacted the banking acts, private firms faced the difficult task of obtaining sufficient capital to undertake ventures which were too large to be financed out of the individual resources of most entrepreneurs. How was the necessary capital for Japan's rapid industrialization obtained, and who controlled the firms? Although they must be accompanied with the usual proviso needed in making historical periodization, these questions can best be answered by examining the years from 1868 to 1940 in three periods. As will become evident, these are fairly distinct periods for the purpose of the analysis of the ownership and control of Japanese industrial firms.

The first period can be thought of as extending from the Restoration into the mid-1880s. This was a period of preparation for modern economic growth, and it continued to the eve of the visible spurt in investment activities in the cotton textile industry. Private industrial firms, such as those of Suzuki in sugar refining and Itō in cotton textiles, began in most instances with capital which the entrepreneurs accumulated themselves and/or borrowed from their friends and relatives. The Oji Paper Company, which was to grow into the largest in the industry, began in 1873 with capital shared by the House of Mitsui and a dozen other merchants.[65] The Tokyo Electric Light Company began construction of its plants in 1886 when, after four years of struggling to raise capital, it finally persuaded sixty-four individuals to invest 200,000 yen.[66] These were also the years during which Hirano

63 Katō, *History of Banking in Japan,* 18.

64 Article I of the Kawase Kaisha Act read in part: 'The *kawase kaisha* were established for the purpose of . . . enriching the nation and . . . the government shall exercise its authority when loans are not repaid upon the promised date.' The government directed *kawase kaisha* to lend money for 'international trade, tea-growing, and purchasing cocoons', all of which were risky long-term loans. (*Ibid.*, 22.)

65 Oji Paper Company, *Oji seishi shashi* [*The History of the Oji Paper Company*], 5 vols. (Tokyo, 1957), vol. I.

66 See Muneo Nitta, *Tokyo dentō kabushiki kaisha kaigyō 50-nenshi* [*The First Fifty Years of the Tokyo Electric Light Company*] (Tokyo, 1936), and the company's *Tokyo dentō kabushiki kaishashi* [*A History of the Tokyo Electric Light Company*] (Tokyo, 1956).

Tomiji, who was to build one of the largest shipbuilding firms in Japan, laboured mightily to accumulate the necessary capital to start a shipyard and to make it sufficiently profitable to obtain a bank loan.[67] These were the years of the industrial pioneers whose meagre capital and abundant determination laid the foundations for the rapid growth to come.

The bankers, still groping for the fundamentals of sound modern banking practices in the new industrial age, were not yet ready to participate in industrial financing. An examination of bank records and recent empirical studies conducted by Japanese scholars make it clear that most bank funds tended to flow to agriculture and commerce.[68] I agree with Patrick's observation: 'It is clear that until the late 1880's most bank loans financed domestic and foreign trade, small-scale units of production in agriculture and processing industries, and, to some extent, the consumption of poor samurai and poor farmers (who, respectively, used pension bonds and land as collateral).'[69]

The zaibatsu, which were to become a dominant force in the economy, were still at the stage of recovering from the financial difficulties which they had met from the forced loans and economic dislocation of the past few decades and were occupied in building up their financial strength. They were still merchant houses at the dawn of a new industrial era. The House of Mitsui, for example, was under the management of Rizaemon Minomura, as described earlier. His forte was more in cultivating the good will of political leaders than in assessing the profitability of industrial ventures. Minomura was successful in getting the House of Mitsui appointed to the profitable position of 'Official Agent' of the new government's *dajōkan-satsu* (Privy Councillor's notes) and was a shrewd speculator in the new currency, taking the best advantage of its fluctuating prices. Mitsui bought a trading company in 1875 from Mitsui's political benefactor, Kaoru Inoue, who entered the new cabinet. Renamed the Mitsui Bussan (Trading Company), it grew rapidly, to earn large profits from government contracts to market coal produced by a government mine and from lucrative

67 The very interesting case of Hirano is not discussed in this chapter because of space limitations. Those interested can examine Mitani, *Detailed Biographies;* Arai Gensui, *Tokyo Ishikawajima Zōsenjo 50-nenshi* [*A Fifty-Year History of the Tokyo Ishikawajima Shipyard*] (Tokyo, 1930); and the Ishikawajima Heavy Industry Company, *Ishikawajima jūkogyō kabushiki kaisha 108-nenshi* [*A 108-Year History of Ishikawajima Heavy Industries, Ltd*] (Tokyo, 1961).

68 See Yamamura, 'The Role of the Samurai'. 69 Patrick, 'Japan, 1868–1914', 279.

dealings in textile goods and the importation of a large number of industrial goods from the West.[70]

Then, in 1876, Mitsui established its own bank, capitalized at 2 million yen. The bank, exclusively controlled by the Mitsui family, began its business with thirty branches located all over the nation. From the beginning this bank enjoyed the same political favours given to the other Mitsui enterprises: namely, the bank received large government deposits and benefited from the tax-collection services which all local branches rendered to the Ministry of Finance. By 1882, the bank was large enough to withstand a momentary crisis which was caused by the establishment of the Bank of Japan, to which the Mitsui Bank immediately lost 6.8 million yen in government deposits.

The second period, from the mid-1880s to the First World War, saw a few important developments which changed the ownership and control patterns of Japanese industrial firms. Most notable is the fact that the largest merchant houses, now financially strong and equipped with their respective thriving banks, took the first steps toward creating their own industrial empires. Beginning in the early 1880s, the largest among them, especially, began to acquire government plants. These acquisitions – twenty industrial plants and mines in all – proved highly profitable. Thus they became an added impetus for these zaibatsu to establish, acquire, and increase their financial control in industrial undertakings. The industrial empires of these zaibatsu had not yet approached the proportions they were to reach after the end of the First World War, but by the first decade of the new century they had become the new industrial economic powers within the nation. Mitsui formally organized a holding company, Mitsui Gōmei, in 1911 to exercise tight financial control over its bank, trading company, mining firms, real estate, and warehousing activities, as well as the Oji Paper Company and a dozen other enterprises. Mitsubishi, too, established its holding company, the Mitsubishi Gōshikaisha, in 1917 to increase the financial control over its firms.[71]

70 Here and elsewhere in this essay the discussions on Mitsui are based on the following sources, in addition to those works of Tsuchiya already cited (*Japan's Political Merchants*, *Business History Study*, and *The Zaibatsu-Builders*): Ryotarō Iwai, *Mitsui, Mitsubishi monogatari* [*The Stories of Mitsui and Mitsubishi*] (Tokyo, 1934); Mitsubishi Economic Research Institute, *Mitsui, Mitsubishi, Sumitomo* (Tokyo, 1955); Hidekichi Wada, *Mitsui kontserun dokuhon* [*The Story of the Mitsui 'Konzern'*] (Tokyo, 1937); Mitsuhaya Kajinishi, *Seishō* [*The Political Merchants*] (Tokyo, 1963); Mitsui Bank, *Mitsui ginkō 50-nenshi* [*A Fifty-Year History of the Mitsui Bank*] (Tokyo, 1926); Mitsui Bank, *Mitsui ginkō 80-nenshi* [*An Eighty-Year History of the Mitsui Bank*] (Tokyo, 1957).

71 For a fuller treatment and useful sources, see Yamamura, 'The Founding of Mitsubishi Zaibatsu'.

Banks during this period began to make long- and short-term loans to industrial firms, and their holdings of industrial shares increased. However, contrary to the long-maintained proposition that the banks, especially the large ones, were a dominant factor in providing industrial capital, a close examination of the data seems to reveal that the importance of large banks as owners of individual shares and as individual financiers during this period has been significantly overstated. One can show this in several ways.

Beginning with the oft-quoted aggregate data, we find for 1899-1902 that the loans made by all ordinary banks using shares as collateral were in the neighbourhood of 25 per cent of all the loans made in each year; when loans made on debentures are added, the figure rises to approximately 30 per cent. These data seem to show the importance of banks in industrial financing, but a closer scrutiny reveals that this first impression is deceptive. In a more meaningful context, we find that the loans made using shares as collateral amounted to about 22 per cent of the total paid-in capital in 1899, 18 per cent in 1900, 12 per cent in 1901, and 11 per cent in 1902. These percentages, however, do not indicate the degree of direct contribution by the banks to industrial financing. Even assuming that all the loans made using shares as collateral were used for financing industry, these percentages must be almost halved before we can consider them as indicators of the degree of the direct contribution of the banks to industrial financing, because only slightly more than half of these loans and investments were for industrial firms. Not only was nearly half of the total paid-up capital for non-industrial firms, but the banks tended to prefer to finance other banks, insurance companies, and established commercial firms.[72]

It is true that some portion of loans made using non-industrial shares as collateral found their way to industry, and the total direct investment by banks in industrial and non-industrial shares amounted to slightly over half of those loans made using shares as collateral. But from what can be observed of the aggregate data, direct bank financing in industrial firms by means of loans and direct investment was limited. That is, as the bank records of the period reveal, the industrial financing made by these banks during the period 1899–1902 was limited in magnitude to no more than 15 per cent of the total industrial paid-up capital –

72 Tōyō Kaizai Shimpō-sha [Tōyō Economic Publishing Co.], *Meiji-Taisho kokusei sōran* [*A Survey of the National Economy in the Meiji-Taisho Periods*] (Tokyo, 1924), 12–13 and 36. The total amount of paid-in capital for each year is taken from Tōkeikyoku [Bureau of Statistics], *Teikoku tōkei nenkan* [*Annual Report of Imperial Statistics*] for the respective years.

often much less – and was not of an order of magnitude to justify the view held by numerous earlier writers who, though differing in their choice of phrases, observed in effect that 'the banks were the major source of industrial financing by the turn of the century'.

Another set of data frequently used is the one calculated by the Industrial Bank of Japan. Earlier authors often cited the data to show that bank loans were the major source of industrial financing by the beginning of the twentieth century. According to these data the sources of 'a total of 247 million yen in industrial funds supplied to industrial corporations between 1897 and 1913 were bank loans (57.7 per cent), new stock issues (32.4 per cent), corporate debentures (6.5 per cent) and internal reserves (3.6 per cent)'.[73] I believe these data are small in coverage and are heavily biased to overemphasize bank loans; this can be seen easily. The new stock issues increased by about 700 million yen during the period 1897–1913. This means that the coverage of the Industrial Bank's data was slightly over 11 per cent of new stock issues. That is, when the bank found that 32.4 per cent of the total industrial funds (247 million) were financed by means of stock issues, the capital so obtained was slightly over 80 million yen, which is 11.4 per cent of 700 million yen. It seems evident that the data covered only this small fraction of all the bank loans made to industrial firms. Also, regardless of the coverage and source, the figure of 3.6 per cent attributed to internal reserves is hardly acceptable, as will be shown shortly. One rather suspects that the data reflect much of the intra-zaibatsu financing, i.e. from zaibatsu bank to zaibatsu-controlled firms.

It is evident from company and bank histories that many of the long-term loans made by the largest banks went to a small number of firms which were closely connected with these banks or ventures and which were organized by the bankers themselves. These were the zaibatsu industrial firms in mining, shipbuilding, and other industries, and they were in many instances firms which were established from the former government plants. The firms receiving long-term loans were small in number compared to the large number of firms which lamented the lack of long-term credit. The largest banks were, in fact, quite frank in admitting such practices. The Bank of Mitsui noted that 'over 7 million yen', or nearly 40 per cent of the total amount lent, went to several firms 'connected' with the bank. During

73 Japan Industrial Bank, *Nippon kōgyō ginkō 50-nenshi shi* [*A Fifty-Year History of the Japan Industrial Bank*] (Tokyo, 1957), 38.

the 1897–8 recession, the bank 'curtailed loans as much as possible to general borrowers', and large loans were confined to the firms in which Mitsui had a direct interest.[74] The Mitsubishi Bank followed the same practice during the period 'by lending only to those firms which are Mitsubishi-related', while 'all branch offices sharply reduced loans to general [non-related] borrowers'.[75] What percentage of the total amount in long-term loans was borrowed by the minority of the zaibatsu firms is difficult to ascertain. One conclusion which can be drawn safely is that it would be extremely difficult to show that a large number of industrial firms enjoyed long-term loans of any appreciable amount. This is especially true since it is well known that the smaller banks were even less willing to make long-term industrial loans.

That bank participation in industrial financing was not as important as has long been believed can be shown when we examine the cotton textile industry, which initiated the first industrial spurt of Japan. The Osaka Cotton Textile Company, the first large-scale firm (10,500 spindles), was established on private capital in 1882. This company, which by growth and the absorption of other firms was to become the giant Tōyō Textile Company, financed its growth by selling increasing amounts of shares and by ploughing back its profits. There is little evidence that bank loans played a significant role in its rapid expansion. The firm began with a capital of 25,000 yen in 1882; but in the following year this was increased to 280,000, and it was doing well enough to declare a dividend of 6 per cent. Over the next several years the firm gradually increased its capital to reach by 1888 the truly large sum – by the standards of the day – of 1.2 million yen, with cash reserves of 124,600 yen. The dividend rates for the years between 1884 and 1888 were 18, 11, 12, 30, and 33 per cent respectively. These rates undoubtedly aided shareholders in buying newly issued shares. By 1914, when the firm merged with Mie Cotton Textiles (Itō Denhichi's company) it had 13,009,225 yen of paid-in capital and 8,124,242 yen of reserve funds.[76]

Except for a few firms such as Kanegafuchi Cotton Textiles, which was taken over by Mitsui interests, the industry as a whole was relatively free of zaibatsu incursion and dependence on banks, and this is clearly seen in the industry-wide figures for 1905, at the height of the boom which followed the Russo-Japanese War. The industry's total

74 Mitsui Bank, *An Eighty-Year History,* 405.
75 Mitsubishi Bank, *Mitsubishi ginkō shi* [*The History of the Mitsubishi Bank*] (Tokyo, 1954), 90.
76 Tōyō Textile Company, *Seventy Years,* 135–52.

assets were 51,469,000 yen with a paid-in capital of 34,332,000 yen, and the total internal reserve stood at 11,598,000 yen. Against this, outside loans of all types amounted to 5,565,000 yen, thus yielding a ratio of industry-wide total loans (short- and long-term) to total assets of 0.11, compared with a ratio of total reserve to owners' equity of 0.34, and one of total reserves to total assets of 0.23. The internal reserve was nearly twice the amount of outside loans.[77]

Behind this industrial expansion, and especially in view of the much less than dominant participation of the banks in such an important industry as the cotton textile industry, we must note the following oft-neglected figures. Even before the turn of the century, public participation in stock-buying had significantly increased. The total number of shareholders in Japan increased rapidly from 108,296 persons in 1886 to 244,585 persons in 1890 and then rose sharply to 684,070 persons by the end of 1898. When these figures are examined for different industries we find that the average number of shareholders per firm increased rapidly for 'modern' industries, while it declined visibly for other types of industries. Between 1893 and 1898, the average number of shareholders per firm rose from 136 to 457 in cotton-spinning, from 714 to 1,040 in railways, and from 4 to 124 in shipbuilding, while the same figure declined from 228 to 28 in cocoon-raising, from 410 to 45 in foreign trade, and from 361 to 93 in land development.[78]

During the third period, the inter-war years, we find that the ownership and control of Japanese industrial firms underwent significant changes. Most notable among them is the rapid rise of the financial control of, and increased ownership of, industrial firms by the zaibatsu banks. Concentration of product and capital markets continued at a rapid pace, and mutual shareholding and interlocking directorships continued to increase. It also was during this period that nearly a dozen holding companies, both large and small, appeared.

77 Fumio Yamada, 'Capital for Japan's Cotton Textile Industry', *Keizaigaku Ronshū* [*Economic Essays,* University of Tokyo], VI, 2 (1962), 147.

78 Toshimitsu Imuda, 'Meijiki ni okeru kabushiki kaisha no hatten to kabunushi-sō no keisei' ['The Development of Incorporated Firms and the Formation of the Shareholder Class in the Meiji Period'], in Osaka Municipal University, Economic Research Institute, *Meijiki ho keizai hatten to keizai shutai* [*Economic Development and Its Leading Agents in the Meiji Period*] (Osaka, 1968). The same author, who made an extensive use of industrial and individual data, provisionally advanced the thesis that the financing patterns should be divided into the following five categories: (1) partnership; (2) mostly by relatives; (3) mostly by non-management shareholders; (4) by management and shareholders from two distinct groups, where the number of shareholders is not large; (5) the same as (4) but where the number of shareholders is large. One of his more important (though still tentative) conclusions is that 'although there was a difference in degree, the basic pattern of financing approximated the process of development of incorporated firms seen in advanced Western nations' (*Ibid.*, 141).

The First World War boom, which made Japan a fully fledged industrial power, profoundly changed banking practices. The largest banks, which were beginning to be called zaibatsu banks, began to advance significant sums in long-term loans to industrial firms in such capital-using industries as the heavy, chemical, and utility industries. More importantly, these new recipients of long-term bank loans were not, as earlier, a small number of firms which had close zaibatsu connections, either having been established partly by zaibatsu capital (such as the Oji Paper Company) or being one of the zaibatsu industrial ventures developed from plants bought by the zaibatsu interests from the Meiji government at the beginning of the 1880s. One could say that the zaibatsu banks became, during the 1920s, investment banks of the German type.

This transition was possible because the formerly bank-dependent zaibatsu-connected firms had by the end of the First World War become self-sufficient in terms of financing their own growth, and the banks themselves became large enough during the 1920s to make this transition possible in practice. The data indicate that these giant banks grew rapidly in strength, both in absolute and in relative terms, through increases in capital, deposits, and the number of mergers. It is well known that depositors sought these giant banks after a series of bank runs in the 1920s.

Facts to substantiate these observations can be found in numerous company histories and aggregate bank data. Preceding more general observations on the destinations of bank loans, several samples from the semi-annual financial reports of zaibatsu-connected firms will be useful in showing the transformation of the financial patterns of these firms, demonstrating that the rapidly growing zaibatsu banks no longer needed to concern themselves with supplying capital to their 'own' firms. These examples are 'representative' firms in that they were selected to reflect the financing patterns of zaibatsu firms during the Taisho and early Showa periods and were chosen from thirty-seven major zaibatsu-connected firms, for which these data are available.[79]

As early as 1907, the Shibaura Seisakusho (Shibaura Machine-Tool

79 Data were obtained from the respective company histories, which the writer was able to obtain since 1962, and from the Yūshōdō Microfilms publication of 'The Annual Financial Reports of One Thousand Firms, 1868–1945' (Tokyo, 1962). As most Japanese writers agree, there were about eighty-five firms which were directly controlled by the four zaibatsu holding companies at the end of the 1920s; the sample of thirty-seven covers about 44 per cent of these firms. The zaibatsu affiliates which were controlled only to a limited degree by zaibatsu subsidiaries or by the zaibatsu holding companies are not included among the eighty-five firms classified as direct subsidiary firms.

Industries) of the Mitsui group had stopped long-term borrowing from the Mitsui and other banks, and no long-term loan was made again until 1934. Neither does any short-term loan appear on the financial reports after 1908. The firm's capital was increased from 2 million yen to 5 million in 1912 before the investment boom of the First World War, and it was increased again to 20 million yen in 1920. A dividend rate in excess of 20 per cent was maintained between 1916 and 1921, and this fact enabled the company to sell its shares easily for the purpose of expansion.[80]

The Dainihon Seruroido KK (The Greater Japan Celluloid Company) of the Mitsui group ceased making short-term loans in 1921, and long-term loans disappeared from the reports in 1926. The long-term loans existing during the Taisho period (1912–25) never exceeded an amount equivalent to a small percentage of the total assets of the company. The firm increased the ratio of reserves to owners' equity (paid-in capital) from 5 per cent to 35 per cent during the period between 1921 and 1929. Share capital increased during the same time from 12.5 million yen in 1919 to 100 million in 1921.[81]

The Mitsui Kōzan KK (Mitsui Mining Company) issued no bonds during the Taisho or early Showa years. Its capital increased from 20 million yen in 1916 to 50 million in 1918, and then to 100 million yen in 1920 in order to finance the expansions of the boom years. Long-term loans were made from Mitsui Gōmei[82] until 1918, although the total amount was small – in the neighbourhood of 0.5 per cent of total assets. Between 1919 and 1929, only six loans were made from Mitsui Bussan (Trading Company) as extended advances to coal and other chemical by-products which the mining company sold to the Bussan. However, these loans from the Bussan did not exceed 1.5 per cent of the total assets of the firm, and steadily increasing reserves reached 12 million yen by 1929.[83]

Even the Oji Paper Company, which had borrowed from the Daiichi and Mitsui banks, became much more financially independent after the war. Short-term loans disappeared after 1919, and long-term loans amounted to no more than 10 per cent of the total assets except twice – once in 1922, when they came to just over 10 per cent, and in 1927,

80 Data are from the Yūshōdō Microfilms; see also Yasuichi Kimura (ed.), *Shibaura seisakusho 65-nenshi* [*A Sixty-five-Year History of the Shibaura Machine-Tool Industries*] (Tokyo, 1940).

81 Data are from the Yūshōdō Microfilms, and from Dainihon Seruroido KK, *Dainihon seruroido kaishashi* [*A History of the Greater Japan Celluloid Company*] (Tokyo, 1952).

82 The Mitsui Gōmei (a legal entity organized by the Mitsui family) owned the Mitsui Bank before 1919. However, when a part of the bank shares were sold publicly in 1919, the Gōmei was observed by the bank.

83 Mitsui Bank, *An Eighty-Year History*, 210–11.

when they were 23 per cent. Most outside capital was obtained by means of bonds, which were issued in an amount equivalent to 23 per cent of the total assets in 1916, while during most of the 1920s the figure fluctuated within the range of 18–26 per cent of total assets. However, the firm's ratio of reserves to total assets was at a higher level (8–14 per cent) compared with the pre-war years, when it was only a small percentage of total assets. The ratio of reserves to owners' equity also increased, from 24 per cent to 44 per cent, during the period between 1917 and 1929.[84]

In the Mitsubishi group, the Mitsubishi Zōsen KK (Mitsubishi Shipbuilding Company) relied on bond financing to the magnitude of 10 million yen against a paid-in capital of 30 million yen in 1918. The bond obligation was gradually eliminated and stood at zero in 1927. No short-term loans were seen after 1919, and only one long-term loan of 0.5 million yen was made in 1930, against a reserve which increased from 2 million in 1919 to 5.8 million by 1930.[85] The Mitsubishi Kōgyō KK (Mitsubishi Mining Company) was even sounder: in 1918 it was capitalized at 50 million yen, and no bonds were sold and no long-term loans made after 1919, while reserves rose from 0.3 million yen in 1918 to 3.2 million yen in 1929.[86]

The Nisshin Seifun KK (Nisshin Flour-Milling Company) stayed clear of long-term borrowing during the Taisho and the early Showa years; it borrowed only during 1922–5 and in an amount equivalent to 4.2 per cent of total assets. No explicit mention is made of short-term loans, and no bonds were sold before 1930. Capital steadily increased from 1.7 million in 1914 to 4 million in 1917, and then to 12.3 million in 1925. Since the dividend rate remained well above the floor of 15 per cent after 1916, with an exceptionally high 30 per cent at the height of the war boom, the firm had no difficulty in marketing its own shares for the purpose of acquiring capital for expansion.[87]

One could easily add many more examples to convey this changing pattern of financing in zaibatsu-connected firms. Suffice it to say that in addition to these firms, there were many more zaibatsu firms which depended only to a very limited extent on long-term loans from their respective zaibatsu banks. In fact, of the sample examined, fifteen firms

84 Yūshōdō Microfilms; and Oji Paper Company, *History*, vol. I.

85 Yūshōdō Microfilms; and Mitsubishi Shipbuilding Company, *Mitsubishi zōsen* [*History of the Mitsubishi Shipbuilding Company*] (Tokyo, 1958).

86 Yūshōdō Microfilms; and Saburō Fumoto, *Mitsubishi Iizuka tankōshi* [*The History of Mitsubishi Iizuka Coal Mines*] (Tokyo, 1961).

87 Yūshōdō Microfilms, and Nisshin Seifun KK, *Nisshin seifun kabushi kaishashi* [*The History of the Nisshin Flour-Milling Company*] (Tokyo, 1965).

in the Mitsui, Mitsubishi, Sumitomo, Asano, and Koga groups – including the Mitsui Kōzan and Mitsubishi Zōsen – made no long-term loans at all throughout the 1920s. It can be safely concluded that zaibatsu-related firms were financially secure by the beginning of the 1920s and required little long-term capital from their parent banks.[88]

In examining bank data, we can confirm the financial independence of zaibatsu firms. If we take the example of the Mitsui Bank, for which useful information is available, we find that by 1930 only 9.8 per cent of the total amount lent went to Mitsui-connected firms.[89] Although direct evidence is not available, one can conclude that all other major banks followed an essentially similar pattern. For example, loans to Sumitomo-related firms by the Sumitomo bank were even smaller because the group's major firms had no long-term loans by the late 1920s.[90]

Throughout the 1920s, the basic pattern was one in which the zaibatsu firms, because of past relationships, enjoyed a high degree of participation from the zaibatsu banks and families, even though these largest firms could easily sell shares to the public. For the subsidiary firms, zaibatsu participation in equity was limited, but these firms too were sufficiently sound to be able to float shares of their own and required few or no zaibatsu loans. By 1928, the share holdings of zaibatsu families, banks, and other zaibatsu firms within the same zaibatsu group were extensive. The percentages of the total paid-up capital supplied by the respective zaibatsu *honsha* (holding company and bank) of the four largest zaibatsu to the so-called zaibatsu firms which they controlled were: Mitsui, 90.2 per cent; Mitsubishi, 69.4; Sumitomo, 79.1; and Yasuda, 32.0. When the percentage of total paid-up capital supplied by other zaibatsu firms belonging to the same zaibatsu group is added, the respective figures rose to: Mitsui, 90.6 per cent; Mitsubishi, 77.6; Sumitomo, 80.5; and Yasuda, 48.0.[91]

That the zaibatsu banks provided during the 1920s an increasing amount of long-term capital to non-zaibatsu firms can be shown easily. First, bonds were a much more important means of obtaining capital than were long-term loans during the 1920s. Of the 352 largest firms

88 The firms are Nihon Cement (Asano), Koga Mining (Koga), Mitsui Bussan, Taiheiyō Coal-Mining (Mitsui), Hokkai Soda (Mitsui), Mitsubishi Papers, Nisshin Steamships (Mitsubishi), Meiji Sugar-Refining (Mitsubishi), Sumitomo Besshi Lead-Mining, Sumitomo Steel Pipes, the Sumitomo Steel Mill, Fujikura Electric Wires (Sumitomo), and Sumitomo Electric Wires.

89 Calculated from data contained in Mitsui Bank, *An Eighty-Year History*, 421–2.

90 Calculated from the Sumitomo Bank data in the Yūshōdō Microfilms.

91 K. Takahashi and J. Aoyama, *Nihon zaibatsu-ron* [*A Study of the Japanese Zaibatsu*] (Tokyo, 1938), 162.

examined by the Mitsubishi Economic Research Institute, bonds accounted for 21 per cent of the total capital, long-term loans 7 per cent, share capital 56 per cent, and short-term capital 15 per cent. Out of twenty-two industries examined by the Institute, thirteen industries depended more on bonds than on long-term loans. The total value of bonds sold during the period 1920–5 was 2,422 million yen, of which only 18.1 per cent was in bonds of zaibatsu-connected firms. The major share of the total, 41.3 per cent, was in bonds floated by utility firms, and 20.7 per cent was for electric railway companies. These were two industries in which zaibatsu interests were extremely small. By 1930, the total value of bonds floated was 2,927 million yen, of which zaibatsu-connected firms accounted for only 15.2 per cent. The zaibatsu firms floating the bonds were small subsidiaries and affiliates, and not major zaibatsu firms.[92]

An important point to be made is that the four largest zaibatsu banks held, by the end of 1929, 27.1 per cent of all outstanding bonds. If the insurance and credit companies of the zaibatsu groups are added, the bond holdings increase to 29.1 per cent of the total.[93] Among the zaibatsu banks, the ratio of bonds to the total negotiable paper ranged in 1924 from 41.7 per cent for the Mitsubishi Bank to 37.0 per cent for the Mitsui Bank.[94]

As noted earlier, the long-term loans made by the zaibatsu banks increased rapidly during the latter half of the 1920s. The Mitsui Bank's ratio of long-term loans to total assets rose from 0.24 in 1912 to 0.44 at the end of 1930. The ratio was somewhat lower during the period 1919–24, but the rising trend is unmistakable. The ratio of long-term loans to total loans rose steadily with no visible departure from the trend throughout the period 1912–30. These data for the Mitsui Bank show a clear departure from the bank's loan practices during the first 'spurt' from 1885 to 1905. The Mitsubishi Bank shows an even more distinct change in its loan practices between the first

92 Calculated from data contained in Japan Industrial Bank, *A Fifty-Year History*, 222–3, and the data sections of Nomura Securities Company of Japan, *Kōshasai nenkan* [*An Annual Report of Government and Company Bonds*] (Tokyo, 1930). The zaibatsu firms are identified by referring to Kamekichi Takahashi, *Nihon zaibatsu no kaibō* [*An Anatomy of Japanese Zaibatsu*] (Tokyo, 1930), 21–2, 55–60, and 140–1, and Ryukichi Minobe, *Karuteru, Torasuto, Kontserun* [*Cartels, Trusts, and Concerns*], 2 vols. (Tokyo, 1931), vol. II. Throughout this chapter, the expressions 'zaibatsu-controlled', 'zaibatsu firms', and 'zaibatsu groups' are used only for those cases which are clearly identifiable – i.e. those in which connections with zaibatsu families and banks can be readily shown by share-holding, interlocking directorships, or loans made. For the pre-1940 years, such identification is quite straightforward because of the evident dependence of zaibatsu subsidiaries and affiliates on the zaibatsu banks and other zaibatsu firms.

93 Takahashi, *An Anatomy of Japanese Zaibatsu*, 44–7.

94 From data contained in the history of each bank and the Yūshōdō Microfilms.

'spurt' period and the First World War. The ratio of long-term loans to total assets rose sharply during the First World War, and it remained, in spite of the gradual decline from the peak of 0.65 in 1917, at a relatively high level throughout the 1920s. The ratio of long-term loans to total loans jumped distinctly during the war and remained at a high level with no visible sign of declining. It is also noteworthy that the Mitsubishi Bank began to purchase an increasingly large amount of negotiable papers (bonds and shares) throughout the period 1912–30, in clear contrast to the pattern observed before 1912. As the Mitsubishi Bank's holdings in the shares of Mitsubishi-connected firms were smaller than any other zaibatsu bank's holdings in the shares of its respective group, the Mitsubishi Bank's high ratios of negotiable paper to total assets and of long-term loans to total assets reflects the bank's increased holdings in bonds and shares of non-zaibatsu firms. Since the Yasuda, Sumitomo, and Daiichi banks also showed similar increases in the importance of long-term loans *vis-à-vis* total assets and total loans, the conclusion that during the 1920s the zaibatsu banks were making long-term loans to non-zaibatsu firms in increasing amounts appears to be well founded.[95]

Banking was increasingly dominated by the zaibatsu banks during the 1920s. It is easy to show that there were significant changes in both the absolute and relative positions of the zaibatsu banks between 1919 and 1927. During those eight years, the zaibatsu banks increased their relative share of the total deposits from 25 per cent to 31 per cent, or from 5,700 million to 9,000 million in absolute amounts. The market share of loans remained virtually unchanged, but the total amount lent by these banks increased from 5,700 million yen to 8,200 million. These developments are especially significant when considered against the fact that the relative share of the paid-in capital of these banks decreased from 21.2 per cent to 19 per cent. Another way of appraising the financial power of the zaibatsu group is to note that eight zaibatsu (including banks, insurance companies, and credit companies) accounted for 45.7 per cent of the total capital plus deposits plus

95 The necessary data and information were obtained from the histories of the banks mentioned. Here the procedure (well accepted by Japanese scholars) of separating long- and short-term loans is adopted to obtain the necessary ratios. The long-term loans are *kashitsukekin* (literally, 'money lent'), which are the sums of the loans made against various negotiable instruments (*tegata kashitsuke* and *shōken kashitsuke*). The total of loans includes – in addition to long-term loans – bills discounted (*waribiki tegata*), call loans, and overdrafts (*tōza kashikoshi:* literally, 'lent for the moment'). There are various difficulties concerning renewed short-term loans and some of the loans made for less than a year, which are put under the heading *tegata kashitsuke,* but adjustments made for these difficulties should not change the ratios observed here by more than a few percentage points.

reserves of all private banks, insurance companies, and credit companies at the end of 1929.[96]

A few important factors contributed to this rapid concentration of the financial market. One of these was the sporadic bank runs which the banking industry experienced after the First World War and the nationwide bank runs of 1927 which resulted from the accumulated ills of the 'earthquake bills' and the practice of banks acting as 'organ banks'. 'Earthquake bills' were those notes which many borrowers were unable to pay because of the earthquake of 1923 and which were guaranteed to banks by the Bank of Japan. These bills resulted in limiting the freedom of the monetary policy of the Bank of Japan and also constrained the activities of banks because the banks had to depend on heel-dragging political decisions by the government as to the amount of loans to be made to banks holding these bills.[97]

The 'organ banks' were the many Japanese banks of the period which became 'organs' of their specific clients. This meant that banks were often forced into the position of making unsound loans to their clients, mostly industrial firms, who were facing financial difficulties. Since the banks were committed to their clients in the sense that large loans had already been made to these firms and their bankruptcy meant the end of the banks themselves, the banks were forced to make further unsound loans. Such a practice could and did lead to nationwide bank runs, as the Bank of Taiwan discovered in dealing with the Suzuki Shōten.[98]

The instability of the banking industry caused many savers to transfer their deposits to larger and better-established banks. The zaibatsu banks, which survived these crises with only an occasional run on their branch banks, naturally were the major beneficiaries of these transferred savings. Throughout the period, also, the government was anxious to stabilize the financial market and chose to actively promote mergers and unifications of weaker (small and/or local) banks. Beginning in 1924, the Ministry of Finance engaged in an active programme to reduce the number of banks in each prefecture, to extend assistance in the evaluation of assets at the time of a merger, and to help select the

96 The eight zaibatsu are Mitsui, Mitsubishi, Sumitomo, Yasuda, Daiichi (i.e. the Big Five, involving twenty-nine banks, four credit firms, four life-assurance companies, and nineteen other types of insurance companies), and the Kawasaki, Yamaguchi, and Kōnoike groups (involving twenty-one banks, three credit firms, seven life-assurance companies, and six other types of insurance firms). The last three zaibatsu are much smaller in size. Takahashi, *An Anatomy of Japanese Zaibatsu*, 39.

97 For detailed descriptions, see Mitsuhaya Kajinishi *et al.*, *Nihon shihonshugi no botsuraku* [*The Fall of Japanese Capitalism*], vol. 1 (Tokyo, 1960), 185–90.

98 *Ibid.*, 157–61.

best-qualified managers for newly unified banks. This programme was carried on throughout the 1920s, and the Ministry's 'persuasion' was extremely effective in numerous instances.[99]

No less important in bringing about the highly oligopolistic structure of the banking industry were the aggressive merger and absorption measures adopted by the largest banks themselves. A typical case is that of the Yasuda Bank. In 1923, the Yasuda Bank absorbed ten other banks scattered throughout the country to create a giant bank.[100] It was common practice at that time for the larger city banks to absorb smaller local banks and make them into branch offices.

The expansion of financial power continued throughout the 1930s, and by 1942 the financial control of the four largest zaibatsu was indeed pervasive. In finance, the four zaibatsu accounted for 49.7 per cent of the total paid-in capital of the banking, insurance, and credit industries. In industry, the same four owned 32.4 per cent of the total paid-in capital of the heavy industries and 10.8 per cent of that in light industry. In addition, the four zaibatsu accounted for 12.9 per cent of the total paid-in capital of utility, transportation, real estate, and trading companies. In the aggregate, the holding companies of these four zaibatsu directly accounted for 24.5 per cent of the total paid-in capital of the industries listed above.[101]

The control exerted by these zaibatsu holding companies far exceeded that expressed by the above percentage figures for paid-in capital. The extent of their control of the various industrial sectors was significantly augmented by their power to grant loans, by the use of interlocking directorships, and by the numerous other leverages which these super-large financial empires had at their command. The extent of these powers can easily be surmised when we discover that by 1944 74.9 per cent of all loans made within Japan were made by the four zaibatsu banks,[102] and each zaibatsu had woven an elaborate net of interlocking directorships. For example Mitsui alone commanded the fate of nearly two hundred large firms, in which it placed key executive officers.[103]

The march toward the concentration of the ownership and control of Japanese industries became visible after the end of the First World

99 Kajinishi Mitsuhaya, *Zoku nihon shihonshugi hattatsu-shi* [*A Revised History of the Development of Japanese Capitalism*] (Tokyo, 1957), 49–50.

100 A detailed description of this merger is found in Yasuda Bank, *Yasuda ginkō 60-nenshi* [*A Sixty-Year History of the Yasuda Bank*] (Tokyo, 1940), 225–48.

101 Holding Company Liquidation Commission, *Nippon zaibatsu to sono kaitai* [*The Japanese Zaibatsu and Their Dissolution*], 2 vols. (Tokyo, 1962), vol. II (*Data*), 469.

102 *Ibid.*, 63. 103 *Ibid.*, 468–72.

War, and it continued at a rapid pace throughout the 1920s and 1930s. There are numerous indicators of a highly concentrated economy, but it is sufficient to note here that 2.59 per cent of all the shareholders in Japan at the end of the Second World War, or slightly over 40,000 individuals, owned over 64 per cent of the total outstanding shares, and less than 10 per cent of those individuals – 3,762 zaibatsu-connected or other extremely wealthy persons to be exact – owned 216 million shares or 48.74 per cent of the total outstanding shares.[104]

Our narrative on the years after the Second World War can be briefly summarized because much has been written in English.[105] The Allied Command, on encountering the highly concentrated ownership and control of Japanese industries, instituted a wide-ranging policy of 'economic democratization' to eliminate what it termed a 'cancerous' zaibatsu dominance. Holding companies were outlawed; giant firms which were virtual monopolists were dissolved, and in the place of each giant, two or more firms were created; the ownership of former zaibatsu banks was taken from the zaibatsu families; mutual share holdings among zaibatsu firms and between zaibatsu banks and zaibatsu firms were made illegal; zaibatsu families were forced to sell their shares through a commission which, in turn, made efforts to sell them to the public; and interlocking directorships were prohibited, and a large number of former officers of zaibatsu firms were purged from such positions.

This was, in fundamental ways, a revolution in the ownership and control patterns of the Japanese economy. The forced sales of their shares, plus the newly instituted capital levies and inheritance taxes, reduced the zaibatsu families' real wealth to about a twentieth of what it once had been before these policies were carried out. The distribution of share holdings was now much more widespread; neither large firms nor banks were owned by a few individuals. Rarely does anyone own more than 5 per cent of the total shares of a large firm or a bank, and majority owners, who were common before the end of the war, no longer exist.

Then, as is well known, the political effects of the Korean War began to dilute this thoroughgoing economic democratization policy, and after the return of sovereignty to Japan in 1952 the Japanese government began to reverse the occupation policies on the ground that these policies were detrimental to rapid economic recovery and

104 *Ibid.*, 450–5.
105 This section on the post-war period is based on Kozo Yamamura, *Economic Policy in Postwar Japan: Growth Versus Economic Democracy* (Berkeley, California, 1967).

growth. Each step need not be retraced here, but by the mid-1960s the ownership and control patterns of Japanese industrial firms certainly did not resemble the patterns which the Allied Command had once tried to establish.

When the twenty-five years of post-war history are reviewed, a few salient points emerge with regard to the ownership and control patterns of Japanese industries. Most obvious is the marked difference in the share-holding patterns of the mid-1960s compared with those observed during the pre-war years. It is true that the onetime ideal of the Allied Command – widely diffused share-holding by millions of 'little people' – has never been realized, that there has been a tendency for the share-holding pattern to concentrate in the hands of a decreasing number of individuals. However, compared to the heyday of the zaibatsu trust companies, the share-holding patterns of today are fundamentally different in that nearly 20 million people, or roughly one in five Japanese, are shareholders. Unlike the pre-war years, 11 million shares out of the total of 20 million shares outstanding are owned by persons owning between 1,000 and 5,000 shares. That is, there is a large number of middle-class shareholders today compared to the highly concentrated pre-war ownership of shares in the hands of zaibatsu interests and a limited number of individuals.

Dramatic examples of this change, which some Japanese economists called 'the revolution in share-holding', can be readily found. The Mitsubishi Heavy Industry Company, which was once owned and controlled by the Mitsubishi zaibatsu, now has 380,000 shareholders. The Yawata Iron and Steel Company, a firm jointly owned by the government and zaibatsu interests, is now owned by 400,000 shareholders. Hitachi Ltd, a diversified electric equipment and machinery manufacturer which was not controlled by any zaibatsu, has 420,000 shareholders. Also, we find that the present pattern of share-holding of the largest banks is even more diffused than for the giant firms. Gone completely is the family-trust ownership and/or control of these banks. Today, only rarely does the largest shareholder own more than 3 per cent of all the outstanding shares, and even legal persons, who jointly own the majority shares of these banks, usually own only from 1 to 3 per cent of all the outstanding shares.

Though the share-holding pattern is diffused, and the zaibatsu as they were known in the pre-war years have disappeared from the economy, the ownership and control patterns of the Japanese economy had, by the mid-1960s, regrouped themselves on various lines. To be sure, though the new groupings are different from the pre-war zaibatsu-controlled ones, there are many resemblances as well. The new groupings, often called *keiretsu* (literally 'lineage'), can be either vertical or horizontal. Vertical *keiretsu* is usually a grouping of smaller firms by a large firm. The large firm is usually in an industry which requires many subcontractors or subordinate firms capable of supplying various inputs to, or relying on the outputs of, the parent firm. The parent firm is often a majority shareholder and/or in a position to make changes in the upper executive levels of the 'child' companies (*kogaisha*). Also, parent companies are often able to secure necessary loans for child firms. In 1962, the Japan Fair Trade Commission found that the 256 largest firms had on the average 16 child companies each, which were defined as those firms of which 10 per cent or more of the shares were owned by the parent firm. The Matsushita Electric Co. headed the list with 193 subsidiary firms.

The horizontal *keiretsu* are groupings of large former zaibatsu-connected firms across industrial boundaries. The new groupings are loose 'community of interest' groups rather than the tightly knit groups dominated by the respective zaibatsu trust and bank. By the mid-1960s these groups were easily identifiable. The presidents of the respective groups have regularly scheduled meetings, and each group strives to have maximum dealings with those within the group instead of with those who are outsiders to the group. Intra-group mutual share holdings increased from the early 1950s to 1957, though the latest observation for 1965 indicated a levelling-off in this trend. The Mitsui group's mutual share holdings in 1951 were 6.2 per cent of the total outstanding shares of the group, and the figure reached 11.0 per cent in 1957, though it again fell to 10 per cent in 1965. For the Mitsubishi group, the figures were 1.3 per cent in 1951, 16.4 in 1957, and 17.0 in 1965; for the Sumitomo groups, the figures were 7.0 per cent, 14.0 per cent, and 19.0 per cent for the same three years.

It is not difficult to understand the rapid post-war development of vertical *keiretsu,* given the post-war economic conditions of Japan – wage differentials between large and small firms, constant investment activities with general credit shortages, and increasingly complex technological requirements. After all, subcontracting and subsidiary firms of various types are common in advanced industrial economies, and the Japanese case is perhaps no more than an accentuated version of Western models.

The horizontal *keiretsu* are much more difficult to interpret. They are products of the historical legacy and the economic rationale. The historical legacy led the former zaibatsu firms to seek out others within the respective confines of their former zaibatsu groupings. The former Mitsui firms tend to borrow from Mitsui banks, and these firms co-operate in investment, technological development, marketing, and many other aspects of their activities. Personal ties and the advantages of familiarity with former fellow zaibatsu-connected firms played a role no less important than the economic advantages which could be gained by belonging to each group.

The new horizontal *keiretsu* is a loose grouping. Unlike the pre-war zaibatsu groups, it is possible for a firm within a group to place its interests before that of the group, and a few have done so. Firms can, and at times do, do business with firms of other groups. Bank loans, for example, for a so-called Mitsui-group firm can and often do come from a Mitsubishi or Sumitomo bank. As among siblings, the new horizontal *keiretsu* is based on the past; and, again as among siblings, the exigencies of the present can and do lead some of the members of the new group to seek new associations or new attachments. Many economists seek the reasons for this new horizontal grouping in purely economic terms. Their efforts, however, cannot be successful unless it is realized that, in the final analysis, these *keiretsu* are based on Japanese group-orientation and the need to identify themselves within a group. After the parents are gone – the dissolution of the zaibatsu holding companies – siblings work together for common causes because of their common lineage. A sibling might for his own interest ignore the interest of the family, but this is much rarer in Japan than in most other societies. In the same way, a Mitsui–*keiretsu* firm, although a rigid code to bind together firms is no longer in force, is quite unlikely to disregard the interests of the group: most workers, whether blue- or white-collar, work for the Mitsui Shipbuilding Company with the emphasis on 'Mitsui' rather than on 'Shipbuilding Company'.

The powerful and pervasive zaibatsu of the pre-war years are gone; the ownership and control patterns of post-war Japan differ fundamentally from those of pre-war years. The same name, the same trademark, and even the same senior officers, along with the new *keiretsu*, may give the impression that the difference is deceptive. But we know that the difference is real. On the other hand, behind these names, trademarks, and senior officers, we discover a living legacy of years past. Economic historians can somehow sense the handiwork of history which makes the ownership and control patterns of today's Japan so very Japanese. This discovery is not contradictory to the fundamental difference in those patterns between pre-war and post-war years, because changes, however fundamental, take place within the confines of a nation's culture and tradition.

THE MANAGERIAL SYSTEM

As economic historians we ask, What are the most significant features of the Japanese managerial system, and how did it evolve as Japan's industrialization proceeded? If one is to briefly highlight the major characteristics of the Japanese managerial system, one might select two as being among the most important: these are industrial paternalism and an emphasis on group harmony and co-operation, as manifested in the so-called *ringi* system of decision-making. We shall thus discuss each in turn, and with these two as the basic building blocks, we shall examine related aspects of the Japanese managerial system in historical perspective.

A highly structured hierarchical society emerged during the Tokugawa period. Apprenticeship in the crafts during this period was rigid and highly formalized. Each apprentice had to observe a long apprenticeship, one which often lasted for nearly a decade or even fifteen years. The relationship between master and apprentice was rigorously defined and highly personal. A master exercised full authority over the persons of his apprentices and expected to receive complete loyalty and obedience from them. Apprentices, in return, received training in the craft, full maintenance, and aid when starting out as new masters. Japanese literature and folklore richly document that the master-apprentice relationships were nearly as absolute as those observed between a lord and his samurai.

The institution of *ie* (house) which developed among the Tokugawa merchants is another example of the hierarchically structured society. An *ie* was a functionally simulated kinship organization built around the head of an *ie*. The relationship between the head of the house and his employees was similar to that between a master and his apprentice. However, for an *ie,* there was another dimension which did not exist in the master-apprentice relationship.[106] That is, an *ie* was an entity, a name to be honoured by all and protected by all at all costs. For well-established and large *ie,* such as the House of Mitsui or Sumitomo, rules which governed their respective *ie* were minutely codified. These

106 Yasuzō Horie, 'The Problem of *ie* in Japanese Business History', *Japan Business History Review,* II, I (July 1967), is a useful re-examination of the concept of *ie*. On many points made in this section, as well as on *ie,* Solomon B. Levine, 'Labor and Collective Bargaining' in W. W. Lockwood (ed.), *The State and Economic Enterprise in Japan,* 633–7, is excellent.

rules defined the intra-*ie* personal relationships, schedules of advancements, and above all the duties and obligations of the head of the house and all its employees.

These examples typify the rigidly hierarchical, group-oriented social structure of Tokugawa Japan.[107] As in the world of samurai, the hierarchy was founded on the principle that the superiors in these social classes were under an obligation to provide for the economic security of their inferiors in exchange for the latter's total loyalty and obedience. Ability and aggressiveness could advance status, but only within a class, and the social position of an individual, determined by birth, allowed virtually no inter-class mobility except in the late Tokugawa period, when the rigid class barriers could no longer be maintained. This was the world of Tokugawa Japan into which modern industry intruded. Larger, more complex human organizations were demanded by the new industries, and the Tokugawa institutions were forced to adapt themselves.

But, the Tokugawa institutions yielded only grudgingly. For the first two decades or so of the Meiji years, or before the coming of the cotton textile boom, we find a period of institutional disorientation. During these politically and economically turbulent years the government built pilot plants, recruited needed labour from the ranks of commoners, and depended on samurai-turned-bureaucrats to manage its plants. Although class distinctions were abolished shortly after the Restoration, they persisted during these decades, preserving much of the Tokugawa hierarchical relationship between management and labour. Case studies show that the government plants were managed as if they belonged to a feudal lord.

The few private firms which began to emerge differed little from the government plants. Private firms had to be concerned with profits, but the adjustments which they made to the requirements of their new industries were too small and few to be considered a first step toward

107 A leading student of Japanese history observed:

> The oldest and in many ways the most deeply rooted of these historically ingrained systems of political organization grew out of the earliest period of Japanese history for which we can reconstruct the political community. We have called this the 'familial' system rather than use the more common term 'clan' which gives rise to too many ambiguous connotations . . . The familial ingredient in Japan's political heritage, while being transformed under changing conditions of culture and political ideology, nonetheless formed a constant and important element linking the social hierarchy to the power structure at all levels. The tendency of the Japanese to fictionalize superior-inferior relations by conceiving of them in familial terms is the best example of this.

John W. Hall, *Government and Local Power in Japan, 500 to 1700: A Study Based on Bizen Province* (Princeton, 1966), 6–7.

modern industrial management practices. True, a few men like Iwasaki, the founder of the Mitsubishi Zaibatsu, adopted daring modern policies while samurai-turned-managers groped painfully for a *modus operandi* in industrial management. But Iwasaki and his kind were still a small minority.[108]

During the early 1880s, the government, as we have seen, sold most of its plants, and the appearance of the private firms in the cotton textile and other industries heralded the first industrial spurt in Japan. This was the beginning of a period which Hazama called the 'primitive' period,[109] which extended into the First World War years. These were the years of rapid increases in industrial output based on newly imported technologies; they were also the years of laissez-faire, the years during which new entrepreneurs pursued profits and exploited western technology while the workers were exposed to the fate of the English workers of a few generations before.

The problems which the new industrial entrepreneurs faced were many, and obtaining a sufficient amount of the desired kind of labour was no less a problem than finding the necessary capital and technology. Skilled workers – those able to operate the Western machines – were few, and the unskilled and semi-skilled had to be coerced into the irksome disciplines of factory work. A new generation of managerial staff, equipped with or willing to learn the necessary administrative and technical skills, had to be found.

Generally speaking, the entrepreneurs found their managerial personnel from the new universities, as was discussed in section I. For the bulk of unskilled labour, the surplus labour of the agricultural sector and poverty-stricken and unemployed lower-class samurai were employed. The new employees – reflecting their past social status – were docile and disciplined to the long hours and often substandard working and living conditions. The management could exert maximum authority over them with a minimum of restraint. The abject condition of the female hands in the cotton textile industry and the miners' working conditions, which were found less desirable than prison life by the journalists of the day, characterized this 'primitive' period.

A large proportion of skilled workers and often semi-skilled workers were employed by the now-familiar method of contracting through an *oyabun*. He was, in most cases, a skilled workman himself who had

108 See Yamamura, 'The Founding of Mitsubishi Zaibatsu'.

109 Hiroshi Hazama, *Nihon rōmu kanrishi kenkyū* [*A Study of Japanese Labour Management*] (Tokyo, 1964), 15. In the area of labour management and the managerial system as a whole, this is the most useful and valuable book to appear since the end of the Second World War.

from several to as many as several hundred *kobun*, the skilled workers who worked under the protection and command of the *oyabun*. The *oyabun* contracted to supply his *kobun* to a firm and functioned as a foreman. The contract was signed usually on a short-term basis, and the wages were paid through the *oyabun*. The system of *oyabun-kobun* was a replica of the master-apprentice system of the Tokugawa period, and the relationship between the *oyabun* and *kobun* was equally pre-industrial in many respects.

Before the First World War, Japanese management enjoyed a period of freedom in dealing with its employees. Still free of social legislation which was soon to contain managerial freedom, employers pursued profit as had their English counterparts a century earlier. Because the Meiji Restoration destroyed those delicately balanced, perhaps more human, relationships of Tokugawa society, unprotected workers were now exposed to the anonymous and often ruthless air of the new industrial age. The shocking documentaries of the operatives of cotton textile factories of the period are a legacy of this transition.

With the new constitution and an increased franchise, the first Factory Act of 1911 was to be expected. Industrial firms, which were now employing most of their labour directly, dispensing with the *oyabun-kobun* system to meet the rapidly increasing needs of skilled personnel for its exclusive employment, opposed the Act. Employers argued that the Act and any other Western-style factory laws were unsuitable for Japan because Japanese society functioned best not on impersonal contractual relationships but on more human, personal, and group relationships. Although a few acknowledged the detrimental effects which these restrictions on the authority of the management might have on rapid capital accumulation and on Japan's ability to be internationally competitive, many argued – and sincerely, if the eloquence of their arguments is to be believed – that Japanese management could more than adequately accomplish what these acts intended.

This was the period during which industrial paternalism – 'a company is a family' – became explicit. The management, under the threat of further laws and leftist ideology, and also to appease the critics of huge profits earned during the First World War, instituted numerous welfare and fringe-benefit programmes. This industrial paternalism was to cushion the sharpening edge of economic and social discontent of the years following the First World War. During the Taisho years (1912–25), punctuated by the rice riots of 1918 and the formation of the Japanese Communist Party in 1922, industrial firms – especially zaibatsu-related giant firms – appealed to the importance of the Japanese tradition of family and widened the scope of employee benefits and welfare programmes of various types.

We have noted earlier that today's employees of the Mitsui Shipbuilding Company identify themselves with Mitsui and are highly conscious of belonging to the Mitsui group, as other employees of any large firm do with their own firms. Between the First World War and the present much has intervened, not the least being the rise of strong, politically oriented labour unions. Despite all these changes, the Mitsui employee's identification with the Mitsui group and the development of the horizontal *keiretsu* of today somehow attest to the fact that management's continued insistence on the importance of 'a company is a family' is not a totally baseless ploy to stave off the political and economic criticisms which it has received. One must not misread the facts of a capitalist economy to the point of believing that warm words and a small contribution to the dowry of a departing female employee are a substitute for shorter hours and higher wages. But, at the same time, cynicism can misread the intentions and practices of Japanese management if carried to the point of ignoring Japan's historical and cultural heritage.

Specialists agree that industrial paternalism continues to be practised in Japan to a degree not found in Western economies. From the first decade of the century, the nature of paternalism changed. It is now much less crude, less offensive – even apologetic. But it is still observable, and Japanese accept the practice of daily exhortations from the company president and compulsory Zen camps for new employees, as their parents accepted their president's concern for the taste of the pickles in an employees' canteen, with gratitude. This was and is possible because the Japanese find a strong need to identify themselves with a group, and they appear to function most effectively within one. To most Japanese, post-war labour unions and active political party activities seem poor substitutes for group identification with a firm, because it is on the job that they spend most of their waking hours, and they find a need to be a part of a co-operative effort. The fact that firms, in recruiting their future executives, seem to favour applicants from one university as opposed to those from others is also an indication that the firms place a premium on cohesiveness and intra-firm harmony, which such a policy can help foster. To this day, some firms are known to be biased toward Tokyo University, while others favour Keio, Hitotsubashi, or other elite universities.

The nature and the extent to which group orientation is ingrained in Japanese culture can best be seen in the *ringi* system of decision-making in Japanese firms. '*Ringi*' is one of those compound words in

Japanese which are most difficult to translate literally; '*rin*' means the act of submitting a proposal to one's superior for his sanction, and '*gi*' means to discuss or to deliberate. Thus, the *ringi* system of decision-making within a group by means of sanctioning proposals originating from one's subordinates.[110]

The system, which has well-developed roots in the Tokugawa *bakufu* and its local offices, was formalized and widely used by the bureaucrats of the Meiji period, and private firms adopted the procedure at the beginning of industrialization. Typically, a small group of office workers within a section propose a particular measure after extensive discussion among themselves. Then, the proposal is submitted to the section chief in charge. The section chief, before making his decision, consults other section chiefs who may be affected or who have an interest in the proposal. If any part of the proposal is objected to, the proposal is returned to the section members for re-examination or is rejected. If the proposal is approved by the section, it will be submitted to a higher group of managerial personnel, who in most cases will be bureau chiefs working under the executive officers of the firm. If the proposal is accepted at this level, it then goes to the executive board and, with its approval, to the president for final sanction.

There can, of course, be variations in this pattern. A section chief might suggest that a proposal be prepared on a specific problem, or on rare occasions a bureau chief or even an executive officer might suggest that a section chief draw up a proposal. However, in such cases, these suggestions, which in fact are orders, do not come to the lower level as orders, because if an order is issued the person who does so will be personally responsible for the proposal. Personal responsibility and identification with a specific proposal must be avoided at all costs, because if the proposal is disapproved the loss of prestige results in the worst social disgrace for any administrator of any rank, and if the proposal is accepted it is socially unacceptable to personally receive credit for the success.

The attraction of such a system within the Japanese social context is obvious. Decisions are made anonymously. No one is either blamed for or credited with the failure or success of a proposal, and all is done in the name of collectivity. Thus, infinite care is taken from the first step so that consensus is obtained within the group which is involved in the deliberation of a proposal. Then, when the proposal is finally approved

110 A thorough analysis of the *ringi* system is available in Akira Yamashiro (ed.), *Ringi-teki keiei to ringi seido* [Ringi *Management and* Ringi *System*] (Tokyo, 1966).

for execution, it is a decision of the entire firm, and all are expected to do their best in order that the proposal accomplish its intended aim.

The shortcomings of such a system are also evident. To begin with, it is cumbersome and slow. Innovative ideas can be stifled at the discussion stage and bold approaches tend to be shelved in the name of consensus, even before they reach the higher-echelon executives. It is, of course, unthinkable to ignore the chain of command within a firm. The high-level decision-makers are forced into the position of viewing a proposal with a strong presumption for approval, and they rarely have access to the facts or the minority opinions necessary to counterbalance the weight of the proposal. Many company presidents, rather than risk prestige, tend to accept all proposals after a few perfunctory questions – the practice which Japanese call '*mekura-ban*', literally 'blind seal'. Most Japanese firms have apparently found that these shortcomings are a bearable price compared to the great merits of the system, the anonymity of decision-making and the rule of consensus. Few prices are too high in Japan for intra-group harmony.

What has been described above is a realistic model of the *ringi* system. Though the basic ingredients of the system – consensus, anonymity, and harmony – are guarded carefully, an increasingly large number of firms have begun to introduce significant variations to this model, and there were always exceptions even during the pre-war years. The reaction time to economic and sometimes political events must now be much shorter than before. Increasing government participation in economic affairs, especially with long-range growth plans, makes it necessary for firms to have long-range plans. The *ringi* system, which is generally sufficient for short-run policy-making and problem-solving, is no longer adequate. Decisions in today's industrial economy must come quickly, and long-run and short-run decisions must be coordinated if both are to be effective.

For these reasons, a majority of firms now have a planning department which specializes in long-run planning, and the decision-making process has been increasingly decentralized to increase autonomy and the speed of decisions. But it is nevertheless true that these innovations are not replacing the *ringi* system but rather are grafted on to it. It is the observation of students specializing in the management system that many of the key decisions are still made on a consensus basis using the *ringi* system, while recent additions such as the planning department and the decentralized decision-making process are more confined to questions which are basically technical in nature. Post-war Japan has experienced periodic revivals of emphasis on the Japanese way of management, alternating with periods of eager adoption of American managerial methods. But on balance the *ringi* system is far from being made obsolete, and it is most likely that as long as the Japanese value consensus, anonymity, and harmony in their corporate life, the system will continue to be used.

CONCLUSION

Japanese industrialization continues to fascinate economists and economic historians because of its rapidity and the uniqueness of its Asian setting. Few economies have accomplished as much in so short a time, and Japan's modernization, accompanying the process of industrialization, profoundly transformed the society during the past century. Thus, it was natural that attempts were and are being made to understand and to explain this feat. These attempts have yielded a set of interpretations and views which try to explain why this Asian nation succeeded in industrializing so rapidly.

The orthodox view explains the success of Japan's industrialization by emphasizing its distinct social and historical uniqueness and its lateness of entry to industrialization. The vision of dedicated and selfless bureaucrats and entrepreneurs, former samurai and those motivated by samurai spirit, battling to industrialize from above to bring the latecomer to the industrial age as rapidly as possible was presented persuasively. And as this view was strengthened and refined during the course of nearly a half-century of its development, it became increasingly difficult to deny its validity.

Another part of this orthodoxy firmly holds to the view that the banks, originally established under government-samurai initiative, played the crucial role of industrial financier, and that by the beginning of the twentieth century they had become the dominant suppliers of industrial capital. The Japanese pattern, it has long been argued, was like that of nineteenth-century Germany, which had also industrialized as a latecomer and which found it needed to mobilize its capital by means of highly oligopolistic banks. But after two generations and two world wars, this orthodoxy too appears to be faced with the necessity of making an accommodation to a series of recent challenges. The students who suggest re-evaluation of the current view are questioning the interpretation and views with findings obtained by more thorough examinations of data and other evidence. These challenges need to be further evaluated; they can, however, no longer be neglected, because they question the fundamental building blocks of the accepted view.

In many respects, the recent wave of explicit questions concerning the existing view has long been overdue. In Japan, the militarism which stifled the freedom of academic pursuits, and the futile *Methodenstreit* on the economic nature of the Meiji Restoration and the Second World War, perhaps retarded a more natural course of re-examination and evolution of these views. For Westerners Japan was long a quaint subject of curiosity, and only after the Second World War was full-scale research begun. And even then, this research was deeply coloured by earlier Japanese works and hampered by a formidable linguistic barrier. In these circumstances, more empirically oriented historical research by both Japanese and Westerners has been delayed.

Thus, the recent re-examinations of the established views have not been surprises for most specialists in Japanese economic history. When the role of the government and the samurai was de-emphasized and put in a new perspective, and when the role of commoners and their profit motivations was given its due place, it appeared that we have merely confirmed what had long been expected. Thus, if the continued re-evaluation of the process of Japanese industrialization can indeed demonstrate that the long-held view must now undergo a fundamental reappraisal and that the suggested new interpretations are to replace the old, one may find Dore's words on Japanese modernization equally applicable to Japan's industrialization:

> In sum, it was important that the Japanese populace was not just a sack of potatoes. The modernization of Japan was not simply a matter of top-level changes. It was also a cumulation of a mass of small initiatives by large numbers of people who could appreciate new possibilities, make new choices, or at the very least allow themselves to be persuaded to do for the first time something they had never done before.[111]

For an economy to industrialize successfully, it requires efforts from the broad spectrum of its people. Industrialization, like modernization, cannot be achieved if the government is compelled to try to motivate 'a sack of potatoes' while the populace remains passive and conservative and clings to its old ways.

However, as parts of pre-Keynesian economic theory found a niche in post-Keynesian economics, some aspects of the orthodox view of Japanese industrialization can and must be accommodated within the new framework which is to be established on the strength of continued research. The tasks involved in establishing a new set of coherent

111 Ronald P. Dore, 'The Legacy of Tokugawa Education', in Marius B. Jansen (ed.), *Changing Japanese Attitudes Toward Modernization* (Princeton, 1965), 104.

interpretations on the nature and roles of entrepreneurship, government, banks, and management will necessarily be those of synthesis, as all such endeavours must be.

When these tasks are successfully accomplished, we should be better able to explain the rapid industrialization of Japan. The role of government can then be evaluated more accurately, and the roles accorded to various social classes can then be seen in a more meaningful light. The story of Japanese economic growth can be told not just with Shibusawa and the zaibatsu but with a full cast including the Suzukis, Itōs, Yasudas, Iwasakis, Minomuras, and Nakamigawas. The role played by the banks and the changing patterns of ownership and control of Japanese industrial firms can also be appraised and understood much more accurately with the use of more detailed data. If further research supports the basic findings expressed in this chapter, then true industrial banking began only in the 1920s, and the earlier patterns of financing approximated to the English pattern rather than that of Germany. This, if established, is an important insight in understanding the development of labour-intensive industries, especially the cotton textile industry, which appears to have depended mostly on share capital and ploughed-back profits rather than on industrial bank loans. In this new perspective, it becomes possible to evaluate much more accurately the evolution of ownership and control patterns in general and the zaibatsu's economic significance.

For a general framework to emerge benefiting from the strength of both the old and the new views, one should recognize the most salient point arising from both views on Japanese entrepreneurship, ownership and control, and the managerial system. That is, Japan was able to industrialize because she was able to adapt her society and culture to the requirements of industrialization. It is a mistake to argue that the early Japanese entrepreneurs were not basically Western in outlook, and therefore that they did not modernize but depended on the 'old vibrant spirit of samurai'. It is a serious error to conclude that the Japanese *ringi* system is not modern because it is not Western. It is also fallacious to say that the new *keiretsu* groupings find no counterparts in the West, and therefore that the emergence of these groupings is a reversion to the pre-war form of economic organization. Many writers tended to emphasize the Japaneseness of the Japanese industrialization or were inclined to stress the Japanese ability to Westernize in order to achieve industrialization. To emphasize Japaneseness while equating modernization and Westernization is to overemphasize the traditional at the cost of ignoring the ability of Japanese society to modernize itself in its own way. To argue that Japan Westernized and sought replicas of Western models is to misjudge the scope and depth of Japanese modernization.

Given the history, culture, and traditions of Japan, her task for industrialization was dual. She had to produce goods by using Western technology while at the same time transforming her society to make it capable of meeting the needs of industrialization. This transformation of society was carried out at two levels. One was in form and the other in substance. Changes in form included the codification of commercial laws following the Western model, the enactment of the Factory Acts, the establishment of planning departments within corporations, and a series of laws enacted under the Allied Command.

But the transformation in substance was accomplished much less visibly and much more continuously. This transformation was profound. The *ie* gradually adopted the interpersonal relationships of the new era, and industrial paternalism emerged. The industrial paternalism of the 1920s was significantly different from the education- and welfare-oriented programmes of today's corporations. But the *ie* still exists. Group identification, the values placed on co-operation and harmony, an assiduous observation of rank differentials, and a premium placed on personal rather than legal relationships – all are transformed characteristics of the *ie*. And, as we have seen, the *ringi* system still continues to be used along with computers in the decision-making process in post-war Japanese firms. The *keiretsu* groupings of the 1960s resemble the pre-war zaibatsu, and some have even spoken of a zaibatsu revival. But neither the *ringi* system of today nor the *keiretsu* groupings are what they appear to be in form. These living institutions change and do not remain what they once were. These changes in substance are the process of Japanese modernization, and it is crucial to realize this fact before we can gain a better understanding of Japanese economic history.

BIBLIOGRAPHY

This bibliography includes only a small number of selected works published in Japanese. Those wishing to find the most useful Japanese works, especially those published most recently, should examine 日本経済史 *Nihon keizaishi*, published in eight volumes, as listed below, by 岩波書店 Iwanami Shoten, Tokyo, 1988–90. These volumes contain fifty-three articles on a wide range of topics by Japanese economic historians, economists, and historians drawing upon the literature as of the late 1980s.

Vol. 1 経済社会の成立: 17–18世紀 *Keizai shakai no seiritsu: 17–18 seiki*, edited by 速水融 Hayami Akira and 宮本又郎 Miyamoto Matao, 1988.

Vol. 2 近代成長の胎動 *Kindai seichō no taidō*, edited by 新保博 Shimbo Hiroshi and 斎藤修 Saitō Osamu, 1989.

Vol. 3 開港と維新 *Kaikō to ishin*, edited by 梅村又次 Umemura Mataji and 山本有造 Yamamoto Yūzō, 1989.

Vol. 4 産業化の時代(上) *Sangyō-ka no jidai (jō)*, edited by 西川俊作 Nishikawa Shunsaku and 阿部武司 Abe Takeshi, 1990.

Vol. 5 産業化の時代(下) *Sangyō-ka no jidai (ge)*, edited by 西川俊作 Nishikawa Shunsaku and 山本有造 Yamamoto Yūzō, 1990.

Vol. 6 二重構造 *Nijū kōzō*, edited by 中村隆英 Nakamura Takafusa and 尾高煌之助 Odaka Kōnosuke, 1989.

Vol. 7「計画化」と「民主化」*"Keikaku-ka" to "minshu-ka,"* edited by 中村隆英 Nakamura Takafusa, 1989.

Vol. 8 高度成長 *Kōdo seichō*, edited by 安場保吉 Yasuba Yasukichi and 猪木武徳 Inoki Takemori, 1989.

Some readers may find Kozo Yamamura's long review of these volumes, published in the *Journal of Japanese Studies*, Volume 17, Number 1 (Winter 1991), pp. 127–43, useful in identifying sources of special interest to the reader. The review contains a brief summary of each of the fifty-three articles, along with Yamamura's critical assessment.

Allen, G. C. *A Short Economic History of Modern Japan 1867–1937*. 3rd rev. ed. London: Allen & Unwin, 1972.

Allen, G. C., and Audrey Donnithorne. *Western Enterprise in Far Eastern Eco-*

nomic Development: China and Japan. London: Allen & Unwin, 1954.

Aoki Koji. *Meiji nōmin sōjō no nenjiteki kenkyū*. Tokyo: Shinseisha, 1967. 青木虹二. 明治農民騒擾の年次的研究. 新生社.

Aoki, Masahiko. *The Co-operative Game Theory of the Firm*. Oxford: Oxford University Press, 1984.

Aoki, Masahiko, ed. *The Economic Analysis of the Japanese Firm*. Amsterdam: North-Holland, 1984.

Aoki, Masahiko. *Information, Incentives and Bargaining in the Japanese Economy*. New York: Cambridge University Press, 1988.

Arimoto Masao. *Chiso kaisei to nōmin tōsō*. Tokyo: Shinseisha, 1968. 有元正雄. 地租改正と農民闘争. 新生社.

Asanuma, Banri. "Manufacturer-Supplier Relationships in Japan and the Concept of Relation-Specific Skill." *Journal of the Japanese and International Economies* 3 (1989).

Baba, M., and M. Tatemoto. "Foreign Trade and Economic Growth in Japan: 1858–1937." In Klein and Ohkawa, eds. *Economic Growth: The Japanese Experience Since the Meiji Era*.

Blumenthal, Tuvia. "Factor Proportions and Choice of Technology: The Japanese Experience." In *Economic Development and Cultural Change* 9 (1980).

Blumenthal, Tuvia. "The Japanese Shipbuilding Industry." In Hugh T. Patrick, ed. *Japanese Industrialization and Its Social Consequences*.

Blumenthal, Tuvia. "Senkanki no Nihon keizai." In Nakamura Takafusa, ed. *Senkanki no Nihon keizai bunseki*. Tokyo: Yamakawa shuppansha, 1981. トゥヴィア・ブルメンソール. 戦間期の日本経済. In 中村隆英. 戦間期の日本経済分析. 山川出版社.

Cargill, Thomas, and Shoichi Royama. *The Transition of Finance in Japan and the United States: A Comparative Perspective*. Stanford: Hoover Institution, 1988.

Cameron, Rondo, et al., eds. *Banking in the Early Stages of Industrialization*. London: Oxford University Press, 1967.

Caves, Richard, and Masu Uekusa. *Industrial Organization in Japan*. Washington, D.C.: The Brookings Institution, 1976.

Chubachi, Masayoshi, and Koji Taira. "Poverty in Modern Japan: Perceptions and Realities." In Hugh T. Patrick, ed. *Japanese Industrialization and Its Social Consequences*.

Cole, Robert E. *Work, Mobility and Participation*. Berkeley and Los Angeles: University of California Press, 1979.

Cole, Robert E., and K. Tominaga. "Japan's Changing Occupational Structure and Its Significance." In Hugh T. Patrick, ed. *Japanese Industrialization and Its Social Consequences*.

Craig, Albert M., ed. *Japan: A Comparative View*. Princeton, N. J.: Princeton University Press, 1979.

Crawcour, E. S. "Changes in Japanese Commerce in the Tokugawa Period." In

Hall and Jansen, eds. *Studies in the Institutional History of Early Modern Japan.*

Crawcour, E. S. "Japan, 1868–1920." In R. T. Shand, ed. *Agricultural Development in Asia.* Canberra: Australian National University Press, 1969.

Crawcour, E. S. "The Tokugawa Heritage." In William W. Lockwood, ed. *The State and Economic Enterprise in Japan: Essays in the Political Economy of Growth.*

Crawcour, E. S. "The Tokugawa Period and Japan's Preparation for Modern Economic Growth." *Journal of Japanese Studies* 1 (Autumn 1974): 113–26.

Crawcour, E. S., and Kozo Yamamura. "The Tokugawa Monetary System: 1787–1868." *Economic Development and Cultural Change* 18 (July 1970): pr. 1, pp. 489–518.

Dore, Ronald P. "Agricultural Improvements in Japan, 1870–1890." *Economic Development and Cultural Change* 9 (October 1960): 69–91.

Dore, Ronald P. *British Factory–Japanese Factory: The Origins of National Diversity in Industrial Relations.* Berkeley and Los Angeles: University of California Press; and London: Allen & Unwin, 1973.

Dore, Ronald P. *Flexible Rigidities.* Stanford: Stanford University Press, 1986.

Dore, Ronald P. "Land Reform and Japan's Economic Development." *The Developing Economies* 3 (December 1965): 487–96.

Dore, Ronald P. *Land Reform in Japan.* London: Oxford University Press, 1959.

Dore, Ronald P. "The Meiji Landlord: Good or Bad?" *Journal of Asian Studies* 18 (May 1959): 343–55.

Dore, Ronald P. "The Modernizer As a Special Case: Japanese Factory Legislation, 1882–1911." *Comparative Studies in Society and History* 11 (1969).

Eads, George C., and Kozo Yamamura. "The Future of Industrial Policy." In Kozo Yamamura and Yasukichi Yasuba, eds. *The Political Economy of Japan, Volume 1: The Domestic Transformation.*

Frost, Peter. *The Bakumatsu Currency Crisis.* Harvard East Asian Monographs, no. 36. Cambridge, Mass.: Harvard University Press, 1970.

Fruin, Mark. *The Japanese Enterprise System: Competitive Strategies and Cooperative Structures.* Oxford: Oxford University Press, 1992.

Fujino, Shozaburo. "Construction Cycles and Their Monetary-Financial Characteristics. In Klein and Ohkawa, eds. *Economic Growth: The Japanese Experience Since the Meiji Era.*

Fukushima Masao. *Chiso kaisei.* Tokyo: Yoshikawa kōbunkan, 1968. 福島正夫. 地租改正. 吉川弘文館.

Galenson, Walter, and Konosuke Odaka. "The Japanese Labor Market." In Hugh T. Patrick, ed. *Asia's New Giant: How the Japanese Economy Works.*

Gerlach, Michael. *Alliance Capitalism; The Social Organization of Japanese Business.* Berkeley: University of California Press, 1993.

Gerlach, Michael. "Keiretsu Organization in the Japanese Economy: Analysis and Trade Implications." In Johnson, Tyson, and Zysman, eds. *Politics and Productivity.*

Gordon, Andrew. *The Evolution of Labor Relations in Japan: Heavy Industry, 1853–1955.* Cambridge, Mass.: Harvard University Press, 1985.

Gordon, Andrew. *Labor and Imperial Democracy in Prewar Japan.* Berkeley: University of California Press, 1991.

Hadley, Eleanor. *Antitrust in Japan.* Princeton, N. J.: Princeton University Press, 1970.

Hall, John W., and Marius B. Jansen, eds. *Studies in the Institutional History of Early Modern Japan.* Princeton, N. J.: Princeton University Press, 1968.

Hanley, Susan B., and Kozo Yamamura. *Economic and Demographic Change in Preindustrial Japan, 1600–1868.* Princeton, N. J.: Princeton University Press, 1977.

Hatai, Yoshitaka. "Business Cycles and the Outflow of Labor from the Agricultural Sector." In Shunsaku Nishikawa, ed. *The Labor Market of Japan*, trans. Ross Mouer. Tokyo: Tokyo University Press, 1980.

Hauser, William B. *Economic Institutional Change in Tokugawa Japan: Osaka and the Kinai Cotton Trade.* Cambridge, England: Cambridge University Press, 1974.

Hayami Akira. *Kinsei nōson no rekishi jinkōgakuteki kenkyū.* Tōyō keizai shimpōsha, 1973. 速水融. 近世農村の歴史人口学的研究. 東洋経済新報社.

Hayami, Akira. "Population Movements." In Jansen and Rozman, eds. *Japan in Transition.*

Hayami, Yujiro, and Ruttan, V. "Factor Prices and Technological Change in Agricultural Development: The U.S. and Japan, 1880–1960." *Journal of Political Economy* 78 (September/October 1970).

Hayami, Yujiro, in association with Masakatsu Akino, Masahiko Shintani, and Saburo Yamada. *A Century of Agricultural Growth in Japan, Its Relevance to Asian Development.* Minneapolis: University of Minnesota Press; and Tokyo: Tokyo University Press, 1965.

Hayami, Yujiro, and Saburo Yamada. "Agricultural Productivity and the Beginning of Industrialization." In *Agriculture and Economic Growth: Japan's Experience.* Kazushi Ohkawa et al., eds. Tokyo: Tokyo University Press; and Princeton, N. J.: Princeton University Press, 1969.

Hayami, Yujiro, and Saburo Yamada, "Technological Progress in Agriculture." In Klein and Ohkawa, eds. *Economic Growth: The Japanese Experience since the Meiji Era.*

Hazama, Hiroshi. "Formation of an Industrial Work Force." In Hugh T. Patrick, ed. *Japanese Industrialization and Its Social Consequences.*

Hazama, Hiroshi. "Historical Changes in the Life Style of Industrial Workers." In Hugh T. Patrick, ed. *Japanese Industrialization and its Social Consequences.*

Hazama Hiroshi. *Nihon rōmu kanrishi kenkyū.* Tokyo: Daiyamondosha, 1964. 間宏. 日本労務管理史研究. ダイヤモンド社.

Hirschmeier, Johannes. *The Origins of Entrepreneurship in Meiji Japan.* Cambridge, Mass.: Harvard University Press, 1964.

Hirschmeier, Johannes. "Shibusawa Eiichi: Industrial Pioneer." In William Lockwood, ed. *The State and Economic Enterprise in Japan: Essays in the Political Economy of Growth.*

Hirschmeier, Johannes, and Tsunehiko Yui. *The Development of Japanese Business 1600–1973.* Cambridge, Mass.: Harvard University Press, 1975.

Huber, Richard. "Effect on Prices of Japan's Entry Into World Commerce after 1858." *Journal of Political Economy* 79 (May/June 1971).

Inukai, I., and A. R. Tussing. "Kogyo Iken: Japan's Ten Year Plan, 1884. *Economic Development and Cultural Change* 16 (September 1967).

Ishii Takashi. *Bakumatsu bōekishi no kenkyū.* Tokyo: Nihon hyōronsha, 1944. 石井孝. 幕末貿易史の研究. 日本評論社.

Jansen, Marius B., and Gilbert Rozman, eds. *Japan in Transition: From Tokugawa to Meiji.* Princeton, N. J.: Princeton University Press, 1986.

Johnson, Chalmers. *MITI and the Japanese Miracle: The Growth of Industrial Policy, 1925–1975.* Berkeley and Los Angeles: University of California Press, 1982.

Johnson, Chalmers, Laura D'Andrea Tyson, and John Zysman, eds. *Politics and Productivity: The Real Story of Why Japan Works.* Cambridge, Mass.: Ballinger, 1989.

Kaneda, Hiromitsu. "Long-Term Changes in Food Consumption Patterns in Japan." In Kazushi Ohkawa et al., eds. *Agriculture and Economic Growth: Japan's Experience.*

Kelley, Allen C., and Jeffrey G. Williamson. *Lessons from Japanese Economic Development. An Analytical Economic History.* Chicago: University of Chicago Press, 1974.

Klein, Lawrence, and Kazushi Ohkawa, eds. *Economic Growth: The Japanese Experience Since the Meiji Era.* Homewood, Illinois: Richard D. Irwin Inc, 1968.

Komiya Ryūtarō et al., eds. *Kōdo seichō no jidai.* Tokyo: Nihon hyōronsha, 1981. 小宮隆太郎. 高度成長の時代. 日本評論社.

Komiya Ryūtarō et al., eds. *Nihon no sangyō seisaku.* Tokyo: Tokyo daigaku shuppankai, 1984. 小宮隆太郎. 日本の産業政策. 東京大学出版会.

Kosai, Yutaka. *The Era of High-Speed Growth.* Tokyo: Tokyo University Press, 1986.

Kosai, Yutaka, and Yoshitaro Ogino. *The Contemporary Japanese Economy.* New York: Macmillan, 1981.

Kumon, Shumpei, and Henry Rosovsky, eds. *The Political Economy of Japan, Volume 3: Cultural and Social Dynamics.* Stanford, Calif.: Stanford University Press, 1992.

Landes, David S. "Japan and Europe: Contrasts in Industrialization." In William W. Lockwood, ed. *The State and Economic Enterprise in Japan: Essays in the Political Economy of Growth.*

Levine, Solomon B. *Industrial Relations in Postwar Japan.* Urbana: University

of Illinois Press, 1958.
Lincoln, Edward. *Japan's Industrial Policies.* Washington, D.C.: Japan Economic Institute, 1984.
Lockwood, William W. *The Economic Development of Japan: Growth and Structural Change, 1868–1938.* Princeton, N. J.: Princeton University Press, 1954.
Lockwood, William W., ed. *The State and Economic Enterprise in Japan: Essays in the Political Economy of Growth.* Princeton, N. J.: Princeton University Press, 1965.
Magaziner, Ira C., and Thomas H. Hout. *Japanese Industrial Policy.* Berkeley: University of California Press, 1980.
Marshall, Byron K. *Capitalism and Nationalism in Prewar Japan: The Ideology of the Business Elite, 1868–1941.* Stanford, Calif.: Stanford University Press, 1967.
Masu, Uekusa. "Industrial Organization: The 1970s to the Present." In Kozo Yamamura and Yasukichi Yasuba, eds. *The Political Economy of Japan, Volume 1: The Domestic Transformation.*
Minami, Ryoshin. *The Economic Development of Japan: A Quantitative Study.* London: The MacMillan Press Ltd., 1986.
Minami, Ryoshin. "The Introduction of Electric Power and Its Impact on the Manufacturing Industries: With Special Reference to Smaller Scale Plants." In Hugh T. Patrick, ed. *Japanese Industrialization and Its Social Consequences.*
Minami, Ryoshin. *The Turning Point in Economic Development.* Tokyo: Kinokuniya, 1973.
Minami, Ryoshin, and Akira Ono. "Wages." In Kazushi Ohkawa and Miyohei Shinohara, eds. *Patterns of Japanese Economic Development: A Quantitative Appraisal.*
Morley, James W., ed. *Dilemmas of Growth in Prewar Japan.* Princeton, N. J.: Princeton University Press, 1971.
Murakami, Yasusuke. *An Anticlassical Political-Economic Analysis: A Vision for the Next Century.* Stanford, Calif.: Stanford University Press, 1996.
Myers, Ramon H., and Mark R. Peattie, eds. *The Japanese Colonial Empire, 1895–1945.* Princeton, N. J.: Princeton University Press, 1984.
Nakagawa, Keiichiro, and Henry Rosovsky. "The Case of the Dying Kimono: The Influence of Changing Fashions on the Development of the Japanese Woolen Industry." *Business History Review* 37 (Spring–Summer 1963): 59–80.
Nakamura, James. *Agricultural Production and the Economic Development of Japan 1873–1922.* Princeton, N. J.: Princeton University Press, 1966.
Nakamura, Takafusa. *Economic Growth in Prewar Japan,* trans. Robert A. Feldman. New Haven, Conn.: Yale University Press, 1983.
Nakamura, Takafusa. *Lectures in Modern Economic History, 1926–1994.* Tokyo: LTCB International Library Foundation, 1986.
Nakamura Takafusa. *Nihon keizai: sono seichō to kōzō.* 2nd ed. Tokyo: Tokyo

daigaku shuppankai, 1980. 中村隆英. 日本経済：その成長と構造. 東京大学出版会.

Nakamura, Takafusa. *The Postwar Japanese Economy: Its Development and Structure.* Tokyo: Tokyo University Press, 1981.

Nakatani, Iwao. "The Economic Role of Financial Corporate Grouping." In Masahiko Aoki, ed. *The Economic Analysis of the Japanese Firm.*

Nishikawa Shunsaku. *Edo jidai no poritikaru ekonomii.* Tokyo: Nihon hyōronsha, 1979. 西川俊作. 江戸時代のポリティカル・エコノミー. 日本評論社.

Nishikawa, Shunsaku. "Grain Consumption: The Case of Choshu." In Jansen and Rozman, eds. *Japan in Transition.*

Nishikawa Shunsaku, ed. *The Labor Market in Japan,* trans. Ross Mouer. Tokyo: Tokyo University Press, 1980.

Nishikawa Shunsaku. *Nihon keizai no seichōshi.* Tokyo: Tōyō keizai shimpōsha, 1985. 西川俊作. 日本経済の成長史. 東洋経済新報社.

Norman, E. H. *Japan's Emergence As a Modern State: Political and Economic Problems of the Meiji Period.* New York: Institute of Pacific Relations, 1940 and later printings.

Ohkawa, Kazushi. *Differential Structure and Agriculture: Essays on Dualistic Growth.* Tokyo: Kinokuniya, 1972.

Ohkawa, Kazushi, B. F. Johnston, and H. Kaneda, eds. *Agriculture and Economic Growth: Japan's Experience.* Princeton, N. J.: Princeton University Press; and Tokyo: Tokyo University Press, 1970.

Ohkawa, Kazushi, and Rosovsky, Henry. *Japanese Economic Growth: Trend Acceleration in the Twentieth Century.* Stanford, Calif.: Stanford University Press, 1973.

Ohkawa, Kazushi, and Miyohei Shinohara, with Larry Meissner, eds. *Patterns of Japanese Economic Development: A Quantitative Appraisal.* New Haven, Conn.: Yale University Press, 1979.

Ohkawa, Kazushi, with Miyohei Shinohara, M. Umemura, M. Ito, and T. Noda. *The Growth Rate of the Japanese Economy Since 1878.* Tokyo: Kinokuniya, 1957.

Okimoto, Daniel I. *Between MITI and the Market: Japanese Industrial Policy for High Technology.* Stanford, Calif.: Stanford University Press, 1989.

Okimoto, Daniel I., and Gary R. Saxonhouse. "Technology and the Future of the Economy." In Kozo Yamamura and Yasukichi Yasuba, eds. *The Political Economy of Japan, Volume 1: The Domestic Transformation.*

Ōkōchi Kazuo. *Sengo Nihon no rōdō undō,* rev. ed. (*Iwanami shinsho,* no. 217). Tokyo: Iwanami shoten, 1961. 大河内一男. 戦後日本の労働運動. 改訂版岩波新書.

Oshima, Harry T. "Meiji Fiscal Policy and Agricultural Progress." In William W. Lockwood, ed. *The State and Economic Enterprise in Japan: Essays in the Political Economy of Growth.*

Patrick, Hugh T. "Japan 1868–1924." In Rondo Cameron et al., eds. *Banking in the Early Stages of Industrialization.*

Patrick, Hugh T., ed. *Japan's High Technology Industries: Lessons and Limitations of Industrial Policy*. Seattle: University of Washington Press, 1986.

Patrick, Hugh T. "The Economic Muddle of the 1920's." In James W. Morley, ed. *Dilemmas of Growth in Prewar Japan*.

Patrick, Hugh T., ed. *Japanese Industrialization and Its Social Consequences*. Berkeley and Los Angeles: University of California Press, 1976.

Patrick, Hugh T., and Henry Rosovsky, eds. *Asia's New Giant: How the Japanese Economy Works*. Washington, D.C.: Brookings Institution, 1976.

Pempel, T. J., and K. Tsunekawa. "Corporatism without Labor?" The Japanese Anomaly." In P. C. Schmitter and G. Lehmbruch, eds. *Trends Toward Corporatist Intermediation*.

Pempel, T. J., ed. *Policymaking in Contemporary Japan*. Ithaca: Cornell University Press, 1977.

Pyle, Kenneth B. "Advantages of Followership: German Economics and Japanese Bureaucrats, 1890–1925." *Journal of Japanese Studies* 1 (Autumn 1974): 127–64.

Ranis, Gustav. "The Financing of Japanese Economic Development." In Kazushi Ohkawa et al., eds. *Agriculture and Economic Growth: Japan's Experience*. Tokyo: Tokyo University Press; and Princeton, N. J.: Princeton University Press, 1969.

Rosovsky, Henry. *Capital Formation in Japan*. Glencoe, Illinois: Free Press, 1961.

Rosovsky, Henry. *Industrialization in Two Systems*. New York: Wiley, 1966.

Rosovsky, Henry. "Japan's Transition to Economic Growth, 1868–1885." In Henry Rosovsky, ed. *Industrialization in Two Systems*.

Rosovsky, Henry. "Rumbles in the Rice Fields: Prof. Nakamura vs. Official Statistics." *Journal of Asian Studies* 27 (February 1968).

Samuels, Richard J. *"Rich Nation Strong Army": National Security and the Technological Transformation of Japan*. Ithaca: Cornell University Press, 1994.

Sato, Kazuo. "Growth and Technological Change in Japan's Non-Primary Economy: 1930–1967." *Economic Studies Quarterly* 17 (April 1971).

Saxonhouse, Gary R. "Country Girls and Communication among Competitors in the Japanese Cotton-Spinning Industry." In Hugh T. Patrick, ed. *Japanese Industrialization and Its Social Consequences*.

Saxonhouse, Gary R. "A Tale of Japanese Technological Diffusion in the Meiji Period." *Journal of Economic History* 34 (March 1974).

Schmitter, P. C., and G. Lehmbruch. *Trends Toward Corporatist Intermediation*. Beverly Hills, Calif.: Sage, 1979.

Sheard, Paul. "The Economics of Interlocking Shareholding in Japan." *Ricerche Economiche* 45 (1991).

Sheard, Paul. "The Main Bank System and Corporate Monitoring and Control in Japan." *Journal of Economic Behavior and Organization* 11 (1989).

Shimbo Hiroshi. *Kinsei no bukka to keizai hatten: zenkōgyōka shakai e no sūryōteki sekkin*. Tokyo: Tōyō keizai shimpōsha, 1978. 新保博. 近世の物価と経済

発展：前工業化社会への数量的接近. 東洋経済新報社.

Shimbo Hiroshi, Hayami Akira, and Nishikawa Shunsaku. *Sūryō keizaishi nyūmon*. Tokyo: Nihon hyōronsha, 1975. 新保博. 速水融. 西川俊作. 数量経済史入門. 日本評論社.

Shinohara, Miyohei. *Growth and Cycles in the Japanese Economy*. Tokyo: Kinokuniya, 1962.

Shionoya, Yuichi. "Patterns of Industrial Development." In Klein and Ohkawa, eds. *Economic Growth: The Japanese Experience Since the Meiji Era*.

Silberman, Bernard, and H. D. Harootunian, eds. *Japan in Crisis*. Princeton, N. J.: Princeton University Press, 1974.

Smethurst, Richard J. *Agricultural Development and Tenancy Disputes in Japan, 1870–1940*. Princeton, N. J.: Princeton University Press, 1986.

Smith, Thomas C. *The Agrarian Origins of Modern Japan*. Stanford: Calif.: Stanford University Press, 1959.

Smith, Thomas C. *Political Change and Industrial Development in Japan: Government Enterprise, 1868–1880*. Stanford, Calif.: Stanford University Press, 1955.

Smith, Thomas C. "Pre-Modern Economic Growth: Japan and the West." *Past and Present* 43 (1973): 127–60.

Sumiya Mikio. *Shōwa kyōkō*. Tokyo: Yūhikaku, 1974. 隅谷三喜男. 昭和恐慌. 有斐閣.

Sumiya Mikio, ed. *Nihon rōshi kankei shiron*. Tokyo: Tokyo daigaku shuppankai, 1977. 隅谷三喜男, ed. 日本労使関係史論. 東京大学出版会.

Sumiya, Mikio, and Koji Taira, eds. *An Outline of Japanese Economic History, 1603–1940*. Tokyo: Tokyo University Press, 1979.

Taira, Koji. *Economic Development and the Labor Market in Japan*. New York: Columbia University Press, 1970.

Takahashi Kamekichi. *Nihon zaibatsu no kaibō*. Tokyo: Chūō kōronsha, 1930. 高橋亀吉. 日本財閥の解剖. 中央公論社.

Takahashi Kamekichi. *Taishō Shōwa zaikai hendōshi*, 3 vols. Tokyo: Tōyō keizai shinpōsha, 1954. 高橋亀吉. 大正昭和財界変動史. 東洋経済新報社.

Teranishi Shigeo. "Matsukata defure no makuro keizaigakuteki bunseki." *Kikan gendai keizai* 47 (Spring 1982): 78–92. 寺西重郎. 松方デフレのマクロ経済学的分析. 季刊現代経済.

Tiedemann, Arthur E. "Big Business and Politics in Prewar Japan." In James W. Morley, ed. *Dilemmas of Growth in Prewar Japan*.

Tauber, Irene B. *The Population of Japan*. Princeton, N. J.: Princeton University Press, 1966.

Tsuchiya Takao. *Zaibatsu o kizuita hitobito*. Tokyo: Kōbundō, 1955. 土屋喬雄. 財閥を築いた人々. 弘文堂.

Tsuchiya Takao. *Nihon no keieisha seishin*. Tokyo: Keizai ōraisha, 1959. 土屋喬雄. 日本の経営者精神. 経済往来社.

Umemura, Mataji. "Population and Labor Force." In Kazushi Ohkawa and Miyohei Shinohara, eds. *Patterns of Japanese Development: A Quantitative*

Appraisal.

Vlastos, Stephen. *Peasant Protests and Uprisings in Tokugawa Japan.* Berkeley and Los Angeles: University of California Press, 1986.

Waswo, Ann. *Japanese Landlords: The Decline of a Rural Elite.* Berkeley and Los Angeles: University of California Press, 1977.

Wray, William D. *Mitsubishi and the N.Y.K., 1870–1914: Business Strategy in the Japanese Shipping Industry.* Cambridge, Mass.: Harvard University Press, 1985.

Yamada, Saburo, and Yujiro Hayami. "Agriculture." In Kazushi Ohkawa and Miyohei Shinohara, eds. *Patterns of Economic Development: A Quantitative Appraisal.*

Yamaguchi Kazuo. *Bakumatsu bōeki shi.* Tokyo: Chūō kōronsha, 1943. 山口和雄. 幕末貿易史. 中央公論社.

Yamaguchi Kazuo. *Meiji zenki keizai no bunseki.* Tokyo: Tokyo daigaku shuppankai, 1956. 山口和雄. 明治前期経済の分析. 東京大学出版会.

Yamamura, Kozo. *Economic Policy in Postwar Japan: Growth Versus Economic Democracy.* Berkeley: University of California Press, 1967.

Yamamura, Kozo. "The Founding of Mitsubishi: A Case Study in Japanese Business History." *Business History Review* 41 (1967): 141–60.

Yamamura, Kozo. "The Japanese Economy, 1911–30: Concentration, Conflict, and Crises." In Bernard Silberman and H. D. Harootunian, ed. *Japan in Crisis.*

Yamamura, Kozo. "Japan's Deus ex Machina: Western Technology in the 1920s." *Journal of Japanese Studies* 12 (Winter 1986): 65–94.

Yamamura, Kozo. "The Meiji Land Tax Reform and Its Effects." In Jansen and Rozman, eds. *Japan in Transition.*

Yamamura, Kozo. *A Study of Samurai Income and Entrepreneurship: Quantitative Analyses of Economic and Social Aspects of the Samurai in Tokugawa and Meiji Japan.* Cambridge, Mass.: Harvard University Press, 1974.

Yamamura, Kozo, and Yasukichi Yasuba, eds. *The Political Economy of Japan, Volume 1: The Domestic Transformation.* Stanford, Calif.: Stanford University Press, 1987.

Yamamura, Kozo. "Pre-Industrial Landholding Patterns in Japan and England." In Craig, ed. *Japan: A Comparative View.*

Yamamura, Kozo. "Success Illgotten? The Role of Meiji Militarism in Japan's Technical Progress." *Journal of Economic History* 37 (March 1977).

Yasuba, Yasukichi. "Anatomy of the Debate on Japanese Capitalism." *Journal of Japanese Studies* 2 (Autumn 1975): 63–82.

Yasuba, Yasukichi. "The Evolution of Dualistic Wage Structure." In Hugh T. Patrick, ed. *Industrialization and Its Social Consequences.*

INDEX

Printed in the United States
By Bookmasters